Deleuze, Guattari and the Schizoanalysis of Postmedia

Schizoanalytic Applications

Series Editors: Ian Buchanan, Marcelo Svirsky and David Savat
Schizoanalysis has the potential to be to Deleuze and Guattari's work what deconstruction is to Derrida's – the standard rubric by which their work is known and, more important, applied. Many within the field of Deleuze and Guattari studies would resist this idea, but the goal of this series is to broaden the base of scholars interested in their work. Deleuze and Guattari's ideas are widely known and used but not in a systematic way, and this is both a strength and weakness. It is a strength because it enables people to pick up their work from a wide variety of perspectives, but it is also a weakness because it makes it difficult to say with any clarity what exactly a 'Deleuzo-Guattarian' approach is. This has inhibited the uptake of Deleuze and Guattari's thinking in the more wilful disciplines, such as history, politics and even philosophy. Without this methodological core, Deleuze and Guattari studies risk becoming simply another intellectual fashion that will soon be superseded by newer figures.
The goal of the Schizoanalytic Applications series is to create a methodological core and build a sustainable model of schizoanalysis that will attract new scholars to the field. With this purpose, the series also aims to be at the forefront of the field by starting a discussion about the nature of Deleuze and Guattari's methodology.

Titles published in the series:
Deleuze and the Schizoanalysis of Feminism, edited by Janae Sholtz and Cheri Carr
Deleuze and the Schizoanalysis of Literature, edited by Ian Buchanan, Tim Matts and Aidan Tynan
Deleuze and the Schizoanalysis of Religion, edited by Lindsay Powell-Jones and F. LeRon Shults
Deleuze and the Schizoanalysis of Visual Art, edited by Ian Buchanan and Lorna Collins
Deleuze, Guattari and the Schizoanalysis of Trans Studies, edited by Ciara Cremin

Deleuze, Guattari and the Schizoanalysis of Postmedia

Edited by
Joff P. N. Bradley, Alex Taek-Gwang Lee and Manoj N. Y.

BLOOMSBURY ACADEMIC
LONDON • NEW YORK • OXFORD • NEW DELHI • SYDNEY

BLOOMSBURY ACADEMIC
Bloomsbury Publishing Plc
50 Bedford Square, London, WC1B 3DP, UK
1385 Broadway, New York, NY 10018, USA
29 Earlsfort Terrace, Dublin 2, Ireland

BLOOMSBURY, BLOOMSBURY ACADEMIC and the Diana logo are trademarks of
Bloomsbury Publishing Plc

First published in Great Britain 2023
This paperback edition published 2024

Copyright © Joff P. N. Bradley, Alex Taek-Gwang Lee, Manoj N. Y. and Contributors, 2023

Joff P. N. Bradley, Alex Taek-Gwang Lee and Manoj N. Y. have asserted their right under the
Copyright, Designs and Patents Act, 1988, to be identified as Editors of this work.

For legal purposes the Acknowledgements on p. xiv constitute an extension of this
copyright page.

Cover design by Charlotte Daniels
Cover image: Abstract Landscape Background (© StudioM1 / iStock / Getty Images Plus)

All rights reserved. No part of this publication may be reproduced or transmitted in any
form or by any means, electronic or mechanical, including photocopying, recording, or
any information storage or retrieval system, without prior permission in writing from the
publishers.

Bloomsbury Publishing Plc does not have any control over, or responsibility for, any third-
party websites referred to or in this book. All internet addresses given in this book were
correct at the time of going to press. The author and publisher regret any inconvenience
caused if addresses have changed or sites have ceased to exist, but can accept no
responsibility for any such changes.

A catalogue record for this book is available from the British Library.

A catalog record for this book is available from the Library of Congress.

ISBN: HB: 978-1-3501-8050-5
PB: 978-1-3501-8550-0
ePDF: 978-1-3501-8051-2
eBook: 978-1-3501-8052-9

Series: Schizoanalytic Applications

Typeset by Deanta Global Publishing Services, Chennai, India

To find out more about our authors and books visit www.bloomsbury.com and sign up for
our newsletters.

Contents

Illustrations	vii
List of contributors	viii
Foreword	xi
Acknowledgements	xiv
Introduction *Joff P. N. Bradley, Alex Taek-Gwang Lee and Manoj N. Y.*	1

Part I Philo-fiction and Schizoid self: Resistance to techno-tethering

1. All power to the cockroaches: Postmedia and the posthuman *Joff P. N. Bradley* — 15
2. The existential territory of Shaheen Bagh: A schizoanalytic cartography *Manoj N. Y.* — 40
3. The schizoanalysis of mechanical surveillance *Alex Taek-Gwang Lee* — 55

Part II Principles of schizo thought — 67

4. Postmedia Hans: Keeping it real with Guattari *Janell Watson* — 69
5. Reflections on postmedia for philosophers *Edward Thornton* — 86
6. Postmedia and dissensus: Reinventing democracy with Guattari *Jean-Sébastien Laberge* — 103

Part III Becoming algorithmic and ecosophical struggles for singularity

7. Assemblage line and tactical fluidity: Along Beijing's lines versus Hong Kong's 'Be Water' *Hsiu-ju Stacy Lo* — 119
8. Cartographies of the gaze of the other/other gazes: Youth, slums, and audiovisual production in the postmedia age *Silvia Grinberg and Julieta Armella* — 135
9. No media ... *David R. Cole* — 149
10. Schizoanalysis and ecology on the other side of postmedia *Mark Featherstone* — 164

Part IV Microtechnologies and resistance: Chaodyssey of postmedia

11 Groups of militant insanity versus the videopolice: The schizoanalysis of radical Italian audiovisual media culture as postmedia assemblages *Michael Goddard* 183

12 Minor video and becoming-Japanese: Towards migrant adolescent molecular revolution *Masayuki Iwase* 197

13 Akira versus Tetsuo: Postmedia chaos as reserve of potentials in Guattarian ecosophy *Toshiya Ueno* 218

Notes 235
Index 240

Illustrations

Figure

4.1	Territories of Hans's rhizome. © Janell Watson	72
4.2	The family territory. © Janell Watson	74
4.3	From the family territory (A) to the territory of the parent's bed (B). © Janell Watson	75
4.4	From the territory of the parent's bed (B) to the mother's face (C). © Janell Watson	77
4.5	Territory of the object of phallic power (D). © Janell Watson	79
4.6	Machinic territoriality of the unconscious fantasy (E). © Janell Watson	81
7.1	*Two Cézanne's*. Courtesy of artist Li Zi-Fong	122
7.2	*The Copy*. Courtesy of artist Li Zi-Fong	123
7.3	*Digital Foundation Makeup*. Courtesy of artist Li Zi-Fong	124
7.4	*Disembody*. Courtesy of artist Li Zi-Fong	125
7.5	*Salamander-Merfolk*. Courtesy of artist Li Zi-Fong	126
7.6	*The Cartesian Headgear*. Courtesy of artist Li Zi-Fong	127
7.7	*The Four Quadrants of an Elephant*. Courtesy of artist Li Zi-Fong	128
7.8	*Sun Wukong in the Matrix*. Courtesy of artist Li Zi-Fong	129
7.9	*Your Left Eye Is My Right Eye*. Courtesy of artist Li Zi-Fong	129
9.1	The four-line matter cloud analysis leading into the singularity of the Anthropocene. © Cole 2017	153
9.2	The argument for social ecology. © Cole 2017	156
9.3	Finance-subjectivity. © Cole 2015	157
9.4	The economic doughnut from Raworth. Figure used with permission from the author	158

Tables

9.1	The educational thinking practice to connect the Anthropocene with 'no media'. © David Cole	159
12.1	Participant Demographics	208

Contributors

Julieta Armella (PhD) is a lecturer of Sociology of Education at the School of Humanities, National University of San Martin (UNSAM), Argentina. She is also a researcher at the Human Sciences Research Laboratory (National Scientific and Technical Research Council/School of Humanities, UNSAM). Her ongoing research project aims to understand the characteristics of the pedagogical apparatuses attending to the processes of digital inclusion in the everyday life of public secondary schools located in contexts of extreme urban poverty. She has published chapters and articles in academic journals in Argentina, Latin-American and international.

Joff P. N. Bradley is a professor of Philosophy and English, Faculty and Graduate School of Foreign Languages, Teikyo University, Tokyo, Japan, visiting fellow at Kyung Hee University, Seoul, Korea, and previously visiting professor at Jamia Millia Islamia, New Delhi, India. He is the vice president of the International Association of Japan Studies. Joff has co-written *A Pedagogy of Cinema* and co-edited: *Deleuze and Buddhism*; *Educational Ills and the (Im)possibility of Utopia*; *Educational Philosophy and New French Thought*; *Principles of Transversality, Bringing Forth a World*; *Bernard Stiegler and the Philosophy of Education*. He published *Thinking with Animation* in 2021. His book *Schizoanalysis and Asia* is due for publication in 2023.

David R. Cole is an associate professor in Education at Western Sydney University, Australia, and the founder of the Institute of Interdisciplinary Research into the Anthropocene: https://iiraorg.com/. He is a philosopher of education and author, having produced more than one hundred significant publications and fifteen books. He believes that the problematics of the Anthropocene can only be approached through collective practice and thought. His latest book is *Education, the Anthropocene, and Deleuze/Guattari*.

Felicity Colman is a professor of Media Arts and an associate dean of Research at University of the Arts, London.

Mark Featherstone is a professor of Social and Political Theory at Keele University, England. His main fields of interest are critical theory, cultural theory and psychoanalysis. He is author of two monographs on utopia and contemporary social and political thought, *Tocqueville's Virus* (2007) and *Planet Utopia* (2017). His latest book is *The Sociology of Debt* (2021). He is the co-editor of the journal *Cultural Studies*.

Michael Goddard (PhD) is a reader in Film and Screen Media at Goldsmiths, University of London. His work falls under three areas: transnational cinema, popular music and media theory. His publications include *Polish Cinema in a Transnational Context* (co-edited with Ewa Mazierska, 2014); *The Cinema of Raúl Ruiz: Impossible Cartographies* (2013); *Reverberations: The Philosophy, Aesthetics and Politics of Noise* (co-edited with Benjamin Halligan and Michael Goddard, 2012) and *Guerrilla Networks* (2018) which excavates a range of 1970s radical media practices; among others.

Silvia Grinberg (PhD) is a professor of Sociology of Education and Pedagogy at the School of Humanities, National University of San Martin (UNSAM), Argentina. She is also a researcher and the director of the Human Sciences Research Laboratory (National Scientific and Technical Research Council/School of Humanities, UNSAM). She has conducted several research projects in the slums of Buenos Aires. She has published six books and numerous chapters and articles in academic journals in Argentina, Latin-American and international publications. With her colleague Julieta Armella is now co-editing a book on education in platform societies.

Masayuki Iwase received his doctorate from the Faculty of Education at the University of British Columbia, Vancouver, Canada (2022). His dissertation is entitled *Minor-Videos and Becoming-Japanese: Problematizing [co][existence] Policies and Envisioning Alternative Futures of Young Migrants' Lives in Japan*. He is currently working as a multimedia specialist in the Learning and Teaching Technology division of the Centre for Educational Excellence at Simon Fraser University, Burnaby, Canada. His most recent publication is 'Towards a Noncompliant Pedagogy of the Image: Reading Negentropic Bifurcatory Potentials in Video Images' (with Joff. P. N. Bradley, 2021) for the *Video Journal of Education and Pedagogy*.

Jean-Sébastien Laberge is a PhD candidate at the School of Political Studies at the University of Ottawa, Canada, and in the History of Arts and Representations Laboratory at Paris Nanterre University, France. He is interested in ecosophical democracy, especially issues related to alterity and dissensus, and contributed a chapter 'Heterogenesis, Ecosophy and Dissent' to *Schizoanalysis and Ecosophy: Reading Deleuze and Guattari* (2017). Laberge is a member of the editorial board of *Chimères – Revue des schizoanalyses* and *La Deleuziana*. Laberge is also researching the impact of Brazil and Japan in Guattari's work as well as his reception in these countries.

Alex Taek-Gwang Lee is a professor at the Department of British and American Cultural Studies and a founding director of the Center for Technology in Humanities, Kyung Hee University, South Korea. He has edited the third volume of *The Idea of Communism* (2016) and published articles in various journals such as *Telos*, *Deleuze and Guattari Studies* and *Philosophy Today*, along with chapters in *Balibar/Wallerstein's "Race, Nation, Class": Rereading a Dialogue for Our Times* (2018), *Back to the '30s?: Recurring Crises of Capitalism, Liberalism and Democracy* (2020), *The Bloomsbury Handbook of World Theory* (2021) and *Thinking with Animation* (2021).

Hsiu-Ju Stacy Lo is a full-time postdoctoral fellow at National Yang Ming Chiao Tung University in Taiwan. Since completing her doctoral dissertation on the so-called jianghu culture and cynicism in contemporary China, she has been investigating digital surveillance and censorship, and their effects on the bodily consciousness and performance in the context of – but not limited to – protest movements in Asia. Her recent publications are concerned with the creative use of technologies and various 'jianghu' tactics in Hong Kong's 'Be Water' movement as well as new media art.

Manoj N. Y. is a visiting fellow at Kyung Hee University, Seoul, South Korea. He is the general secretary of Deleuze and Guattari Studies in India Collective and co-editor of *Deleuze, Guattari and India: Exploring a Post-postcolonial Multiplicity* (2021).

Edward Thornton is a lecturer in Philosophy at the University of Aberdeen, Scotland. Dr Thornton has a special interest in the work of Deleuze and Guattari, including in Guattari's psychoanalytic, ecosophic and political writings. He also writes about psychoanalytic theory and has conducted work on the history of institutional psychotherapy and institutional pedagogy. Before moving to Aberdeen, Dr Thornton worked at Royal Holloway, University of London, where he also completed his PhD in philosophy. The research conducted for this project formed the basis of an upcoming monograph titled *On Lines of Flight: Deleuze and Guattari's Philosophy of Transformation*.

Toshiya Ueno is a professor in the Department of Human Science, Wako University, Tokyo, and a leading expert on critical theory, cultural studies and postmedia ecosophy. His current project is the transversal and comparative analysis of Guattarian ecosophy and Japanese postwar intellectuals.

Janell Watson is a professor of French at Virginia Tech, USA. She is the author of *Literature and Material Culture from Balzac to Proust* and *Guattari's Diagrammatic Thought*, as well as numerous articles on critical theory and culture. She is the editor of *The Minnesota Review: A Journal of Creative and Critical Writing*.

Foreword

Desiring somatic time

Felicity Colman

'I want to watch the end of the world with you: a live feed of the last moments on a big screen TV' (Signal message 2022)

Becoming exhausted. Exhaustion. Exhausting energy. Expended energy. Will go to sleep in x minutes if not connected to a power source. Power platforms unavailable due to [grid overload/ natural: manmade disaster/warzone]. The energy of media forms requires living capital to power, to generate, to connect, to plug into, to power up and down. The energy of the world is harnessed by political concepts and given form by media platforms; sounds, images, actions captured as generically recognizable movements. Screen time big time. In 2022, TikTok gives selfie game-time warzone forms for the complicit user/generator of thermal energy forms. Images of dead bodies and destroyed things power the news edited to the beat of commercially recognizable audio tracks in frenetic, repetitive and banal circuits. Revealing the powering up; media platforms facilitate the processes of authority generation; with codesigning tools coded for users to make more by deforming the codes carried by the sound images. Injecting more energy in staged transmission, the flows generate forms until the circuit is exhausted and other energy vectors input to generate processual movements which are harnessed for different labour systems and provide a limitless supply of ideological data banks for the latest despotic leader. There is no longer concealment of or from this problematic vampirism of humanitarian or even ecological power; it is a human-made, human-desired, human-destructive drawing-off of energy resources. Media exhaustive platforms suck human energy; require human energies to exist to be fired up, to circulate, to command. AI; as if the machines could work without the sentient energies. Sentient creatures only know themselves and their identifiable community groups through mediated frameworks of existence; the recordings; their endless photographs and mindless time stamping; I am designated as a this or that; I was here or there, here's the shop sign, the dog shite, the food, the explosion, the dead body, the body in motion, here is the poverty of the political discourse that surrounds my designation in spacetime. How can I document faster and faster new experiences, the freakish, how can I tag and metatag this exhausting exhaustive processual framework; freely feeding the machinic big daddy main framework? The semiotics and emoji are slippery familiar and basic; does difference matter?

Articulation of the slipperiness of existence is a thought experiment that has an ongoing genealogy of consequences; challenging the community structures that have produced it, and shifting liability firmly onto the singular body. Through the exhaustion, barely graspable thoughts, and event affects can be linked (rationally or otherwise) to actual and virtual sites, faceless bodies, indeterminate and absolute belief systems. Feelings are numbed, muted, silenced. Despite the endless platforms for narrativizing and representing, no one is actually listening, or responding. What has happened to concepts such as 'peace', 'non-violent actions', 'thought' (Lambert 2010)? Aesthetic codes may offer some limited relief, but who has time for those? Existence is made definitively capturable, submitted to the public realm with ease, freely feeding commercial exploits, exploiting and exhausting energy sources even further. This is a state deeper than submission. Willing exhaustive submission to the massed platforms of violence towards others, and the banal algorithms for the distribution of energy through modes of power. But exhaustion is a human expression, tied to the uses of our physical bodies (Schaffner 2016), so how do we understand it (and other somatic temporal affects) through the practice of schizoanalysis of the postmedia situation?

The 'collective interactivity' of media forms that Félix Guattari had in mind in the 1980s are yet to arrive (Broeckmann 2013). In the intervening years since Guattari's sketch of the datafied society, the complexities of the technological paradigm he indicated have both expanded and simultaneously contracted the human existential remit. The production of subjectivity, as Guattari details, consists of the articulation of continuous acceleration towards its own solipsistic capitalist future made on an endless production route. This kind of future, as Guattari reminds us, is predicated on the 'machinic subjectivity of a new type' wherein one must try to rethink human subjectivity (2013: 11–15).

In posthuman terms, 'humans' are a bundle of bioinformatics becoming algorithmic; we are data sets, organized by cultural systems coordinated by energy forms. In the era of unregulated networked platforms, the data sets that we produce and feed are continually harvested, valued and sold. Our bioinformatics are assigned and sorted by codes, arranged, mapped, rearranged by the network effect feeding the systems. Humans have created their own meta-cognitive worlds. In generating these worlds, societies set up various kinds of models that govern the production and control of information, models that control the experiences (chemical, social, educational) of information, and models which map users' systemic patterns. The energy forms to drive these systems is designed to exhaust completely the somatic time of humans. But this is not Deleuze 2.0 control society. Governance of this time is driven by what Guattari identified as the 'semiotic operator' of capitalism (1996: 202); where the movement of information is through social operations (such as we can easily identify through technological platforms). In the 2020s, we can further describe the modalities of this algorithmic governance of bioinformatics, where the technological operations of the semiotic operators are mis/directed and un/generated, through the algorithmic condition of the market today. To elaborate on this, we can identify that through the capitalist market system's flows of information and things (the inequitable, exploitative use and distribution of resources); the multiple modalities that 'govern' the dataflows which are chaotic, random and contingent. Governance is done through algorithmic conditions that are willingly fed energy by its subservient subjects. To be respondable to these conditions, we can adopt a Spinozist modal framework; to recognize the regime requiring the energy; recognize how our own resources are limited and finite, and as Guattari implores, understand that our existence is not reliant upon an authorization of modes of existential energy (the pleasures of life).

Developing the tools of critical care that Guattari offers in his work (finding the existential energies) as a way forward out of the affects of those collective apparatuses of subjectification and the contemporary postmedia bind is a task that requires attention to both the technicalities of the operational factors of machinic frameworks, and also attention to existential concepts and their realization. The chapters in this volume each attend to this task. How exactly do we 'keep it real' as Janell Watson encourages; describing how postmedia subjects continue to invest in limitations on desire, and thus thwart their own existential energetic possibilities. *What is it that you desire?* is perhaps the ethically determining question for how the twenty-first century will play out. Frightening in postmedia terms as we feed the authority producing the violence; exhausting ourselves. Time to set aside the self-imposed limit of being live-stream passive and complicit users. Care and peace in the twenty-first century call for a considered development of tools of schizoanalysis as a practice that can engage with the psychotechnologies of postmedia forms (Stiegler 2010: 202); releasing humans from their submissive states and providing methods for intervention. Repair of the communities that support and provide nurture for the existential subject is desperately needed.

References

Broeckmann, A. (2013), '"Postmedia" Discourses: A Working Paper', *Abroeck*, Available online: https://abroeck.in-berlin.de/postmedia-discourses/ (accessed 04 May 2021).
Guattari, F. (1996), 'Capital as the Integral of Power Formations', in C. Wolfe and S. Cohen (trans.), S. Lotringer (ed.), *Soft Subversions*, 202–24, New York: Semiotext(e).
Guattari, F. ([1989] 2013), *Schizoanalytic Cartographies*, trans. A. Goffey, London: Bloomsbury.
Lambert, G. (2010), 'Perpetual Peace Project | Concept', *Perpetual Peace Project*, Available online: http://perpetualpeaceproject.org/concept.php (accessed 14 May 2021).
Schaffner, A. K. (2016), *Exhaustion: A History*, New York: Columbia University Press.
Stiegler, B. ([2008] 2010), *Taking Care of Youth and the Generations*, trans. S. Barker, Stanford: Stanford University Press.

Acknowledgements

This book emerges (much belatedly) from joyful face-to-face, pre-corona meetings across the world with friends and colleagues devoted to the work of Gilles Deleuze and Félix Guattari. The editors of the book worked on the critical postmedia project as part of the Indian government's SPARC project 2019–20 and during that time, we visited each other in India, Japan and Korea for workshops, conferences and even worked together for the inaugural World Congress on Deleuze and Guattari in Delhi. The academy of scholars in this book are all part of this intellectually thriving network. Indeed, it features a collection of essays from writers based in East and South Asia, Europe and the UK, Australia and both North America and Latin America. In Tokyo, Delhi, Seoul, London, Toronto, Taipei, Sydney, Beijing, Manchester and many other places our paths have crossed. For the editors, the decision to gather friends together to write on postmedia is a necessary one, as there is a desperate need to account for the mental and existential problems afflicting and affecting the youth in swelling conurbations across the planet, where tens of millions of inhabitants cluster together. It is Guattari more than anyone else who has guided us to account for the new forms of mental pollution which remote-control entire populations.

This co-edited book is also one of the outcomes of the MHRD-SPARC project P750, funded by the Indian government. The joint project, led by Lee, Manoj N. Y., Bradley and Professor Biswajit Das, which ran from 2019 to 2021, was entitled Critical Post-Media Studies in Asia: A Comparative Study of India, Japan and South Korea, and was hosted by the Centre for Culture, Media and Governance, Jamia Millia Islamia, New Delhi, India.

The co-editors wish to thank the excellent copyediting work by Kartikeya Jain who stuck with the project throughout the coronavirus pandemic.

Introduction

Joff P. N. Bradley, Alex Taek-Gwang Lee and Manoj N. Y.

This book on the philosophies of Deleuze and Guattari and what the editors term *critical postmedia* is principally concerned with thinking the unthought in schizoanalysis – the *what-is-yet-to-come* from schizoanalysis. We take it that schizoanalysis is not simply a method to forecast or predict what is not yet actualized in the present but precisely a mode of creation and resistance. In this sense, schizoanalysis is akin to 'virtual' criticism, that is, the 'creation' of a condition for critique. As schizoanalysis is in the political sense expressive of the fabulatory, this volume does not merely aim to reiterate the theses of orthodox media studies nor for that matter to regurgitate the prescient comments Guattari made about the postmedia era in the 1980s and early 1990s. Instead, this volume aims to reproduce or reinvent the condition on which the critique of the media serves *as resistance*. We are thus aiming for a political dissensual fabulation (Bogue 2010). Therefore, critical postmedia studies can be understood as a metamodelization exercise (Watson 2009) which, on two fronts, can grapple with established 'university discourse' on media studies and philosophize what has not yet been adequately discussed in such a 'normal' scholarship.

This volume is especially focussed on updating the insights of Guattari with respect to his utopian prospectus of a postmedia dissensus. While it has become increasingly difficult to believe that postmedia and indeed schizoanalysis can alone somehow *help us* to think beyond our increasingly serial and paranoid societies of control, this is the difficult task which the contributors to this volume resolutely embrace. As Guattari says in 'Remaking Social Practices', change, the real root-and-branch transformation of the way of things, does not emerge spiritually or majestically – preordained from above as it were – but it must be 'endlessly reconquered' by those participating in the here and now: 'Ethical and aesthetic values do not arise from imperatives and transcendent codes. They call for an existential participation based on an immanence that must be endlessly reconquered' (Guattari 1996: 266).

In the flat, platformed world of incessantly whirring machines, the task is to constantly metamodel new ethico-aesthetic paradigms in order to think otherwise than the status quo. While the development of postmedia over the last thirty years has produced what Mark Featherstone calls 'a digital dystopia with far greater reach than the old mass media of the 20th century ever had,' in his chapter 'Schizoanalysis and Ecology on the Other Side of Post-Media,' there is nevertheless something in critical postmedia research which still has value. Our job, our collective remit, is simply to respond to the perennial question: what is to be done?

The academy of scholars in this volume are excellently and eclectically mixed, some established academics, some up-and-coming scholars, but all of them share a passion for Deleuze and Guattari and for expressing the futural role and nature of the unconscious, the possibility of utopia, and for a mode of thinking which searches for a way beyond the impasse and nihilism of the present moment. Our manifesto thus remains doggedly positive. Our belief is that schizoanalysis is a way to think about the unconscious and its relationship with the future and one of the continuing tasks of schizoanalysis in its current iteration is to account for the impact of technologies on the human psyche. This is why critical postmedia research is a heuristic and necessary tool: if it is to mean anything it must mean the radical critique of the present. This means that when we look at the question 'what is the schizoanalysis of postmedia?' we must write *beyond postmedia* in terms of the futural unconscious. We are writing a kind of utopia beyond the crushing sense of mass media and beyond the outdated paradigm of what postmedia has become since the early 1990s. We are writing a new kind of prospectus for the future as such; it is in these terms that I think the readers of this book should approach the wonderful ecosophical texts that lie within.

We know that Guattari first used the concept of postmedia in the mid-1980s and developed it during that decade through to the early 1990s. Writing on the cusp of the World Wide Web revolution which was to come only a few years after his death in August 1992, like most people of his time he could never have fully anticipated the radical transformation in intelligence and knowledge which was to come. Nevertheless, he conjured up the idea of a post-mass media age, where individuals, groups and communities could have more control of their lives and could be somehow less consumed by images by way of creative and productive universes of references engineered by the technological era. In the 1980s, he drew on his experience of pirate and community radio and conjectured what was to come from the French proto-internet Minitel system, and thereupon outlined the prospects of a new era of dissensus. This was consistent with his ecosophical vision, which was a treatment and reading of social and mental ecologies alongside the environment proper. This, he believed, allowed for a better understanding of the struggles in the depressing political 'winter years' in the 1980s. Simply, to change, protect and have responsibility for the environment in the long term one needs a fundamental change in mentalities. And conversely to change mentalities one needs to change the environment. This is the social ecology which lies at the heart of the ecosophical project.

The critical postmedia perspective challenges the view that mere participation in micro or minor, miniaturized media is inherently liberatory. This is so because the new modes of mediation which were once imagined to liberate desire and to create new democratic practices, to manifest more openness and freedom, have left us spinning in the 'neuroleptic' void. We are more and more enchained to all manner of addictions. What has happened to desire and libidinal energy, to processes of subjectivation which activate 'disjunctive synthesis of singularities and chains'? What has happened to the micro politics of desire? Where are the new social practices? Against the stark reality we face and the difficulty in answering these questions, it is fair to ask oneself: why write a book on schizoanalysis when we know postmedia has led to no workable alternative but rather to more entrenched patterns of passivity, cynicism and resignation?

We know microdevices such as smartphones leave the subject in greater stupefaction and disavowal. The modern subject of cognitive capitalism stumbles from one place to another in and through different modes of addiction, alienation and trauma. Consensual, hypnotic, trance-like, in a zombie-like state. Inert. Minds elsewhere, in the ether – in new forms of collective hallucination, at once insensitive to the immediate milieu and somnolent, in suspended animation, unable to ward off the secreted madness of new technologies. What has happened to the production of subjectivity? Why does the idea of resingularization through postmedia experimentation seem foolhardy and impossible? This is no glorious scene of co-participation and co-creation but rather one of intoxication, dependency, addiction and deadly repetition. Critics will say the euphoria of 1968 in which people demanded the impossible got the better of the French intellectual class, including Deleuze and Guattari. The utopia once foreseen has turned to dust. As a result, we are left with a veritable remodelling of the unconscious with retrofit molar identities and shrink-wrapped capitalist subjectivities, and our time is now more cynical about any realistic change. Critics will ask: what are the prospects for revolutionary machinic desire and for molecular revolution when the proletarian class is no more?

Our answer is that even in the politically bleak years of Guattari and indeed for us, the ecosophically prescient writings of Guattari intimate at the perpetual emergence of new modes of valourization in everyday life – friendship, sexual identity, the transformation of work, a new sense of solidarity, a new ethico-aesthetic paradigm and new forms of resistance. We hear the refrain again and again, that capitalism produces subjectivity the same way it produces commodities like shampoo or cars, but that is the point to underscore. New subjectivities can turn out *for better or worse*. This is to invoke the molecular revolution in everyday life. Yet what do we have at present? A child learns more language from the toy given by an exhausted parent, who stands close by but is entombed and distracted in the funk and jouissance of the smartphone. A smartphone app displays a grid directing a concerned parent to the whereabouts of their child. Familial relations are mediated through GPS satellites and tracking devices. Direct communication of the parent and the child about issues of truancy and refusal at school would destroy the semblance of normality in the family. It is off the table. Better to mediate relations through technology. Better the app does its impersonal work. An app shows a pizza delivery boy snaking his way through busy mid-evening traffic. A man sits alone at home after a hard day at work, too exhausted to shop and cook an evening meal. He watches the screen. In control of his consumption. The pizza arrives. Words are not exchanged, neither is money as digital money is now the norm. Pure autistic communion. An app shows the delivery itinerary from a warehouse. The young unemployed lad has paid extra for next day delivery and believes he directs and is in control of his consumption. With little else going on in his life, he is the master and the delivery service the slave. He thinks the worker is the Monkey King and he the Buddha plays with his movements through his index finger. The bored, unemployed man pays what money he has and demands what he wants. The delivery service – one among many competing others – works for him not the other way around. Relations of consumption and service are mediated and transparent. Raw capitalist relations mean nothing less than the implosion of society. Again, we must ask where lies the contemporary political promise of the postmedia era? Where is the possibility of the eventual 'reinvention of democracy', the strengthening of the heterogeneity and singularity of each member of society?

To care for the world, to have an ethics of responsibility for the planet demands the reinvention of the body, the mind and language itself. This is a constant Guattarian refrain. In other words, a new comportment to the world and to existence as such. A critical postmedia is henceforth pharmacological and therapeutic: it questions forms of subjectivation which engineer not only heterogeneous media ecologies but also new subjectivities and collective assemblages. Postmedia and schizoanalysis whence combined can become a powerful unified theory in the critique of the pre-assembled subjectivities produced by neoliberalism or Integrated World Capitalism. Guattari's desire for processual potentiality and the prospects of a less consensual postmedia was part of his search for new paths of singularization and universes of creative enchantments, a life beyond the living planetary hell in which billions toil and endure.

In *Schizoanalytic Cartographies*, Guattari was very much aware of the 'invasive grip' of computer-assisted data banks, which we now might call algorithmic governmentality, and said there was literally no domain of opinion, thought, image, affect or narrativity which could realistically escape from this new form of governmentality or control. Nevertheless, in the age of planetary computerization, and through the miniaturization of technologies, Guattari foresaw the faintest possibility of a passage away from oppression, alienation, the stupidity of consensus and empty speech, to a new society of liberation, a 'diagrammatics of communism' (Guattari and Negri 2010: 99) and following Hans Jonas, a futurally oriented ethics of responsibility.

A critical postmedia worth its name must, therefore, robustly account for how capitalism commandeers desire – and schizoanalysis is really always about desire – how it clamps down upon the desire of people young and old, how it cuts people off from the world around them, how it intensities a process which leads people to turn in upon themselves, an inward movement leading to the deadly ipseity of the self. A critical postmedia worth its salt must robustly search for 'potential zones of resistance against the uni-dimensionality of subjectivity' (Guattari 1994). This is to search for 'a possible heterogeneity of subjectivity'. A zone of resistance might be a moment of crisis, says Guattari, out of which a desire may flourish for the affirmation of existence. A zone of resistance might be found in communities of resistance or the refusal to endure forms of discrimination, racism or sexual categorization. Guattari proffers a clear utopian motif:

> I wait in an utopian dream, that there are means of recomposition of subjectivity coming particularly from the Global South, with its considerable demographic expansion and all of the pressure that the South will deploy in direction to the North and from that point on creates recompositions that are more ideological and militant for inflecting power relations on an international level from another direction for creating other voices of resolution not only in economical conflicts but also in inner-ethnic conflicts and all these situations, that nowadays is so monstrously displayed all over the planet. (Guattari 1994; Melitopoulos 2016: 33)

Such a utopian motif would look beyond crushing systems of alienation, oppressive mass-mediatization and infantilized consensual politics. It would ask after 'the unconscious turned towards the future': it would demand the reconfiguration of desire and challenge the 'computational, telematic, robotic, bureaucratic, biotechnological revolutions' which crush desire at every turn. If this is not timely it is difficult to fathom what is. In the reformulation of critical postmedia which appears in these pages, there is a call to make use of the following observation by Guattari regarding societies of control:

> Thus, control today is less a matter of the direct subjection of individuals to 'visible' systems of authority, to publicly organised apparatuses of standardisation, than of a multitude of more or less private institutional forces, associations of all kinds – sporting, social and cultural, community groups, young people's clubs, churches and so on. (Guattari and Rolnik 2008: 249)

Guattari is clearly prescient here in noting how desire and power function stealthily and imperceptibly through *private institutional forces*. One only thinks about what Guattari would make of the addictive qualities of social networking and online gaming in our time. That said, this book is not a sociology of postmedia but a critical postmedia prospectus affirming the schizoanalytic project in the twenty-first century. Simply we must better understand how power and control functions and how desire is funnelled away from its creative exploration. While we search for molecular potentiality in youth, ecosophy, postmedia and schizoanalysis are not merely empirical studies of molar desire. Again, we do not aim to write another boring media studies book. We are tasked with understanding the workings of info-semiocapitalism and its deleterious effects on desire. Why do we give away our cognitive labour so freely? Why do we participate in the production of signs, symbols and knowledge and why do we thirst for the mad enjoyment of producing capitalist subjectivity, for the passion to exploit ourselves to the point of collapse and exhaustion? Part of this task is to understand the obsessive refrains or ritournelle which keep us inhumated in our pitiful lugubrious state.

~

The writers of this book took to their individual task as follows. They appear here as in the order of the book. We have chosen to group the chapters into four divisions: Philo-fiction and Schizoid self: Resistance to techno-tethering; Principles of Schizo Thought; Becoming Algorithmic and Ecosophical: Struggles for Singularity; and Microtechnologies and Resistance: Chaodyssey of Postmedia.

The first chapter entitled 'All Power to Cockroaches: Postmedia and the Posthuman' is an idiosyncratic reading of ecosophy, schizoanalysis and postmedia wherein Bradley cleverly weaves a discussion on postmedia with questions of transhumanism and trauma, Kafkaesque literature and science fiction. He draws from neuroscience and the neuro-totalitarianism of semiocapitalism to launch a critique against the transhuman phantasmagoria of permanent digital connection. Bradley considers postmedia in terms of the trauma and memory of both human and non-human varieties to provide an ethical critique of neuroscience. He does this by underscoring his belief that schizoanalysis can help us think about this new reality we humans may endure. By citing the example of the Backyard Brains advertisement for RoboRoach on Amazon's website, Bradley explores the schizoanalytic cartography of new modes of control in the digital age, drawing inspiration from Guattari but also from Bernard Stiegler and Franco Berardi. The milieu of the devastated 'poor in world' cockroach, he argues, is symptomatic of contemporary fascistic tendencies, and exemplifies the innovative and polyphonic architectonics of control (collective algorithmic unconscious). The new form of algorithmic subjectivity which knowingly accepts the domination and is controlled by the 'ghostly, ethereal transcendental subjectivity' (world brain) constitutes a new class, a proletarian mass which is deprived of knowledge and skills. Here Bradley argues that the new alliance of machines with the planetary unconscious which Guattari envisaged must be critiqued for its limits and shortcomings as there is no room for dissensus in this 'hyper-consensual dystopian nightmare'. The cockroach is not merely a metaphor but an 'itinerant probe head' for seeking out future nightmarish posthuman and human subjectivities. Yet, while addressing the limitations of the liberatory promise of postmedia and the posthuman paradigm, this chapter demands a transvaluation of all values by affirming the philosophical lines of flight offered by schizoanalysis.

In the chapter 'Existential Territory of Shaheen Bagh: A Schizoanalytic Cartography', we find a truly unique application of Guattari's schizoanalytic cartography. To date, few have applied Guattari's four-fold schema to the Indian context and here Manoj N. Y. does so in a singularly brilliant fashion, focussing on Shaheen Bagh in Delhi, the epicentre of the protest against the Citizenship Amendment Act employed by the central government of India in late 2019. Manoj N. Y. breaks fresh ground in applying the four-fold to the subjective mutations and alternate assemblages of subjective production that emerged during the December 2020 protests at Shaheen Bagh. He finds in the territories which spontaneously emerged in Delhi, an amalgam of intensive, creative forces which opposed the politics of hatred and communalism articulated by the Hindutva state machine in India. Moreover, for Manoj N. Y., the existential territory of Shaheen Bagh destabilized the neighbouring assemblages and paved the way for 'the precipitation of new flows'. By scrutinizing the protest through a dissenual postmedia lens, Manoj N. Y. finds in the anti-CAA slogans, chants of Azaadi (freedom), poetic utterances, the traditional ritual of kolam (drawing using rice flour in certain Hindu traditions), graffiti and placards, the formation of what he calls the refrains of freedom. These new rhythms and affects expand beyond the immediate context and call the whole of the Indian government into question. Images of and quotes from Gandhi and Ambedkar, as well as the language of the Indian nationalist movement, constitutional morality, Dalit politics, the Muslim culture of north India, secular thought, protest poetry, the memories of the Occupy movement, receive creative expression on the streets as well as in the dissemination of digital images. Manoj N. Y. finds that in the territorial multiplicity of Shaheen Bagh, the incorporeal transformation of the thoughts, memories, experiences of the lives of students brought a new universe of possibility into being. What Manoj N. Y does in this chapter is to map this 'abstract diagram of dissent' to suggest the creative repetition of events across the Indian continent. He reminds us that the existential territory of Shaheen Bagh will remain one of the most important universes of reference 'for the protests to come'.

Throughout Lee's timely chapter 'The Schizoanalysis of Mechanical Surveillance' is an investigation into the relationship between surveillance, privacy and capitalist assemblages. Lee brings forth a timely discussion on the juridico-politics of mechanical surveillance in global capitalism and its transition from knowledge to data. Written with the Covid-19 pandemic in mind, and with a focus on the semiotics of Delhi's metro system, Lee rightly notes the risks to individual and bodily autonomy, the balance between collective security and private life, and the threat to human dignity and human rights. He finds a curious regime of truth and form of disciplinary power emerging in the Indian capital. But Lee is optimistic that resistance can take place in the new tele-technological situation and does not find Big Brother omnipresent or omniscient. Yet, he questions the threat of 'Big Other' and finds 'the obscurity of privacy is nothing less than the legitimacy of surveillance'. To demonstrate this, Lee sketches a history of technological governmentality to understand the emergent form of surveillance capitalism. From Heidegger to Derrida and Stiegler, Lee traces the philosophical interventions into the development of surveillance capitalism and provides an insight into the society of control. After wedding analyses of Foucault, Derrida, Heidegger, Benjamin, Zuboff and others to think through the spatial and temporal ecologies of vast urban technopoles like Delhi, Lee turns to Guattari to explore the delirium of postmedia subjectivity and possible 'venues of resistance'. Following Guattari, he claims 'chaosmos' within the technological network of computing surveillance can be such a venue of resistance. As such, Lee breaks fresh ground in juxtaposing Derrida and Stiegler's understanding of the tele-technological mechanism with the schizoanalysis of postmedia to seek out the escape routes from our unconscious compulsion vis-à-vis mechanical surveillance.

In the next section, and in his 'Reflections on Post-Media for Philosophers,' Edward Thornton focuses on the complex relationship between the nature of subjectivity and the process of mediation, especially in the context of intricate and sophisticated media technologies which are reconfiguring subjectivity in radical ways. By way of Berardi and Appich, it is argued that postmedia discourses address the role of the medium in reconfiguring subjectivity in terms of disruptive political engagements and rhizomatic collective assemblages of enunciation and in so doing revamp the conventional norms of social mediation. In an important sense, Thornton suggests that postmedia studies moves away from the normal philosophical tradition of construing subjectivity as a given fact, and instead asserts the role of heterogeneous components that cannot be 'reduced to a single semiotic entity'. In the formulation of postmedia by Félix Guattari, there is no outright jettisoning of the concept of subjectivity, but rather the focus is more on the contingent nature of subjectivity and media *as assemblages of subjective production*. Thus, the question of what the medium precisely is should not be simply addressed as one of structuring the subject, but rather as a milieu in which the subject emerges. In short, this chapter scrutinizes the question of medium vis-à-vis the notion of subjectivity in the context of postmedia studies by exploring the possibilities of what the discipline of philosophy can offer us in this endeavour.

In her contribution, in 'Postmedia Hans: Keeping It Real with Guattari', Janell Watson discusses how machinic enslavement is required for capitalist exploitation and how the Oedipalization of production functions as its axis of sustainability. Endorsing Guattari's anticipation of the post-industrial accumulation system, she relocates the story of Hans, Freud's famous analysis of a Viennese familial relation, in today's condition of deterritorialized labour. With Lazzarato and Franco Berardi, Watson points up the way in which the Oedipalization of Hans's unconscious operates in the mode of cognitive capitalism. Watson demonstrates that the theoretical framework of schizoanalytic cartography promises creativity and social engagement. She sheds light on this alternative approach to desire and demonstrates the political implications of de-Oedipalization in the twenty-first century through the radical reformulation of psychoanalytic presuppositions.

In Jean-Sébastien Laberge's chapter, 'Postmedia and Dissensus: Reinventing Democracy with Guattari', we find a focus on postmedia dissensus and its relevance to the 'resingularization' of democracy. Laberge explores in depth the manifold theoretical notions integral to the critical understanding of postmediatic dissensus and Guattari's activism. This chapter argues that transversality and molecular revolution are two integral concepts pertinent to the concept of postmedia and as such critically evaluates their role in dissensual practices. Contra the forms of centralism identified in the functioning of trade unions, political parties and groupuscules, Laberge argues that transversality is crucial for decoding the degree of openness in institutional settings. Molecular revolution is also crucial in locating and creating forms of heterogeneity, multiplicities of divergent subjectivities and spaces for experimental politics. While laying down the theoretical ground for postmedia, this chapter makes use of specific examples from Guattari's activism – such as Minitel, the Alternatik network, the Rainbow network and Guattari's engagement with the ecology movement.

In Part III, Hsiu-ju Stacy Lo in her 'Assemblage Line and Tactical Fluidity': Along Beijing's Lines versus Hong Kong's 'Be Water' provides a striking analysis of the 'Be Water Movement' in the Chinese context and shows the reader the practical aspect of the 'lines'. Lo deals with Li Zi-Fong's computer-generated art compared to the 'Be Water Movement' in Hong Kong and emphasizes the affective overlapped image in both Li's work and the image of a girl's damaged eye in the city. This is a beautiful evocation of how machinic assemblages meet the liquid forces of movement and how images consisting of lines dismantle and deconstruct given identities. The analysis of Li's artwork provides us with an excellent example of theory *as practice* grasped from Guattari's perspective.

Following on from Lo, in their collaboration 'Cartographies of the Gaze of the Other/Other Gazes: Youth, Slums and Audiovisual Production in the Postmedia Age', Silvia Grinberg and Julieta Armella interrogate the postmedia society from the deep analysis of audiovisual production in the Global South. They focus on how young people living in slums in Buenos Aires rearrange the given media differently and organize and resist through such practices. According to Grinberg and Armella, young people in the slums are no longer the petrified object of a stranger's gaze but rather the engineers of singularity, raising the possibility of embracing otherness *without reservation*. Through interviews regarding landfill and ecological problems and by examining the creative and artistic expression of young people, Grinberg and Armella find youth performing a cartography of *other gazes*.

In David Cole's chapter, we find a thought-provoking reflection on the state of 'no media'. This is grasped in the context and prospect of planetary extinction, environmental crises and the event of the Anthropocene. While we find that through the saturation of cinematic and mediatic images the conjuring of counter-ideas to the status quo by 'idiot-media-consumers' becomes an ever-fainter prospect, Cole claims there remains the possibility to revive social ecology and to move towards the dissolution of the 'idiot/mesmerising/nullifying' media. By looking at Deleuze and Guattari's prescience on this issue, Cole points to ways to rethink approaches to education and economics. In terms of the latter, the economic analysis presented by Cole engages with Guattari's notion of semiocapitalism and Raworth's doughnut economics and addresses educational issues through Deleuze's third synthesis of time in *Difference and Repetition* (1994) to open a new pathway for postmedia.

Equaling concerned with the endemic crises of capitalism, Mark Featherstone, in his chapter entitled 'Schizoanalysis and Ecology on the other side of Postmedia', addresses the contemporary global crisis in terms of the struggle between primitive nationalists and the sci-fi futurists, but suggests that what is left untouched is precisely the philosophical structure of capitalism. Thus, Featherstone suggests a political reading of this 'apocalyptic realism' and suggests an alternate vision of the future, 'a minor utopianism' in the works of Guattari and Deleuze. In this endeavour, the onus is on the schizoanalytic critique of capitalist subjectivity which can be traced to *Anti-Oedipus* (1977), *A Thousand Plateaus* (1987) and *What Is Philosophy?* (1994) and the analytical reading of the nature of contemporary semiocapitalism which fragments, codifies and commodifies the subject. Though the focus is on the philosophical structure of Guattari and Deleuze's work, this chapter argues that it is imperative to update the utopian aspect of postmedia which affirms the dismantling of mass media.

In the last section, Michael Goddard's 'Groups of Militant Insanity versus the Videopolice: The Schizoanalysis of Radical Italian Audiovisual Media Culture as Postmedia Assemblages', applies Guattari's conceptions of minor cinema and the postmedia era to explore how anti-psychiatry was taken up both in the Radio Alice free radio station and cinematic culture in Italy in the 1970s. In terms of the latter, emphasis is placed on the work of Marco Bellocchio, Elio Petri and especially Alberto Grifi. While Grifi's work *Anna* (Grifi and Sarchielli 1975) is a relatively well-known anti-psychiatric video experiment, Goddard explores how a schizoanalytic approach runs through his 1970s work in proximity with the Creative Autonomia movement which gave rise to Radio Alice. However, these currents were already present in key works of Marco Bellocchio and Elio Petri, especially in *Fists in the Pocket* (Bellocchio 1965), *Matti da slegare* (Fit to be Untied 1975) and *La classe operaia va in paradiso* (The Working Class Goes to Heaven, Petri 1971). However, in *La classe operaia va in paradiso*, Goddard finds the exploration of sound especially significant as it indicates the schizoanalytic inter-relations between class struggle, sexuality and psychic and emotional states. What is also brought out in this chapter then is that this forms the basis for Radio Alice's reinvention of radio as a delirious machinery for the militant destabilization of the state, capital and mass media. It becomes clear that in many of these media phenomena it is not just anti-psychiatric representation that is expressed, but what emerges is a minor politics in tune with the transformation of cinema, video and radio. Emergent are schizoanalytic ecologies which work to break down to varying degrees the distinctions between producers, technologies and consumers. Goddard suggests that while militant insanity ultimately lost out to the video police (mass arrests and the rise of Berlusconi's media empire), it nevertheless provides a rich legacy for the potential reinvention of the postmedia era in the twenty-first century.

Turning to Japan in the last two essays, Masayuki Iwase first applies concepts from Deleuze and Guattari to understand the reality of immigrants living in Japan in 'Minor Video and Becoming-Japanese: Towards Migrant Adolescent Molecular Revolution'. He picks up on the issue of the coexistence between Japanese and incoming non-Japanese foreigners within the archipelago and extrapolates from this reality a critique of noo-politics characteristic of the societies of control. For Iwase, TV and present-day social media are the main enhancers of perpetuating the Japanese-non-Japanese binary, which infiltrates into the nervous systems of machinically enslaved viewers. A-signifying dispositifs are utilized to sensationalize 'Japanese uniqueness' – to the detriment of the other. He uses the video project of his students to point to a counter and 'minor video of desire' that destabilizes the coexistence of an unchanging binary. In approaching the postmedia situation through an analysis of migration and its effects, Iwase clarifies how 'foreignness' is invented and consists of immigrants' identities. Iwase points to the paradox between law and the nation-state – where the asymmetrical structure always facilitates the ontological repetition of 'pure nation'. For Iwase, while mass media plays a pivotal role in promoting this discrepancy, it also preserves a possible space for an emergent micropolitics. And last but not least, Toshiya Ueno writes an imaginary account of Tetsuo and Akira, characters drawn from popular anime, and uses this as a prism through which to explicate the intellectual history of postmedia in 1980s Japan. In 'Akira versus Tetsuo: Postmedia Chaos as Reserve of Potentials in Guattarian Ecosophy', Toshiya Ueno draws on his personal knowledge and experience of meeting Guattari in Japan to explain the importance of postmedia for Japanese intellectuals such as Tetsuo Kogawa and Akira Asada. This intellectual history which is unfamiliar to many researchers outside of Japan is important because it helps to answer the question: Can postmedia be equated with new media or multimedia after the mass-media era? Ueno answers this question by refusing a simple sociological reading, suggesting ecosophy is not media ecology *per se* but a 'virtual ecology' in the Guattarian sense. Ueno compares Akira with Tetsuo in the Japanese context, but extends his discussion to the politics of postmedia chaos. Ueno reminds us of the interview with Tetsuo Kogawa during Guattari's visit to Japan and juxtaposes this encounter with the episode of Asada Akira, one of Japan's most famous postmodernist intellectuals. Ueno clarifies Guattari's concept of postmedia and its theoretical breakthrough, and his argument reveals the hidden story of Guattari's relation to Japan. By this revelation, Ueno suggests the lingering potentiality of Guattari's ecosophical aesthetics-politics.

References

Bogue, R. (2010), *Deleuzian Fabulation and the Scars of History*, Edinburgh: Edinburgh University Press.
Guattari, F. (1994), 'Avez-vous vu la guerre?', *Chimères: Revue des schizoanalyses*, 23 (1): 1–12.

Guattari, F. (1996), *The Guattari Reader*, ed. G. Genosko, Oxford: Blackwell Publishers.
Guattari, F. and S. Rolnik (2008), *Molecular Revolution in Brazil*, trans. K. Clapshow and B. Holmes, Cambridge: MIT Press.
Guattari, F. and A. Negri (2010), *New Lines of Alliance, New Spaces of Liberty*, ed. S. Shukaitis, trans. M. Ryan, J. Becker, A. Bove and N. Le Blanc, London: Minor Compositions.
Melitopoulos, A. (2016), *Ways of Meaning: Machinic Animism and the Revolutionary Practice of Geo-Psychiatry*, PhD diss., Goldsmiths, University of London.
Watson, J. (2009), *Guattari's Diagrammatic Thought: Writing between Lacan and Deleuze*, London: Bloomsbury Publishing.

Part I

Philo-fiction and Schizoid self
Resistance to techno-tethering

1

All power to the cockroaches

Postmedia and the posthuman

Joff P. N. Bradley

I shall begin and end with the question of the 'remote-controlling of human individuals' (Guattari 2000: 38–9) – '*over and underneath*' speaking heads. For this task, I refer to two initial statements from Kafka and Guattari, both discussing the monstrous, the machinic, the unconscious and our embroilment within all of that. Kafka writes (2009: 29): 'As Gregor Samsa woke one morning from uneasy dreams, he found himself transformed into some kind of monstrous vermin [*Ungeziefer*]' and Guattari (2016: 223) asks: 'Why not admit that a machinic consciousness exists – for example in the case of the enslavement of the driver to his machine?. . . A thousand machinic propositions constantly work over every individual, over and underneath his speaking head.' The statements shall serve as philosophical probe-heads guiding the direction of what is to come.

Scurrying madly across this manuscript are also innumerable and abominable cockroaches, monstrous vermin and perverse insects – black insect laughter, undreaming insect eyes and mangled insect screams which reveal vast inhuman landscapes. Such infestations may intrude upon any straightforward humanist enterprise, aspiration and reading. There is a veritable becoming-cockroach of the reader and writer at work. In the first part of this chapter, I explore the concept of transhumanism, memory and trauma through two odd sources: (1) a consideration of the neuroscience of the RoboRoach device and (2) Dennis Potter's British TV drama *Cold Lazarus* which aired on British TV in 1996. My aim is to raise ethical questions around brain research and how science fiction and postmedia studies can help us think about the new entomon-reality we live *within*. Arguing from an idiosyncratic reading of ecosophy, schizoanalysis and postmedia, and including the ruminations of Bernard Stiegler and Franco Berardi, thinkers heavily influenced by Félix Guattari, I end by explaining why I am – and we as a species ought to be – in solidarity with the cockroaches. It will be seen that the abominable cockroach is more than a Kafkaesque metaphor to describe what we are becoming; it is rather a veritable probe-head (O'Sullivan 2006), rethinking the conventional and seeking out non-human futures. There is, thus, a certain destruction of metaphor at work. Of course, there is a history of thinking about the human-machine interface entomologically in a number of writers and thinkers. We find the insect metaphor used in *Naked Lunch* by William Burroughs in relation to control and Kevin Kelly uses entomological metaphors, such as the hive, superorganism in *Out of Control*. But here, with less metaphor and more metamorphosis, our understanding of the cockroach is neither imaginary nor symbolic but machinic, technological and concrete. Yet, I situate myself in-between the critique of the 'remote-controlling of human individuals' and the searching or 'guidance device' of the probe-head which escapes forms of control. The question is how to maintain unicity, 'despite the diversity of components of subjectivation that pass through me' (Guattari 1995a: 16). I want to understand the becoming machinic and mechanico-metamorphosis of the cockroach in terms of concepts drawn from Guattari's *The Three Ecologies* and his inchoate postmedia theory. These heuristic concepts, I argue, chart a path from postmedia to the posthuman and the transhuman as such and demonstrate the continued importance of the postmedia prospectus as a mapping out of the unconscious *geared towards the future*. My insistence is that there is much still to be gleaned from Guattari's prescient speculations. Schizoanalysis, if it is to mean anything, must remain occupied with the myriad productions of computer-aided subjectivity and with it the plasticity of the brain – insect or otherwise. What I am attempting to do in this chapter is, therefore, to write a schizoanalytic cartography of the cockroach, to understand the *Umwelt* of the cockroach as such, and to remodel Guattari's notion of postmedia in order to understand the changing, polyphonic terrain and milieu in which techniques and technologies take on different mutational forms. This is a bold and committed project of dissensual metamodelization.

In the second part of the chapter, I think about the idea of 'collective intelligence' and stress the importance of the work of Pierre Lévy in Guattari's thought and how this might allow us to construct a new vocabulary to question what might be called the neuro-totalitarianism of the unconscious (Berardi 2014). The focus here is not so much on the noosphere as an ethereal and transcendental possibility but on collective consciousness as a form of grammatization or virtual hypomnemata (Stiegler 2010: 33). For Bernard Stiegler, grammatization explains 'the history of the exteriorisation of memory in all its forms: nervous and cerebral memory, corporeal and muscular memory, biogenetic memory' (2010: 33). This is to understand the connection between collective consciousness and memory in order to appreciate the nature of the expansion of consciousness and how it is connected with postmedia. I want to think collective intelligence alongside the idea of the World Brain or superorganism.

The conclusion highlights the dangers and possibilities of computer-aided subjectivity, the contemporary manipulation of brain science for marketing and entertainment purposes, and the ethical consequences of brain research, the latter of which Guattari would frankly call *mental pollution*. What I am saying is that there is both simultaneously a mental pollution of the cockroach and of the human remote-controlled populations moored to smartphones. It is the task of schizoanalysis to understand this strange ecology and collusion, and our *unnatural participation* within it.

Part 1: Cockroaches, transhumanism, trauma and memory

> Slowly he pushed himself towards the door, still groping clumsily with his antennae, whose value he was only now learning to appreciate, in order to check what had happened there. (Kafka 2009: 44)

I am traumatized by the depiction of a cockroach as a primitive cyborg with its antennae tethered to the internet ether. I know there are other examples of this cyborg insect phenomenon such as the remote-controlled beetle developed by Dr Hirotaka Sato, an aerospace engineer at Nanyang Technological University in Singapore (Baharudin 2016), but for some reason I feel perturbed by the ethical indifference to the pain of the insect.

Imagine a cockroach equipped with a circuit board and a backpack of sorts connected via Bluetooth to an iPhone, which allows the user of the iPhone to direct the motor skills of the insect. What are the ethical ramifications of this endosomatic toy ostensibly sold as a teaching aid for introductory classes on neuroscience to school children? What incorporeal universes of reference are opened up by it? What are the ramifications for what we can understand to be the transhuman? What is at stake in the trauma and memory of the cockroach?

My own personal trauma regarding this image began by chancing upon the Backyard Brains advertisement for RoboRoach on Amazon's website. The equipment for the RoboRoach is proclaimed as revolutionary and billed as the world's first commercially available cyborg. The RoboRoach is advertised as a way to introduce advanced neuroscience to adolescents and young students interested in this exciting scientific field. The advertisement says you can perform your own advanced neural interface surgery to remotely control the movement of a cockroach from your smartphone or tablet. It goes on to say you can perform multiple experiments by using reusable Bluetooth, the LTE-enabled backpack and a small battery. The experiments allow you to make electrodes for three RoboRoaches. The advert says there are free online resources, experiment and surgery instructions. The cockroach is not included but can be sourced elsewhere, it happily proclaims. The product was sold for $99 on Amazon. In 2013, at the TEDGlobal conference in Edinburgh, Backyard Brains company representative Greg Gage explained the operation on the cockroach:

> This prototype called the RoboRoach is our latest invention. We're going to hook it up to an iPhone when you pair it to the Bluetooth off your iPhone, you can then send the small impulse to the backpack, which goes into either the left or the right antenna and it will turn it. (Wakefield 2013)

The functors of the fourfold metamodel

In *Chaosmosis*, Guattari analyses subjectivity in terms of four functors:

(T) finite existential territories;
(F) material, energetic and semiotic fluxes;

(Φ) concrete and abstract machinic phyla; and
(U) virtual universes of value.

Using Guattari's fourfold subjectivity (Berressem 2020: 8), the four functors or quadripartitions can be used as a metamodel to map the diverse domain or existence of the devastated 'poor in world' cockroach (Watson 2009: 123; Heidegger 2008). This is not a structuralist and Lacanian matheme of the unconscious, not merely a surplus or excessive graffiti of the unconscious, but an experimental diagrammatics exploring the pulsating circulation of affects in the non-human world of the cockroach. It is also a criticism of the petrified relations in societies of control in which nothing circulates or escapes, and nothing resingularizes. There is no pulsation. Through the capture and exploitation of affects, what we are left with is a black hole of subjectivity, a deadly refrain spinning on its axes. Why? The existential territory (T) of the cockroach's computer-aided subjectivity is nondiscursive and real but only virtual, a refrain occupied and disturbed by brain surgery. The cockroach becomes solipsistic or autistic, cut off from its environment, from reality as such. The cockroach sees and moves but its reaction and memory of its environment will be reset once the electrodes are removed. It apprehends the imagination and existence of another self. Pierre Lévy's 'ontological iron curtain' is removed and there is a gain in ontological consistency – but at what cost? What is the nature of the being in the world of the cockroach?

The material fluxes (F) [actual and real] of the cockroach's partial, computer-aided, polyphonic subjectivity are intensities of play, emotion and semiotics. Again, there is learning, the fascination with the mind control and manipulation of a living creature via smartphone and Bluetooth, maybe even voice control. The permutations are endless. The finger swishes on the phone and the living being moves according to the signs and signification of the data handset, but against its own volition. A schizoanalytic subjectivity emerges where flows of signs intersect with machinic flows, but at what price?

The actual and potential Phylum (Φ) of the cockroach's computer-aided subjectivity include the abstract machine overseeing the exploitation of this living creature. The machinic Phyla traces the technological lineage of techniques to exploit the neural circuits of insects. Funding models, advertising space, blueprints for new neuroscience research, plans submitted to ethics committees, rules and regulations on the online purchase of insects of the order Blattodea, faster phone chips, greater processing power, the remote-controlling of brains from space via satellites whizzing around the earth, drone control – plans and diagrams realized in the matter and energy of the flows. The abstract machines and machinic phylum (technological lineage) govern the potential for greater exploitation and control, in a creative process of experimentation and actualization (Watson 2009: 126).

The virtual possibility of incorporeal universes (U) of the cockroach's computer-aided subjectivity is non-signified and nondiscursive. It can be concrete, oneiric, pathological or aesthetic. There must be a collective desire and imaginary for this exploitation and the acceptance of neuroscientific research for utilitarian ends (children's educational benefit, breakthrough in brain disease, etc.). There must be a collective enunciation of desire and assemblage of enunciation for such a project.

Incorporeal universes, the set of values, universes of reference, virtual possibilities – all hover above the abstract machine. Will the dreams and visions of the cockroach one day be screened back to the smartphone for vicarious and scopophilic viewing pleasure? Will or can we ever know what the cockroach is thinking? Here incorporeal universes of reference, incorporeal universes of value and the existential territory of the cockroach combine to forge a machinic and mutant proto-subjectivity. A new perverse logic of the Body without Organs (BwO), the body without a brain, the acephalous body without self-direction, the body wired to Bluetooth signals, battery packs, smartphones, and flows of money to buy the wares of neuroscience toys, flows of packets of data to watch online lectures and demonstrations. The proto-subjectivity of the machined and machinic cockroach is 'permanently electrocuted' (Berardi 2015: 72) and permanently subjectivated according to the technical lineage of the machinic phylum. The mutational assemblage of machinic and biological components is co-functioning, in 'sympathy' and 'symbiosis'. Crystals of singularization and points of bifurcation emerge to suggest the creation of irreversible 'mutant universes of reference' (Watson 2009: 129), but while the assemblages of enunciation productive of this proto-subjectivity are necessarily collective, proto-subjectivity is at once technological and abstract, a 'collective agent of enunciation,' and essentially overseen by a death-drive abstract machine running smoothly and autopoietically in the machinic unconscious.

On the worst reading of our historical moment, the chance for affirmative metamorphosis and change seems to be slipping by, day by day. The spasm fecund with the possibility of chaosmosis, that is, the possibility of rebalancing the rhythms of the body, the local milieu and the 'envelope' of information surrounding the earth, seems beset on a painful nihilistic contraction, a death drive of destruction and mental implosion. There is a derailing of the natural spasm, a de-sensitizing of the body, a loss and exploitation of memory, and instead of a new rhythm of life and a new sense of coexistence with the cosmos there is more and more chaos and less and less chaosmosis. Correspondingly, there is a shrinking of the possibility of transforming the social brain for the betterment of mankind. More than this, social life suffers a profound shock provoking 'pathological effects on the living terminal, the human mind which has physical, emotional and cultural limits' (Berardi 2014: 35).

Umwelt of the cockroach

A capitalist subjectivity manufactures the artificial organs of the cockroach, enjoys the cockroach, plays with the cockroach, consumes the cockroach. The *Umwelt* of the cockroach is the paragon of a society of drones (Shaw 2017: 65–6). *Umwelt* becomes *Unwelt* or *unworld*. The *Umwelt* of the cockroach demonstrates the fascism of our days – the desire to control the brain of another living creature. Indeed, the automatic control of populations in the age of cybernetics is fascistic according to Norbert Wiener (2013). With a swish or swoosh of your finger on your phone or tablet, you in effect direct the motor skills of a living being.

Mnemotechnology

I am situating the manifestly unethical sales product of RoboRoach in terms of the wider question of the World Brain, or what we might call the transhuman cerebrum (Bradley 2018). There are even more recent scandalous examples of this, including Pager, the ping-pong-playing macaque monkey (Wakefield 2021). The cockroach-iPhone assemblage is literally a gadget consciousness (Hands 2019) in the sense that the iPhone stores tertiary retentions as a mnemotechnology: 'Whenever we communicate via gadgets we also lay down a digital memory and extend the life span of that moment into the technology and beyond' (Hands 2019: 96). This is all enframed within the question of trauma, the trauma of the cockroach brain, the trauma of the human brain and the 'remote controlling' of populations. Echoing Guattari's concerns over the social class formations of remote-memory-control, Slavoj Žižek (2017) asks: 'There is first the big question of power – who will be controlled in this digital space?' Yet, Žižek is not seduced by the speculation regarding the collective brain singularity; the question for him is more phenomenological. It is a question of the self-experience of living beings. Yet, Žižek asks (2017): 'Will we still experience ourselves as free beings, or will we be regulated by digital machinery, without ever being aware that we are regulated?' This is precisely the question I am raising *vis-à-vis* the invasive control of the cockroach.

What is the self-experience of the cockroach? RoboRoach gives us a prime example to think about this question. The memory of the cockroach is manipulated and dominated unbeknownst to the insect. But more than this: we can say the cockroach is not alone, as vast swathes of humanity are increasingly controlled by micro, digital technologies such as the ubiquitous smartphone. These are not the mad ramblings of the schizo-paranoiac but a crucial question for critical postmedia studies and schizoanalysis. In what way is the living being controlled by algorithms, by what I call the 'collective algorithmic unconscious'? South Korean philosopher Byung-Chul Han shares this dystopic concern but thinks beyond it and says the following: 'In Orwell's *1984* society knew it was being dominated. Today, we are not even aware of the domination' (2018). The dystopian mentality would put the point like this: as a species we are increasingly unaware we are dominated by Big Data, the Big Other (Zuboff 2015), by social networking and algorithmic governmentality (Rouvroy and Stiegler 2016). But what would it mean to say that we are aware of this domination? Let me put it like this. Clearly, I am writing this chapter, which means to say that I think one can know one is being dominated – but in what sense are we in collusion with this domination? This is somewhat different from the reality of the cockroach which is not at liberty to discern its own domination. Žižek suggests that to link the brain with artificial intelligence will create a privileged class that will retain self-identity and free will and with it, immense control. The rest of us will become the new proletariat – we could say a disindividuated and proletarianized mass, that is to say, a class without skill and knowledge as Bernard Stiegler argues (2013). In the cockroach's case, the loss of motor skills – its proletarianization, its becoming-worker without knowledge or skill – is precisely through the brain becoming linked directly to artificial intelligence. The memory and control of its own body is proletarianized. This seems to me to encapsulate the failure of the experiment of the World Brain, the failure of the World Wide Web in its current iteration. Information is literally in the hands of Thumbelina who is holding the smartphone which controls the cockroach (Serres 2015). Knowledge is replaced by information and entertainment. For me, this reality demands that we must rethink what the World Brain can be, and what this means for the memory of mankind. It is here Stiegler (2016) has much to contribute to critical postmedia studies in his theory of automatic societies. And in Guattari's language, this is a question of how we can create new incorporeal universes of reference and non-dominated forms of knowledge. Again Žižek (2017) is concerned about these problems too, suggesting the following: 'Never forget that attempts to control us always begin like this. You begin with all these humanitarian causes, heart diseases and so on, and then sooner or later you move to police control.' This is correct, but we must extend Žižek's criticism because his thesis has no theory of memory and no theory of resistance. It is my belief that critical postmedia is a corrective to this.

Backdoor Brains makes a similar argument suggesting that through the introduction of more advanced neuroscience classes in schools and colleges, humans can make rapid advances in terms of Parkinson's disease and so on, that is diseases concerned with the loss of memory. The loss of memory of the cockroach, therefore, has a utilitarian function. The more we know about the loss of memory of the living being, the more we can make medical advances *for us humans*. Again, to return to Žižek, he says he is not a pessimist on this question, as something new is happening which is affecting our most basic experience of who we are as human beings. Something fundamentally new is at work in the world, which we need to account for. Again, it is not so much the cockroach that is dominated by the 'miniaturisation of technologies' (Guattari 2000: 40), it is we as human beings who are knowingly dominated. We love our intoxicants. The question then is the pharmacological possibility which arises from the miniaturization of technologies, that is what is affecting our most basic experience of who we are as living beings. This is what must be accounted for. Yet, there are optimists like Guattari who say that humans need to get more into the machine, we need to become more aligned with the machine, we need to forge a new alliance with machines and he makes the interesting move to rethink the alliance with machines in terms of planetary consciousness. Here schizoanalysis thinks the limit of the postmedia at the point at which it opens out onto the posthuman. Guattari demands a fundamental recomposition of the social brain and a new *alliance* with machines:

> The new planetary consciousness will have to rethink machinism, will have to rethink distributed cognition and the social brain. We frequently continue to oppose the machine to the human spirit. Certain philosophies hold that modern technology has blocked access to our ontological foundations, to primordial being. And what if, on the contrary, a revival of spirit and human values could be attendant upon a new alliance with machines? (Guattari 1996a: 267)

This planetary consciousness can be called the machinic global machinic phylum and for Guattari we must rethink what machinism is in its essence. For Guattari it suggests a rebirth, a revival of spirit, a revival of human values through the alliance with machines. This is something quite different from what Teilhard de Chardin (1881–1955) or Vladimir Vernadsky (1863–1945) discuss in terms of the noosphere or 'the skin of the earth'. But what is interesting is how these ideas connect with Elon Musk and his desire to have satellites encircling the earth, beaming data directly into the brains of humans and indeed other living beings.

All of the above clearly has repercussions for what media is and what the postmedia era has become. It seems there is little scope for dissensus and there are of course pessimists questioning what it is to be transhuman in this hyper-consensual dystopian nightmare. One such pessimist is Paul Virilio who insists that when people vaunt the World Brain by declaring that humans are no longer human but neurons inside the world brain and that interactivity favours this phenomenon, for them, 'it's more than just a question of the society of control. It's a cybernetic society, the very opposite of freedom and democracy' (1996: 80). This is consistent with Žižek's arguments above. In Virilio's argument what we find is a criticism of Deleuze's society of control thesis (1992) and what we can take from this is an understanding of the limits of what the postmedia era promised and what it has become in reality.

Thus far, we have found that the cyborg cockroach engineered by Backdoor Brains acts as a microcosm or paragon of what the cybernetic society might become, signifying a loss of freedom through direct control of the brain. Interactivity is taken over by artificial intelligence, by algorithms, by the collective algorithmic unconscious, by the smartphone controlling the motor functions of an insect. For the cockroach, interactivity means the temporary loss of motor skills. The living organism – its movements, vibrations, thresholds – is dominated by something with a ghostly, ethereal transcendental subjectivity, which we can call the World Brain. In other words, the cockroach is 'mnemotechnically captured and industrially automated' (Pringle, Koch and Stiegler 2019: xii). The question is whether the human animal is also becoming *noetic hymenoptera* (Stiegler 2016: 213).

Universes of reference

Was he a beast, that music should move him like this? (Kafka 2009: 66)

I want to make sense of the remote-controlling of life through the 'organisation of memories' of both the human and animal kingdom. Becoming-animal or becoming-cockroach is to plunge into an ethological, vital milieu, populated with molecular, neurological becomings. In *The Three Ecologies*, Guattari discusses the emergence of animal-, vegetable-, Cosmic-, and machinic-becomings in a world of anonymous, impalpable matter in constant variation and connection, and looks to account for the winners and losers of the technological and data-processing revolutions in terms of institutional governmentality:

> The unconscious remains bound to archaic fixations only as long as there is no investment . . . directing it towards the future. This existential tension will

proceed through the bias of human and even non-human temporalities such as the acceleration of the technological and data-processing revolutions, as prefigured in the phenomenal growth of a computer-aided subjectivity, which will lead to the opening up or, if you prefer, the unfolding . . . of animal-, vegetable-, Cosmic-, and machinic-becomings. At the same time we should not forget that the formation and 'remote-controlling' of human individuals and groups will be governed by institutional and social class dimensions. (Guattari 2000: 38–9)

In *Schizoanalytic Cartographies*, Guattari questions why 'the immense processual potentialities carried by all these computational, telematic, robotic, bureaucratic, biotechnological revolutions so far still only result in a reinforcement of previous systems of alienation, an oppressive mass-mediatisation, infantilising consensual politics,' and asks: 'What will enable them finally to lead to a postmedia era, setting them free from segregational capitalist values and giving a full lease of life to the beginnings of a revolution in intelligence, sensibility and creation?' (2013: 12). This is my argument in essence regarding the cockroach. It seems to me that the biotechnology and robotic revolutions have *for some absurd purpose* produced the abomination of the iPhone-directed cockroach in societies of alienation infantilized by the mass-media industries. Guattari also writes of the emergence of universes of reference in his short but influential essay 'On Machines':

> Thus we have a new machine. Today, children who are learning language from a word-processor are no longer within the same types of universes of reference as before, neither from a cognitive point of view (of how there may be another organisation of memory, or rather memories . . .), nor in the order of affective dimensions and social or ethical relationships. (Guattari 1995b: 11)

I am quite sure that Guattari would be equally incensed over the disruption and despoiling of memory, by the 'black hole of involuntary memory' (Deleuze and Guattari 1987: 186) wrought by social networking in the first two decades of the twenty-first century. In this world of Twitter, Skype, WeChat, Line. Instagram, WhatsApp, Facebook, Uber Eats, Tik-Tok, Zhibo live-streaming (Bradley 2017), Pokémon GO (Bradley 2019), Zoom lectures, online gambling (Bradley 2016) and instantaneous pornography, we find little that is enduring and stable. In *Schizoanalytic Cartographies*, Guattari admitted to utopian hopes that would transform the planet, a place 'lived as a hell by four-fifths of its population today, into a universe of creative enchantments' (2013: 11). But what is this universe of creative enchantments? One suspects the apps on our smartphones today – apps aggressively advertised to make our lives more convenient – will soon be obsolete, and replaced by ever more sophisticated neuro-marketing ideas to gain and garner attention. Here it is a struggle to think that they make us more creative in any naïve sense. And down the line one suspects there will be little to remember of them as other more addictive suitors will immediately take their place. Indeed, readers of the above lines in a decade or two may well wonder why and how such fads seized the 'infantilized subjectivity' of billions of people across the planet in such a frenzied fashion and state. This is especially so when we see the following newspaper story on video gaming trends:

> According to a new report, 'Cloud gaming: Enabling a next generation gaming and streaming paradigm', commissioned by InterDigital, the video gaming market is now among the largest entertainment industries in the world. Currently, more than 2.3 billion individuals play video games, and the number of gamers is expected to grow substantially over the next four years to more than 3.5 billion gamers by 2024. (Skeldon 2020)

It is to Guattari we turn to understand the mental pollution which has excrescently emerged from the data-processing revolution, and why things have not turned out *for the better*. Given his concern with the machinic production or manufacture of subjectivity, Guattari was keen to understand the effects of the information revolution and the role of artificial intelligence not only on the environment but also on the mental and social ecologies of the brain. Guattari believed the molar and molecular effects of the machinic phylum on the human subject's relationship with the non-human had to be accounted for in terms of a possible new collaboration with machines. This gave Guattari hope but also necessitated caution as the new social and technical machines generated by the machinic phylum produce corporeal and incorporeal universes of reference which can either liberate or subjugate subjectivity. The miniaturization of technologies offered a promise along with a danger, as the incorporeal universes of reference generated could transform human perception in fabulous and imaginative ways, but they could also leave users intoxicated with machines and bound to new forms of slavery. We are indeed at an *unavoidable crossroads*. Our wires are crossed. Our signals are scrambled. Our antennae are out of order.

Towards the end of his life, Guattari was concerned with challenging the conspicuous, perceived and pervasive lack of collective imagination regarding the future. It is this myopic vision regarding the future which I wish to update and apply to the contemporary moment. My task is to defend the prospectus of the postmedia as an influential paradigm which continues to account for the changing formations of media and communications and indeed the science of the brain in the twenty-first century. That Deleuze and Guattari were writing on the 'cusp' (Abbinnett 2017: 113) of the internet revolution is very important because it raises questions about the limits of their speculation, but it also shows how their prescient thinking can help to make sense of the present moment and crisis in which it is so very difficult to envisage the future in any positive sense. Guattari's visionary cartography helps us make sense of the age of the smartphone and the app (Hands 2019) and indeed the voluntary servitude which we all suffer. The danger of voluntary servitude is picked up by Guattari who writes that social control in the 1980s was achieved by peaceful albeit surreptitious means. It is the jingles or refrains, the schizophrenic voices in our heads that keep the populace in its state of unfreedom. Guattari writes:

> Certainly social control has never been achieved with as little violence as it is today. People are kept the prisoners of their environment – of the ideas, the taste,

the models, the ways of being, the images constantly presented to them, even the turns of phrase that run through their heads. (Guattari and Rolnik 2008: 249)

And contrasting the visible 'apparatuses of standardisation' with less direct 'private institutional forces' (in our time think of the seductive, indeed sedative and addictive qualities of social networking), Guattari discerns what will become the lot of our digitally intensive times. He writes of the multitude of private institutional forces:

> Thus, control today is less a matter of the direct subjection of individuals to 'visible' systems of authority, to publicly organized apparatuses of standardisation, than of a multitude of more or less private institutional forces, associations of all kinds – sporting, social and cultural, community groups, young people's clubs, churches and so on. (Guattari and Rolnik 2008: 249)

Given the exponential use of social networking and the blinkered and paralysed time people spend on the internet, given the 'perseveration' (the pathology of attention) in front of computer screens – that is, the often excessive degree of time spent beyond a desired goal, or perhaps in Guattari's words, the deadly refrain or repetition despite the absence or cessation of a stimulus, given the addictive nature of computer games and internet use deprived of a positive 'state of flow' (Csikszentmihalyi 2016), given the emergence of the 'limbic Capitalocene,' that is 'a phenomenon of addictive consumption induced by generalised proletarianisation' (Moore et al. 2019), given the abstract relationality in society between people, between young and old, between parent and child, between teacher and student, from all of these manifestations, I believe Guattari is on to something in cartographically tracing the 'private institutional forces' which have become little more than marketing tools rather than generators of new forms of knowledge.

It is therefore timely to appreciate Guattari's understanding of the machinic and the possibility of a new alliance with machines and how this can be applied to the contemporary moment. This can be explored through the concept of universes of reference and how such universes have somehow been monopolized by a consensual mass media, Big Data and the marketization of the internet. This I demonstrate through an analysis of the contemporary use of neuroscience and in Part II later through a reflection on science fiction in which we find the memory of mankind manipulated for the entertainment industries rather than the knowledge sector. Indeed, it seems fitting to use science fiction to remind ourselves of this fact because Guattari also drew on the genre, writing the screenplay *A love of UIQ* (Guattari, Maglioni and Thomson 2016a; Bradley and Weber 2018), which drew heavily on science fiction themes. Again, this was a concern with thinking the future, with thinking utopia and thinking the possibility of a new arrangement of things in the emergent postmedia era. This is consistent with Guattari's understanding of the machinic unconscious and how the unconscious has a role in thinking the future. Indeed, in *Soft Subversions*, we find Guattari interested in exploring the unconscious 'turned towards the future' (Guattari 2011; Guattari and Lotringer 2009).

Schizotherapy and the proletarianized cockroach

The proletarianization of the senses of the cockroach by the exploitation of its retentional system demonstrates the disastrous reality of new manifestations of proto-subjectivity in contemporary postmedia. The cockroach falls into a black hole, where motricity, gestures and skills become – in the short term at least – decoupled from its body and brain. The cockroach struggles to free itself from an imposed territory. The message from the iPhone makes the cockroach forget (Hands 2019: 100). This reality suggests the permanent electrocution of the brain and the collapse of the chaosmic spasm. From this, it is difficult to see how one can 'ward off the ordeals of barbarism, the mental implosion and chaosmic spasm looming on the horizon' (Guattari, Bains and Pefanis 1995: 135). There seems little opportunity for a 'new syntony, a new attunement with the surrounding universe' (Berardi 2019b: 223), a new phase of syntony, of sympathy or the ability 'to feel for other bodies, to share the same pathos' (223). Pessimistically, the realization of 'a harmonic order by way of resingularisation' (2019a: 24) seems in vain as there is now a desperate struggle to find a new sense of osmosis, equilibrium, harmony 'beyond a condition of spasm' (223). For the cockroach, machinic chaosmosis is the living dead. Berardi writes:

> If chaosmosis is the process through which singular creativity gives its own order to the chaotic constellations that circumscribe the conscious organism, then schizoanalysis proposes to act as an ecology of the mind and a therapy of becoming world. (Berardi and Mecchia 2008: 114)

The exploitation of the retentional or mnemonic system of living beings for entertainment and marketing purposes effectively blurs the distinction between life and death, sleep and wakefulness, conscious and unconscious. In terms of the human population, the general intellect is at the whim of the marketing industries. As Featherstone says: '[I]ntegrated world capitalism penetrates through to the level of subjectivity and essentially turns humans into zombies, staggering through their environment in a liminal state somewhere between life and death' (2016: 252)

Part II: Lévy and collective intelligence

Both Guattari and Pierre Lévy share a common interest with respect to the 'growth of a computer-aided subjectivity,' with the expansion of consciousness (*l'expansion de la conscience*). This is part and parcel of Guattari's prospectus for the postmedia era as he remained concerned with the possibilities which are opened up by the computer revolution, the aforementioned 'new alliance with machines'. Lévy is important for Guattari because it is he who thinks beyond 'the ontological iron curtain' between the human and the machine. As we have seen, Guattari was concerned with the production of 'new ecosophical assemblages of enunciation' (Guattari 2000: 38, 53), with 'creative processuality'. The postmedia era thus takes on an ethical and eco-systemic necessity. He writes in *Utopia Today*: 'It is true. I'm crazy about machines, concrete and abstract, and I have no doubt that a fabulous expansion will eventually break down all the conservatisms that "keep us in place" in this absurd and blind society' (Guattari 2009: 307). While Guattari looked at the postmedia era as a way to escape control and the abuse of power in 'absurd and blind' societies, he also observed there was always the possibility of society turning into systems of subjection and enslavement. Society can always turn out badly. Populations can be 'remote controlled' in so-called societies of hymenoptera – slave-like societies modelled on insects like the bees and ants. He writes:

> [A] blind and catastrophic fear can seize the most developed human society and lead it to set up systems of subjection and enslavement bringing it closer to societies of hymenoptera (production for production's sake, systematic segregation, generalized gulags). (2011: 128)

In Deleuze and Guattari's much-cited example and affirmative sense of the wasp and the orchid, much can be gleaned to celebrate the machinic and mutual involution between unnatural natures. In Deleuze and Guattari's thought, the wasp and the orchid crystallizes the movement of deterritorialization and reterritorialization, the movement of the rhizome, cross-contamination, pollination, transformation and communication, and 'a veritable becoming, a becoming-wasp of the orchid and a becoming-orchid of the wasp' (1987: 10). The wasp, an organism of fauna of the order hymenoptera, and the orchid, an organism of flora, enter into unnatural participation, dismantling or disrupting the distinction between themselves. The wasp and the orchid become a multiplicity, an animistic assemblage. The wasp enfolds itself as part of the orchid's reproductive apparatus. The wasp-orchid assemblage operates via a relay between organic and inorganic life.

What have we become? The cockroach is of organic life, the iPhone, the 'libidinal parasite' (Pasquinelli 2008) *par excellence*, of the inorganic. The cockroach and iPhone form a multiplicity or assemblage. The cockroach becomes part of the iPhone's apparatus (mobile appendage) and the iPhone becomes the organ of the cockroach (controlling the motor skills). There is a blending of the inorganic and organic. The environment is transformed through the co-evolution and co-becoming of the two. Life takes on a posthuman dimension. The cockroach is mnemotechnically captured and industrially automated as noetic *hymenoptera*. What other new systems of virtual connectivity or constellations of universes emerge from this? The possibility of becoming animal, vegetable, Cosmic, and machinic – a central concern of schizoanalysis – appears altogether foreclosed by societies of hymenoptera, by systems of enslavement and subjection (Lazzarato 2014). In the remote-controlling and nooshock of individuals, the remote-controlling of hymenoptera populations by systems of virtual connectivity (*hypomnemata*), the wasp becomes the war machine, the possibility of which 'is constituted through the experience of sensory and noetic degradation that is produced through the capitalising power of technoscience, and the new possibilities of self-expression opened up by systems of virtual connectivity (*hypomnemata*)' (Abbinnett 2017: 113).

For Guattari, extra or non-human, a-signifying, intensive regimes and the prepersonal part of subjectivity are crucial for generating new heterogenic becomings of subjectivity. Writing in 1989, Guattari was far-sighted in noting the effects of the acceleration of the technological and data-processing revolutions but he could have never foreseen what was to come. Yet, Guattari's postmedia theory remains essential to decoding the manifold production of machinic subjectivities. It remains relevant for understanding how people go 'crazy' for machines, for a 'machinic kind of buzz'. André Gorz's question why people upon returning home exhausted from work 'automatically' turn on the TV to experience artificial and personal reterritorialization remains important. In our time we may ask: Why it is that people touch their smartphone screens hundreds of times a day in a kind of automatic reflex, a desire for *permanent electrocution*? In *Anti-Oedipus*, Deleuze and Guattari note how people become entranced by capital, how capital entertains 'the reflux of organised, axiomatised stupidity' and how workers rediscover their 'little desiring-machines'. In the postmedia era, the key question for Guattari was how to proliferate an inventive machinic and collective passion 'without crushing people under an infernal discipline' (Genosko 2002: 126). This remains a question for schizoanalysis in the twenty-first century.

World Brain

A proliferation of names and concepts come to mind when we think about the notion of the World Brain. Chief among them, of course, are Diderot and D'Alembert of the Encyclopaedist movement in France in the mid-eighteenth century. In the early twentieth century, Vladimir Vernadsky adopted the concept of noosphere or global consciousness and Teilhard de Chardin embraced an idealist philosophy which predicted the evolution of the human mind into the noosphere; this, he believed, would eventually signal the emergence of the 'spirit of the Earth'. Growing interest in the notion of the global human mind in the nineteenth and twentieth centuries by writers such as H. G. Wells, who wrote *The World Brain* in 1938, came when the machine age and technology revolution had yet to be fully realized. Nowadays, the World Brain has more contemporary rivals, for example, the global brain (Bloom 2000), as well as the global mind and social brain. There is also Lévy's notion of 'collective intelligence' and virtualization (1999), Kevin Kelly's hive mind, and ongoing discussions regarding the melding of human and machine by Elon Musk and long-standing critiques of such a reality by Virilio and indeed Stiegler's notion of the 'global mnemotechnical system' (Bradley 2018).

Cold Lazarus

To continue the transhuman nightmare I am exploring and its connection with memory manipulation and loss, let us briefly consider Dennis Potter's *Cold Lazarus* (1996), the British science fiction TV drama set in the twenty-fourth century in which society is held to ransom by the virtual world. In this society, which is controlled by large corporations, memories from deceased human brains, some of which lived in the twentieth century, are retrieved through cryogenic techniques for the vicarious pleasures of citizens. The problem is one of those brains, Feeld's brain, becomes miraculously and traumatically aware of its resurrection. This is the veritable realization of Berardi's cognitive worker or neuro-worker affected by psychopathological 'syndromes and stress' (2014: 98).

Feeld's brain bears witness to the memories of lost loved ones brought back to consciousness. The brain caught in Feeld's process of desubjectification, the dissolution of the self (*depouillement*) suffers excruciatingly as a consequence. Feeld's brain is Beckett's 'unnamable's cogito,' a 'hive of words,' a vortex of manufactured desires, a maelstrom of voices:

> It must not be forgotten (sometimes I forget) that all is a question of voices. I say what I am told to say, in the hope that some day they will weary of talking at me. The trouble is I say it wrong, having no ear, no head, no memory. Now I seem to hear them say it is Worm's voice beginning. (I pass on the news, for what it is worth.) Do they believe I believe it is I who am speaking? (That's theirs too. To make me believe I have an ego all my own, and can speak of it, as they of theirs: another trap to snap me up among the living). (Disembodied narrator in Beckett's *The Unnameable*, 1958)

It is right to ask as Lyotard does in *The Inhuman*, 'Can thought go on without a body?' (1991: 8). And Žižek is right to note thought is not 'happily floating in its hallucinations' but contorted and radically divided. In Feeld's nightmare, speech is imposed on it from outside, it is not speaking but is spoken and dominated by an external Other. Nothing belongs to Feeld's brain. In the end the brain explodes, its manufacture is burst asunder (Žižek 2020: 111). The horror of this experience represents some of the ways in which the World Brain and the retentional systems and forms of knowledge have become a matter of control and trauma – by a new form of the *malin génie*. Indeed, like Guattari, Virilio, a man of much presentiment, describes the 'eradication of memory, like that of biological diversity, as a necessary step in the program of transnational capitalism' (quoted in Conley 1997: 89). The loss of memory is a triumph for capitalism. In *Cold Lazarus*, through advanced psychotechnologies or mnemotechnics brains are brought back from the dead to reshape human experience and perception in a commercially desirable way. Research and knowledge are not undertaken for lofty scientific reasons alone. That past memory, experience and knowledge might shape the future of mankind in a progressive way is eclipsed by the demand to entertain living brains. What is exploited by marketing and the media industries is the extraction and exploitation of human memory for erotic titillation and base entertainment purposes. Neurons in the brain are reactivated and somehow projected onto a televisual screen. In this future society deprived of empathy and care, this is to resurrect the memories of the past, the cerebrum, the human cerebrum of the past, to see what others thought and desired. It seems to me that the premise of Potter's TV drama explores what is symptomatic of the current crisis of the media and indeed the current crisis of postmedia. It serves as a prism through which we see a stifling lack of dissensus in the media and indeed in the creative use of miniaturized technologies. It suggests that we are verily becoming crushed people living under the 'infernal discipline' which Guattari identifies. Moreover, we suffer a lack of 'educational Renaissance' in the words of H. G. Wells, who saw much possibility in the idea of the World Brain. For Wells, the world's soul could be an awakening of thought, not a forgetting of thought or deletion of memory. For him, there lay the possibility of a planetary cerebrum, a planetary brain or mind, a planetary memory for mankind. This would lead to a World Encyclopaedia of pure knowledge and the idea that the World Brain would lead to a collective 'tethering' of mankind.

Let me return to *Cold Lazarus* as it explores, in some ways, the unbinding of the drives from desire and acting out of asocial drives. Feeld's brain at the end of the story explodes, destroying the research lab. It becomes an explosive device of an altogether different meaning from the sense of the human as matter *at its most incendiary stage* in Teilhard's work. In *Cold Lazarus*, the brain becomes conscious that it is being exploited and dominated and it seeks retribution. My point is that as the brain and memories of Feeld and the cockroach are both exploited by marketing, by microtechnologies, by the algorithms of social networking, Big Data and Google, what meaning can we give to this in terms of the postmedia paradigm?

Teilhard talks of the possibility of a super consciousness, a 'harmonized collectivity of consciousnesses equivalent to a kind of super consciousness, with the earth not only covered by a myriad of grains of thought, but wrapped in a single thinking envelope until it forms but a single vast grain of thought on a planetary scale. The plurality of individual reflections being grouped and reinforced in a single unanimous act of reflection' (2003: 178). The idea of enshrouding the earth with a hyper-intelligent consciousness is one also espoused by Elon Musk who envisions a satellite system forming a transhuman neural net, directly connected to the neural cortex. Yet, this transhuman fantasy appears something quite distinct from Teilhard's, who describes intelligence as superhuman and enveloped, a becoming transcendental, connected with the universe and with God in the final instance. But it also shares some characteristics with Stiegler's philosophy which describes the processes of exosomatization and uses Heidegger's notion of *Gestell* or enframing, in the sense of the biosphere becoming technosphere, the biological organism becoming a technological organism. Elon Musk talks of NeuroLace, or more recently of Neuralink, demonstrated through Gertrude the pig who has had a computer chip inserted into her brain, a brain-to-machine interface and means for consciousness to merge with artificial intelligence. Again, such a case seems to be exemplified by the cockroach. NeuroLace entails the injection of a grid of wires into the brain, 'insinuating itself with living neurons and eavesdropping on their chatter, offering electronics a way to interface with your brain activity' (Musk 2016).

My argument about RoboRoach is that it is a reality that NeuroLace might follow on a wider scale. This entails an ethical question regarding the memory of mankind. Who controls this memory and has access to this memory? Who can exploit and dominate memory? These are questions that need to be answered by the transhumanists. Musk says we have already become cyborgs. With our digital devices, he says humans have more power than the president of the United States had only a few decades ago. But what we find in *Cold Lazarus* is the exploitation of memory, the explication of the concept of necromancy in Vernadsky and the concept of 'noetic necromass' (Stiegler 2018). This is to produce an artificial retention and accumulated knowledge as the version of the necromass. Pleasure in *Cold Lazarus* is through the exosomatization of memory, the visual projection of memory. Those in the past contribute to the noetic necromass. From a schizoanalytic perspective, *Cold Lazarus* reveals what thinking has become, what artificial desires are, that is part of exosomatic evolution and the realization of exosomatic organs. In order to reach beyond the limits of marketing, control and technological manipulation, mental ecology has to be continually rethought as it cannot rely on the conventions of orthodox discourse. It must introduce dissensus into the mix, to resist the status quo.

But Integrated World Capitalism as a globalizing entity is not only a technological matter but a machinic one. Guattari will grant the machinic primary ontological importance, with concrete, singular instantiations of technology granted a secondary role. Erich Hörl (2014) makes the point that Guattari's machinic theory emerged from the 'originary connection' of desire and technics: 'Guattari has reformulated his machinic theory of desire as a question of subjectivation under media-technical conditions and he has postulated as part of this project nothing less than the originary connection of desire and technics' (2014: 4). The point here is that the machinic – not technics – is the concept through which to think the technological machine as one of machinic *agencement*, composed of autopoietic and allopoietic structures (Guattari 1995a). Moreover, we can say that machinery *per se* need not be construed as purely technological. For example, tool use (a technical object) presupposes a machine (abstract machine) with social dimensions. If this is the case, any machine or technology is social before it is technical. Why? Because technical machines are tied to more complex assemblages overseen by the formative power of a distinct socius. Technology as such assumes a social form. It is always a question of machinic evolution. In 'On Machines', Guattari explains the point with great perspicacity:

> In the history of philosophy the problem of the machine has generally been regarded as secondary to a more general system – that of technē and technique (*la technique*). I would propose a reversal of this point of view, to the extent that the problem of technique would now only be a subsidiary part of a much wider machine problematic. Since the 'machine' is opened out towards its machinic environment and maintains all sorts of relationships with social constituents and individual subjectivities, the concept of technological machine should therefore be broadened to that of machinic *agencements*. (1995b: 9)

Machinism is both positive and productive while technology or technics on the other hand is perceived as impersonal, enframing and somehow out of control. Machinism is about plugging in and creating weapons from experimentation. It is also about resistance. Technology is perceived as passing over the subject and the individuation process to something alien and dominant. Rejecting the dualism of nature and artifice and suggesting 'biological' evolution has always been a question of technics, as Deleuze and Guattari insist in *A Thousand Plateaus*: 'There is no biosphere or noosphere, but everywhere the same mechanosphere' (Deleuze and Guattari 1987: 69; see also Ansell-Pearson 2012: 125). Their theory of creative involution thus subsumes the noosphere under the term *mechanosphere*. Yet, for Genosko (2016: 43), the machine is in no way synonymous with Teilhard's (or indeed Vernadsky's or H. G. Wells's) sense of the noosphere or World Brain. The noosphere or conscious mind as a skin wrapped around the planet is rather more akin to an 'etherialised version of the megamachine', argues Genosko citing Mumford in *The Myth of the Machine* (1970: 314). Yet, if Genosko is right to note that the noosphere is part of an evolutionary process not unlike Guattari's machinic evolutionism of 'collective apparatuses of subjectification' then a case can be made for thinking 'collective intelligence' (Lévy 1999) in terms of the noosphere. Indeed, Guattari in 1992 speaks of the necessity of a 'new planetary consciousness,' a new alliance with machines. This new planetary consciousness is described as a 'mecanosphere surrounding our biosphere' (Guattari 1996a: 267). Moreover, it is less 'the constraining yoke of an exterior armor' but rather the 'abstract, machinic efflorescence, exploring the future of humanity' (267–8).

Remaking social practices and planetary consciousness

Attempting to anticipate the rapid transformations brought about from the information processing revolution, Guattari foresaw in the postmedia era the opportunity to change media and subjectivity for the better, from one of consensus to dissensus. In terms of his dissensual, at once abstract and concrete, 'psychological metamodelisation' (Guattari 1995a: 11), Guattari searched for ways to move beyond the infantilizing subjectivity engineered by mass media. This was important for Guattari because the world appeared ethical and politically decapitated – in other words, a body without brain. The question Guattari poses is how to reconnect the head to the body, and rejoin science and technology together in terms of human values. *This acephalic reality is the cockroach's fate and nightmare.* Like the cockroach in the time of the Anthropocene and a form of acephalic, runaway capitalism, '[h]umanity seems to have lost its head, or more precisely, its head is no longer functioning with its body' (Guattari 1996a: 262). The functioning of the current mass media, and television in particular, for Guattari ran counter to the dissensual postmedia era: 'The tele-spectator remains passive in front of a screen, prisoner of quasi-hypnotic relation, cut off from the other, stripped of any awareness of responsibility' (1996a: 263). Again, the cockroach clearly expresses this 'quasi-hypnotic relation'. Guattari was concerned with the creation of new collective assemblages of enunciation, which might occur between lovers in the home, at school, in the local neighbourhood and so on. Influenced by Hans Jonas's 'ethics of responsibility', the postmedia era had to be explored with an urgent sense of responsibility, responsibility for the future, for the present, for the other, for those who are yet to come, that is, the children of the present generation and beyond. And yes, for the cockroaches. Yet, Guattari is somewhat optimistic about what technology can deliver for mankind. Shortly before his death in 1992, he writes in the compelling and inspirational 'Remaking Social Practices': 'Technological evolution will introduce new possibilities for interaction between the medium and its user, and between users themselves' (1996a: 263).

What Guattari is asking for is a change in mentalities to prevent the catastrophes – ecological, social and political – facing mankind. This call assumes even more seriousness in the time after Fukushima and in the wake of the Anthropocene and climate change. For him a change in mentality was a necessary step on the way to responding to the 'presentiment of catastrophe which can release an unconscious desire for catastrophe, a longing for nothingness, a drive to destruction' (1996b: 2). Clearly, this sense of presentiment weighs down on the present just as it did in the 1980s and early 1990s. The thoughts on the postmedia era are clearly connected with the founding of an ecosophy which would integrate environmental ecology with social ecology and mental ecology. This is a machinic ecology, which is neither strictly posthuman nor post-natural. Guattari writes: 'Without a change in mentalities, without entry into a postmedia era, there can be no enduring hold over the environment' (1996a: 264). What is the nature of the planetary consciousness which Guattari called for? For Guattari, such a planetary consciousness would produce different values systems, different constellations of universes, universes of reference, different and contrary to globalization. He writes:

> An essential condition for succeeding in the promotion of a new planetary consciousness would thus reside in our collective capacity for the re-creation of value systems that can escape the moral, psychological and social bulldozer of capitalist valorization, which is only centered on economic profit. (1996b: 3)

As Guattari is concerned with the production of subjectivity, and the gelling or gaining of consistency of incorporeal universes, he was searching for a new consistency and difference to the mass mediatized universe of values. Yet, and to return to my obsession, nothing 'gels' in the brain of the cockroach as it is manipulated by a nearby iPhone. When Guattari writes that the 'current crisis of the media and the opening up of a postmedia era are the symptoms of a much more profound crisis' (Guattari 1996a: 266), his thoughts clearly resonate with the contemporary moment in which the internet in its current iteration is precisely experiencing a crisis of its initial formation. The growing demand – led by Sir Tim Berners-Lee and others – for a new kind of World Wide Web, a freer, open and new reconfiguration of information science, a new kind of communication, is emerging from a profound crisis which sees endemic levels of internet and game addiction, social withdrawal and loneliness.

This is why the paradigm of the postmedia era has not gone past its sell by date because we are still concerned with computing and technological machines as vehicles to create new kinds of collective territories for the family, the community, between ethnic groups, for all oppressed groups. This thought clearly speaks to the present moment and the proliferation of forms of 'machinic solitude'. This kind of machinic solitude is precisely what the million-strong *hikikomori* suffer from in Japan (Saitō 2013). But again, Guattari is trying to extract moments of potential from this machinic intoxication. This is again the difficult task of schizoanalysis. Guattari finds in the use of TV and computer games by children the potential for new forms of sociality – *a return of ourselves to ourselves*. A new kind of machinic relation.

Romantic and ruthless deterriorialization

The romantic in me writes: Resisting Oedipalization and defamiliarizing the face, the war machine of the cockroach scurries and scutters across a smooth space directed by its probe-head that latches on to lines of flight, or cutting edges of deterritorialization, to explore the 'prodigious idea of Nonorganic Life' (Deleuze and Guattari 1987: 411). The war machine rips the skin away to explore the inhuman virtuality of the BwO which 'lies beneath' the familiar face. The cockroach literally becomes an itinerant 'probe-head' (*têtes chercheuses*), an impersonal, abstract and active guidance device seeking out future subjectivities. To paraphrase Deleuze and Guattari in *A Thousand Plateaus*, the probe-head dismantles the strata, breaks through the 'walls of significance', pours out of the 'holes of subjectivity' – toys with the politics of real, functional becoming. The probe-head steers the familiar world into a future of uncertainty and seeks out mutant forms of subjectivity; it traverses cutting-edge lines of positive deterritorialization (Deleuze and Guattari 1987: 190–1). The probe-head of Gregor becomes cockroach to escape where his father could not, 'to flee the director, the business, and the bureaucrats, to reach that region where the voice no longer does anything but hum: "Did you hear him? It was an animal's voice" said the chief clerk' (Deleuze and Guattari 1986: 13). One can call this the new alliance of machines. Indeed, the transhuman probe-head of the cockroach is a becoming machine, a nonsignifying and nonsubjective corporeal force transforming humanity. The probe-head of the cockroach redirects the memory of man into an indiscernible non-human space of experimentation, in the space and time of becoming-animal as such. The hydroida-order of the probe-head of the cockroach erupts multiple probe-heads, releasing inhuman intensities that inspire the abominable metamorphoses of man. The familiar face of man is erased as molecular becomings swarm and multiply, distort and reconfigure. The probe-head renders strangely inhuman the face of man.

> Beyond the face lies an altogether different inhumanity: no longer that of the primitive head, but of 'probe-heads'; here, cutting edges of deterritorialisation become operative and lines of deterritorialisation positive and absolute, forming strange new becomings, new polyvocalities. (Deleuze and Guattari 1987: 190–1)

Conclusion

What is the nature of our new planetary consciousness, the 'mecanosphere surrounding our biosphere'? For Guattari, as we have seen, it is not 'as the constraining yoke of an exterior armour, but as an abstract, machinic efflorescence, exploring the future becomings of humanity' (Guattari 267–8). David Cronenberg too picks up on this when he asks: 'Is Gregor's transformation a death sentence or, in some way, a fatal diagnosis? Why does the beetle Gregor not survive? Is it his human brain, depressed and sad and melancholy, that betrays the insect's basic sturdiness?' (Cronenberg 2014: 11). Yet, when Guattari speaks about the following, we can surmise that he is clearly talking about the early forms of the internet (Mintel). In the opening up of a postmedia era, he finds a 'mutation of subjectivity'. I believe we need to rethink our machinic intoxication, enslavement and 'machinic solitude'. Again, this is why postmedia still has something to say.

While computer-aided subjectivity may deprive the modern human subject of volition, or at least the right to its own cognition, computer-aided subjectivity clearly opens up forms of machinic becoming and manifests new universes of reference. This was the case with the cockroach and Feeld's brain. In this new mechanosphere, the psychic world of the cockroach world is tranquilized via technics; Feeld's brain and the cockroach's brain are tormented by the entertainment industries and traumatized by the memory of mankind. Nature becomes artifice, and artifice natural. Freedom operates through artificial, constructed modern spheres. The 'remote-controlling' of human individuals and groups is pervasive. The brain of the cockroach is hacked and manipulated. With this in mind, a new cartography is demanded, to map the psychosocial, psychotechnical, mechanospherical and infospherical world of the cockroach-cyborg. Without a radical reordering of the world, there can be no exit from 'the chrysalis of noetic hymenoptera' (Stiegler 2016: 30) and no passage towards new subjectivities of liberation and freedom. There is no intense line of flight. There can be no art of dissensus. Even the becoming-cockroach of Kafka's Gregor is doomed to experimental failure.

My endeavour has been to contrast collective consciousness alongside both the World Brain and the internet under digital capitalism. Held privately and externally, knowledge has become more commodified and reified. Consequently, we have lost the authentic relation to the world and its social being. The postmedia era which Guattari envisioned has not turned us more towards others but pushed us further away into our 'machinic solitude' and machinic enslavement. Collective consciousness has been thoroughly perverted and corrupted by marketing, which commands the attention of consumers. The promise of the collective consciousness has turned into an 'all-too-human cerebrum satisfying the drives' (Bradley 2018: 413). The corporatism of knowledge enslaves the individual more thoroughly than covert displays of power.

Are we conned by technology? And why do we still desire our own repression? In answering this, a schizoanalysis of postmedia demands nothing less than a *transvaluation of all values* pertaining to the promise of technology. If we adopt Guattari's definition of schizoanalysis as 'the analysis of the impact of Assemblages of enunciation on semiotic and subjective productions in a given problematic context' (Guattari 2013: 18) then this definition can work alongside contemporary forms of schizotherapy to 'disentangle mental contents and psychic activity from the obsessive refrains that are entangling the activity of the mind' (Berardi 2015: 209). Indeed, Berardi talks about the need to entangle the autonomy of the general intellect from its 'neuro totalitarian jail' (Berardi 2015: 251) in which 'the embodied self is totally aligned with the global circuitry of semio-capitalism through the mapping and manipulation of neural networks' (Featherstone 2016: 263–2). Schizoanalysis must continue to offer escape plans from exhaustion, collapse, self-indulgent nay-saying, obsessive refrains and the remote-controlling of subjectivity. While the postmedia paradigm understands the emergence of the individual, the subtlety of control, the insidious remote-controlling of populations, we need to contest the hell of the cockroach tethered to the iPhone, the prospects and hell of Feeld's consciousness and memory tethered to the entertainment industry. This is too much to bear. We are at the end of our tether (Wells [1945] 1974). My rallying cry is a schizoanalytic one, it is a call for the liberation of the unconscious: Cockroaches of all countries unite. We have nothing to lose but our tethering.

References

Abbinnett, R. (2017), *The Thought of Bernard Stiegler: Capitalism, Technology and the Politics of Spirit*, London: Routledge.

Ansell, P. K. (2012), *Viroid Life: Perspectives on Nietzsche and the Transhuman Condition*, Hoboken: Taylor and Francis.

Baharudin, H. (2016), 'NTU's Cyborg Beetles: Netizens Upset over "Animal Torture"', *Straits Times*, 8 (December): 8–12.

Beckett, S. (1958), *The Unnamable*, New York: Grove Press.

Berardi, F. (2008), *Félix Guattari: Thought, Friendship and Visionary Cartography*, ed. and trans. G. Mecchia and C. J. Stivale, Basingstoke: Palgrave Macmillan.

Berardi, F. (2014), *Neuro-totalitarianism in Technomaya Goog-colonisation of the Experience and Neuro-plastic Alternative*, Los Angeles: Semiotext(e).

Berardi, F. (2015), *AND Phenomenology of the End: Cognition and Sensibility in the Transition from Conjunctive to Connective Mode of Social Communication*, Los Angeles: Semiotext(e).

Berardi, F. (2019a), *Breathing: Chaos and Poetry*, Los Angeles: Semiotext(e).

Berardi, F. (2019b), 'I Can't Breath as Schizo-analysis: Chaosmosis, Poetry and Cinema (Interview with Franco 'Bifo' Berardi by Mitra Azar)', *La Deleuziana*, 9: 219–30.

Berressem, H. (2020), *Félix Guattari's Schizoanalytic Ecology*, Edinburgh: Edinburgh University Press.

Bloom, H. Global Brain: The Evolution of Mass Mind from the Big Bang to the 21st Century. New York: Wiley, 2000.

Bradley, J. P. N. (2016), 'Guattari and Pachinko: Deadly Ritournelle, Himatsubushi-Tinguely Machines', *Journal of International Association of Japanese Studies*, 2: 13–22.

Bradley, J. P. N. (2017), 'Zhibo, Existential Territory, Inter-Media-Mundia: A Guattarian Analysis', *China Media Research*, 13 (4): 77–89.

Bradley, J. P. N. (2018), 'Cerebra: All-Human, All-Too-Human, All-Too-Transhuman', *Studies in Philosophy and Education: An International Journal*, 37 (4): 401–15.

Bradley, J. P. N. (2019), 'Schizoanalysis of PokemonGo', *China Media Research*, 15 (4): 78–91.

Bradley, J. P. N., and S. Weber (2018), 'On Nonhuman Machinic Love', *Trans-Humanities*, 11 (2): 173–204.

Conley, V. A. (1997), *Ecopolitics: The Environment in Poststructuralist Thought*, London: Routledge.

Cronenberg, D. (2014), 'Introduction: The Beetle and the Fly', in S. Bernofsky (trans.), *The Metamorphosis: A New Translation*, 9–17, New York: W. W. Norton & Co.

Csikszentmihalyi, M. (2016), *Flow and the Foundations of Positive Psychology: The Collected Works of Mihaly Csikszentmihalyi*. Springer.

Deleuze, G. (1992), 'Postscript on the Societies of Control', *October*, 59 (1): 3–7.

Deleuze, G. and F. Guattari (1986), *Kafka: Toward a Minor Literature*, trans. D. B. Polan, Minneapolis: University of Minnesota Press.
Deleuze, G. and F. Guattari (1987), *A Thousand Plateaus*, trans. B. Massumi, Minneapolis: University of Minnesota Press.
Featherstone, M. (2016), 'Chaosmic Spasm: Guattari, Stiegler, Berardi, and the Digital Apocalypse', *Communication and Media*, 11 (38): 243–68.
Genosko, G. (2002), *Félix Guattari: An Aberrant Introduction*, London: Continuum.
Genosko, G. (2016). *Critical Semiotics: Theory, from Information to Affect*, London: Bloomsbury.
Guattari, F. (1995a), *Chaosmosis: An Ethico-Aesthetic Paradigm*, trans. P. Bains, and J. Pefanis, Sydney: Power Publications.
Guattari, F. (1995b), 'On Machines', trans. V. Constantinopoulos, *Journal of Philosophy and the Visual Arts*, 6 (8): 8–12.
Guattari, F. (1996a), *The Guattari Reader*, ed. G. Genosko, Oxford: Blackwell.
Guattari, F. (1996b), 'Remaking Social Practices', trans. S. Thomas (revised by Brian Holmes), Raumstation, n.d. Available online: http://raumstation.cc/content/archiv/poetiken_der_existenz/Guattari_Remaking_Social_Practices.pdf (accessed 2 January 2020).
Guattari, F. (2000), *The Three Ecologies*, trans. I. Pindar and P. Sutton, London: Athlone Press.
Guattari, F. (2009), *Soft Subversions: Texts and Interviews 1977–1985*, ed. S. Lotringer, trans. C. Wiener and E. Wittman, Los Angeles: Semiotext(e).
Guattari, F. (2011), *The Machinic Unconscious: Essays in Schizoanalysis*, trans. T. Adkins, Los Angeles: Semiotext(e).
Guattari, F. (2013), *Schizoanalytic Cartographies*, trans. A. Goffey, London; New York: Bloomsbury.
Guattari, F. (2016a), *A Love of UIQ: A Screenplay*, trans. S. Maglioni, and G. Thomson, Minnesota: University of Minnesota Press.
Guattari, F. (2016b), *Lines of Flight: For Another World of Possibilities*, trans. A. Goffey, London: Bloomsbury Academic.
Guattari, F. and S. Rolnik (2008), *Molecular Revolution in Brazil*, trans. B. Holmes and K. Clapshow, Cambridge: MIT Press.
Han, B-C. (2018), 'In Orwell's '1984' Society Knew It Was Being Dominated. Not Today', *El Pais*, 7 February. Available online: https://english.elpais.com/elpais/2018/02/07/inenglish/1517995081_033617.html (accessed 2 January 2020).
Hands, J. (2019), *Gadget Consciousness: Collective Thought, Will and Action in the Age of Social Media*, London: Pluto Press.
Heidegger, M. (2008), *Basic Concepts of Ancient Philosophy*, trans. R. Rojcewicz, Bloomington: Indiana University Press.
Hörl, E. (2014), 'Protheses of Desire: On Bernard Stiegler's New Critique of Projection', *Parrhesia*, 20: 2–14.
Kafka, F. (2009), *The Metamorphosis and Other Stories*, trans. J. Crick, Oxford: Oxford University Press.
Lazzarato, M. (2014), *Signs and Machines: Capitalism and the Production of Subjectivity*, Los Angeles: Semiotext(e).
Lévy, P. (1999), *Collective Intelligence: Mankind's Emerging World in Cyberspace*, Cambridge: Perseus Books.
Lyotard, J-F. (1991), *The Inhuman: Reflections in Time*, trans. G. Bennington and R. Bowlby, Cambridge: Polity Press.

Moore, G., N. Mylonas, M-C Bossière, A. Alombert and M. Pavanini (2019), 'Planetary Detox and the Neurobiology of Ecological Collapse', *Arguments on Transition*. Available online: https://internation.world/arguments-on-transition/chapter-9/ (accessed 2 January 2020).

Mumford, L. (1970), *The Myth of the Machine: The Pentagon of Power*, New York: Harcourt Brace Jovanovich.

Musk, E., K. Swisher and W. Mossberg (2016), 'Elon Musk | Full Interview | Code Conference 2016' [video], *Youtube* (2 June). Available online: https://www.youtube.com/watch?v=wsixsRI-Sz4 (accessed 2 January 2020).

O'Sullivan, S. (2006), 'Pragmatics for the Production of Subjectivity: Time for Probe-heads', *Journal for Cultural Research*, 10 (4): 309–22.

Pasquinelli, M. (2008), *Animal Spirits: A Bestiary of the Commons*, Rotterdam: NAi Publishers.

Potter, D. (1996), *Karaoke and Cold Lazarus*, London: Faber and Faber.

Pringle, T., G. Koch and B. Stiegler (2019), *Machine*, Minneapolis: University of Minnesota Press.

Rouvroy, A. and B. Stiegler (2016), 'The Digital Regime of Truth: From the Algorithmic Governmentality to a New Rule of Law', *La Deleuziana*, 3: 6–29.

Saitō, T. (2013), *Hikikomori: Adolescence Without End*, trans. J. Angles, Minneapolis: University of Minnesota Press.

Serres, M. (2015), *Thumbelina: The Culture and Technology of Millennials*, trans. D. W. Smith, London: Rowman & Littlefield.

Shaw, I. G. R. (2017), *Predator Empire: Drone Warfare and Full Spectrum Dominance*, Minneapolis: University of Minnesota Press.

Skeldon, P. (2020), 'Half the World's Population Will be Gamers by 2024 – So How Will Telemedia Monetise It?' *Telemedia Online*, 16 July. Available online: https://www.telemediaonline.co.uk/half-the-worlds-population-will-be-gamers-by-2024-so-how-will-telemedia-monetise-it/ (accessed 2 January 2020).

Stiegler, B. (2013), *Uncontrollable Societies of Disaffected Individuals*, trans. D. Ross, Cambridge: Polity.

Stiegler, B. (2016), *Automatic Society, Vol. 1: The Future of Work*, trans. D. Ross, Cambridge: Polity.

Stiegler, B. (2018), 'Artificial Stupidity and Artificial Intelligence in the Anthropocene', trans. D. Ross, *Academia.edu*, 23 November. Available online: https://www.academia.edu/37849763/Bernard_Stiegler_Artificial_Stupidity_and_Artificial_Intelligence_in_the_Anthropocene_2018_ (accessed 2 January 2020).

Stiegler, B. and D. Ross (2010), *For a New Critique of Political Economy*, Cambridge: Polity Press.

Teilhard, P. C. (2003), *The Human Phenomenon*, trans. S. Appleton-Weber, Brighton: Sussex Academic Press.

Virilio, P. and P. Petit (1996), *Politics of the Very Worst: Paul Virilio: An interview*, ed. S. Lotringer, trans. M. Cavaliere, New York: Semiotext(e).

Wakefield, J. (2013), 'TEDGlobal Welcomes Robot Cockroaches', *BBC*, 10 June. Available online: https://www.bbc.com/news/technology-22786371 (accessed 2 January 2020).

Wakefield, J. (2021), 'Elon Musk's Neuralink Shows Monkey Playing Pong with Mind', *BBC*, 9 April. Available online: https://www.bbc.com/news/technology-56688812 (accessed 2 January 2020).

Watson, J. (2009), *Guattari's Diagrammatic Thought: Writing between Lacan and Deleuze*, London: Continuum.

Wiener, N. (2013), *Cybernetics; or Control and Communication in the Animal and the Machine*, Mansfield Centre: Martino Publishing.
Wells, H. G. ([1945] 1974), *Mind at the End of its Tether*, San Francisco: Millet Books.
Žižek, S. (2017), '"Who Will Control Merged Human-AI Digital Space?" Slavoj Zizek on Musk's Brain Implant Venture', *RT*, 31 March. Available online: https://www.rt.com/news/383029-human-ai-implant-slavoj-zizek/ (accessed 2 January 2020).
Žižek, S. (2020), *Hegel in a Wired Brain*, London: Bloomsbury.
Zuboff, S. (2015), 'Big Other: Surveillance Capitalism and the Prospects of an Information Civilization', *Journal of Information Technology*, 30: 75–89.

2

The existential territory of Shaheen Bagh

A schizoanalytic cartography

Manoj N. Y.

The Shaheen Bagh protest in New Delhi, which lasted for more than a hundred days, can be identified as a singularity in the history of social movements in India apropos the participation and leadership of Muslim women. It started off in the evening of 15 December 2019 when the Jamia Millia Islamia (henceforth Jamia) students, who were protesting against the Islamophobic CAA-NRC citizenship laws, were brutally attacked by the Delhi police on campus. The territory of Shaheen Bagh, a colony home to a largely Muslim community and part of the larger Jamia Nagar area (Farooqi 2020), is redrawn by the event-driven singularity of the Jamia students' protest, which effectuates a complex mode of subjectivation resulting in the recomposition of their existential embodiment. Though the deterritorialization of Shaheen Bagh can be considered an immediate response to the brutal crackdown on the students of Jamia, the history of exclusionary politics played by the Hindutva state machine and the constant vilification of Muslims in India on multiple grounds constituted the virtual plane of the event. Territory cannot be considered as static though it has the potential to become a black hole, an impasse which restrains the deterritorialization. Rather it is a multiplicity in itself, virtually real, replete with intensive forces in relation to the constellation of universes of reference, the economy of flows and the machinic phylum constituting new assemblages of enunciation. This is an attempt to explore the schizoanalytic cartography of the existential territory of Shaheen Bagh and its becoming, focusing on the formation of new relational fields, its specific modes of existence and the new modalities of knowledge that the event imparts. Shaheen Bagh in fact proposes a politics of resistance, the quest for an alternative and the imagination of a new earth and new people against the oppressive state apparatus intensified into a logic of capture.

Before going into a detailed analysis of the existential territory of Shaheen Bagh, let us clarify why a schizoanalytic metamodel is proposed in lieu of a sociological, discursive or empirical approach. Though the prefix 'post' attached to the concept postmedia signifies an ambiguous relation with the existing (mass media) framework, as is the case with postmodernism and post-colonialism, Félix Guattari conceived the schizoanalytic cartography of postmedia as a political project which proposes new practices of subjectivation vis-à-vis 'the disengagement of the postmodern type' (Guattari 2013: 42). The immersive habitat and life forms facilitated by the complex machines of integrated world capitalism offers new modes of 'enrichment and impoverishment' (Guattari 2013: 1) different from that of the collective apparatus of subjectification which engenders the archaic or capitalist form of subjectivity. Guattari developed Lewis Mumford's concept of megamachine, not in terms of the human-machine binary, but articulating a new framework to understand the production of subjectivity as fundamentally machinic and complex, pertinent in the era of planetary computerization (Genosko 2015). The immensely complicated information flows and the new modalities of communication offered by the new informational machine have radically reconfigured the essential notion of the self-contained subject harboured in the heart of Western metaphysics, as nothing more than 'heterogeneous components both human and non-human, organic and inorganic, semiotic and material, archaic and modern, signifying and a-signifying' (Genosko 2015: 8). The accelerated potential of machines to record the states of fact does not necessarily confer them a 'diabolical power' as Guattari (2013) argues; rather machines are considered as 'hyperdeveloped and hyper concentrated forms of certain aspects of human subjectivity' (Guattari 2013: 2).

Though the double bridge laid between the machine and human contributes to the formation of a new individual and collective assemblages of enunciation and modular subjectivities, the peril of social subjection is still retained in its structure. The political project of schizoanalytic cartography focuses on the liberative ruptures that could be identified with the molecular alternate practices of dissensual postmedia (against the delirium of consensual mass media) which escapes the fluid and self-modulating expanse of the societies of control. Guattari evinces the tension between the two while conceding the 'invasive grip' of data banks and telematics, and exemplifies its double bind – an apparent democratization of data complicated by the closure of its elaboration and planetary stirring of cultures punctured by the striated forms of racism and valorization of molar cultural forms (Guattari 2013: 1).

Schizoanalytic cartography is a pedagogic intervention in tackling the innovative forms of experience, collective expressions and disparate practices against the normative formal diagrams or modelling of capitalism and psychoanalysis. The four-fold functors of schizoanalytic ecology – universe of reference (virtual possible), existential territories (virtual real), signaletic flows (actual real) and machinic phylum (actual possible) – posited against the Oedipal diagram of psychoanalysis opens up the chaotic void and schizo possibilities rather than confining the new field of relations and experiences to already existing traditional and normative diagrams. The domain of flows (F) and the machinic phyla (Φ) constitute the vertical axis of the actual which is extensive, objective, abstract and defines the world as given, while the domain of territories (T) and universes of reference (U) constitute the axis of the virtual which is intensive, subjective and defines the world as giving (Guattari 2013; Berressem 2020; Bradley 2019; Watson 2011).

Though the world first appears to us and the emergence of the schizo subject takes place in the actual real domain of flows, it opens up into the domain of actual possibilities which is the machinic phyla, an abstract machine or a rhizome. Similarly, the virtual real domain of the fluid existential territory opens up into the domain of the virtual possible domain of the universes of reference by means of fractalization. Though the virtual and actual are conceived as diagrammatically complimentary, the fully virtual plane of immanence holds primacy over the actual plane of consistency. But it is important to note that the reciprocal presupposition and the principles of composition of the four functors constitute the schizoanalytic ecology. The processual and ecological nature of this diagram evades the danger of schematism and the plane of transcendence (n + 1) that could stabilize the constantly changing machinic milieu (Berressem 2020: 54).

The fourfold functors which constitute schizoanalytic ecology cannot be limited to the domain of the given as it focuses on the domain of giving which 'promote[s] the concatenation of affects, of sense and pragmatic effects' (Guattari 2013: 19). Guattari conceives the complex conceptual four-fold topology as a 'metamodel' which can address the modes of subjectivity that cannot be grasped in the contours of the traditional subject–object divide, in the modes of linguistic articulations or neurosis. Rather it is an 'instrument for deciphering modelling systems in diverse domains' and thus 'a matter of constituting networks and rhizomes in order to escape the systems of modelisation in which we are entangled' (Guattari 2013: 17). The non-subjective semiotic assemblages, the non-semiotic assemblages and subjective non-conscientialized semiotic assemblages that constitute the event are more pertinent and what is required is a metamodelling of these heterogeneous domains. Here, in this analysis, the focus is on the formation of the existential territory of Shaheen Bagh and the political and ethical possibilities that it envisages in the fight against communalism and religious fundamentalism in India. The transversal connections and the process of heterogenesis and singularization that belie the constitution of the protest site necessitate a 'radical' empirical approach, a schizoanalytic metamodel, which can provide both abstract and concrete renderings of the situation.

Territorialization and the occupy

Territory can never be considered static; rather it must be intensive and processual against the geometrical conception of space as an inert container. Thus, territory is conceived as an affective dimension which exists between the individual and the milieu, a sort of dynamic individuation. Thus, individuation, affect and milieu (*Umwelt*) become particularly important in the formation of a territory in the Deleuzo-Guattarian sense. This should be posited against the conception of space apropos phenomenology in the theoretical structure laid out by Henri Lefebvre (1991). Space is conceived in terms of a synergetic schema which holds physical, social and mental space which are perceived, lived and conceived, respectively. The space of representations which is otherwise known as 'lived space' in Lefebvre's vocabulary is the most crucial in our analysis. This was not purely Lefebvre's concept, as it has its antecedence in Heidegger, Bachelard and Merleau-Ponty. Home becomes a metaphor to explain the existential space, the way of inhabiting a space or a corporeal transformation of an abstract space.

To quote Bachelard, 'A house that has been experienced is not an inert box. Inhabited space transcends geometrical space' (Bachelard 1994: 47). The same idea is articulated by Merleau-Ponty when he speaks of an existential space vis-à-vis geometrical space which is 'to live it, to take it up, assume it and discover its immanent significance' (1992: 258). In Lefebvre's thesis, space is entangled with the existing mode of production as it is a reproduction of the same and also a product wherein existing social relations are reflected. Hence it is 'operational and instrumental' (Lefebvre 1991: 11) as the 'class struggle is inscribed in space' (Lefebvre 1991: 68). In the apparent Marxist tone, the politics of space is rendered in terms of allocation of space apropos class distinctions and critical understanding of social planning as the reproduction of the existing class structure. Hence, space is political.

This conception of space could explain the social conflicts and the segregated spatiality embedded in the social space of Shaheen Bagh. Otherwise famous for its shopping space of factory outlets, Shaheen Bagh was relatively unknown among the other Muslim-populated pockets adjacent to it like Jamia Nagar, Zakir Nagar, Ghaffar Manzil, Noor Nagar and Batla House (Farooqi 2020: 13). Apart from the spatial isolation, the internal economic segregation was polarized between the intellectual elites teaching at Jamia and the labouring class comprising 'migrant construction workers, plumber, carpenters, vendors' adds to the spatial segmentation (Bhatia and Gajjala 2020: 6287). Besides the other vectors of internal conflicts and segregation among these colonies, all these ghettos populated by Muslims elicit a particular response, which becomes evident in their collective appraisal as 'mini-Pakistans' in the discursive spaces of mainstream Hindutva folds.[1] The subjectivation of the Muslim women of Shaheen Bagh, who occupy an exceptional existential territory and exhibit a new language of protest starkly different from that of the normative register and the spatial performative of protest often witnessed in Jantar Mantar in Central Delhi, raises the question of spatial segregation and embodied comportment of the places they inhabit. But the explanations on these grounds apropos the social production of space will be explicating the limitations of the phenomenological constitution of space. Lefebvre's conception of space can be located as an abstraction of subject-oriented spatial analysis of phenomenology and thus, it still retains its transcendental nature as in Kant's metaphysics. A Deleuzian approach will open up the possibilities of overcoming the subject–object chasm to focus on territories, events and assemblages which they call 'geophilosophy' (Deleuze and Guattari 1994). The political act of reconstructing the territory through 'occupying' the space calls for a new subjectivation and a new earth. Thus, it is not an occupation of the existing territory, but a construction of the territory in terms of its rhythms. The occupation of Shaheen Bagh is also situated in the larger problematic of creating territories in political terms and transforming it apropos the dynamics of the Occupy movement that we witnessed across the world, from the Arab Spring to the Jamia Square.[2]

The protest site of Shaheen Bagh was a long stretch of land and people, which was initially overcoded and negotiated by the flows of market and the virtual world of polities (the imminent threat of Hindutva) and relations of the sovereign nation-state. With this occupation of a minor sort driven by the singular event of the Jamia protests, the territory of Shaheen Bagh underwent a deterritorialization, a line of flight that creates a rhizomic world and subjective resingularization. The new assemblage that reconstitutes the existential territory of Shaheen Bagh has destabilized the neighbouring assemblages and paved the way for the precipitation of new flows. The transferential grafts effectuated by the new complexes of subjectivation reveal the existence of other possible worlds by escaping the 'repetitive impasse' and recomposing their existential embodiment. The ghetto of Shaheen Bagh was reterritorialized into a protest space, turning the 13A road linking the arterial Mathura Road in Delhi with the suburb of Noida into a realm of a dissident aesthetic and political project. This collective expression of dissent which is inherently political and aesthetic, and 'making dissident of subjectivity' (Guattari 1986: 68 as quoted in Watson 2012: 310), offered a new hope for the people calling for new images of existence and existential territories. As Janell Watson (2012: 311–12) argues, Guattari privileges the analysis of universe of references (U) embodied in existential territories (T) as they form the nondiscursive, intensive and virtual domains of the assemblage and become quintessential for the other two quadrants to function. It is in this domain that the subjectivity emerges and 'the amorphously coalesced collective disruptions' (2012: 310) exhibit a sense of ethological proto-subjectivity. As it is claimed before, the constitution of existential territory in Deleuze and Guattari's framework is not conceived in terms of spatial consistency and, thus, is not fundamentally geographical.

From the chaos to home: Existential territory of Shaheen Bagh

In this section, the onus is on the formation of the existential territory of Shaheen Bagh informed by the varied universes of reference, the flows, collective assemblages of enunciation, machinic assemblages of bodies and the abstract machine or diagram. An assemblage is essentially a multiplicity, 'a symbiosis, a "sympathy"' (Deleuze and Parnet 1987: 69). Thus, assemblage is a dynamic concept which has content and expression on the horizontal axis and territorialization/reterritorialization and deterritorialization on the vertical axis. Further, Deleuze and Guattari identify a machinic assemblage of bodies which is 'of actions and passions, an intermingling of bodies reacting to one another' and collective assemblages of enunciation, which is 'of acts and statements, of incorporeal transformations attributed to bodies' (Deleuze and Guattari 1987: 88). Assemblages cannot be deciphered without analyzing their virtual component, the abstract machine that is built into any assemblage as an overarching logic which is subjected to mutation as well. As Patton (2000: 45) argues, the abstract machine, an informal diagram, becomes the virtual double of the assemblage, on which it is embedded, and is ontologically prior to the content and expression. It is the virtual multiplicity which effectuates concrete machines and reshapes the social, material and energetic flows through their reciprocal interaction. The fluid structure of the assemblage is guaranteed by the heterogeneous nature of the components, and a cartography of its constituted elements allows us to decipher its rhizomic, nomadic and fluid nature. All these concepts in their interconnections assert the logic of multiplicity central to the notion of the assemblage.

Territorialization, for Deleuze and Guattari, is an act which is neither restricted to the intentional consciousness of the subjects who occupy, nor does it presuppose any essential or prior territory and relations. Rather territorialization is a dynamic individuation which produces its own conditions by proposing a radical immanent politics. Thus, the differential relation between intensities articulated in the field of the virtual facilitates the process of actualization as differentiation constituting the process of individuation as a virtual–actual complex. The concept of affect is crucial in explaining the occupation of Shaheen Bagh, by explicating the relation between milieu, territorialization, individuation, ritournello (refrain) and their associated concepts, and the becoming of it by invoking the constellation of universes. According to Guattari (2013: 204), affect is not an extensive but an intensive 'process of existential appropriation by continuous creation of heterogeneous duration of being'. Thus, an ethico-aesthetic paradigm against scientific accretion is privileged as the concept of affect possesses the 'potential for singularisation, for heterogenesis, in other words the eventual compositions, the "haecceities" that it promotes' (204). This is quite relevant in explaining the territorialization of Shaheen Bagh, the protestors' attempt in constructing a home, an earth, amidst the chaos and atmosphere of fear surrounding them, that could initiate pertinent ethical and political deliberations.

In the theoretical parlance of Deleuze and Guattari, the discerning of territory and the act of territorialization is deliberated in the context of ethology, which deals with the territorializing and non-territorializing animals. Here the concepts of milieu, rhythm, ritournello, motif, counterpoint, the different sorts of assemblages (intra, infra and inter) and the forces of chaos, earth and cosmos are critical in explaining the notion of territory and the act of territorializing. Though the idea is primarily drawn from ethology, Deleuze and Guattari move further away from the functional aspect of animal behaviour (mechanistic stimulus response model) to its expressive aspect and thus from the directional to the dimensional aspect (Deleuze and Guattari 1987: 315). The imminent threat of crumbling into chaos is always there for the territorial assemblage, irrespective of the coherence or stability it has achieved. There is a possibility of becoming dysfunctional or obsolete because of an internal element of an assemblage that could throw them into the danger of chaos, a threat posed by an external element which could destabilize the assemblage or an internal element escaping the valency of the assemblage, as there are no natural elements to a territory. Thus, the milieu in its basic form is susceptible to be drawn to the forces of chaos. It is from chaos that a milieu, 'a synthesis of unification' (Deleuze 1990: 102) can be deciphered and thus rhythm becomes milieu's response to chaos (Deleuze and Guattari 1987: 313). Here rhythm, according to Deleuze and Guattari, is not a meter or a periodic repetition, but 'a difference that is rhythmic'. Milieu is not territory, rather it is sub-territorial; 'a block of space-time constituted by periodic repetition of the component' (1987: 313). Here, the milieu constituted by the selection of a specific component from the undifferentiated chaos creates a centre focusing on the aspects of infra assemblage.

The stratified territorial assemblage of Shaheen Bagh was disrupted and unclasped from the original signification, collapsing to the imminent threat of chaos as the news and video footage of police firing on and brutalizing the students of Jamia reached them (Ausaf and Salam 2020; Mustafa 2020). It was panic, fear, disbelief and anguish which spread across the ghettos of Shaheen Bagh. There was a clear disorientation that dismantled the territory of Shaheen Bagh as there were no point of references for them to make connections and distinctions. The initial chaos that prevailed at Shaheen Bagh, the space of disorientation, slowly developed into a feeling of communitas as women in the community started a sit-in on the road chanting prayers and slogans of 'Azaadi' and 'Inquilab', creating a sonorous envelope around them, pointing to an orientation towards a 'calm and stable centre in the heart of chaos' (Deleuze and Guattari 1987: 315). Here, there is no specific spatial demarcation, but a sonorous orientation, a rhythm which calms and stabilizes the chaos of darkness. This orientation is not centred on an already anticipated space or a territory but a 'momentary determination of a centre', as there was 'no grand plan, no design and no intention to start a movement from Shaheen Bagh' (Pasha 2020: 48). Furthermore, Shaheen Bagh was 'endowed with a different vantage point of belonging' (Farooqi 2020: 14) vis-à-vis the performative mainstream protests held at Jantar Mantar, as it was a relatively unknown, interior ghettoized space. As more and more women joined the sit-in, the stratified territorial assemblage was creatively appropriated and made open to possibilities to mark a new territorial limit. The coded milieu was decoded to become a territory – as it was recoded into a new assemblage. The becoming expressive of the refrain or ritornello, which is 'an aggregate of matters of expression' (Deleuze and Guattari 1987: 322) becomes the 'territorializing mark: a signature' (315). The milieu becomes a territory when the momentary centre becomes a stable and expressive entity created by the refrain, as the fluid structure of protest emerged from the initial chaos gradually.

Refrain or ritornellos becomes a central concept to explain the phenomenon of territorialization or creation of home amidst the chaos that we find as a characteristic of most Occupy movements. The becoming expressive of Shaheen Bagh was marked by multiple ritornellos invoking a constellation of various universes of reference, not subjecting the constitution of territory into the principle of one or any form of transcendence. The territory was marked by the ritornellos of *azaadi* (freedom) and the visual image, and later graffiti, of 'the reprimanding finger' of the Jamia student 'who stood up to the shielded and armed police men in her act of parrhesia' (NY Manoj, Bradley and Lee 2020). Various placards and posters expressing solidarity with the students of Jamia and anti-CAA slogans became the first expression of the protest. The spatial demarcation was in fact done by the police using barricades separating the ghetto from the rest of the neighbourhood and closing down the highway leading towards the protest site. The expression of these ritornellos 'draws (the) territory and develops into a territorial motif and landscapes' (Deleuze and Guattari 1987: 322). The refrain of freedom becomes the territorial motif and the assemblage of the Hindutva and the state machine becomes the counterpoint, which adapt and counter-adapt their ability to capture and evade each other. In short, the 'territory is in fact an act that affects milieus and rhythms, that territorializes them' (Deleuze and Guattari 1987: 314). Territory raises the issues of consistency and the notion of ritornello explains it without reducing it to a mere geographical conception of spatiality. Here the ritornello focuses on the intra-assemblage which gives stability to it and transforms the amorphous screams and fears into chants and performance by invoking multiple universes of references. Since there is no overarching principle of ordering reality, there is neither a preconceived notion of a territory nor a particular destiny attributed to it. It becomes a superposition of disparate rhythms. Thus, any attempt to understand the territory becomes a concrete analysis of assemblages which is nothing but non-totalizable multiplicities.

Machinations of dissent: Shaheen Bagh as an intensive spatium

Thus, through the identification of a centre at Shaheen Bagh and then creating a territory or home around the centre by means of expressive acts, the inhabitants and the community organize and assemble it as an intensive spatium. The form of expression informs the way in which the regime of signs (mythical, religious, secular, poetry) instils an incorporeal transformation in the bodies of Shaheen Bagh assemblages. The substance of bodies that form the machinic assemblage of desire are the informational machines, communication technologies, graffiti, murals, posters, placards and substance of the regime of signs comprising poetic utterances of dissent, constitutional phrases, the loaned word *Azaadi* (freedom), the protest slogans of various Occupy movements in West Asia, Quranic verses, etc. Multiple peoples entered into an existential constellation with refrains of freedom that resonated across the territory through its artistic, political and cultural expressions. The highway occupied by the protesters was ascribed a dimensional depth as the materials, practices and discourses transformed it into a space of art and protest, which is nothing but the organization of a space, marking a home. It becomes purely expressive, stripping off the functional aspects attributed to it. The territorialization of the milieu is marked by the iconic expressions of the protest such as the transformation of the bus stop into a library, the becoming of the foot overbridge as an artistic museum and as a haven for artists, students and poets, the installation of the 35-foot tall iron and mesh map of India weighing over 2 tonnes with the inscription of anti-CAA slogans, the simulation of detention centres heralding the dark days ahead, the art installation of India Gate with the names of those who had lost their lives in anti-CAA protests, graffiti art etched on the road stretching around 100 metres, the national symbols of flags and the Constitution, and various posters carrying the images of and quotes from Gandhi and Ambedkar.

In the becoming of the protest site, art proliferated everywhere crossing the boundaries of material substrate so that even debris were converted into pieces of art, along with an endless proliferation of digital images. This significantly raised concerns regarding the specificity of the medium which opens up ways to rethink the practices of art. The existential territory of Shaheen Bagh opens up to multiple universes of value and reservoirs of residual cultural objects which function as a component of the passage to various other assemblages. This connection with the virtual world of values qualifies the existential territory and it becomes an embodied existential territory as there are no abstract universes of value. The existential embodied territory of Shaheen Bagh is replete with nationalistic images and the invocation of constitutional values.

The pathway of self-referencing is crucial in creating the singularities, expressive of stable configurations of subjectivity, which escape the black hole. The assemblages formed of multiple exchanges between individuals, groups and machines create new material of expression which recomposes the existential contours of territory by escaping the repetitive impasses, the rigid predetermined logic of the control regime. The singularities are event-driven, thus they can be considered a liberation from the black hole of territorialization and this process of subjectivation is the effect of heterogeneous elements which are transversally connected. Thus, the singularization, which is the concatenation of 'rhythms of lived experience, obsessive refrains, identificatory emblems, transnational objects, fetishes of all sorts' (Guattari 2013: 4), and transversalization open up the field of existential territory to the creative domain of virtual and incorporeal universes. There were various universes of reference including the invocation of Gandhi and Ambedkar, the Indian nationalist movement, constitutional morality, Islamic Universe, the secular universe, the universe of various protest poetry traditions, the other Occupy movements across the world, the universe of the liberal left, the universe of Dalit politics, the Muslim culture of north India, their language, attire and poetry and the mythical world (Manoj, Bradley and Lee 2020; Ausaf and Salam 2020; Mustafa 2020).

It is the abstract machine of dissent that could be identified in the territorial multiplicity of Shaheen Bagh, which had art and technology as the concrete machines effectuating the diagram. The content and expression of the assemblages cannot be read in terms of the signifier–signified relation as proposed by structuralism. Deleuze and Guattari propose a new theory of language based on pragmatics, that is, the study of the use of language in social context contra structuralism. Taking it further, beyond the theory of discursive formation in Foucault and withstanding the residue of structuralism in Hjelmslev, Deleuze and Guattari (1987) focus on the potentialities and variations that could be identified in the virtual structure of language – collective assemblages of enunciation which could effectuate incorporeal transformations. The collective assemblages of enunciation will always be located in space and time indicating the social context of the use of language and they will also appear in relation with the machinic assemblages of bodies. As Deleuze and Guattari affirm, 'there are no individual statements, only statements producing machinic assemblages' (Deleuze and Guattari 1987: 36). In precis, it is not the language or the subject that speaks, rather both are effects of 'interpenetrating multiplicities that at any given moment form a single machinic assemblage' (1987: 36). The plane of expression and content, though reciprocally presupposed, have got a different history and are thus, asymmetric components. To be more precise, they are independent of each other, though they are related. The collective assemblages of enunciation in fact put forth the possibility of an encounter, a diagram for a political practice, as it does not cater to the logic of ordinary discursive analysis. Rather it challenges the semiotic regime of signification and contributes to 'enacting existential crystallizations' (Guattari 2013: 4).

This incorporeal transformation equips the bodies to intermingle with new bodies and with the old bodies in significantly different ways. Thus, the order word is endowed with a potential of disordering and transformation for what Deleuze and Guattari (1987) call passwords. This could be a metamorphosis machine which facilitates the becoming war machine of language itself. So, for Deleuze and Guattari, language is not a simple tool for communication, rather it is primarily illocutionary. This means that language is performative, explicating an intrinsic relation between speaking and acting. This effectuates the collective assemblages of enunciation which is capable of bringing incorporeal transformations in the machinic assemblages of bodies. It is the abstract machine which is mutational, in which the linguistic and non-linguistic variables interact reciprocally and are selected by the assemblage. In the context of Shaheen Bagh assemblages, the machinic assemblages of bodies (content) and the collective assemblages of enunciation (expression) are two independent formations which do not establish a necessary relation but a contingent one. They need not last long also, as there could be vectors of disintegration functioning in it which lead to deterritorialization. The Shaheen Bagh assemblage invokes the protest poetry of various universes, predominant being the poem 'Hum Dekhenge' (we shall see) of Faiz Ahmed Faiz, which caught the ire of the Pakistani autocratic regime of General Zia-ul-Haq (Kumar 2018) in the 1980s and 'Dastoor' (constitution) of Habib Jalib, which was written in protest of the arbitrary introduction of the constitution by General Ayub Khan, with the provocative line 'aisay dastoor ko, Subh-e-benoor ko, main nahin manta, main nahin manta' (Such a constitution, such a dark dawn, I refuse to accept, I refuse) (Rahman 2020). The provocative slogans calling forth a revolution across the world by Lebanese protesters, slogans of the Sudanese protestor Alaa Salah, the protest song of Tahrir square (ala ala ala tahrir, ala ala ala soura), the usage of the Palestinian phrase 'intifada inquilab' in protest songs, the poetry of Varun Grover which expresses the voice of dissent, and Amir Aziz's 'Sab Yad Rakha Jayega' (Everything will be remembered) were all part of the enunciative assemblage (Manoj, Bradley and Lee 2020). As Guattari noted, 'a polyvocity (then) of components of semiotization' were in 'search for their existential consummation' (Guattari 2013: 203).

Though the first two aspects of the territorialization focus on the assemblages in their attempt to ward off the chaos, the onus of the third aspect is to preclude the possibility of the ritournello becoming static or cliché. The inter-assemblage opens up a crack in the circle which signifies the openness of the home by creating vectors of change and novelty (lines of flights). Thus, the ritournello is not simply a shielding of home from the chaos, but it opens up to the formation of multiple territories in its deterritorialization and invokes different existential territories. The abstract machinic phyla which form the realm of the actually possible interact with the material and energetic semiotic flows which constitute the actual real of the four-fold functors in its operation. The existential territory of Shaheen Bagh informed by the incorporeal universes of values opens to the material and energetic semiotic flows, the actual real dimension of existence. Here, the flows become the medium of the abstract diagram of dissent, which according to Guattari becomes a dissensual processual postmedia practice. The schizoanalytic subjectivity emergent at the intersection of machinic and sign flows, and constituent of the transformative potentials of various modalities of assemblages exceed the archaic collective and individual subjective territories and the domain of consciousness.

Here the focus is specifically on the media flows, especially that of the new assemblages of digital media, a broader ensemble of internet tools, which Guattari pronounces promising, as it could effectuate a resingularization of subjectivity through the production of affective intensities and techno-regimes of expression against the signifying imperium of mass-mediatic flows. The focus would be on the deterritorialization of components of subjectivity and process of extension and multiplication of the existential territory in unprecedented ways, by inserting 'subjectivity into incorporeal network' (Genosko 2009: 91). There were various impersonal or masked Twitter accounts like Jamia Resists, Shaheen Bagh Official, anonymous Instagram and Facebook accounts and mailing services, which constantly updated information regarding the protests, the change in venues and timing (in the case of solidarity marches). Through the calls for Twitter storms, they were in fact enacting a desire driven by dissensus through an affective modulation of bodies by frequency negotiating physical proximity of bodies. The protesters used internet spaces like Twitter, Facebook, Instagram and other social media apps to propagate images and videos, along with the live-streaming of performances, street plays and protests, enabling the protest to deterritorialize the physical space, placing it at the intersection of a series of flows. This could be analyzed in terms of the semiotic typology of Guattari, especially that of the a-signifying semiotics which is non-representational and keeps the 'semiological linearity of the structural signifier which imposes itself despotically over all other modes of semiotisation' at bay (Guattari 1995: 49).

The deterritorialization is not restricted to the domain of digital ecology. In fact, many Shaheen Baghs were created across the country with protesters chanting slogans of freedom and verses of resistance. The domain of protest art was also deterritorialized with the exceptional instance of using the traditional ritual of kolam (drawing using rice flour in Hindu tradition) in expressing solidarity to the protest, which again was circulated via digital medium. With the interface of digital ecology, the affective images and videos of the protest circulated across spaces extending the materiality of the protest camp to enter into asynchronous political participation, invoking 'an infinity of existential operators permitting access to mutant creative universes' (Guattari 2009: 299). By becoming the producer of the images of the protest art, performances and illustrations, the protesters become part of artistic practice through the technological medium. This is referred to as 'amateurism of artistic practice' facilitated by the technological turn, and also the becoming political of art 'by betraying what is perceived as art' (Manoj, Bradley and Lee 2020). The mechanical reproducibility of the art through a technological medium should be analysed from the perspective of difference and repetition, as the images in their incessant repetitious production create different sorts of affects in different people in the act of repetitious viewing. These repetitious views are not the repetition of the same, but a repetition of difference, a becoming which is not based on sameness or identity. In short, the question of subject or the linguistic signifier cannot constitute the problematic in the domain of the unconscious as its manifestations emerge out of a-signifying ruptures.

The assembly of protesters at Shaheen Bagh encountered a crisis with the global pandemic, as it provided an occasion for the government machinery to impose sophisticated mechanisms of control over the protesters. It has to be noted that towards the end of February 2020, the imminent danger of rhythm becoming cadence was materialized as the assemblage seems to have lost the dynamic interaction among the fourfold functors by becoming static. The pandemic situation raised a health emergency to which the states across the world responded with the aid of sophisticated technologies of surveillance, such as detecting geolocation, various surveillance apps and facial recognition. The protesters were evicted from Shaheen Bagh in the context of the pandemic which dissolved all the forms of assembling as social distancing became the new norm. The techno-regimes of expression were dissolved and the state apparatus appropriated the same technological assemblages to block the political becomings and dissensual media practices. Further, the state made use of these technological assemblages to crush dissent and panic among the populations. The Indian government used facial recognition apps and other technological devices to identify the protesters and later jail them (Nileena 2020; Trivedi 2019). The tools or war machine of protesters become an important component of the apparatus of capture employed through the liquid surveillant assemblages of the state. Janell Watson (2012) raises this point in her critique of the utopian dimension attached to the technological regime of postmedia constellations, as they can serve the purpose of the apparatus of control with a significant shift in the constitution of assemblage. This unravels the creative tension inherent in the postulation of postmedia between the liberative ruptures and the apparatus of control. Apart from being interactive and dissensual, she stresses the processual aspects of the postmedia assemblage to focus on the 'existential condition of the subjective mutation' (Watson 2012: 315). The discussion on postmedia was not 'overtly technological' but focuses on the question of 'new emancipatory social practices and above all alternative assemblages of subjective production' (Genosko 2013: 16).

Conclusion

I would like to address the pertinence of this theoretical deliberation on the existential territory of Shaheen Bagh in the context of Indian politics. Here, the focus is on the potential of the subjective mutation, alternate assemblages of subjective production and emancipatory social practices rather than the technological premise. In this specific context, the existential territory of Shaheen Bagh incites a response to the constitution of Hindutva heterotopia which employs exclusionary spatial strategies that segregate groups that 'do not fit Hindutva's template of an ideal citizen of the Hindu nation' (Anand 2005: 204). Here, this protest proposes an alternate ethical frame of valuation which destabilizes the notion of minority communities as dangerous and threatening. As Britta Ohm (2021: 758) argues, the protest of Shaheen Bagh charted a 'territory of empowerment that was diametrically opposed to the ghetto' and offered an 'alternative and sheltered' mode of communication in opposition to the 'aggressive conditions' of the mass-mediatic violence. The sonoric disruptions and the constitution of this territory articulated by the protesters expose the ideology of communalism and hatred, and the ways of normalized and institutionalized violence that is at the heart of the Hindutva movement in India.

The discussion on the concepts of heterotopia and utopia anticipates certain spatial configuration and strategies. This is extremely pertinent even in the analysis of nation as imagined communities, which brings in the notion of an identifiable territory and an abstract space (imagined). The physical territory can be a necessary condition, but not a sufficient one for the nation to exist (Deshpande 1995: 3220). Hindutva is a potent political project actively engaging in the relation between the abstract space and concrete territory fundamental to the nation through certain social practices, appropriating, deploying and controlling the exercise of power. According to Foucault (1997), utopia is 'an unreal space' that evinces a 'direct or inverted' relation with the real space, but with no reference to a concrete place. But heterotopia is a more potent concept as it exists in reality for Foucault. The mirror becomes a heterotopia, though it is a placeless place, when it 'exerts a counteraction on the position that we occupy' (Foucault 1997: 334) in the sense that it 'enables the people to see themselves reflected in some utopia' (Deshpande 1995: 3221). Ram Rajya and Hindutva are potent examples of such a kind of heterotopic construction which consciously engages with the spatial strategies of political exclusion and hatred. Shaheen Bagh as an existential territory offers a response to this virtual problem embedded in the very notion of Indian nationness. The assemblage of Shaheen Bagh offered a counter strategy to encounter this and, in this assemblage, the components of Gandhi and Ambedkar emerge as intense centres which evade or are always being subtracted from the apparatus of capture employed by the state and the Hindutva machine. To conclude, the existential territory of Shaheen Bagh will remain one of the most important universes of reference for protests to come and the possibility of new subjectivities, as the poet Amir Aziz said, 'tum zameen pe zulm likh do/aasmaan pe inquilab likha jayega' (If you write injustice on the earth/we will write revolution in the sky).

References

Anand, D. (2005), 'The Violence of Security: Hindu Nationalism and the Politics of Representing "the Muslim" as a Danger,' *The Round Table*, 94 (379): 203–15. Available online: 10.1080/00358530500099076 (accessed 15 March 2021).

Bachelard, G. (1994), *The Poetics of Space*, trans. M. Jolas, Boston: Beacon Press.

Berressem, H. (2020), *Félix Guattari's Schizoanalytic Ecology*, Edinburgh: Edinburgh University Press.

Bhatia, K. and R. Gajjala (2020), 'Examining Anti-CAA protests at Shaheen Bagh: Muslim Women and Politics of the Hindu India', *International Journal of Communication*, 14: 6286–303.

Bradley, J. P. N. (2019), 'Schizoanalysis of PokemonGo', *China Media Research*, 15 (4): 78–91.

Deleuze, G. (1990), *The Logic of Sense*, trans. M. Lester and C. Stivale, New York: Columbia University Press.

Deleuze, G. and F. Guattari (1987), *A Thousand Plateaus*, trans. B. Massumi, Minneapolis: University of Minnesota Press.

Deleuze, G. and F. Guattari (1994), *What is Philosophy?* trans. H. Tomlinson and G. Burchell, New York: Columbia University Press.

Deleuze, G. and C. Parnet (1987), *Dialogues*, trans. H. Tomlinson and B. Habberjam, New York: Columbia University Press.

Deshpande, S. (1995), 'Communalising the Nation-Space: Notes on Spatial Strategies of Hindutva', *Economic and Political Weekly*, 30 (50): 3220–227. Available online: http://www.jstor.org/stable/4403567 (accessed 10 January 2021).

Farooqi, I. (2020), 'Citizenship as Participation: Muslim Women Protestors of Shaheen Bagh', *Economic and Political Weekly*, LV (4): 13–15.

Foucault, M. (1997), 'Of Other Spaces: Utopias and Heterotopias', in N. Leach (ed.), *Rethinking Architecture: A Reader in Cultural Theory*, 330–6, New York: Routledge.

Genosko, G. (2009), *Félix Guattari: A Critical Introduction*, New York: Pluto Press.

Genosko, G. (2013), 'The Promise of Postmedia', in C. Apprich, J. B. Slater, A. Iles and O. L. Schultz (eds), *Provocative Alloys: A Postmedia Anthology*, 14–25, Lüneburg: Mute Books.

Genosko, G. (2015), 'Megamachines: From Mumford to Guattari', *Explorations in Media Ecology*, 14 (1–2): 7–20. Available online: https://doi.org/10.1386/eme.14.1-2.7_1 (accessed 1 April 2021).

Guattari, F. (1995), *Chaosmosis: An Ethico-Aesthetic Paradigm*, trans. P. Bains and J. Pefanis, Bloomington: Indiana University Press.

Guattari, F. (2009), *Soft Subversions: Texts and Interviews 1977–1985*, ed. S. Lotringer, trans. C. Wiener and E. Wittman, Los Angeles: Semiotext(e).

Guattari, F. (2013), *Schizoanalytic Cartographies*, trans. A. Goffey, London: Bloomsbury.

Kumar, K. (2018), 'Who is afraid of Faiz?', *The Hindu*, 18 May. Available online: https://www.thehindu.com/books/books-authors/who-is-afraid-of-faiz/article23918842.ece (accessed 15 March 2021).

Lefebvre, H. (1991), *The Production of Space*, trans. D. Nicholson-Smith, USA: Blackwell Publishing.

Manoj, N. Y., J. P. N. Bradley and A. T-G. Lee. (2020), 'Gadfly or Praying Mantis? Three Philosophical Perspectives on the Delhi Student Protests', *Educational Philosophy and Theory*. Available online: 10.1080/00131857.2020.1823211 (accessed 10 January 2021).

Merleau-Ponty, M. (1992), *The Phenomenology of Perception*, trans. C. Smith, London: Routledge.

Mustafa, S., ed. (2020), *Shaheen Bagh and the Idea of India*, New Delhi: Speaking Tiger.

Nileena, M. S. (2020), 'Amid Lockdown, Delhi Police Target and Arrest Anti-CAA Protesters from Jamia Nagar', *The Caravan*, 15 April. Available online: https://caravanmagazine.in/politics/anti-caa-protesters-jamia-arrested (accessed 1 June 2021).

Ohm, B. (2021), 'Media against Communication: Media/Violence and Conditionalities of Muslim Silencing in Northern India', *Media, Culture & Society*, 43 (4): 750–63. Available online: https://doi.org/10.1177/0163443721994531 (accessed 04 April 2021).

Pasha, S. (2020), 'Women, Violence and Democracy', in S. Mustafa (ed.), *Shaheen Bagh and the Idea of India*, 43–66, New Delhi: Speaking Tiger.

Patton, P. (2000), *Deleuze and the Political*, London: Routledge.

Rahman, S. (2020), 'Habib Jalib, his Dastoor – Why the People's Poet and His Words are Inspiring India's Youth', *The Indian Express*, 2 January. Available online: https://indianexpress.com/article/lifestyle/art-and-culture/habib-jalib-his-dastoor-why-the-peoples-poet-and-his-verse-are-inspiring-indias-youth-6194746/ (accessed 12 February 2021).

Salam, Z. U. and U. Ausaf (2020), *Shaheen Bagh: From a Protest to a Movement*, New Delhi: Bloomsbury.

Trivedi, S. (2019), 'Delhi Police Using Facial Recognition System to Identify Protesters', *The Hindu*, 31 December. Available online: https://www.thehindu.com/news/

cities/Delhi/delhi-police-using-facial-recognition-system-to-identify-protesters/article30437756.ece (accessed 15 March 2021).

Watson, J. (2011), *Guattari's Diagrammatic Thought: Writing Between Lacan and Deleuze*, London: Bloomsbury Academic.

Watson, J. (2012), 'Culture as Existential Territory: Ecosophic Homelands for the Twenty First Century', *Deleuze Studies*, 6 (2), 306–27.

3

The schizoanalysis of mechanical surveillance

Alex Taek-Gwang Lee

The relationship between surveillance and privacy is a crucial feature of modernity and capitalist assemblages. The Covid-19 pandemic is a serious challenge to the traditional idea of privacy established in the eighteenth century in Europe, understood as a keystone of individual autonomy and human dignity and the foundation of other human rights. The issue of privacy was initially about the protection of one's body and home and now leads to a problem revolving around the control of personal information. Today's situation stirs up the controversy further as what emerges on a global scale is a more enhanced tension between collective security and private life. This global crisis of privacy is not accidental and tentative but rather the necessary homeostasis of modern life. Therefore, the new problematic of privacy is an excellent starting point for introducing a new approach to understanding the relationship between surveillance and modernity revealed by the twenty-first-century pandemic.

Pandemic and privacy

The meaning of privacy is obscure, not only in its daily usage but also in its geographical reception. For instance, I found a sign in Delhi's metro stations, which informed the passengers that 'you are under surveillance'. The sign image, adopting a smiling cartoon character of a female police officer, does not mean that you are controlled or have no privacy, but rather you are safe and that there is no crime. The sign is only for potential criminals, not for 'lawful citizens'. In this sense, surveillance brings forth the invisible separation within the community, which divides something into the legal and the illegal. The implication of surveillance, therefore, is related to juridical subjectivity.

Delhi's metro sign tells us about the multifaceted nature of privacy. The concept of privacy is not singular but rather plural, as it rests upon geographical differences. Of course, these different standards of privacy have been occasionally criticized by the Universal Declaration of Human Rights (Shah 1997: 35–43). For European or American visitors, the message in Delhi's metro station would be problematic and violate their right to privacy. However, for those local passengers, in particular, female commuters, the word indicates the promise of security. Does this case show the other side of surveillance? Does the different signification of personal safety suggest a tricky aspect of privacy? If surveillance presupposes legal approval, its existence implies a disturbing truth – people agree to hand over the right to control their data to the authorities.

This ambiguous aspect of surveillance would be the voluntary compliance with surveillance that Michel Foucault points out in his analysis of the power/knowledge relation (Foucault 1998: 63). According to Foucault, power has no agency and no structure but is pervasive. We do not obey the rule of authority but rather are forced to follow the regime of truth. The regime does not mean sovereign acts of domination and coercion, rather it facilitates the constant flux and negotiation (Foucault 1998: 63). Scientific discourse and institutions produce and sustain the regime of truth, and the educational system continuously reinforces its general politics.

The regime of truth is the consequence of disciplinary power, such as Bentham's model of the panopticon. The self-monitoring prisoner in the panopticon obeys the rule of surveillance. The fear of surveillance resides in the knowledge of the norms by which they know they are being watched. However, what must be stressed here is that Foucault does not presuppose any transcendental form of Big Brother keeping a close watch. He presumes that the principle of surveillance is founded on the self-knowledge of the observation. Those who are monitored *want* to be an upstanding and good person, that is, the rule of surveillance already functions as a normative imperative sustaining our daily life. Delhi's metro signs convince us that the obscurity of privacy is nothing less than the legitimacy of surveillance.

The legitimacy of surveillance relies on two features of privacy: the need for privacy and the right to privacy. The former is related to the classical sense of the distinction between the private and public, while the latter is rooted in the historically developed concept of a right to control personal information. Leading up to the eighteenth century in Europe, the right to privacy was a juridical issue, a question of the right to open or read private letters. Legal issues gradually turned to questions about the collection of personal information. It was the colonization of America when the focus of privacy shifted onto the physical distance between the individual realms because land ownership in the new continent forged a secure base for the privilege of privacy (Wagner 47). By then, the home as such became seriously regarded as the first place of privacy, and this dramatic change has pinned down the concept of privacy until today.

As a historical by-product, there is a tension between the need for privacy and the right to privacy. The latter has increasingly extended its management of personal information since the rise of cognitive capitalism. What becomes significant in the new capitalism is not who has privacy but who owns the information. The administration of information is about the right to privacy, the legal permission to read personal letters. Jacques Derrida clearly points out that every right is 'right of inspection' (Derrida and Stiegler 2002: 33). According to him, 'there is no right that does not consist in conferring upon a power a right to control and surveillance, therefore, a right of inspection, in a situation where nothing guarantees it "naturally"' (2002: 33). In this sense, surveillance always presupposes a right tacitly but legally yielded to authority.

Derrida continues to argue that 'what links the juridical, or juridico-political, to seeing, to vision, but also to the capture of images, to their use' comes along with a question as to 'who, in the end, is authorised to appear [*se montrer*] but above all authorised to show [*montrer*], edit, store, interpret, and exploit images' (2002: 33–4). What must be stressed here is that Derrida focusses on the connection between the right of inspection and the right of editing and showing. Today, those who are authorized to modify and display the images are people themselves. With this modification and exhibition, tele-technology brings forth 'artifactuality' in Derrida's sense, not the truths of the world. The rapid advancement of 'tele-technologies', as well as mobile devices, dramatically transforms the classical definition of surveillance. Still, it is not technology as such but the legal approval to the right to inspect the personal data behind its mechanism which determines the transition. In short, the rise of cognitive capitalism implicates the legal permission of surveillance.

Knowledge versus data

Indeed, the advent of cognitive capitalism is deeply related to this paradigm shift. As Yann Moulier-Boutang conceptualizes, cognitive capitalism is 'a paradigm, or a coherent research program, that poses an alternative to post-Fordism' (Moulier-Boutang 2011: 113). Cognitive capitalism can be grasped by the transformation of three economic elements such as the form of accumulation, the mode of production, and the way of exploitation, and its main feature resides in the progress of new technologies since 1975. However, Moulier-Boutang makes a sharp distinction between his concept of cognitive capitalism and 'information society'. For him, the term *information society* is a misleading definition of the capitalist changeover embedded in the shift of three economic foundations. In this new type of capitalism, 'the object of accumulation consists mainly of knowledge, which becomes the basic source of value, as well as the principal location of the process of valorisation' (Moulier-Boutang 2011: 57). The knowledge-centred economy leads to reshaping the traditional division of labour and facilitates the emergence of the horizontal structure enforced by a data-collecting system like the internet.

Furthermore, it is undeniable that cognitive capitalism paves the way towards surveillance capitalism along with the advancement of technological means. To some extent, surveillance capitalism can be called one of the many features observed in cognitive capitalism, however, in my opinion, what makes a difference between these types of capitalism lies in the role of *learning* in accumulation. Consistent with the paradigm of cognitive capitalism, the production of knowledge through knowledge, that is, its exploitation of the invention power, is crucial for its accumulative process. In this procedure, knowledge takes the place of a commodity; however, this replacement does not mean the commodification of knowledge but rather the redesigning of property rights and the expansion of possible wealth externally. For this reason, cognitive capitalism unveils the foundation of surveillance capitalism: the commodification of personal data.

Data is the raw material for the accumulation of surveillance capitalism, and the extraction and analysis of human behaviours are its imperative. Google is the pioneering company par excellence which invented the paradigm of surveillance capitalism, while Ford Motor Company and General Motors are the chief progenitors of industrial capitalism. Shoshana Zuboff, who coined this term, points out that 'although surveillance capitalism does not abandon established capitalist "laws" such as competitive production, profit maximisation, productivity, and growth, these earlier dynamics now operate in the context of a new logic of accumulation that also introduces its own distinctive laws of motion' (Zuboff 2019: 66–7). The new logic of accumulation, based on the 'economies of scale in the extraction of behavioural surplus' (Zuboff 2019: 87), gives rise to the necessary construction and modification of behavioural means that 'incorporate its machine-intelligence-based "means of production" in a more complex system of action, and the ways in which the requirements of behavioural modification orient all operations toward totalities of information and control, creating the framework for an unprecedented *instrumentarian power* and its societal implications' (Zuboff 2019: 67).

The shift from knowledge to data denotes the difference between cognitive capitalism and surveillance capitalism. Even though the arrival of surveillance capitalism does not mean the end of cognitive capitalism, as the two types of accumulative systems coexist and cooperate, knowledge in cognitive capitalism is not a commodity as such, but the commodity structure to bring on the symbolic exchange of the non-exchangeable. Cognitive capitalism finds its origin in the increased significance of knowledge and its eruption driven by higher levels of education and the expansion of immaterial and intellectual labour. In this way, the main feature of cognitive capitalism is embodied by the qualitative dominance of *living knowledge* (mobilized by labour) over *dead knowledge* (incorporated in fixed capital). The initiative of the knowledge built in living labour is the main trait of cognitive capitalism. This transformation sheds light on the decline or crisis of the Smithian and Taylorian model of labour division and technical progress inherent in industrial capitalism. The mutation of accumulation is fundamental, and the so-called information technology revolution is not the single determinant for the mode of production.

As previously discussed, technological progress is one of the elements to accelerate the paradigmatic conversion to solve the crises of capitalism, and is one of the 'guardians' of innovation, that is, the juridical agreement is always a hidden impetus behind the shift. As far as the 'revolution' takes place as part of capitalist accumulation, whether cognitive or something else, technology cannot go beyond the principle of the early capitalism that Karl Marx already discusses in his unfinished work. Marx states that the juridical relation, 'whose form is the contract, whether as part of a developed legal system or not, is a relation between two wills which mirrors the economic relation' (Marx ([1867] 1990): 178). Marx's analysis of the link between the legal system and accumulation reveals the fact that cognitive capitalism and surveillance capitalism are founded on the new juridical norms of privacy, for example, the legitimate permission to use personal data for economic purposes.

Cognitive capitalism effectuates the decline of the traditional working class and the expansion of knowledge by bringing in the cognitive dimension of labour into the relations of production. Cognitive assemblages organize desire with the axiomatics of human capital. Mass education and popular intellectuality are the prerequisites for the success of the new accumulation and gradually necessitate Taylorism and Fordism, the scientific theories of organizing labour and production, as ways to confront the crisis.

The ideological imperative of cognitive capitalism demands worker autonomy and thus renders manual labour obsolete. For this reason, the spirit of cognitive capitalism springs out from the obsession of *self-directed learning*. According to Malcolm Knowles, self-learning is 'a process by which individuals take the initiative, with or without the assistance of others, in diagnosing their learning needs, formulating learning goals, identifying human and material resources for learning, and evaluating learning outcomes' (Knowles 1983: 18).

The duty of self-learning constitutes the ethics of new Protestantism in the phase of cognitive capitalism. It seems to herald the return of the nineteenth-century self-help maxim in industrial capitalism. To some degree, the motto of self-learning in knowledge-based accumulation is akin to a form of popular stoicism which encourages mass self-guided improvement for individual welfare and well-being. Even though *cognitive capitalism* is a term to indicate the new stage of accumulation, Marx already discussed the cognitive dimension of work. In Marx's sense, knowledge is incompatible with labour, and the economic conditions and the social formations of knowledge rely upon the creative power of living labour. Marx argues:

> Nature builds no machines, no locomotives, railways, electric telegraphs, self-acting mules, etc. These are products of human industry; natural material transformed into organs of the human will over nature, or of human participation in nature. They are *organs of the human brain, created by the human hand*; the power of knowledge, objectified. The development of fixed capital indicates to what degree general social knowledge has become a *direct force of production*, and to what degree, hence, the conditions of the process of social life itself have come under the control of the general intellect and been transformed in accordance with it. To what degree the powers of social production have been produced, not only in the form of knowledge, but also as immediate organs of social practice, of the real life process. (Marx [1857] 1993: 706)

What Marx points out here is that the 'general intellect' is the knowledge built in the 'conditions of the process of social life' and could transform the social foundation by its changeability. Therefore, the transition towards cognitive capitalism is, in this sense, nothing less than the consequence of a capitalist attempt to control the 'general intellect' over the collective workers' hegemony within the knowledge-based accumulation system. The dynamic criss-cross of conflicts forces capital to reconstruct its established modality and bring forth the new structure of accumulation and production. Neoliberalism, as a theory of governmentality, is introduced here to reregulate the relations between capital and the creative power of labour. For Marx, machines are 'organs of the human brain' and 'the power of knowledge'. These objectified neurological organs determine the degree of the real subsumption of the labour process by capital. Industrial capitalism and its utilitarian theory of governmentality were not interested in the cognitive dimension of labour power, but the disciplinary control of work. The cognitive dimension of labour power embedded in 'general intellect' was repressed in industrial capitalism and is now re-appropriated by the new phase of accumulation, that is, cognitive capitalism as the autonomy of work through social cooperation is progressively enhanced.

Meanwhile, the notion of surveillance capitalism seems more focussed on the technological mediation of behaviour modification through 'a pervasive global architecture of ubiquitous computational knowledge and control constructed and maintained by all the advanced scientific know-how that money can buy' (Zuboff 2019: 308). Zuboff warns of the danger that 'Big Other', corporations such as Google, Amazon and Facebook, would use the collected personal data for their commercial purposes. However, the companies do not sell the congregated data to the market. What they want to do with Big Data is to create the perfect model of 'artifactuality' to anticipate consumers' behaviour. In a nutshell, surveillance capitalism could be defined as an accumulative system to extract private human experience as free raw material and transform it into behavioural data. Is this statistic quantification of human behaviour a new feature of capitalist accumulation? The principle of surveillance capitalism, the translation of human behaviour to data, is already suggested by the Austrian economists such as Ludwig von Mises.

Mises argues that a man is a living datum and 'there is no yardstick that a scientific investigation can apply to human action other than that of the ultimate goals the acting individual wants to realise in embarking upon a definite action' (Mises 1963: 651). He intends to set up the theory of human behaviour, a so-called praxeology, and believes that 'human action is necessarily always rational' (Mises 1963: 19). His theory presupposes that human behaviour has intended purposes, but this idea of rationality is not a necessary condition for the actuality of the market system. The market operation has nothing to do with the 'conscious' choice of rational action. Mises's theory of the data economy ignores the unconscious level of the market system and reserves the introduction of psychology to the economic theory. This psychological model of the data economy paves the way towards the elaboration of surveillance technology to control unconscious compulsions. Ironically, there lies a passion for the reality behind the advent of mechanical surveillance.

The juridico-politics of surveillance capitalism

What is at stake in the discussion of surveillance capitalism is the function of technology, in particular, the high development of computation which enables 'Big Other' to extract the personal data from human behaviour. The accumulation of Big Data is the consequence of the 'scientific investigation' but has no direct relation to production itself. The logic of surveillance capitalism is not like one of cognitive capitalism, but rather removes the cognitive dimension from labour. Surveillance capitalism does not need any creative knowledge or invention power but the extraction of data from personal experiences. In this sense, it is not easy to define surveillance capitalism as the fundamental transformation of the production modality, even though 'new automated protocols are designed to influence and modify human behaviour at scale as the means of production is subordinated to a new and more complex *means of behaviour modification*' (Zuboff 2019: 19). The original point of Zuboff's arguments here is that 'Big Other' does not intend to sell the collected data, but instead use it to reorient the subjective desires for future market trends. She discloses the manipulation behind the data economy. However, Zuboff seems to overlook the fact that those companies desperately collect personal data to bring forth the 'general' model of human behaviour. The generalization of desiring-machines is impossible, and even further the machinic desires escape from the rigid scale of mechanical surveillance. Mechanical surveillance necessarily preserves a chaotic vantage point through which the unconscious impulse sneaks away.

Zuboff's understanding of technology seems inclined to Martin Heidegger's critique of modern technology. For Heidegger, technology is not a means to an end and has nothing to do with human activity (Heidegger 1977: 16). Technology already presupposes the modification of our behaviour. In Heidegger's sense, technology is a way of revealing its origin. The mode of revealing, the technical aspects in its right, turns extremely 'unreasonable' in the mechanism of modern technology. The revealing of modern machines is the challenging demand for extracting and storing up the concealed energy of nature. Heidegger denotes this process of challenging forth as 'unlocking'. He argues that 'the revealing reveals to itself its own manifoldly interlocking paths, through regulating their course' (Heidegger 1977: 16). This process of technological revealing constructs its own rule against the natural one. The self-regulation of technology is a 'setting-up', mobilizing people into ordering and concentrates them upon framing the real as standing reserve: Enframing. Heidegger conceptualizes the essence of Enframing as 'setting-upon gathered into itself which entraps the truth of its own coming to presence with oblivion' (Heidegger 1977: 36). Because of Enframing, nature and human beings are regarded as raw materials for mechanical operation. Surveillance technology, in this sense, could be one of the typical examples that prove the extreme challenging forth revealing.

However, Heidegger insists on the possible change of Enframing. He admits that 'if Enframing is a destining of the coming to presence of Being itself, then we may venture to suppose that Enframing, as one among Being's modes of coming to presence, changes' (Heidegger 1977: 37). Therefore, Heidegger's critique does not aim at rejecting the Enframing of technology, but rather changing our orientation, that is, 'self-adapting', to technology. In Heidegger's sense, a 'destining' (*Geschick*) means the adaptation of oneself to the enframed reality. Any destining always conserves potential changeability, yet this change does not mean a way to make any technology better. A crucial question concerning the use of technology is not how to improve its function but how to escape its influence. In short, it is our attitude towards technology that his critique proposes to change. The juridico-politics of surveillance emerges at this point: the control of the ethical attitude towards technological governmentality. The limit of Heidegger's critique lies in his ignorance of juridical implication of technology. If technology is revealing, its operations cannot be separated from the legal permission. Any object within the framework of capitalist accumulation is supposed to be commodified with juridical axioms. In this sense, the technological appropriation of information does not work alone. Without juridico-politics, technology cannot have a right to penetrate the veil of privacy. As Derrida says, 'there is a juridical technology, and no judgement, no justice is neutral or innocent with regard to technics in general' (Derrida and Stiegler 2002: 62).

Mechanical surveillance and postmedia

Surveillance is the internal logic of modernity. What we newly face up to within the current phase of surveillance capitalism is the rise of mechanical surveillance. Mechanical surveillance is machine-based surveillance, facilitating an algorithmic operation. Artificial intelligence is one of those technical instruments to set forth the mechanical surveillance. Automation is the condition of mechanical surveillance and the progress of the early observation system. As Foucault points out, the structure of the panopticon is the origin of a modern surveillance system (Foucault 1995: 196). The centralized power controls the population and modifies its behaviour. However, it is not only the structure of the building, but the norms imposed by the gaze of surveillance which enforce prisoners to modify their behaviour. Automation is nothing less than the internalization of the surveillance gaze and the decentralization of the panopticon structure. The omnipresent surveillance constantly reproduces 'artifactuality'. As Derrida points out, this mechanical operation already assumes the juridical right of inspection (Derrida and Stiegler 2002: 33). This 'invisible hand' of juridico-politics is the principle of the centralized media hegemony. Derrida's conceptualization of tele-technology aims at the critique of the homogenous 'artifactuality' produced by the panopticon-like media system. Mechanical surveillance is in this sense the essential principle of the media industry. However, mechanical surveillance is not a 'Big Brother' to control everything. Its function seems to exclude human agency from its system, yet, its mechanism necessarily contains the possible alterative use within itself because of its juridico-politics.

When the Gulf War broke out in 1990, Guattari (1990) wrote an essay, '*Vers une ère post-média*' (Towards a Postmedia Era), in which he put forward the form of non-hegemonic media. He ponders the images of warfare on the television and states that those images made us lift off into 'an almost delirious universe of mass-media subjectivity' (Guattari 1990: 1). Against the efficiency of the media mechanism, he suggests 'molecular alternative practices' of media, that is, the performance of postmedia. For Guattari, the practices of postmedia must be the expressive mediation against the mechanical representation of reality, since the 'good old day' of media is nothing less than the scientific and positivist imagination. There is no powerful Big Brother in the new tele-technological situations, but many potential resistances within them. In this sense, what is urgently needed is to invent the milieu of postmedia, in other words, the concept of it which stands in and for itself. Guattari emphasizes the 'minor' use of technology. The concept of a minority implies the affirmation of differences, that is, those which are not subsumed to the generalization of the majority. The minor use of tele-technology is nothing less than the practices of postmedia, in my term, the schizoanalytic reversion of mechanical surveillance. Surveillance is not a self-fulfilling system but always requires its 'supplements' from the outside of its mechanism. As Derrida puts it, television broadcasting no longer delivers original news, but somebody's scripts on the prompter. The information has already been altered by somebody else. Derrida also states that 'when a journalist or politician seems to be speaking to us, in our homes, while looking us straight in the eye, he (or she) is in the process of reading, on screen, at the dictation of a "prompter", a text composed somewhere else, at some other time, sometimes by others, or even by a whole network of anonymous authors' (Derrida and Stiegler 2002: 4).

Derrida's analysis of the broadcast system reminds us of Walter Benjamin's conceptualization of photography and cinema as the typical consequence of technical reproduction (Benjamin 2003: 120). Benjamin emphasizes what is brought in by a machine's replacement of an artist and the automatic operator of sensorium. Interestingly, Benjamin also shed light on the 'optical unconscious', which is invisibly preserved in the technological representation. This unrepresented locus of technical reproducibility is the point of resistance. Benjamin argues:

> *In photography, exhibition value begins to drive back cult value on all fronts.* But cult value does not give way without resistance. It falls back to a last entrenchment: the human countenance. It is no accident that the portrait is central to early photography. In the cult of remembrance of dead or absent loved ones, the cult value of the image finds its last refuge. In the fleeting expression of a human face, the aura beckons from early photographs for the last time. This is what gives them their melancholy and incomparable beauty. But as the human being withdraws from the photographic image, exhibition value for the first time shows its superiority to cult value. (Benjamin 2003: 257–8)

The 'nostalgic regress' of technical reproduction seems the 'past tense' of mediatic assemblages, but, according to Benjamin's concept of the standstill dialectic, the 'Angelus Novus' from the bygone days is the image of the utopian impulse towards the future. For Benjamin, the exhibition value of technology, in other words, the modernity of media, is the necessary condition of a cultural transition by which quantitative value turns qualitative value. According to Benjamin, the ocular-centric quantification of objects, that is, the mechanism of modern surveillance, however, preserves the resistance of the optical unconscious within its representation.

If surveillance is the fundamental element of modernity, or further the mechanism of democracy, what makes a difference between yesterday's capitalism and today's capitalism? As Heidegger describes technology as revealing, technological development is closely related to the increment of transparency. The degree of transparency is how many have the rights to edit and show the personal information. Mechanical surveillance is the democratic distribution of the panoptic gaze. That gaze belongs to the subjectivity, which seems excluded from the scope of mechanical surveillance, yet, continuously returns as the void of the mechanism. Its presence seems transcendental but at the same time immanent. The new mode of surveillance disguises itself as a neutral instrument free from the juridical question as to the right of inspection. The function of machines is centred in the serial process of the surveilling operations. No authority is needed here, but programmed algorithms, which rely on total artifactualities worked out for their precise purpose. It does not matter whether the surveillance is effective or not, but what is important is that people recognize its omnipresence.

The silent topos of 'chaosmos' within the network of computing surveillance is the venue of resistance. As Derrida claims, 'we are given this imperative – to think the political beyond the political, as it were, or the democratic beyond democracy – by technics concretely, urgently, every day – both as a threat and as a chance' (Derrida and Stiegler 2002: 65). Derrida suggests 'critical culture' as a kind of education, but such critique should be undertaken with two concerns: the first concern is national, ethnocentric actuality, and the second concern is the advancement of tele-technology or the 'centralising appropriation of artifactual powers for "creating the event"' (2002: 5). The apparent internationalization of regional information paves the way towards the justification of national resistance and the technological monopolization of actuality promotes real-time communication only in the present time. The schizoanalysis of these mediatic assemblages comes up with the alternative approach to the split aspects of the hegemonic broadcast capital. Derrida's understanding of the tele-technological mechanism leads us to the schizoanalysis of postmedia, that is, the schizophrenic escape from the deadlock of the national and international actualities. Schizoanalysis as such is the resistance to forge the 'virtual lines' of flight towards the ontological heterogeneity against the homogeneity of the centralized media.

The escape of the unconscious compulsion from the mechanical surveillance of homogeneous real-time communication is always on the verge of danger to push the use of technology up to its limit. As Deleuze and Guattari confirm, the minor use of technology produces its many techniques, that is, the liberation of technics to multiplicity. The pandemic situation proves that surveillance capitalism is sufficiently adaptive and subtle to sustain its own system dynamics. However, it also shows the ambivalence of surveillance technology, in that people do not want to neglect surveillance, but rather strongly demand that the authorities put their security under constant surveillance. This excessive drive brings forth the vulnerable point of technology and the minor use of the techniques against its instrumental purpose.

References

Benjamin, W. (2003), *Selected Writings, Volume 4 1938–1940*, ed. H. Eilain and M. W. Jennings, London: Belknap.

Derrida, J. and B. Stiegler (2002), *Echographies of Television: Filmed Interviews*, Oxford: Polity.

Foucault, M. (1995), *Discipline and Punish: The Birth of the Prison*. trans. A. Sheridan, New York: Vintage.

Foucault, M. (1998), *The History of Sexuality: The Will to Knowledge*, trans. R. Hurley, London: Penguin.

Guattari, F. (1990), 'Vers une ère post-média'. *Terminal*, 51. Available online: https://www.revue-chimeres.fr/Felix-Guattari-Vers-une-ere-post-media-octobre-novembre-1990-Terminal-No-51 (accessed 2 October 2020).

Heidegger, M. (1977), *The Question Concerning Technology and Other Essays*, trans. W. Lovitt, New York: Garland Publishing.

Knowles, M. S. (1983), *Self-Directed Learning: A Guide for Learners and Teachers*, London: Prentice-Hall International.

Marx, K. ([1867] 1990), *Capital: A Critique of Political Economy Volume One*, London: Penguin.

Marx, K. ([1857] 1993), *Grundrisse: Foundations of the Critique of Political Economy*, London: Penguin.
Moulier-Boutang, Y. (2011), *Cognitive Capitalism*, trans. E. Emery, Cambridge: Polity.
Shah, P. (1997), 'International Human Rights: A Perspective From India', *Fordham International Law Journal*, 21 (1): 24–44.
Von Mises, L. (1963), *Human Action: A Treatise on Economics*, San Francisco: Fox and Wilkes.
Wagner, W. J. (1971), 'The Development of the Theory of the Right to Privacy in France', *Washington University Law Review*, 45 (1): 45–70.
Zuboff, S. (2019), *The Age of Surveillance Capitalism: The Fight for a Human Future at the New Frontier of Power*, London: Profile Books.

Part II

Principles of schizo thought

4

Postmedia Hans

Keeping it real with Guattari

Janell Watson

Can those of us who dwell in the twenty-first-century metropolises of semiocapitalism learn anything from Freud's famous child patient Hans, who lived with his parents and rival sibling in bourgeois industrial-era Vienna and who at age 5 developed a phobia of horses?[1] Although phobia is typically classified as a neurosis rather than a psychosis like schizophrenia, Deleuze and Guattari describe Hans's phobia as a schizo line of escape from a social apparatus of capitalist subjectivation: the Oedipal family. In the introduction to *A Thousand Plateaus*, the second volume of *Capitalism and Schizophrenia*, they explain that Hans 'tries to build a rhizome' but that his parents and Doctor Freud 'kept on BREAKING HIS RHIZOME and BLOTCHING HIS MAP', the very map on which Hans plots his escape (Deleuze and Guattari [1980] 1987: 14). In *The Machinic Unconscious*, Guattari literally draws a map of Hans's attempts at rhizome construction, creating a diagram entitled 'The Rhizome of Little Hans' Phobic Encircling' ([1979] 2011: 175; see Figures 4.1–4.6). The drawing indicates Hans's deterritorializing lines of flight, as well as the breaks and blotches imposed by his parents and Freud, whom Deleuze and Guattari blame for stratifying the boy's rhizome with their Oedipal significations and developmental schemas ([1980] 1987: 14).

Even though this actual case of phobia developed around 1900, prior to the reign of mass media, I suggest that in diagramming Hans's phobia, Guattari was already mapping a postmediatic subjectification. As Guattarian media studies scholars rightly insist, the notion of postmedia first and foremost designates a mode of subjectivation, rather than a set of technologies or a historical period (Genosko 2012, 2013; Godard 2013; Ueno 2012; Bradley 2019). The forces of capitalist subjectivation hinder entry into the postmedia era. In his 1989 book, *Schizoanalytic Cartographies*, Guattari laments that the early technologies of the postmedia era to come had so far resulted only in 'a reinforcement of previous systems of alienation' (Guattari [1989] 2013: 12). Oedipalization is a system of alienation operating in conjunction with the capitalist machine of alienating subjugation. In his 1985 essay 'Entering the Postmedia Era', Guattari calls for 'redefining the unconscious from outside the confining frames of psychoanalysis', which is exactly what his mapping of the Hans case aims to do

(Guattari 2009b: 301). Diagonal lines escape the confines of the Oedipal strata that Freud and the parents tried to impose on the boy. Little Hans drew lines of flight that pointed to a way out. The rhizome of his lines of escape into phobia can help us confront the blockages that are breaking the rhizomes and blotching the maps that could potentially produce postmediatic subjectivities. Postmedia Hans can learn cartography from his Viennese ancestor.

Machinic enslavement or line of flight?

Capitalist sign machines, aided and abetted by psychoanalysis, the media, and contemporary culture, produce 'a specific and fundamental commodity: the individuated subject', argues Maurizio Lazzarato in *Signs and Machines: Capitalism and the Production of Subjectivity* (2014: 100). Drawing on Deleuze and Guattari's schizoanalysis in describing labour under post-industrialism, Lazzarato and Franco Berardi describe information-age capitalism as 'putting subjectivity to work' or 'putting the soul to work', respectively (1996: 143; 2009: 24). Guattari had already sensed the growing importance of subjectivity in capitalist production, for example, when in 1973 he writes that Oedipalization serves capitalism by forming 'a deterritorialised worker . . . who follows the progress of technology' and 'who develops a certain creativity, a certain participation' (Guattari 2009a: 237). The keywords 'technology', 'creativity' and 'participation' suggest that Oedipalization was already grooming Hans for cognitive labour, standardizing his creativity and interest in technology, so as to facilitate his integration into axiomatic capitalism. As Guattari puts it, 'from birth through family, television and social services, a child is "set to work" and is engaged in a complex process of formation, with a view of adapting the child's various modes of semiosis to upcoming productive and social functions' (2009b: 259).

Hans's father and Freud, the former's mentor, were already immaterial labourers, as both were doctors, professionals in the service sector. They integrate their 'scientific labor' of analysing the boy's phobia into their service sector labour of providing care, as is consistent with production in the age of material labour (Lazzarato 1996: 136). Unlike industrial labour, immaterial labour integrates the consumer into the production process (138, 142). At the beginning of 'Analysis of a Phobia in a Five-Year-Old Boy', the case study that his immaterial work produced, Freud acknowledges the collaboration of his disciple-client, Hans's father (1955: 5–6). The psychoanalyst, who met Hans only once, based his case study on the father's notes and copious letters, from which Freud quotes liberally.

The key difference between industrial-era and post-industrial labour, suggests Lazzarato, lies in the mix between 'two heterogeneous power apparatuses': the older apparatus of *social subjection* (signifying semiologies of discourse, narrative, mythologies, refrains, faciality) and today's technologically enhanced apparatuses of *machinic enslavement* (a-signifying semiotics of processes, operations, policies, plans, algorithms) (Lazzarato 2014: 12–14, 24–5, 122–5; see also Genosko 2016: 105–8). The two apparatuses function hand in hand. Social subjection, which begins at home in the family, assigns 'an identity, a sex, a body, a profession, a nationality, and so on'

(Lazzarato 2014: 12). Machinic enslavement integrates human labour as one of its parts (Lazzarato 2014: 119). As Guattari puts it, 'Individuals are modelled to adapt, like a cog, to the capitalist machine' (2009a: 237). The factories of the industrial era were already powerful human-machine assemblages. Today's machines are enhanced by cybernetic systems of control, global information systems, transnational financial networks, and vast corporate entities whose bosses answer to shareholders and boards. The familialist 'father-boss-king' paradigm no longer provides the employment model under the current regime of capitalist production (Guattari 2009a: 240).

I imagine twenty-first-century Hans growing up to become a doctor like his predecessor's father. Post-industrial Hans works for a large healthcare corporation, functioning as a cog within a larger enterprise, rather than as an independent professional with his own practice. Lazzarato ascribes the 'shift from individuated subject'– the physician who owns a private practice – to 'subjectivation carried out by capitalist machinisms' such as the process-and-procedure machines of the healthcare conglomerate's human resources department (Lazzarato 2014: 95). The contemporary corporate machine enslaves by deploying an a-signifying semiotics of processes, operations, policies, plans and algorithms. Its machines are not intersubjective, despite their human components, but instead function as points of intersection or connection for machinic processes (2014: 27).

However, these capitalist megamachines continue to rely on social subjection to produce the subjectivities that serve them (29). Lazzarato suggests that the globally distributed products of the American culture industry, the social side of machinic enslavement under semiocapitalism, 'has worked to neutralize and stifle heterogeneity by exploiting, like psychoanalysis, personological and familialist signifiers' (108; see also 160–4). Media, interactive or not, transmit the signifiers of the Oedipal family. Guattari cites the Hans case as an example of 'submitting the child to the Oedipian code' (2009a: 240). More than a century since Hans developed his phobia of horses in the streets of Vienna, this code dominates cartoons, television series, movies, children's books and toys, which prominently feature Oedipal households. Family structures in the United States and elsewhere have been impacted by historical changes such as the sexual revolution, feminism and LGBTQIA+ rights, but the father-mother-children domestic model remains the standard against which other household types are implicitly compared. The family remains a force for integrating middle-class children into the capitalist megamachine, even in the twenty-first century.

Guattari charts Hans's escape from social subjection by way of Oedipal familialism, but his diagram also charts the zones in which lines of flight can emerge from machinic enslavement. Enslaving machinic assemblages, with their algorithms and depersonalized procedures, destroy the previous social encodings of archaic cultural traditions, opening up possibilities for creating the new political subjectivations (Lazzarato 2014: 122, 134–8). Gary Genosko observes that 'Semiocaptialism did not crush Guattari's belief that a resingularizing combination of social experimentation and new technology was the best hope for exiting mass media and entering the universe of postmedia' (Genosko 2016: 115; see also 45–6). Guattari describes Japan as 'a society of "machinic mutants"', for better and for worse. He declares that 'I'm crazy about machines, concrete and abstract, and I have no doubt that a fabulous expansion will eventually break down all the conservatisms that "keep us in place" in this absurd and blind society' (2009b: 307). Postmedia Hans must learn cartography from the Hans of Vienna circa 1900, if he is to escape both subjection and enslavement to become a marvellous machinic mutant.

Hans at home (A)

Guattari warned about 'violent deterritorializations in the social field' unleashed by capitalism (Genosko 2013: 22). The Oedipian code offers protection against these potentially catastrophic social and psychic deterritorializations because it 'provides the family with an artificial consistency', explains Guattari (2009a: 240). He will later call this artificial consistency 'existential territory'.[2] No creature, fictional or living, can thrive without a territory, whether on the earth's surface or on an existential territory. The territories essential to all social and psychic formations are constituted on the plane of consistency, which is what Guattari draws when he maps the adventures of Hans in *The Machinic Unconscious*, the illustration on which the figures that follow are based. He lays out the plane as a graph on which he plots the strata, the diagonal lines of flight, and the points of subjectification from which territories, assemblages and rhizomes come into existence (Guattari [1979] 2011: 175; Figures 4.1–4.6). The legend to Guattari's map says that Hans's 'phobic assemblage is constituted through a series of ordeals which successively take place' on five territories, arranged from most to least territorialized: the family territory (A), the parents' bed (B), faciality of the mother (C), the phallus (D), and the machinic unconscious fantasy (E) ([1979] 2011: 175; Figure 4.1).

The private family dwelling, urban or suburban, house or apartment, provides a territory for Hans and his family in Vienna, ensuring their physical and psychic

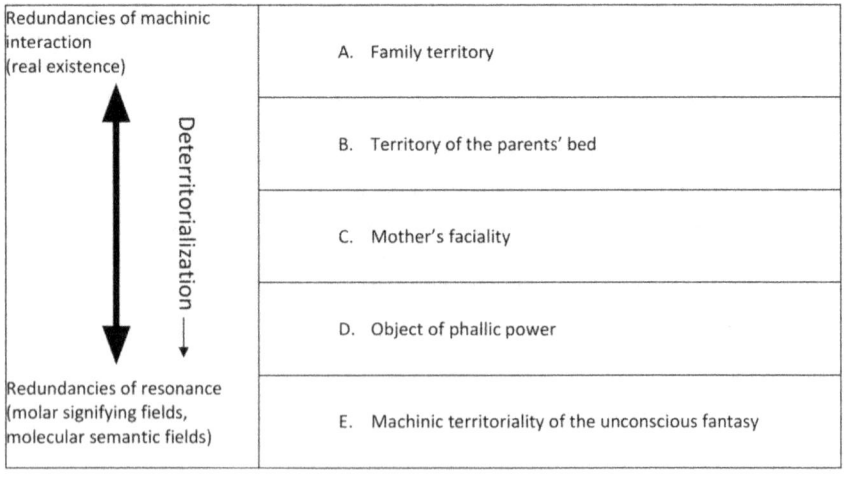

Figure 4.1 Territories of Hans's rhizome. © Janell Watson.

survival. Already in 1900 the modern Viennese family occupies a space more deterritorialized than those of the clan, tribe or multigenerational extended family and yet, Berardi observes, the industrial bourgeoisie maintained territorial ties to the bourg, where capitalists invested in the physical property of factories, built environments and material assets. Berardi maintains that today's semiocapitalist class has pushed deterritorialization to extremes, to the point that the twenty-first century's 'predatory financial class has no territorial affinity'. In an economy dominated by the knowledge and service sectors, 'workers no longer meet in the physical space of the factory and if they do it is usually provisional, temporary, precarious' (Berardi in Hugill and Thorburn 2012: 215–16). He concludes that cognitive labour forms 'a proliferating virtual class' that 'does not need to be linked to a place' (Berardi 2011: 3).

I find such claims of placeless-ness to be exaggerated. The industrial-era Oedipal dwelling indeed persists in Berardi's description of the twenty-first-century virtual class' 'air-conditioned arks' that 'float on the waves of the digital deluge' (Berardi 2009: 104). I have driven or ridden past thousands of these arks in the vast expanses of cognitariat suburbs that surround tech hubs such as Dallas, Houston, Raleigh-Durham, Atlanta, Nashville, Washington, DC or Shanghai. In these relatively affluent suburbs filled with immaterial labourers, the bourgeois household endures as a model for living under semiocapitalism, despite the appealing image of constantly travelling nomadic tech workers, whose networked connections allow them to work from a beach, a mountaintop or any café. Most instead live in a private apartment or house in a metropolitan area, like Hans and his family in 1900. Perhaps the modern nuclear family endures because the cognitariat has yet to find a more viable existential territory.

Berardi describes the encapsulated isolation of cognitariat living: 'Those who can, isolate themselves in a pressurised and hyperconnected capsule. They are physically removed from other human beings (whose existence becomes a factor of insecurity)' (2009: 104). This sense of insecurity when faced with other humans produces 'panic', he says. Is today's cognitariat (Berardi's term) more isolated from the broader social world than Hans and his family were? I suggest that Hans's social phobia corresponds to the panic that Berardi diagnoses among knowledge workers, whose precarious conditions have transformed the other into a competitor (Berardi 2009: 98–103). The other threatens to invade the capsule. Fear of the social domain results. Capitalism favours social phobia, the withdrawal from the social sphere, hence the political significance of Hans and his retreat into phobia.

Freud's Hans already lives within the confines of Berardi's 'pressurized and hyperconnected capsule'. Enclosure in an Oedipal household reinforces modern social institutions that isolate bodies into separate boxes – what Foucault calls *quadrillage* in *Discipline and Punish*, and what could be called encapsulation, after Berardi. Modern bourgeois children, at least the privileged ones that frequently appear in story books or on screen, are given their own beds and bedrooms, just as modern prisoners are put in cells, soldiers in barracks, pupils at desks, or patients in hospital rooms. In a capitalist society, with its kinship networks loosened by geographic mobility and individualism, initiation into the social order begins during infancy, which is why mother-child relations are so tightly controlled by psychologists and educators (Guattari 2009a: 240).

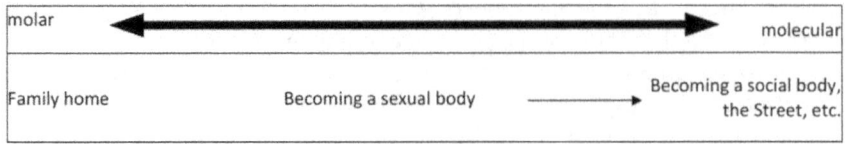

Figure 4.2 The family territory. © Janell Watson.

Little Hans would like to explore the rest of the building beyond the family apartment, and he is fascinated by the activity in the street outside the house. He 'tries to build a rhizome, with the family house but also with the line of flight of the building, the street, etc.' (Deleuze and Guattari [1980] 1987: 14; Figure 4.2). Hans longs to join the street-savvy boys who play on the loading dock he sees outside his house, but as a good bourgeois son, his social interactions remain limited to the company of his mother, father, little sister, grandmother and a group of children he sees only during summer vacations in the country. Hans desires the street, he desires exploration, he wants to pee like a horse, he wants to climb onto the loading dock with the horses and the working-class boys. The parents restrict his access to the street, insist that he always be accompanied by a parent or nursemaid, blocking his line.

Privatized Eros

Guattari's diagram shows that the pathway from home to street passes through the boy's 'becoming a sexual body' (Figure 4.2). He had already made explicit the political stakes of the Hans rhizome in his 1973 essay on cinema and desire, in which he argues that the modern family facilitates the child's entry into the dominant order of capitalism by imposing a privatized, genitally focussed, narcissistic sexuality that obeys the axiomatic of capital: the love object must always participate in the system of private ownership. By the early twentieth century, suggests Guattari, power had taken refuge in the nuclear family, the Oedipal triangle of mother-father-child. 'The struggle between the sexes, generations and social classes has been reduced to the scale of the family and the self', he writes (2009a: 239). In order to divert desiring energies away from social struggles in the streets and channel them into the private realm, capitalism 'puts models of childhood, fatherhood, motherhood and love in circulation' because 'in order to form a worker, one must start in the cradle, discipline his Oedipal development from within the family'. Social desire is replaced by an individualized, privatized, proprietary Eros, which introduces 'a bourgeois owner into the heart of each worker'. Sexualization diverts energies away from collective politics and towards a mentality of bourgeois ownership, guarding against any class struggle that might have ensued from social desire (Guattari 2009a: 237).

Guattari distinguishes between Eros and desire, defining Eros as sexual and personal, and desire as transsexual, social and politically engaged (2009a: 244–5). Unlike privatized Eros, the 'revolutionary libido' is necessarily collective and social.[3] Oedipalization focuses on the development of the child's sexual body (Eros), at the expense of the larger social body (desire). Privatizing desire by redirecting it towards an apolitical Eros, the bourgeois family colludes with capitalism by redirecting affective energies away from the social collective and thus away from any kind of political action. The eroticized libido constantly circulates between social repression and individual semiotization (Guattari [1979] 2011: 164).

Puberty can supply desiring energy not only to the sexual body but also to the social body, observes Guattari, citing subversions on a larger social plane, as in the examples of youth gangs, Woodstock or May 1968 (Guattari [1979] 2011: 161). In a 2012 interview in which he comments on twenty-first-century social movements around the world, Berardi laments that 'the dictatorship of financial capitalism has compressed the social body'. He urges activists on the left to work towards rebuilding a sustainable social body. For him, 'it is about reactivating the sentience of the social body much more than it is about political organization' (Berardi in Hugill and Thorburn 2012: 213). This view of desire was prevalent during the 1970s, observes Franco Berardi, who attributes Europe's radical social movements of that decade to the intuition that 'desire is the determining field for every social mutational process, every transformation of the imagination, every shift of collective energy'. According to this view, which Guattari maintained throughout his life, desire is 'the engine of collective action' (Berardi 2009: 93). Guattari's reading of Hans's predicament highlights the importance of the care and maintenance of a sentient social body, a molecular desiring body rather than a molar eroticized one.

The family in bed (B)

From the sexual-body-becoming, Guattari draws three lines (Figure 4.3). First, the now-abandoned molecularizing horizontal line to the broader social world of horses, trains, and the street. Second, a vertical line leads downwards, then makes a horizontal left turn into the molar zone, winding up at 'becoming guilty' and 'in the parental bed'. Forced to flee from the street (molecular) to the bed (molar), 'the child is made to take root in the family . . . be traced onto the mother's bed', trapping him within a cell, the bedroom, a territory encapsulated within the capsule of the private dwelling

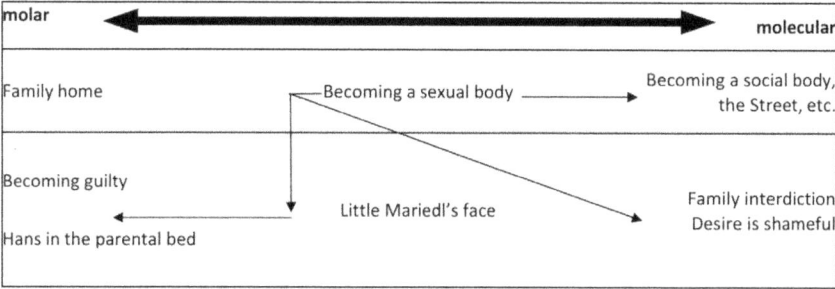

Figure 4.3 From the family territory (A) to the territory of the parent's bed (B). © Janell Watson.

(Deleuze and Guattari [1980] 1987: 14). His mother allows him to cuddle with her in bed whenever he wants, but the father makes them feel guilty for it. A third line, deterritorializing and diagonal – a schizo vector – leads to a dead end constructed by the adults: 'family interdiction, desire is *shameful*' (Guattari [1979] 2011: 175; Figure 4.3). Why would the schizo line of flight lead to interdiction and shame? Why place guilt in the map's molar zone and shame in the molecular zone? Guattari explains that a child may organize 'a repressive *jouissance* within the framework of a rhizome' in order to refuse 'a certain type of logical discursivity'. He claims that 'the singularity traits carried by abstract machines' may enable an escape from the very repression in which the child invests, thus Hans draws a line of flight towards interdiction and shame, located in the molecular zone, opposite the molar zone of discursivity (Guattari [1979] 2011: 163).

Between the lines leading from the sexual body, the vertical line to guilt and the diagonal line to shame, lie the 'faciality traits of the little Mariedl', a 14-year-old girl whose company Hans enjoyed during family vacations at a lake resort (Figure 4.3). He tells his parents he wants to sleep with her. They of course refuse, telling Hans that Mariedl must sleep with her own family. Later, upon Hans's return to Vienna, he tells his mother that he dreamed of being alone with Mariedl. Freud immediately links the desire for Mariedl to a desire for the mother, imposing an Oedipal interpretation in which Mariedl figuratively represents the mother. For schizoanalysis, however, Mariedl is not an object but a face, or rather a constellation of faciality traits. Faciality is an a-signifying semiotic component that can emerge at any point within a rhizome, with lines proliferating from it in all directions. In the case of Hans, the parents do their best to block any lines departing from Mariedl's faciality traits.

Literal lines

On the map, the horizontal and vertical lines indicate the strata laid down by the adults, with their Oedipal interpretations and familial identifications. These are criss-crossed by the child's diagonal lines of flight (Figures 4.2–4.6; Guattari [1979] 2011: 166, 175). These are the lines to which Deleuze and Guattari refer when they write that 'we are made of lines', insisting that they are speaking literally and not metaphorically, a claim that François Zourabichvili examines in his book on literality (2011: 65). Deleuze and Guattari suggest that Hans is literally made of the lines of escape that he maps and of the stratifying lines imposed by Freud and his parents. Zourabichvili distinguishes literal meaning from figurative meaning and proper meaning (*sens propre*). Insisting that 'literal' does not mean 'proper', he argues that literality is 'a process that operates between the significations in ordinary language usage' (56). Literality, he claims, is the plane of consistency itself, the space on which proper sense meets literal sense (54). A plane for encounters, literality has to do with relations (54). The plane of consistency is 'the transversal of all the supposed proper domains on which everything can enter into relation with everything else (rather than everything resembling everything else)' (Zourabichvili 2003). The adults' interpretive figuration, based on resemblance, are to be contrasted against the boy's rhizomatic lines, based on relation.

Zourabichvili's distinction between literal relations and figurative resemblances aligns with Guattari's distinction between capitalist Eros and sociopolitical desire. When Guattari writes that Eros 'polarizes the desiring-production in a game of mirrors that cut it from all access to the real', 'mirrors' evoke resemblance, the signifying figuration that severs relations to the real. He adds that, in cutting off desire from the real, Eros 'catches it in phantasmatic representations', which is to say figurative resemblances (Guattari 2009a: 244). Literality corresponds to what Guattari calls 'access to the real', which Hans pursues with a series of molecular becomings, whereas the figurative corresponds to the 'phantasmatic representations' of Oedipal interpretation supplied by Dr Freud. A map operates not by representation or resemblance, but rather 'is entirely oriented toward an experimentation in contact with the real' (Deleuze and Guattari [1980] 1987: 12).

Psychoanalysis, with its interpretations based on resemblance, misunderstands 'the assemblages a child can mount in order to solve a problem from which all exits are barred him: a plan(e), not a phantasy' (Deleuze and Guattari [1980] 1987: 259–60). Schizoanalytic cartography lays everything out on the plane of consistency, the plane of literality: lived events, historical determinations, concepts, individuals, groups, social formations (Deleuze and Guattari [1980] 1987: 9). Hans's phobia acquires its existential consistency as he pursues his literal lines of flight, seeking to escape the figures imposed upon him by the adults: the horse is your mother, your father, the phallus. Phantasy is representational, the plane is relational. Hans is not fantasizing about penises and horses. He is building his rhizome, assembling its components on the plane of consistency.

The plane of consistency provides an alternative to Lacan's Real-Imaginary-Symbolic topology which, in his 1957 seminars on Hans (which Guattari likely attended), he overlays upon actual maps of downtown Vienna. He shows Hans's house in relation to the street, train tracks and loading dock (Lacan 1994: 309–14, 326–7). Lacan traces the actual routes that Hans and his father actually followed, comparing them to the logically impossible paths through town that Hans imagines in his daydreams. He compares the actual and dreamed maps of excursions taken by father and son, in order

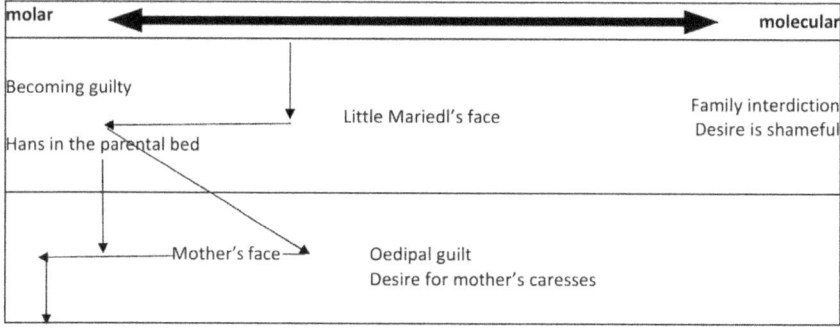

Figure 4.4 From the territory of the parent's bed (B) to the mother's face (C). © Janell Watson.

to illustrate 'the laws made manifest by the structuration not of the *real*, but of the *symbolic*' (Lacan 1994: 309, my emphasis). For Lacan, Hans's fantasized journeys are possible only in the order of the *imaginary*. However, he insists that the destination of Hans's explorations should be the *symbolic*, not the traumatizing *real*. Whereas Lacan attributes a sort of mathematical logic to the symbolic order, the logic of Guattari's plane of consistency is machinic, not mathematical. Guattari maps Hans's rhizomatic existential territory in search of real relations on the plane of consistency.

Mother's face (C)

The father begins to turn Hans away from the parental bed, scolding the mother for permitting the boy to cuddle with her whenever he wants. Barred from the bed, Hans responds by following two new deterritorializing lines and a third, reterritorializing line (Figure 4.4). Within the molar zone, a deterritorializing vertical vector leads from the bed to 'Faciality traits of the mother' (Guattari [1979] 2011: 175). A diagonal schizo vector of deterritorialization leads from becoming-guilty-in-the-parental-bed towards Oedipal guilt and a desire for mother's caresses. Caught between guilt and shame, Hans enters into 'an economy of transgression' imposed by his father's interdictions (Guattari 2009a: 244). The burgeoning family tree invades the boy's rhizome.

A third line, horizontal, leads from the mother's caresses to her faciality traits in the molar zone, reterritorializing Hans' desire. Faciality functions not as an image, but rather as a semiotic operator that helps assemblages cohere and persevere in their existence, giving them existential consistency. Faciality and refrains function as what Guattari calls 'components of passage', operators with the potential to set off new lines of flight or new connections with other assemblages. For schizoanalysis, different faces function differently. The mother's face is no mere substitute for Mariedl's, no mere displacement of love from one object onto another.

A-signifying components like faces proliferate in novels as well as in schizoanalysis. In the lengthy reading of *La recherche* with which he ends *The Machinic Unconscious*, Guattari follows Proust's cartography of the 'semiotic collapse' which is Swann's love (Guattari [1979] 2011: 231). He studies Swann's obsession with Odette's face, approaching this faciality effect not as a symptom to be interpreted, but rather as an operator that holds together Swann's debilitating love rhizome. A neurotic black hole opens up over Odette's faciality, capturing Swann, absorbing all of his creative energies. The black hole effect is not inevitable; faces can also set off passional lines of flight (Deleuze and Guattari [1980] 1987: 587). Other outcomes are possible, as in the example of Proust's narrator, for whom Albertine's face retains the multiplicity of her group of girlfriends. Unlike Swann, the narrator avoids the black hole effect and becomes a writer, a creator of new lines of flight (Guattari [1979] 2011: 316–18).

Blocking the boy's wish to sleep with Mariedl and his desire for his mother's caresses, Freud and the father Oedipalize the latter's face, so that it functions as a resonance chamber within which capitalist Eros and symbolic representation converge and vibrate together. Like a black hole, the mother's face draws Hans's desires and energies into it.

On the map, Mariedl's face lies in the centre of the horizontal continuum between molar and molecular, whereas the mother's face lies well within the molar zone. This positioning of the mother's face is not inevitable or fixed, but rather imposed by the Oedipal restraints on desire. For Hans, the faciality traits of Mariedl remain connected to the group of other children he plays with during vacations, and in that sense she belongs to a multiplicity, as did Albertine for Proust's young narrator. However, interdiction and interpretation prevent Hans from setting off on a passional line of flight from Mariedl's face. Thus diverted, Hans moves onward along another diagonal line, towards the faciality traits of his mother, in the molar zone. Recall that Proust's narrator fixates on his own mother as a young child, then moves from her to the young girls at the beach. Hans's rhizome grows differently. Hans avoids falling into a neurotic black hole like Swann, but only by following the complicated paths that will eventually lead from mother's face to the phobic object.

The proprietary phallus (D)

To escape the pull of his mother's face, Hans sets off on yet another deterritorializing diagonal line of flight, but first he pauses on the penis, masturbation and withdrawal into the body, still on the molar side of the map (Figure 4.5; Guattari [1979] 2011: 175). Hans's desire has, at least for the moment, been eroticized through its redirection towards the pleasures of the penis. Kicked out of the parental bed, he fixates on his penis and masturbation, withdrawing into his body. All desire has been diverted towards genital pleasure. 'They radicled him to his own body' (Deleuze and Guattari [1980] 1987: 14). To 'radicle' is to root – the opposite of connecting rhizomatically. This rooting in the organic body traps Hans in the realm of molar existence, blocking the way of molecularized desire in the social realm.

The penis itself, an organ of the material body, subject to natural biological encodings and chemical signals, has no inherent meaning or special relationship to power. Hans semiotizes his penis as an a-signifying component in touch with the real, describing it literally, as a pee-pee machine. Prior to the onset of the phobia, the curious boy would often watch draft horses pull heavy carts laden with goods. Observing a horse urinate, he admires its large penis, which he calls a 'pee-pee maker'. Horses pee. Hans pees. His baby sister pees. So do his little girlfriends. Even his mother pees. They all have pee-pee makers too. Exploring his world, not only at home but also in the streets, Hans became a student of pee-pee makers, seeking opportunities to look at those

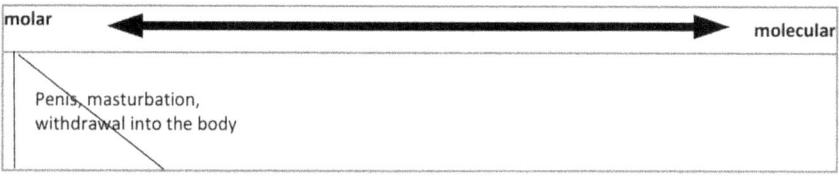

Figure 4.5 Territory of the object of phallic power (D). © Janell Watson.

of others. He observes pee-pee makers wherever he goes, on vacation with his little friends, in the streets filled with carriage horses and draft horses, at the zoo. Engaging in comparative pee-pee studies, he wonders why his younger sister has such a small one, and imagines that his mother's must be as large as a horse's, but even though he has watched mom urinate many times, he has never seen her pee-pee maker. The boy wants to know how various animals and humans pee, but the parents refuse to directly answer his literal questions about the functioning of the pee-pee maker. 'It is obvious that girls have a pee pee-maker because they effectively pee: a machinic functioning rather than an organic function', observe Deleuze and Guattari ([1980] 1987: 256). The penis, for Hans, is a machine.

Semiotizations in touch with the real do not pass through representation, signification or symbolization. Dissensual desire operates through a semiotics of the real, whereas modern capitalist Eros deploys a semiotics of representation, which relies on figuration. If the phallus is a symbol, the penis is a semiotic operator that allows Hans to make connections among the disparate assemblages of his young life – parents, friends, horses, zoo animals. Hans speaks literally about his literal penis, while his parents, as advised by Freud, respond by talking about the figurative phallus.[4] The doctor encourages the family to symbolize the penis, to convince Hans that the large penises of horses and zoo animals remind him of his father. The penis is biologically an organ, figuratively a symbol, literally a pleasure-giving urinating machine. Which semiotic politics will prevail – biology, figuration or literality? The adults choose figuration. Hans speaks literally, but psychoanalysis only listens figuratively, responding to questions about urination by talking about the symbolic phallus. 'Professor Freud's intervention assures a power takeover by the signifier, a subjectification of affects' (Deleuze and Guattari [1980] 1987: 14). The pee-pee maker has been turned into a signifier for its erotic function, a subjugating tool of Eros.

The parents, with Doctor Freud's help, attempt to insert the penis into a private erotic assemblage, hoping to replace Hans's socially engaged pee-pee maker with a power-hungry but a-political and anti-social egocentric phallus. They do their best to overcode the penis with symbolic meaning. You desire a large phallus because you wish to rival your father. You want to have sex with your mother. You feel guilty for masturbating, as you should. You are afraid that you may be castrated like your sister. To transform the penis into a phallus is to eroticize desire, privatizing it, cutting it off from the social and the political. Hans's little pee-pee machine, which guided him in his sociological study of real pee-pee machines, becomes co-opted into Oedipal genitality. As the lines across Hans's territorial explorations show, the adults in Hans's life police childhood sexuality not by forbidding it, not by eliminating it entirely, not by directly steering it, but rather by setting up roadblocks, traps and diversions. Hans negotiates these ingeniously. He is an escape artist. What takes place during the father's conversations with Hans is not an authoritarian laying down of the law, but rather the substitution an Oedipal model of sexuality for Hans's transsexual, transgender, transpersonal, socially oriented desires. His father tries to distract him with figures, symbols, representations. Hans continues laying down literal lines.

Phobic escape (E)

The adults' lines head straight left or straight down, culminating in 'Professor Freud's interpretations' and 'Faciality of transfer'. These stratifying lines in the molar zone are drawn as a two-way arrow that connects the faciality of the mother to the interpretations of Freud (Figures 4.1, 4.4 and 4.6). 'Freud explicitly takes Little Hans's cartography into account, but always and only in order to project it back onto the family photo' (Deleuze and Guattari [1980] 1987: 14). Interpretation and transference set up a redundancy, juxtaposing the faces of the mother, the father, Freud and the horse-as-paternal-signifier, which resonate together and in sync with capitalist Eros. Hans himself is 'photographed under the father', who for Freud is symbolized by the frightening horse whose blinders resemble the father's glasses and who kicks its legs, reminding Freud of a woman's leg movements during sex (Deleuze and Guattari [1980] 1987: 14).

Hans's lines of escape zig-zag downward across the rhizome, upper left to lower right, from the territory of the family house (molar machinic redundancies) to the highly deterritorialized phobic object (molecular redundancies of resonance), first passing through a series of becomings: becoming imperceptible, becoming guilty, becoming a sexual body, becoming a social body and becoming animal. 'The only escape route left to the child is a becoming-animal . . . (the becoming-horse of Little Hans, a truly political option)' (Deleuze and Guattari [1980] 1987: 14). 'Little Hans becomes horse' is another statement that Deleuze and Guattari claim must be taken literally rather than metaphorically, about which Zourabichvili muses (2011: 65). Unlike interpretation, becoming is a matter of relations rather than of resemblance, as Deleuze and Guattari repeatedly insist. Psychoanalysis maintains that the horse with its big widdler resembles the father, imposing figuration. Schizoanalysis says that Hans becomes horse through literal relations, because becoming-horse is doing as a horse does – *faire le cheval* in French (literally, to 'make' or 'do' horse). The boy becomes horse by prancing, kicking, biting and peeing. Becoming is a schizo deterritorialization.

Hans responded to his parents' and Freud's imposition of Oedipal sexuality by developing his famous phobia of horses and the street, which on the map leads to the

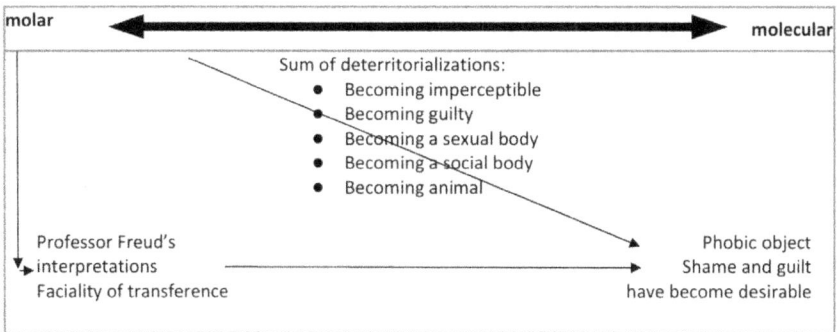

Figure 4.6 Machinic territoriality of the unconscious fantasy (E). © Janell Watson.

'Phobic object' and the desirability of 'shame and guilt' (Guattari [1979] 2011: 175–6; Figures 4.3–4.6). Hans tells his father that he fears a specific scenario based on his experiences with real horses: a big horse with a black mouth lying on its back kicking its feet. Freud says it's a fantasy symbolizing the father (with his moustache and big penis) and mother (kicking her feet) in bed. Hans says it's a real horse, literally chomping on a black bit, who has been beaten and whose heavy load has made it fall over. Family triangle or social rhizome? Bed or street? The phobic object – horses and the streets on which Hans might encounter them – emerges 'on the machinic territoriality of the unconscious fantasy', on the molecular side (Guattari 2011: 175; Figure 4.6).

Becoming horse is 'an experimentation in touch with the real', writes Guattari ([1979] 2011: 171; see also Deleuze and Guattari [1980] 1987: 12). Hans builds his rhizome by surveying his surroundings, establishing relations, making connections with what he finds there. Why does he become horse? A component at hand. He sees horses every day. He sees their pee-pee makers. He sees their blinders and muzzles. He sees them bite. He sees them being beaten. He sees them fall. He makes connections, forges paths, seeks entryways and finds exits. These real connections, paths, entrances, exits and becomings semiotize a world, build a rhizome, produce a lifestyle (Guattari [1979] 2011: 133). Becoming horse, one of his deterritorializing lines of flight, was for Hans a 'political option', according to Deleuze and Guattari, because it was 'the only escape route left to the child' ([1980] 1987: 14).

Through his becomings, Hans refuses the figurative interpretations suggested by Freud. Unfortunately, this escape through becoming-horse is 'perceived as shameful and guilty'. The adults continue their campaign to privatize the boy's roaming desires, creating diversions and detours 'until he began to desire his own shame and guilt, until they had rooted shame and guilt in him, PHOBIA' (Deleuze and Guattari [1980] 1987: 14). Hans had already encountered shame and guilt as his desire was diverted towards the parents' bed (Figure 4.3). According to Guattari, the phobia develops when shame and guilt themselves become objects of desire. Capitalist Eros 'proliferates alongside the law; it makes itself the accomplice of what is forbidden; it channels the libido to the forbidden object', it is 'the interiorization of repression' (Guattari 2009a: 244–5). The parents allow Hans into their bed, but they make him feel guilty for it. They allow him to play with his little friends, but they introduce shame. His libido becomes trapped between 'dominant reality' and 'licit pleasure'. Desire is forced into this space between reality and pleasure, a space which straddles a frontier, a limit. Shame and guilt police this frontier. The imposition of Oedipal significations diverts desire from its objects (horses, little friends, the mother's caresses) and leads it to invest instead in the limits imposed on desire (shame and guilt) (Guattari 2009a: 236).

On what basis do Deleuze and Guattari claim that phobia is a political option? Hans deterritorialized along two pathways: the vertical lines of capitalist Oedipalization that culminated in Freud's interpretations then across the rhizome towards the phobia, and the diagonal schizo lines of flight that also lead to phobia. Forced to choose between neurotic interpretation or schizo possibility, Hans invested in the phobia rather than retreating into the family capsule of Oedipal triangulation. Boldly choosing the fully deterritorialized molecular zone of the phobic formation, he opened up new possibilities by entering the molecular zone rather than remaining stuck in the reductive molar models of psychoanalysis and capitalist Eros. The molecular zone of desire is also the zone of machinic enslavement. Social subjection operates in the molar zone. Postmedia Hans must escape both molar alienation and molecular enslavement by following lines of flight that establish real relations of desire (Guattari [1979] 2011: 193). He must embrace the machines that abolish the last of the archaic social subjections without becoming an enslaved cog.

Conclusion

The Hans rhizome is not a map to be followed, but a schizoanalytic cartography that must be redrawn every time, if there is to be any hope for creativity or social engagement. Nonetheless, the Hans case does suggest a basic approach to the problem of panic-inducing encapsulation modelled on the modern nuclear family with its competitive rivalries and forbidden desires. First, desire must be allowed to freely invest the social sphere. Second, a semiotics capable of engaging real sociopolitical-economic relations must replace the fixed scripts of Oedipal Eros, constantly reiterated through romantic comedy or popular music. This literal semiotics of real relations must create lines of escape not only from the figurative semiotics of standardized Eros, but also and especially from the detrimental diagrammatic axioms and algorithms of semiocapitalism.

Those of us dwelling in twenty-first-century metropolitan agglomerations would do well to follow Hans's example by engaging in a semiotic politics of the real, but the real seems increasingly distant, if 'real' is to be understood as the opposite of 'virtual'. Hans of 1900 Vienna interacts with the real horses of material labour, as the animals haul carts loaded from the train station in front of his house, at the loading dock. Postmedia Hans will interact with the on-screen horses of immaterial labour, on his laptop. Is it even possible to experiment with the real in our age of hyper-mediatization? Today's media machines efficiently capture desire, their a-human algorithms feeding postmedia Hans a steady stream of media images and videos of virtual horses as well as links for purchasing related products like stuffed ponies, horse-themed picture books or plastic equestrian sets. Hans became horse in relation to the real horses that he encountered daily in the streets of early twentieth-century Vienna. He can relate to these horses, which pee just like he does, despite the difference in the size of their penises. Hans's world was populated by real horses with real penises, but urban and suburban metropolitan children today know only cartoon or toy horses which have no urinary equipment. Toy horses have no pee-pee makers. Automobiles have replaced horses in modern urban streets. Neutered dogs and cats have replaced copulating barnyard animals. Organized youth sports have replaced unsupervised outdoor play. First-person shooter video games have replaced hunting. Violent war movies substitute for compulsory military duty for most populations. Coquettish Disney princesses, lovesick boy bands, sanitary sexual education courses, and internet pornography introduce pre-adolescents to mainstream sexuality. Hollywood and Bollywood saturate the planet with love stories. Media dissemination multiplies faciality with thousands of family photos broadcast alongside celebrity faces made standard through cosmetic surgery and digital enhancement. Twitter blurs the line between celebrities and real-life friends. YouTube and TikTok makes all of us into potential media stars.

Is it possible to semiotize a horse literally, if he appears only on a screen rather than on the street or in a stable? Can domestic pets or cartoon creatures inspire animal becomings? Real desire and real relations must break through the glimmering fascination exerted by the ubiquitous onslaught of mass media disguised as social interaction. Like Hans, we must attempt to live literally, despite the barrage of figurative representations emitted by screens and loudspeakers. To enter into the postmedia era, it will be crucial to focus on real problems and struggles, rather than succumbing to the distractions of hyper-eroticized representation. To speak, write or read, literally is to speak, write or read directly about desire, the social and the political – all at once. Keep it real.

References

Berardi, F. (2009), *The Soul at Work: From Alienation to Autonomy*, Los Angeles: Semiotext(e).
Berardi, F. (2011), 'The Future after the End of the Economy', *e-flux*, 30: 1–7.
Bradley, J. P. N. (2019), 'Schizoanalysis of PokemonGo', *China Media Research*, 15 (4): 78–91.
Buchanan, I. (2013), 'The Little Hans Assemblage', *Visual Arts Research*, 39 (1): 9–17.
Deleuze, G. and F. Guattari ([1980] 1987), *A Thousand Plateaus*, trans. B. Massumi, Minneapolis: University of Minnesota Press.
Deleuze, G., F. Guattari, C. Parnet and A. Scala ([2003] 2006), 'The Interpretation of Utterances', in David Lapoujade (ed.), *Two Regimes of Madness: Texts and Interviews 1975–1995*, 89–112, New York: Semiotext(e).
Freud, S. ([1909] 1955). 'Analysis of a Phobia in a Five-Year-Old Boy', in J. Strachey (trans.), *The Standard Edition of the Complete Psychological Works of Sigmund Freud Vol. X (1909), Two Case Histories*, 1–150, London: Vintage. Available online: https://www.pep-web.org/document.php?id=se.010.0000a (accessed 11 May 2013).
Genosko, G. (2012), 'Félix Guattari in the Age of Semiocapitalism', *Deleuze Studies*, 6 (2): 149–169.
Genosko, G. (2013), 'The Promise of Postmedia', in C. Apprich, J. B. Slater, A. Iles and O. L. Schultz (eds), *Provocative Alloys: A Postmedia Anthology*, 14–25, Lüneburg, Germany: Mute Books.
Genosko, G. (2016), *Critical Semiotics: Theory, From Information to Affect*, London: Bloomsbury.
Goddard, M. (2013), 'Félix and Alice in Wonderland: The Encounter Between Guattari and Berardi and the Postmedia Era', in C. Apprich, J. B. Slater, A. Iles and O. L. Schultz (eds), *Provocative Alloys: A Postmedia Anthology*, 44–61, Lüneburg, Germany: Mute Books.
Guattari, F. (2009a), *Chaosophy: Texts and Interviews 1972–1977*, Los Angeles: Semiotext(e).
Guattari, F. (2009b), *Soft Subversions: Texts and Interviews 1977–1985*, Los Angeles: Semiotext(e).

Guattari, F. ([1979] 2011), *The Machinic Unconscious: Essays in Schizoanalysis*, Los Angeles: Semiotexte.

Guattari, F. ([1989] 2013), *Schizoanalytic Cartographies*, trans. A. Goffey, London: Bloomsbury.

Hugill, D. and E. Thorburn (2012), 'Reactivating the Social Body in Insurrectionary Times: A Dialogue with Franco Bifo Berardi,' *Berkeley Planning Journal*, 25: 210–220. Available online: https://escholarship.org/content/qt7z74819g/qt7z74819g_noSplash_955f94a5dc36596793c29047f977861b.pdf (accessed 31 October 2020).

Lacan, J. (1994), *Le Séminaire de Jacques Lacan, Livre IV, La relation d'objet 1956–1957*, Paris: Seuil.

Lazzarato, M. (1996), 'Immaterial Labor', in M. Hardt and P. Virno (eds), *Radical Thought in Italy: A Potential Politics*, 133–147, Minneapolis: University of Minnesota Press.

Lazzarato, M. (2014), *Signs and Machines: Capitalism and the Production of Subjectivity*, trans. J. D. Jordan, Los Angeles: Semiotext(e).

Ueno, T. (2012), 'Guattari and Japan', *Deleuze Studies*, 6 (2): 187–209.

Zourabichvili, F. (2003), *Le vocabulaire de Deleuze*, Paris: Ellipses.

Zourabichvili, F. (2011), *La littéralité et autres essais sur l'art*, Paris: Presses Universitaires de France.

5

Reflections on postmedia for philosophers

Edward Thornton

In 1966, well before he had met Deleuze, Félix Guattari published an article in *Cahiers de Philosophie* – the philosophy journal of the Sorbonne – titled 'Reflections on Institutional Psychotherapy for Philosophers'. This article is fascinating for a number of reasons, not least because of the way in which it prefigures, in certain interesting ways, the philosophical work that Guattari would complete with Deleuze in their *Capitalism and Schizophrenia* series. In effect, Guattari uses the article to highlight several philosophical issues that had arisen in his practical work as a psychoanalyst – concerning especially the relationship between subjectivity and group relations – which he felt that the history of modern European philosophy had not sufficiently addressed, and set out some suggestions on how those trained in philosophy might respond to them.

In this chapter, I aim to do something similar for those engaged in experiments with postmedia technologies. I will begin by laying out what I see as the key theoretical discoveries that have emerged from experiments in postmedia. In this section, I will concentrate on Guattari's work but will also draw more broadly from a number of other writers, including Franco 'Bifo' Berardi. Here I will aim to show that those working with disruptive media technologies – including those investigating the powers of free radio – have exposed certain undertheorized aspects of the nature of subjectivity and its relationship with the process of mediation. Following this, I will turn to the history of philosophy and offer a brief overview of the role that mediation plays in the various ways that the subject has been thought in the European philosophical tradition. Here I will concentrate on the canonical theorizations of subjectivity offered by Descartes's *cogito* and Kant's *transcendental I of apperception*, respectively. My aim here will be to shine a light on the fact that such theorizations already rely on a complex, if implicit, understanding of the role played by media and mediation in the construction of the subject. Finally, in the last section, I will offer some reflections on the ways in which contemporary philosophers might respond to postmedia theory through a re-engagement and critique of the work of Descartes and Kant. Here I will pay some attention to the schizoanalytic work carried out by Guattari and Deleuze, especially in *A Thousand Plateaus*, and will use these activities as suggestive invitations for future work in postmedia philosophy.

It is worth pointing out from the beginning that my engagement with Descartes and Kant is not intended as an apology for modern European philosophy. It is an attempt to map out both the resistances and the opportunities that lie within this tradition, as they relate to the activities of postmedia studies.

Postmedia theory and subjectivity

Postmedia studies is built on the recognition that our modes of subjectivity are determined, at least in part, by the ways in which we interact. If it is the case that our interactions are constrained by the technological and socio-economic possibilities of the media technologies that we use, then our subjectivation is systematically conditioned by the parameters of our media technology. In this sense, we can see postmedia theory as an extension and a critique of accounts of subjectivity informed by structural linguistics. According to such accounts, to be a subject is to speak, and for this reason our subjectivity is conditioned by the signifier.[1] In postmedia theory, however, direct speech is only one of many various forms of human interaction, complemented by those which use the written word, the printed word, the printed image, the broadcast word, and the televised image, to name but a few. These various technologies of mediation add a layer of heterogeneity to the otherwise hegemonic norm of speech as the medium of the subject, but they do not allow the subject to exist outside of the context of its mediation.

It would be easy enough – especially from the point of view of one trained in philosophy – to assume from the name that postmedia theory would be an attempt to argue for, and offer a representation of, the possibilities for human life in a world in which social relations are no longer mediated by the technologies of television, radio, print, video, and internet communication. This vision of postmedia theory is incorrect on two counts. First, the 'post' in 'postmedia' is not a temporal one, supposedly looking forward to a time after technological mediation, or even after our current mode of technological mediation. On the contrary, the word *post* here should be understood more as a 'beyond'. Postmedia studies sets out to think through the possibilities for social interaction and for subjectivity that lie beyond those offered by the relatively narrow social functions performed by media technologies today. In this sense, the concerns of postmedia theorists may embrace, rather than flee from, the fact of mediation. Second, the fields of postmedia studies and of postmedia activism are defined less by what they say about the mediation of subjectivity and more by how they aim to utilize media technologies to intervene in and reinvent subjectivity. What is awkwardly named postmedia *studies* is a form of study in the specific sense of being a practical experimental technique for discovering new modes of life.

Most work in postmedia studies is more directly political than this initial sketch might suggest. This is because of the fact that, when we investigate the ways in which subjectivity is produced and managed by media technologies, it becomes apparent that these activities are closely related to what Foucault might call practices of 'governmentality' (Foucault 1991: 87). The internal dynamics of television – to take perhaps the most obvious example – are structured in such a way that the viewers become passive receivers of information, unable to *speak back* in the language of the medium and only able to *listen*. As Berardi has put it: 'The television medium is structurally constructed to transform people into spectators' (2005: 20). This is exacerbated by the socio-historical facts concerning who is able to produce and distribute television content. Viewers are alienated from the production of television's messages and only come into contact with them as directives issued from on high. By recognizing the way in which such a dynamic of passive spectatorship might affect one's horizon of possibility for political engagement, postmedia theorists have attempted to dismantle the hierarchies that exist within these media and reformulate them to allow for new modes of political subjectivity to emerge. As Berardi puts it, postmedia activism seeks 'a sociality in which communication flows are no longer directed from above towards a passive audience' but instead 'function as a very tight network of rhizomatic exchanges between transmitters who are on the same plane' (2005: 16). This move is political because it involves a reformulation of the political subject and specifically one which allows for an increase in collective speech and collective action. As Clemens Appich has argued, the postmedia age envisioned here is best understood as 'a transformation of classical media structures towards new collective assemblages of enunciation' (2013: 123). Postmedia studies is thus a deconstructive as well as a constructive practice, which involves dismantling the norms of contemporary social mediation and rebuilding new forms of media interaction that allow for a collective self-determination of the people.

While this initial overview of postmedia theory has been brief, my aim here is only to offer a schematic overview of the theoretical norms within postmedia studies. Abstracting for a moment from the specific problems that arise with each new media technology, what motivates postmedia theory as an activity is the recognition that there are various different models or modes of subjectivity that arise with alternative uses of media technology, and, therefore, that both the question of who we are and of the social and political reality that we inhabit are conditioned by our uses of the media. Postmedia studies and experiments in postmedia activism are based on this idea, namely that we can become different kinds of subjects. While there may be a political charge behind this claim, underpinning it are at least two challenging philosophical presuppositions. The first of these is that different modes of subjectivity are possible in the first place. In contradistinction to those philosophical traditions that take the structure of subjectivity as a pre-given fact about human life – and one which must be uncovered and analysed – postmedia studies treats subjectivity as something which is produced and which can be produced differently. While philosophers from at least Descartes to Sartre have asked the question 'what is subjectivity?', those working in postmedia studies are asking 'what can we do with subjectivity?' and 'how can we make subjectivity differently?' In an essay titled 'Entering the postmedia era', Guattari writes the following:

> Unlike the transcendental subject of philosophical tradition (the-closed-in-on-itself monad that structuralists claim to have opened to alterity solely by virtue of the linguistic signifier), pragmatic enunciative arrangements escape in all directions. Their subjective formations, at the intersections of heterogeneous components, cannot be reduced to a single semiotic entity. (2009b: 303)

In these two sentences, Guattari sums up the precise way in which the activities involved in postmedia studies require different philosophical starting points from those relied upon in the majority of other academic fields. Guattari refers to the subject of post-Kantian philosophy, and specifically to the idea that the subject is a transcendental structure or a necessary presupposition of experience. He also refers to structuralist linguistic theory and the idea that the subject is a kind of grammatical necessity for speech. Against these, Guattari points out that behind experience and behind any individual speech act we do not find any entity or any invariable structure which we could name as 'the subject'. Instead what we find is a collection of 'heterogeneous components' which happen to be assembled according to one organization, but which may very well be organized differently.

It is important to note, however, that Guattari's presupposition of the lack of any essential nature of subjectivity does not amount to a rejection of the category of subjectivity as such. From the quotation given earlier, and from its historical position within a milieu of post-structuralism and postmodernism, we may assume that Guattari wishes to do away with talk of subjectivity altogether. We may be inclined to read Guattari as pronouncing the death of the reader, the viewer or the listener as a subject of the media, just as Barthes had announced the death of the author. This is far from the case. In fact, for Guattari, rather than showing that subjectivity is dead, postmedia studies uncovers the contingency of subjectivity by investigating the practices of subjectivation which underlie it. Here Guattari refuses to accept the existence of a single conceptual entity named 'the subject' while he carries out his analysis of subjectivity in general. The necessity of holding on to the category of subjectivity even while dismissing the idea of the subject, as an entity, is particularly apparent when we remind ourselves of what it is like to try to study any particular medium. If we go back to the example of television, we see that, while there is no need to posit a transcendental subject as the receiver of a television broadcast, we cannot study television without something to play the functional role of the viewer. As Boris Groys has put it, 'the media themselves – as far as they become the object of our contemplation, observation and analysis – have to be shown to us by a (mediating) subjectivity that is witnessing and presenting their functioning' (2011: 9). I will return to this idea of a functional subjectivity later on, but for now all I want to point out is the idea that postmedia studies treats subjectivity as something changeable, something which varies according to the mode of mediation it is tied up with, and something which can be experimented upon and thus transformed.

Beyond the idea that subjectivity is not an inviolable norm, we find the second grounding presupposition of postmedia studies, namely that each different mode of subjectivity is essentially tied to the specific dynamics of the medium – or the media landscape – that expresses it. What I mean to point out here is the idea that while subjectivity is variable in form, its variation is not unconnected from the functional role that it fulfils in a specific process of mediation. As the dynamics of television change, the functional role of the subject of television changes with it. In the experiments with free radio, the subject of the radio is altered, but only as it exists in direct relationship with the medium of the radio. Processes of mediation do not act upon an already formed subject in order to change it. Subjectivities only emerge within media landscapes and cannot be thought as external to them. As Berardi writes:

> We should not analyse the media as if they were only the instruments for the implementation of social interests and political agendas. We should not presuppose the existence of an already structured subject behind or inside the info-machine. The subject is not pre-existing, it is rather the outcome of the actual working of the info-machine. (2012: 3)

Guattari goes even further than Berardi in defining media specifically as 'assemblages of subjective production' (2009a: 293). For Guattari, the very practice of experimentation that postmedia activists carry out requires us to treat subjectivity and its mediation together. Media technologies are nothing other than assemblages of subjective production, while subjects are nothing other than functional components in processes of mediation. This is what I am calling the second grounding presupposition of postmedia studies, namely that subjectivity and mediation cannot be understood in isolation from one another. The challenge that is implied by this insight will be important for us in a moment, when we turn to some of the more traditional articulations of the subject in the history of modern European philosophy and consider the processes of mediation examined there.

Before I move on, however, I would like to make one final point of clarification concerning the discourse of postmedia studies. This clarification concerns the way in which the word *medium* is used within this discourse. It is possible to use the word *medium* in at least two distinct ways, the first of which treats a medium as something that exists between two entities and allows them to communicate or to interact, while the second treats a medium as an environment that entities exist within. Speaking of the use of this term in philosophical hermeneutics, Jeffery Bineham explains the first of these options thus: 'the term medium generally connotes an intervening substance or vehicle through which material, impressions, and messages are conveyed' (1995: 1). For example, we may think of air as 'a medium by which sound waves reach ear drums', and we may thus conclude that 'the medium stands between two or more objects that exist independently of one another', namely the speaker and the listener (1995: 1). In contrast to this, Bineham discusses an alternative use of the word *medium* in which 'a medium can also be the pervasive and enveloping substance within which one lives, one's element, one's environment, or the conditions of one's life', in this case, the medium can be understood 'as the symbolic equivalent to a biological petri dish: it is the culture within which people develop and from which worlds grow, and it contains the symbolic substance that is the nutrient for society' (1995: 2). When we look closely at the way in which postmedia theorists use the term, we find that the second of these two options is much more common. When postmedia theorists discuss the medium of the radio, this medium is not taken to exist between subjects. Instead, subjects are, or can be, constituted within the environment of radio technologies. Speech on the radio is an expression of subjectivity and the subject who speaks is a kind of modulation within the environmental field of the medium. It is in this sense that Guattari defined a medium as an assemblage of subjective production. Any particular medium – be it speech, radio, television or the internet – is not a go-between connecting subjects in communication, but a milieu which expresses itself through the production of subjectivities. Taken together with the two presuppositions discussed above, we can formulate the basic picture of postmedia theory in the following way: there is no essential nature of *the* subject, subjectivity can be produced in a variety of different ways depending on the dynamics of the medium in which it is called upon to play a functional role. Furthermore, the medium in question is not something which structures the subject from the outside, but forms the environmental medium, or milieu, in which subjectivity is expressed.

Given this picture, what role might we expect the discipline of philosophy to add to the activities of postmedia studies? In order to answer this question, we can return to the analogous case of Guattari's comments in 'Reflections on institutional psychotherapy for philosophers' and consider the request that he makes of philosophers there. In this text, Guattari outlines a general problem that faces practitioners of social experimentation. He writes that, when 'operating daily in the "praxis" of a living institution' experimental practitioners such as himself regularly 'notice that the reason for our efficacy or our failures escapes us and that the theoretical references that have currency in universities generally fail to respond to problems' ([1972] 2015b: 123). In these cases, those attempting to bring about changes in the ways that institutions operate – be they psychotherapeutic institutions or the institutions of media communication – are at a loss to explain why certain experiments have succeeded and why others have failed. Guattari lays the blame for this fact at the feet of academic philosophy. He critiques academic philosophers for their 'fantasy of creating a homogenous, complete and definitive "system" of concepts that could serve as a reference for all scientific disciplines' ([1972] 2015b: 122), claiming that this fantasy leads philosophers to ignore the specifics of the practical fields of action of individual sciences. In opposition to this, Guattari calls on philosophers 'to begin a specific process within each science that would lead it to play the role of assistant during all of the times when their internal theoretical approaches threatened to lead them astray, due to the lack of sufficient refinement of their conceptual tools' ([1972] 2015b: 122). In effect, Guattari is asking philosophers to involve themselves in the practicalities of life, not by giving up on the task of conceptual analysis, but by paying attention to the conceptual difficulties that arise in situations of action.

I have referred to the founding theoretical positions of postmedia studies as presuppositions. I have done this because in the majority of cases, these positions are not argued for as theorems but are taken as the necessary point of departure for interventions in postmedia activism. Such presuppositions are not, however, unproblematic. Issues arise in practice – say, during an attempt to reformulate the dynamics of mass-media radio broadcasts – that require one to use the language of these conceptual presuppositions to explain why a certain experiment in this practice has been successful and why another has not. Philosophy can play the role of assistant in these cases by taking the concepts presupposed in this field seriously and then attempting to refine them in such a way that the explanations required will not lead into confusion. In the remainder of this chapter, I will make some suggestions for how academic philosophy might play this role for postmedia studies.

Subjectivity and mediation in Cartesian philosophy

The canonical theorizations of subjectivity in the history of the European philosophical tradition are far from silent on the topic of mediation. In fact, perhaps the two most influential of such theorizations – those of Descartes and Kant, respectively – offer their definitions of the subject through an analysis of mediation. In this section and the next, I will offer a brief overview of these conceptualizations of subjectivity and try to show that they can offer us a starting point for a philosophical response to the presuppositions of postmedia studies.

To recognize the role that mediation plays in the account that Descartes gives of subjectivity in the *Meditations*, it is important to focus our attention on what he has to say about the *immediacy* of thought. Descartes is a direct realist, who argues that our access to reality is mediated by our thoughts and our ideas, which stand between the thinker and reality. Thus, while reality is known mediately, thought is known immediately. Descartes defines 'thought' as 'everything that is in us in such a way that we are immediately aware of it' and defines 'ideas' as 'the form of any given thought, immediate perception of which makes me aware of the thought' ([1641] 2017: 94). For Descartes, the essential epistemic problem which faces the thinking subject is the fact that our experience of reality is not direct and unmediated. This means that we can never fully trust our experience of reality, because we have no guarantee that the mediation it has undergone has not distorted it. As Bernard Williams explains, Descartes believes 'that everything "outside myself" is known only through the medium of ideas, which represent reality, and are themselves the immediate objects of the mind's cognition' (2015: 44). As reality is separated from me by my ideas of reality, I can never overcome my doubts about the nature of that reality.

However, according to Descartes, the epistemic gap between the subject and reality, which is produced by the unfortunate fact of its mediation, does not make all knowledge impossible. While reality may be unknowable in a direct way, the thoughts which act as the medium of my experience are known immediately and, therefore, are beyond the reaches of the methodology of radical doubt. I can doubt whether the object in front of me really exists, but I cannot doubt that I am having an experience, even if this experience may not be a fair representation of the object in question. Crucially, for Descartes, even in the very act of doubting, I am immediately aware of my own thought and for this reason I can be confident in the existence of myself as a thinking thing. Because the thoughts which I have immediate access to are *my* thoughts, even in the act of recognizing their dubitability I am immediately aware of myself as the thinker of those thoughts. It is the performative act of thinking which defines the subject, and which makes the self-knowledge of the subject the ground of all other possible knowledge.

If we attempt to apply this philosophical picture of subjectivity to the problems that arise in postmedia studies, then we are immediately confronted with two issues. The first of which concerns the incongruity between Descartes's use of the word *mediation* and that most commonly used in postmedia studies. As I mentioned above, the majority of those working in postmedia studies treat a medium in the environmental rather than the communicative or representational sense. Rather than taking a medium as a kind of conduit for communication which exists between a subject and an object, postmedia theorists treat the medium as an environment or a theoretical space which the subject and object in question both inhabit. At first glance, this does not seem to be the case for Descartes, for whom thoughts are representations of reality which allow for communication, however imperfectly, between the thinking subject and the outside world. If we are to draw some useful lessons out of the Cartesian picture, then we will need to find a way to counteract this tendency and to retheorize the medium of thought as more than a bridge which connects the interiority of the subject with the exteriority of the world.

The second issue that arises with any attempted application of Descartes's philosophy of the subject in the context of postmedia studies concerns a mismatch between the philosophical problems that he is responding to and the practical problems with which postmedia theorists are grappling. Descartes's whole philosophical project concerns the possibility of knowledge. As such, the mode of subjectivity that concerns him is that of the thinking subject. Within the purview of this problematic, we can see why Descartes decides to focus on the subject of thought, rather than on the subject of action. In brief, it is only the subject as a thinking thing which can know itself. Descartes makes this point explicitly in one the replies to his critics which is appended to the main body of the *Meditations*:

> I may not, for example, make the inference 'I am walking, therefore I exist', except in so far as the awareness of walking is a thought. The inference is certain only if applied to this awareness, and not to the movement of the body which sometimes – in the case of dreams – is not occurring at all, despite the fact that I seem to myself to be walking. Hence from the fact that I think I am walking I can very well infer the existence of a mind which has this thought, but not the existence of a body that walks. And the same applies in other cases. ([1641] 2017: 83)

Descartes's reasoning is relatively straightforward here: if I am concerned with the question of knowledge, then no act other than the act of thinking will be sufficient to show me its nature. While my contemplation of my act of walking is known immediately to me, the fact of my walking is only known via the medium of contemplation, so that only the former can act as a ground for indubitable knowledge. Descartes's focus on the thinking subject, rather than the subject of action, is determined in advance by the fact that the problem which concerns him is the problem of knowledge. Outside of the world of academic philosophy, however, a range of other problems manifest themselves. In these cases, if we simply rely on a theorization of subjectivity drawn from Cartesian philosophy, then we will find our conceptual tools insufficient for making sense of our predicament. I will return to this problem in a moment, but first I want to see what can be salvaged from Descartes's work and what can be repurposed in order to help us with the development of a postmedia philosophy.

If we take a step back from Descartes's philosophical concerns with the foundations of knowledge, then it is still possible to appreciate his claim that the production of subjectivity in any medium relies on the reflexivity of that medium. For Descartes, the thinking subject only comes into view with the application of thought to itself. An analysis of any act of thinking that is directed towards something outside of thought, be it another object outside of the self, or the body as the objective instantiation of the thinker, must posit the pre-existence of the thinking subject in question. However, an analysis of the act of self-contemplation need not posit a pre-existing subject, because it offers an account of the genesis of that subject. In his or her act of meditation, the Cartesian subject comes to produce him or herself as a subject of thought. In a sense, then, Descartes's focus on the reflexivity of thought need not assume a communicative or representational mode of mediation after all. When the thinker contemplates the act of their own walking, there is a separation or gap between the walker and the thinker which is bridged by the representation of the act of walking. However, when a thinker contemplates the act of thinking, there is no such gap to be filled. In this case, the medium of thought is not something in-between the thinker and the thought object. Instead, the medium of thought is the precondition for the distinction between the subject and the object of thought. In the specific case of reflexive thought, the identity of the thought in question is challenged by a differentiation internal to thought. We could speak here of the 'thinkingness' of the thought, on the one hand, and the 'thoughtness' of the thought, on the other. Another way to put this would be to say that, in order to be a thought (noun), the thing in question must also be thought (verb). When the medium of thought takes thought itself as its object, the subject of thought arises as that which the object of thought is differentiated from.

This analysis is still restricted to the specific Cartesian example of the medium of thinking. However, we may ask what this example can teach us about mediation in general. To generalize from Descartes, we can say that the mode of subjectivity connected to any medium, is produced by the folding back of that medium onto itself. When the medium mediates itself, subjectivity arises. What would this mean for our understanding of the mode of subjectivation at play in a specific form of technological mediation? To take radio as an example, this analysis would suggest that the mode of subjectivity specific to the medium of the radio is produced when a radio broadcast is not only used by one subject to communicate with another, but when it is used as a self-broadcast. That is to say, when a subject locates itself in both the broadcasting and the broadcasted.[2]

Speaking of the phenomenon of free radio in France, Guattari writes that 'free radio is a completely different use of the radio media . . . It's about finding a different use, a different listening relation, a kind of feedback' (2007: 149). The feedback referenced here can be understood as akin to the reflexivity of Cartesian self-reflection. When a group sets out to produce a free-radio station, what is broadcast is not only a kind of informational content to be distributed to others. In fact, at one point Guattari will say that the free-radio stations 'were vehicles that did not convey anything in terms of content' (2007: 147). Instead, the group constituted itself as a subject of the radio by broadcasting in its own voice. Just as the thinking subject is produced in Cartesian self-reflection, the radio subject is produced in the kinds of self-broadcast instigated by free-radio collectives.

From this brief foray into Descartes's philosophy of subjectivity, we can see one example of the way in which the history of European philosophy provides both tools and blockages for our attempt to produce a mode of philosophy that can speak to the concerns of postmedia studies. When Descartes decides to focus on the epistemic question of the foundation of knowledge – which leads him to take the thinking subject as the foundation of all subjectivity – he commits the offence that Guattari spoke about in his evaluation of academic philosophy in 'Reflections on Institutional Psychotherapy for Philosophers'. There Guattari spoke of the 'fantasy' of creating a 'complete and definitive "system" of concepts that could serve as a reference for all scientific disciplines' ([1972] 2015b: 122). However, if we shift the focus of Descartes's analysis, and if we look at his implicit theorization of mediation, which lies beneath his more explicit theorization of thought, we find a number of tools that might be of use to the postmedia activist. The one that I have attempted to highlight here concerns the relationship between the reflexivity of a medium and the mode of subjectivity of that medium. What Descartes's philosophy suggests is that subjectivity arises in a medium when that medium is turned inwards to mediate itself.

Mediation and temporal synthesis in Kant's transcendental subject

As with Descartes, the mode of subjectivity that concerns Kant is that of the thinking subject. In this sense, Kant is no closer to providing the basis for a postmedia philosophy of subjectivity than Descartes is. However, also like Descartes, Kant offers his analysis of subjectivity by way of an investigation into the question of what is mediated for the subject and what is presented immediately to them. Furthermore, while Kant's analysis of mediation gets us no closer to the subject of intersubjective action, it does offer some further insights into the function by which immediacy and subjectivity are linked. Specifically, what is useful for the postmedia theorist in Kant's work is his account of the subject's role in the temporal synthesis of experience. Kant thus adds two things to Descartes's account of subjectivity, both of which we may attempt to wrestle out of Kant's narrow concern with the subject of knowledge and apply to the more pressing concern of the nature of the subject of our social mediation. First, Kant recognizes the active role that subjectivity plays in synthesizing its reality. Second, Kant argues that the activity of this synthesis is facilitated by the form of time.

But what does it mean to say that Kant recognizes the active role that subjectivity plays in synthesizing reality? For Kant, it is possible for a subject to investigate the structure of reality, specifically because it is the subject that generates this structure in the act of representing it. While for Descartes the act of representation was a way of picturing reality, according to Adam Dickerson, 'Kant sees the key to an account of representation as lying in an act of synthesis' in which 'representations are the immediate objects of our awareness' but 'our knowledge of an independent reality is neither inferred from nor reduced to our knowledge of those representations' (2004: 13). Essentially, according to Kant, the subject is not simply the receiver of a picture of reality, but the agent which constructs the form that reality must take. Under this theorization, the apparent *immediacy* of thought takes on a new meaning. As Dickerson continues, because it is the case for Kant that 'our internal states constitute the *medium* of representation and to represent an object is to be aware of something *in* that medium', it is important that this medium 'not be assimilated with the object represented *in* that medium' (2004: 5, 13). So, while the subject does not create the content of their experience from scratch, it is the activity of the subject to synthesize the raw material of sensation into something which can be experienced. As such, while the subject only has a mediated access to the contents of experience, the subject has an immediate access to the structure of experience, which it has synthesized itself.

Kantian metaphysics can be understood as an investigation into the method by which the subject manages to synthesize their lived reality. One key insight here is that, because the act of synthesis involves the comparison of concepts that are not presented simultaneously in experience, the synthesis of reality must take place within the medium of time. This is how Kant articulates this point:

> Granted, then, that we must advance beyond a given concept in order to compare it synthetically with another, a third something is necessary, as that wherein alone the synthesis of two concepts can be achieved. What, now, is this third something that is to be the medium of all synthetic judgments? There is only one whole in which all our representations are contained, namely, inner sense and its *a priori* form, time. (Kant [1781] 1929: 192)

We do not need to accept Kant's whole metaphysical system to take on board what he is pointing out here. If subjectivity provides reality with its structure, then the subject has an immediate access to this structure. In the case of the subject of knowledge – or the *thinking* subject – which Descartes and Kant are both fixated on, this fact provides the subject with justification for claims about the necessary structure of reality. As time is the form of our inner sense, we are justified in making claims about the nature of time.

But how might Kant's analysis of the role of subjectivity in synthesizing its reality be applied to other forms of subjectivity? For example, how might the mode of subjectivity involved in listening to the radio, watching the TV, or browsing the internet also come to provide the structure of that medium? Moving from a Cartesian to a Kantian conceptualization of subjectivity allows us to recognize the way in which subjectivity is essentially active. Following from Kant, we can say that the less one becomes active in synthesizing the structure of the medium that one inhabits, the less one gains subjectivity within that medium. To be the thinking subject of experience, one must actively synthesize what emerges from sensation into something with a spatial and, crucially, temporal structure. On the same accounts then, we might say that the mode of subjectivity specific to the radio, to stick with our earlier example, must be one which is involved in synthesizing the medium of the radio itself and thus providing it with its structure. We might say that one who passively receives radio broadcasts as if they were imagistic representations of reality fails to gain subjectivity in this medium. In this case, it might be better to say that one is *subject to* the radio, but not a *subject of* the radio. On the other hand – and much like the Kantian subject of experience – the subject of the radio would be one who actively synthesizes the medium of the radio, and thus has a special kind of immediate relationship with it.

This lesson is an instructive one because the activity of the subject in synthesizing experience also puts constraints on the nature of the form of subjectivity in question. For Kant, the medium in question is that of thought, and specifically the act of representation in thought. In this case, if the subject can only become aware of itself through the act of such cognitive representation, then the subject will never be anything other than an abstract and transcendental 'I', which cannot be given any other attributes besides those allowed for within representation. Speaking about the role of self-awareness in Kant's account of subjectivity, Andrew Brook explains: 'When the medium of awareness of oneself is the doing of acts of representing, the medium imposes sharp constraints on what the resulting awareness can be like' (2001: 24). This claim has an immediate resonance with one of the key presuppositions of postmedia studies which I articulated at the outset, namely that different forms of subjectivity are essentially connected to different media. Kant is saying that, *as the subject of cognition*, the subject must have a specific structure. However, if we look at this same comment from another angle, we could read it as saying that any form of subjectivity which arises in a medium other than thought need not be conditioned by the specific structure of representation that Kant has analysed.

In summary then, we can say that Cartesian and Kantian philosophy fail to provide an adequate conceptual framework for postmedia theory because they focus solely on the subject of knowledge. However, it might still be possible to extract some of the insights provided by Descartes and Kant's account of the immediacy of subjectivity and rework them for a new postmedia philosophy. What I have suggested here is that one of the fruitful places to look for such insights is in Descartes and Kant's claims about the relationship between immediacy and subjectivity. At a glance, what we have found is that these elements suggest that the subjectivity that is specific to any medium is produced by a kind of self-reflexive folding of that medium, whereby the medium comes to mediate itself. We have also found it suggested that to be a subject of any particular medium one must be active in synthesizing that medium – and the structures by which that medium is presented – rather than a passive receiver of the contents contained within the medium in question.

Of course, these insights are rather meagre, and do not immediately provide much solace for the postmedia theorist looking for some conceptual tools to make sense of their experiments. In the next section, I will consider just how far philosophers must go beyond this initial picture to become relevant for the activity of postmedia experimentation.

Schizoanalysis and postmedia philosophy

In our preceding investigations of what might be salvaged from two of the central figures of the Western philosophical canon, we have found some hints for how we might begin to develop a philosophy that can respond to the two presuppositions of postmedia studies. As we saw at the beginning, postmedia studies works on the basis that there is no essential nature of *the* subject and that subjectivity can take various forms, depending on the dynamics of the medium in which it is embedded. What we have also seen, however, is that philosophy's stubborn attachment to the *thinking* subject as the archetype for all subjectivity has not allowed philosophers to examine the specific dynamics of the various forms of subjectivity that arise in activities other than that of pure thought.

With this in mind, we can now make sense of why – when speaking of the problems that arise in the practical modelling of subjectivity – Guattari writes that 'university philosophical research remains dry and desiccated on these questions' and that 'it has even constructed a system to resist access to them' ([1972] 2015b: 130). Philosophy's resistance to even accepting the practical problems of postmedia studies for investigation occurs in two steps. As we have seen, the first step involves focussing all attention on the specific question of the nature of the *thinking* subject, but what makes this focus all the more damaging is that it also has the effect of individualizing all subjectivity. In his writings, Guattari recognizes that 'from the perspective of certainty of the individual cogito, group subjectivity seems unstable', but he argues that a sufficient analysis of group subjectivity is 'the only guarantee for grasping the meaning of even the slightest human gestures and words' ([1972] 2015b: 125). Thus, reversing the more traditional philosophical order of priority between the one and the many, Guattari claims that 'group subjectivity' is 'an *absolute precondition* for the emergence of any individual subjectivity' ([1972] 2015b: 125). The specific dynamics of the medium of thought, along with the specific philosophical drive towards the certainty of knowledge, led thinkers like Descartes to focus all of their attention on the experience of the thinking subject. However, in doing this, such thinkers cut the subject off from the social and political milieu in which it actually emerges, acts and interacts.[3] As Guattari writes: 'An entire philosophical tradition has had to take vast detours, starting with the individual *res cogitans*, to miss all or part of the *res publica*' ([1972] 2015b: 125). If we are interested in providing philosophical support for postmedia experimentation, then we will need to find a way to reverse this trend and to think the intersubjectivity of the subject.

Perhaps, then, we should not be surprised to find that when Guattari begins working with Deleuze, one of the main tasks they set themselves is to offer a philosophy of group subjectivity.[4] Already in *Difference and Repetition*, Deleuze had developed a critique of Descartes, Kant and a host of other key thinkers in the history of Western thought, for taking a particular 'image of thought' for granted, and one which takes 'the pure self of "I think"' as an 'implicit presupposition' or starting point (2004: 164). Expanding on Deleuze's metaphysical critique of identity to incorporate the question of the subject, in *Anti-Oedipus* Guattari and Deleuze set out to think both the pre-individual difference out of which a subject can emerge and the group dynamics of the social sphere into which this emergence occurs. Of course, Deleuze and Guattari's schizoanalytic project is not simply a new mode of philosophy. We might do better, in fact, to think of it as a post-psychoanalytic exercise. Regardless of its theoretical targets, however, the practical purpose of the shift to schizoanalysis is precisely the desire to develop a theory of group subjectivity that can be used in the kinds of practical activities of experimentation that are well known to both institutional psychotherapists and postmedia activists.

The theory of group subjectivity developed by Guattari, especially as it appears in his working relationship with Deleuze, has been relatively well documented.[5] What I would like to pick up on here is a slightly different aspect of schizoanalysis, which may help us respond to the insights we have already drawn from Descartes and from Kant. What I am referring to is the way in which schizoanalysis recasts the act of thinking in a way which avoids the dangers of representation that we have already come across. If it is the focus on the *thinking* subject which has led philosophers to privilege the individual, then perhaps a critical investigation into the nature of thought might help us to break from this individualism. As we saw previously, Descartes's direct realism leads him to conceptualize the act of thinking as essentially representative, in the sense that to think is to reach out to the external world through the mediation of a representative image of that world, where the image represented is given to us immediately in thought. Without discarding the idea that to think is to represent, Kant offered an alternative theorization of representation. For Kant, the subject's act of representation is not simply an attempt to copy over an external reality into the internal theatre of the mind, but to synthesize the structure of reality by applying concepts to it. In the Kantian picture, the subject has immediate access to the structure of reality precisely because this structure is constructed by the mind's application of concepts to sensation. In Deleuze and Guattari's schizoanalytic approach, both of these modes of thinking about thought – both of which take representation as essential to the act of thought – are rejected. As Deleuze and Guattari write in *A Thousand Plateaus*, 'schizoanalysis . . . undertakes not to represent, interpret, or symbolise, but only to make maps' (2004: 250). Here I will offer a brief analysis of the non-representative mode of thinking that Deleuze and Guattari aim to develop and to say why such a methodology will be productive for any future project in postmedia philosophy.

In the opening chapter of *A Thousand Plateaus*, Deleuze and Guattari make a distinction between rhizomatic and arborescent modes of thinking. One of the key differences between these two activities of thought is said to be that the former proceeds by 'mapping', while the latter relies on the act of 'tracing' (2004: 13). For Deleuze and Guattari, the world is never static but is in constant processes of self-transformation. For this reason, any attempt to simply represent the world in thought will always be outdated before it can ever be used. According to Deleuze and Guattari's terminology, the 'logic of tracing and reproduction' simply aims to 'describe a de facto state . . . something that comes ready-made' (2004: 13). However, in seeking out some 'profound structure' which is supposed to be unchanging, this activity misses what is active and what is genetic in any process (2004: 13). In the case of Descartes and Kant's respective attempts to think the nature of subjectivity, the incessant focus on representation led these philosophers to see their task as one of tracing the essential structural unity of subjectivity. The problem with this method is that the image of the thinking subject that emerges from this practice can never be successfully reapplied to the various modes of subjectivity that deviate from the norm of the reflective cogito. Deleuze and Guattari, therefore, take up a different set of aims. Instead of attempting to trace out the eternal and essential structures of subjectivity, Deleuze and Guattari aim to map the ongoing dynamics of particular instances of subjectivation. Unlike the act of tracing, the act of mapping happens in an ongoing way; with each further step into an unknown territory, the map is extended. As Deleuze and Guattari write: 'What distinguished the map from the tracing is that it is entirely oriented towards an experimentation in contact with the real' (2004: 13). If we treat thought, not as representational, but as creative and experimental, then perhaps we will be in a better position to think through the different dynamics of subjectivity that arise in different media and postmedia conditions. For Deleuze and Guattari, a shift away from the representational model of tracing, and towards the experimental model of mapping, allows for the possibility that philosophy might be able to offer conceptual insight into the practical and political problems that arise in activities such as postmedia activism:

> Schizoanalysis, as the analysis of desire, is immediately practical and political, whether it is a question of an individual, group, or society. For politics precedes being. Practice does not come after the emplacement of the terms and their relations, but actively participates in the drawing of the lines; it confronts the same dangers and the same variations as the emplacement does. (2004: 225)

What this quotation from *A Thousand Plateaus* suggests is that thinking about the subject should not precede any practical and political experimentation with subjectivity. That is to say, the philosopher should not and cannot offer a theory of subjectivity in advance, and then hope that it will apply to all cases of subjectivation. Similarly, the act of thinking about subjectivity need not come after the act of experimentation. Instead, via the process of conceptual mapping, we can think the subject in its practical and political activity. *A Thousand Plateaus* is frustratingly silent on the topics which concern postmedia studies: there are examinations of painting, mathematics, geology, war and much more, but there are no comparable analyses of television, radio or other forms of social mass-mediation. However, there is nothing to stop us utilizing Deleuze and Guattari's philosophical methodology of mapping in these cases. What I am trying to suggest here is that schizoanalysis gives us a method for thinking through media-relations that need not begin with a preconceived idea of subjectivity. As Brian Massumi writes in the translator's introduction to the book, 'each section' of *A Thousand Plateaus* 'tries to reconstitute a dynamism that has existed in other mediums at other times' (2004: xv). Rather than trying to offer a representative picture of any part of reality, schizoanalysis attempts to think alongside the dynamics of an activity and to reconstitute that activity in the medium of thought.

Throughout this chapter, I have attempted to show that one of the methods by which philosophers have attempted to avoid the practical problems of subjectivity that arise in cases such as postmedia activism is by restricting their focus to the *thinking* subject. If Deleuze and Guattari are simply offering an alternative and non-representational theorization of *thought*, then might it be said that schizoanalysis will make philosophy's mistakes again? The reason why I don't think that this is the case is that when schizoanalysis thinks about thought, it does not take thinking to be the archetypal activity of the subject. In a schizoanalytic study of any particular media technology, for example, the question asked would not be 'how does the subject of this form of media think?' but 'how can we think the subject of this form of media?' In the case of the radio, such an approach would not take the subjects of the radio to be essentially thinking subjects, and then to ask how these subjects think. Instead, the idea would be to try to investigate the dynamics of subjectivation that are enabled by radio technology and then to try to map these dynamics in thought. It is this map that will then be useful for answering the kinds of questions that Guattari has raised. If we can map out the dynamics of a real system as we experiment with it, then we will be able to use this map in order to make sense of why some of our experiments have been successful and why others have not.

Of course, this process of mapping the dynamics of various media systems is already happening. Postmedia theorists have been carrying out this process from the beginning of the first experiments in postmedia activism. Unfortunately, however, academic philosophers have very rarely involved themselves with these ways of thinking. Armed with an outdated set of conceptual tools, many philosophers find that their understanding of subjectivity is inapplicable in practical and problematic situations of subjectivation. What I have tried to suggest here is that this separation of powers between academic philosophy and practical experimentation – including but not restricted to the experiments of postmedia activists – need not continue. The history of modern European philosophy has a lot to contribute to the question of how different modes of subjectivity can be produced in relations to different processes of mediation. As we have seen from our studies of Descartes and Kant, this tradition includes a rich seam of reflection on the nature of subjectivity as it emerges in the medium of thought. However, in order to bring these contributions to the practical stage, philosophers must see themselves as working alongside those conducting experiments, in order to aid with the process of conceptual mapping, and they cannot assume that the tracings of subjectivity drawn out from figures, such as Descartes and Kant, will ever be directly applicable to the concerns of practical and political work.

References

Apprich, C. (2013), 'Remaking Media Practices – From Tactical Media to Postmedia', in C. Apprich, J. B. Slater, A. Iles and O. L. Schultz (eds), *Provocative Alloys: A Postmedia Anthology*, 122–40, Berlin: Mute Books.

Berardi, F. (2005), 'Les radios libres et l'émergence d'une sensibilité post-médiatique', *Multitudes*, 2 (21): 15–22.

Berardi, F. (2012), 'The Paradox of Media Activism: The Net is Not a Tool, It's an Environment', *Ibraaz*, 2 November. Available online: https://www.ibraaz.org/essays/49 (accessed 1 December 2020).

Bineham, J. (1995), 'The Hermeneutic Medium', *Philosophy & Rhetoric*, 28 (1): 1–16.

Brook, A. (2001), 'Kant, Self-Awareness and Self-Reference', in A. Brook and R. D. Vidi (eds), *Self-Reference and Self-Awareness*, 9–30, Amsterdam: John Benjamins Publishing.

Deleuze, G. (2004), *Difference and Repetition*, trans. P. Patton, London: Continuum.

Deleuze, G. and F. Guattari (2004), *A Thousand Plateaus*, trans. B. Massumi, London: Continuum.

Descartes, R. ([1641] 2017), *Meditations on First Philosophy: With Selections from the Objections and Replies*, ed. and trans. J. Cottingham, Cambridge: Cambridge University Press.

Dickerson, A. B. (2004), *Kant on Representation and Objectivity*, Cambridge: Cambridge University Press.

Foucault, M. (1991), 'Governmentality', trans. R. Braidotti and revised by C. Gordon, in G. Burchell, C. Gordon and P. Miller (eds), *The Foucault Effect: Studies in Governmentality*, 87–104, Chicago: University of Chicago Press.

Genosko, G. (2002), *Felix Guattari: An Aberrant Introduction*, London: Continuum.

Groys, B. (2011), 'What is German Media Philosophy? Subjectivity as Medium of the Media', *Radical Philosophy*, 169 (5): 7–9.

Guattari, F. (2007), 'Interview with Félix Guattari for the Journalism Course at the Pontificial Catholic University (PUC), São Paulo, August 26, 1982', in S. Rolnik (ed.), K. Clapshow and B. Holmes (trans.), *Molecular Revolution in Brazil*, 145–58. Los Angeles: Semiotext(e).

Guattari, F. (2009a), 'Postmodern Deadlock and Postmedia Transition', in S. Lotringer (ed.), C. Wiener and E. Wittman (trans.), *Soft Subversions: Texts and Interviews 1977–1985*, 291–300, Los Angeles: Semiotext(e).

Guattari, F. (2009b), 'Entering the Postmedia Era', in S. Lotringer (ed.), C. Wiener and E. Wittman (trans.), *Soft Subversions: Texts and Interviews 1977–1985*, 301–6, Los Angeles: Semiotext(e).

Guattari, F. ([1972] 2015a), 'Machine and Structure', in A. Hodges (trans.), *Psychoanalysis and Transversality: Texts and Interviews 1955–1971*, 318–29. New York: Semiotext(e).

Guattari, F. ([1972] 2015b), 'Reflections on Institutional Psychotherapy for Philosophers', in A. Hodges (trans.), *Psychoanalysis and Transversality: Texts and Interviews 1955–1971*, 121–35. New York: Semiotext(e).

Guattari, F. ([1972] 2015c), 'Introduction to Institutional Psychotherapy', in A. Hodges (trans.), *Psychoanalysis and Transversality: Texts and Interviews 1955–1971*, 60–75. New York: Semiotext(e).

Kant, I. ([1781] 1929), *Critique of Pure Reason*, trans. N. K. Smith, London: Macmillan.

Lacan, J. (1977), *The Seminar, Book XI: The Four Fundamental Concepts of Psychoanalysis*, trans. A. Sheridan, London: Hogarth Press and Institute of Psycho-Analysis.

Sartre, J-P. (1962), *Transcendence of the Ego*, trans. F. Williams and R. Kirkpatrick, New York: Noonday Press.

Thornton, E. (2017), 'The Rise of the Machines: Deleuze's Flight from Structuralism', *The Southern Journal of Philosophy*, 55 (4): 454–74.

Watson, J. (2009), *Guattari's Diagrammatic Thought: Writing Between Lacan and Deleuze*, London: Continuum.

Williams, B. (2015), *Descartes: The Project of Pure Enquiry*, London: Routledge.

6

Postmedia and dissensus

Reinventing democracy with Guattari

Jean-Sébastien Laberge

This contribution aims to account for the idea of a 'passage from the consensual mediatic era to a dissensual postmediatic era' (Guattari 2013a: 13) by situating it in the project of the reinvention of democracy instigated by Félix Guattari. Let us immediately begin with the continuity between transversality, which was conceptualized in the 1960s as a critique of democratic centralism and the valourization of autopoiesis, and the idea, which will appear twenty years later, of a dissensual postmediatic era. At the same time, the concept of postmedia responds to two problems: postmodernism and mass media, two distinct effects of the molecular revolution that are nevertheless linked by the passivity they foster. In this sense, the idea of a postmediatic era is intimately linked to the concept of reinventing practices based on dissensus to experiment with new means of 'telematic consultation' and to rearticulate social movements and political parties. This contribution develops and clarifies the articulation of these different aspects.

For this purpose, a first detour is made by the Guattarian concepts of transversality and molecular revolution. Having thus become interested in the impact of new information and communication technologies [ICTs], in the distinction between the subject group and the subjugated group, and in the critique of centralism that it implies, the concept of postmedia is situated in relation to that of mass media. In order to situate the context and to illustrate the resingularization of the practices that the entry into the postmediatic era values, we will then look at the experiments instigated by Guattari at the time he proposed this concept. The example of the Minitel and the Alternatik network (1986–91) thus shows how the potentialities conveyed by ICTs make it possible to reinvent the means of consultation. In continuity, the following section instead emphasizes the importance of dissensus in this passage by first distinguishing between postmediatic and postmodernist conceptions of it. Considering the role of consensus in democratic centralism and its production by the mass media, dissensus makes it possible to rearticulate social movements and political parties in order to make room for singularities and assume pluralism. Once again, to situate his theoretical proposal, we will turn to Guattari's militancy. The examples of the Arc-en-ciel network (1986–8) and Guattari's dual membership in the French political parties Les Verts and Génération Écologie (1990–2) will then be discussed to illustrate the dissensual functioning characteristic of the postmediatic era. The idea of a dissensual postmedia era is thus to be understood in the context and the problems of its conceptualization and through the experiments undertaken in France by Guattari, which give it consistency.

Postmedia

In 1985, the concept of postmedia emerged in Guattari's work, that is to say, at a time when it was now fashionable for some people 'to consider themselves outside of time, beyond history, claiming to be postmodern and postpolitical, but never, unfortunately, postmedia' (Guattari 2009: 58). Guattari – who had just officially joined the French party Les Vert – was working on *Schizoanalytic Cartographies*' chapter 'From postmodernism to the postmedia era', but also on completing the collection *Les années d'hivers*.[1] In his preface to this book, Guattari points out that by refusing to explore what new technologies 'offer in terms of the development of means of expression and collective consultation, and the multiplication of decision-making bodies', the Socialist Party of French president François Mitterrand will have 'perhaps missed an unhoped-for entry into a postmedia era of liberation from the collective subjectivity of its prefabrication and its guidance by institutions and collective normalization equipment' (Guattari 2009: 34). It should, therefore, be emphasized that postmedia is not simply opposed to any sense of an infantilizing mass media but to the set of collective equipment that prefabricates normalized subjectivities. In this sense, and against the apathy of those who prophesize the end of the social and the political, Guattari calls tirelessly for the experimentation of new practices to get out of serialization. In order to understand what he means by prefabricated collective subjectivity and its links with postmedia, it is necessary to present transversality and molecular revolution as conceptualized by Guattari.

Transversality

Several aspects of the concept of transversality extend into that of postmedia. At the outset, let us say that transversality is an autopoietic mode of an organization whose openness to otherness implies a continual resingularization and an emphasis on the transmonadic character of the enunciation. First, drawing inspiration from Jean-Paul Sartre, who scales collectives from seriality to groups-in-fusion in *Critique of Dialectical Reason I*, Guattari distinguishes, respectively, the subjugated group from the subject group, that is, between groups that receive their determination from the outside and those that found themselves by claiming to assume an internal law. 'One can say of the subject group that *it enunciates* something – whereas of the subjugated group only that "its cause is heard"' (Guattari 2015: 107 (revised); cf. 64) inasmuch as the latter conforms to the prevailing denotations and the former establishes its own discursivity. Transversality refers first of all to this self-founding[2] capacity of the subject group, which is directly involved in its enunciation, in contrast to the centralism of the subjugated group, which thus organizes, subordinates and confiscates the enunciation. It is, therefore, a question of distinguishing two ways of assembling, of making a group, in such a way that transversality responds first of all to the totalizing centralism that is traditionally that of the trade unions and the parties. '"Transversality", after all, is no more than an attempt to analyze democratic centralism!' (Guattari 2015: 380n19).

It should be noted that this distinction between subject and subjugated groups, like all those discussed here, does not function as a binary opposition but rather as two poles between which the groups oscillate. We thus speak of a 'coefficient of transversality' understood as the 'degree of openness' of a group to the heterogeneity of its elements, that is, to its own otherness (Guattari 2015: 112; cf. 1995: 69). It could be said that the transversality of a group amounts to the heterogeneity expressed in it. At what point does a group relax the rules of consensus and allow divergent perspectives to express themselves? The transversal *mode* of organization is, by the very fact, a *way* of being, a *disposition* to heterogeneity, an openness to otherness inseparable from an appreciation of dissensus. In this perspective, Guattari considers that dissensus is the rupture of meaning, the test of the nonsense lived as the concrete experience of finitude (Guattari 2015: 120).[3] In the case of the subjugated group, nonsense is felt like an external phenomenon to be guarded against.

In contrast, in the case of the subject group, it is experienced as an internal rupture that allows a (re)singularization that enriches the enunciation. In other words, by assuming its finitude, the subject group acquires the dynamism that allows it to continually reinvent itself. By becoming mired in a phantasm of eternity with a totalization that claims universality, the subjugated group condemns itself to a sclerosing fixation, that is to say, to the passive empty repetition of the normopath subjugated to dominant meanings. The reification carried out by the subjugated groups thus always implies an irremediably reductive binarism. All or nothing! Either these prevailing meanings or the end of the world! You are either with us or against us, any dissent is perceived as an existential threat. This is unfortunately typical of the temperament of parties, trade unions and *groupuscules* of all kinds.

It should also be stressed that the combination of heterogeneous elements characteristic of transversality makes it possible to emphasize the fact that enunciation always takes place at the interface of several perspectives. It is even from its capacity to resonate in different universes that it derives its consistency. Transversality is a connection that is neither vertical nor horizontal, but which passes impromptu from one register to another, thus assembling itself across hierarchies to cross the different elements in a singular way. Transversality 'tends to be achieved when maximum communication takes place between the different levels and especially in the different directions. It is the very object of the search of a subject group' (Guattari 2015: 113 (revised)). From this perspective, transversality illustrates the transmonadic aspect of the enunciation of the subject group, which combines divergent, dissensual perspectives according to a multivalent logic, hence its richness and complexity.

Molecular revolution

The idea of a molecular revolution posits that the transformations of the means of production instigated by the ICTs are also mutations in the processes of individual and collective subjectivation that drastically modify sociopolitical arrangements (Guattari and Robin 2016: 134; Guattari 2012: 65). In short, the techno-scientific revolution of ICTs is bringing about a revolution in subjectivity, and also in social and political life. These are qualitative changes that irrevocably transform the whole of our relationships, both with ourselves, with others and with the environment (Guattari 2019: 7; 2013a: 37). The information revolution thus marks the end of a certain model of humanity and its sociopolitical relations.

Countless ways of doing things fall into disuse, leading to a generalized feeling of loss of reference. However, this should not be seen as a disappearance of the social or the political, as postmodernism asserts, but rather as a mutation. The break-up of the nuclear family allows for the emergence and experimentation of other ways of organizing sexual relations. The result is not only the diversification of family assemblages, but also a reaffirmation of the traditional family. In other words, either an opening and resingularization or closing and fixation, which Guattari will later call heterogenesis and homogenesis, respectively. The molecular revolution is thus inseparable from the affirmation of a multiplicity of singular and divergent subjectivities, new sensibilities and ways of living: feminists, homosexuals, regionalists. By overturning the old ways of doing things, this revolution creates spaces for experimentation. However, what Guattari is particularly interested in are the new potentialities conveyed by ICTs, which allow the emergence of innovative practices and the creation of new spaces of freedom. ICTs have thus rendered a multiplicity of practices obsolete while bringing the potential of a multiplicity of other practices still unsuspected. Guattari set up a Centre d'initiative pour de nouveaux espaces de liberté [CINEL] (Initiative Centre for New Spaces of Freedom) which accompanied him in several of his postmediatic experiments.

Mass media

Guattari distinguishes between two types of mass media uses, which are never in themselves mass mediatic or postmediatic. According to him, there is a tendency towards hyper-concentrated systems with the aim of 'shaping opinion, a reinforced adaptation of attitudes, unconscious patterns of the population to the dominant norms' and a tendency 'towards miniaturised systems that open up the possibility of collective appropriation'. So that we find, on the one hand, 'more and more centralism, conformism, oppression' and, on the other hand, 'the perspective of new spaces of freedom, self-management, fulfilment of singularities of desire' (Guattari 2012: 353). Guattari points out that the dominant use of the means of communication, such as that which characterizes the format of television broadcasts, 'inevitably leads to an absolute passivity on the part of the consumer. However, nothing at the outset imposed such a political choice from a technical point of view! It was possible from the outset to design equipment for production and consumption adapted to "subject groups" and not to subjected groups' (Guattari 2012: 354).

The passivity that defines mass media has two aspects. First, it refers to an infantilization which is a corollary to the evacuation of all singularities and thus to the confinement to reductive stereotypes which obliterate complexity: 'There is an infantile attitude in mass-media dependency, which consists in expecting the television mechanism to provide you with answers and behavioural models . . . that are totally stereotyped! Indeed, there is never any question of pain, cancer, finitude or desire in these machines' (Guattari 1990: 91). In other words, 'Everything that bothers, everything that is singular, everything that makes us come out of our shell is put in brackets' (Guattari and Favereau 1991: 13). This closure to otherness blocks all opportunities for resingularization and enrichment of the mass-media consumer, but it also condemns us to a simplifying apprehension of the problems, an infantile understanding that ignores the complexity of the issues.

The second aspect is that by conveying standardized opinions that shape consensus, which thereby manufactures consent, the mass media substitutes itself for democratic consultation (Guattari 2013b: 433). In politics, the mass-media game of the star system with its charismatic leaders, particularly in electoral processes – the democratic paroxysm of our societies – far from facilitating access to information that promotes the understanding of complex political issues, impoverishes today's political culture.

Postmedia

Guattari considers that with the new technologies, such as the Minitel, which will soon be discussed, 'it is conceivable that in all areas relating to democratic life, particularly at the most local levels, new forms of telematic consultation will become possible' (Guattari 2013b: 51). Telematic consultation decentralizes and can lead to the recomposition of practices, that is to say: 'Reinvention of a less formal democracy better in touch with the productive social machinery, management of the mass media in the sense of their reappropriation by users, what [Guattari] called: the entry into a postmedia era' (Guattari 2013b: 530). This is the most important aspect of the postmedia era: to keep up with the current changes 'it will be necessary to reinvent the State and democratic consultation. . . . In opposition to the mass media dumbing down, it will be a question of preparing for the entry into a postmedia era, where singularity and dissensus will be the order of the day' and Guattari specifies that 'this is conceivable, on the one hand, because of technological developments . . . and, above all, through collective experiments directly undertaken by the "users"' (Guattari 2013b: 517; cf. 42, 429). In this sense, Guattari calls for a 'postmedia era that would give the Assemblages of subjective self-reference their full scope' (Guattari 2013a: 6), that is, the use of ICTs, but more generally all collective equipment. This perspective is inseparable from the potentialities conveyed by ICTs since 'it is only in the context of the new "deals" of the production of computational and telematic subjectivity that this voice/pathway of self-reference will succeed in acquiring its full capacity' (Guattari 2013a: 6). The postmedia era will be that of self-referentiality made possible by new technologies, the reinvention and multiplication of the means of consultation at all levels, a form of democracy that makes room for singularities. For Guattari, the characteristic autopoiesis of the postmedia is inseparable from the autonomy and self-management characteristic of democracy.

Minitel 3615 ALTER – 1986–91

It was in 1982 that the French State marketed the Minitel – acronym for *Médium Interactif par Numérisation d'Information Téléphonique* (Interactive Medium by Digitizing Telephone Information) – in its 'all-in-one' form (screen-keyboard-modem) which, among other things, made it possible to send instant messages, consult directories, check cinema or train timetables and even buy tickets. In 1985, there were more than 1 million Minitels in service and 6.5 million in 1990. Considering that the World Wide Web appeared in 1992, France was largely a forerunner and constituted an exceptional case.

At the very moment when Guattari conceptualizes the dissensual postmedia era, he also engaged in its experimentation by instigating the Alternatik network constituted by the Minitel 3615 ALTER service and the association Les Amis d'Alter which will federate up to twenty-five associations. When it was launched in the autumn of 1986, 3615 ALTER offered a virtual space where each association could both disseminate information and set up places for exchange, forums allowing both real-time coordination and 'the expression of the "dissensual" point of view of those who do not think or feel like others' (Guattari 1986a: 2). In the text presenting the Alternatik network, Guattari clearly mentions that this telematic service aims to initiate 'the exit from the oppressive consensual era, under the aegis of the major media, to enter the postmedia era of a reappropriation of new technologies' (Guattari 1986a: 3). By experimenting with Minitel in this way, the Alternatik network 'tries to mobilize creativity and collective intelligence to liberate/construct its potential' (Guattari 1986a: 2). The 3615 ALTER service thus supports the idea of molecular revolution by networking a multiplicity of associations and alternative practices, thus encouraging exchanges and, above all, allowing experimentation with innovative forms of consultation.

In November 1986, when the 3615 ALTER service was launched, a student protest movement took shape in France. This movement mobilized this brand-new Minitel service to set up a coordination system.[4] The movement quickly expanded exponentially, and the government had to withdraw its reform the following month. In 1988, it was then the nurses who launched a massive strike movement which also used this service to coordinate itself. Guattari points out that they, after the students, 'were able to use the Minitel for transversal communication: to make the field practices dialogue, to confront individual points of view with the collective movement, and to allow minority positions to be taken into account' (Guattari 1989: 14). The Minitel instigated a paradigm shift in the mode of organization of struggles.

However, this was not Guattari's first postmedia experimentation since Radio Tomate (1981–3) informed his understanding of telematics. Following the experience of Radio Tomate, Guattari emphasizes that free radio 'is an instrument for experimenting with new modalities of democracy, a democracy capable not only of tolerating the expression of social and individual singularities, but also of encouraging their expression, of giving them the importance they deserve in the global social domain' (Guattari 1986b: 12). At Radio Tomate, a multiplicity of styles and formats coexisted in a self-managing formula. As Bernard Prince and Emmanuel Videcoq of CINEL note:

> The internal layout of these information and communication machines that were Radio Tomate and the Minitel ALTER is the trademark of postmedia. Indeed, it is based on proximity networks and the new information and communication technologies; it transforms the individual from a simple receiver and consumer of information to a fully-fledged transmitter and actor . . . it is always a question of making singularities, a multiplicity of desires and expression cooperate, while avoiding the deleterious traps of (hierarchical and centralized) power and control structures. (Prince and Videcoq 2008: 182)

This desire to contest hierarchical centralism is a defining aspect of the new practices characteristic of the postmedia age.[5] The Alternatik network thus proposes 'a new type of relationship, less hierarchical, more "transversal" and, consequently, richer between' a diversity of approaches, between Paris and the peripheries, but also between 'the "out loud" speakers and those who would never dare raise their hands in a public meeting' (Guattari 1986a: 2). Telematics allows new forms of organization which can overcome the pitfalls of centralist structures and can lead 'to the development of a more democratic expression than that of traditional general assemblies . . . They shake up hierarchies, organisational burdens, and welcome minority voices' (Guattari 1989: 14). For Guattari, this revolution in the means of consultation is not just wishful thinking but a tangible result confirmed by different groups' actual use of 3615 ALTER.

Dissensus

It is important to note that at the same time that Guattari began experimenting with Minitel and generalized the use of the concept of postmedia, he also adopted the concept of dissensus. So that by the spring of 1986, he speaks of a 'dissensual postmedia era'.[6] It is in an interview from 14 October 1985 that we find the first occurrence of the term *dissensus* in Guattari's work. However, it was Yann Hernot who proposed it in his question:

> You would then join Lyotard's position of dissensus. Absolutely, at least on this point, replies Guattari. Where I would no longer agree with him is that, for me, dissensus is absolutely not antagonistic to the organization of a social struggle at all other levels. And it is precisely new pragmatics that needs to be supported, putting in place social practices that will make it possible to hold these contradictions together. (Guattari and Hernot 1986: 55)

Dissensus is, therefore, not an aporia but rather the renewal of practices. Make no mistake, the renewal of practices to make room for dissensus is not limited to the new media but aims at the resingularization of activism and consultation to rearticulate movements and parties and to re-dynamize the social and the political.

Guattari is firmly opposed to the postmodernism of François Lyotard, who concludes that dissensus leads to aporia, that is, the very impossibility of politics. Guattari notes that, at this level, Lyotard agrees with Jean Baudrillard and asserts that the postmodern position is the crowning achievement of disengagement (Guattari 2013a: 38–9; 2000: 41; 2013b: 513–14). Far from being dead or simulacra, the social and the political have *certainly* been transformed, and it is important to take note of this: not only are notions such as the working-class obsolete, but 'previous social practices, those of syndicalism and various grist of the parties of the left, have completely failed!' (Guattari 1996: 127). In its wake, it is, therefore, a matter of reinventing practices that respond to current conditions by making it possible to address a multiplicity of issues and divergent perspectives *transversally*. In this sense, Guattari proposes to rearticulate social movements and political parties according to a multivalent logic, which will be discussed next. Dissensus does not prevent consensus or circumstantial agreement from being reached, let alone consultation, but it does indicate the need to reinvent democracy and to enter a postmedia era.

Moreover, if there is a decoy to be wary of, it is rather the reductive ideal of consensus which obliterates nuance and singularity. Guattari's positive and dynamic conception of dissensus is not only opposed to the negative and sterile understanding that postmodernism has of it but also to the consensus shaped by the mass media, with its polls and experts. Consensus synthesizes the plurality of a social movement into the unity of a political party.[7] The control of the central organ of a party over the expression of the movement it claims to represent is, after all, characteristic of the so-called democratic functioning of our societies. In this sense, once again, far from favouring the innovative potential of the social movements that support them, political parties tend to organize them on the basis of power struggles and their Jacobin interests.

For his part, by promoting autopoiesis and the multiplicity of singular perspectives, Guattari opts for pluralism and the challenge to coexistence that it poses. The postmedia reinvention of the means of democratic consultation does not simply aim at the enunciation of a multiplicity of divergent desires, but also at the coexistence of these conflicting subjectivities. Guattari is very clear on this point: 'It is about living antagonism, dissensus, without pretending to magically resolve it, transcendentally . . . The world of values is fundamentally contradictory, antagonistic, conflictual; democracy consists in managing this world with its contradictions, its risks, its embarrassment' (Guattari 2013b: 339–40). How can we create dissensus and bring together a multiplicity of divergent perspectives? In short, how is pluralism managed in the postmedia era? Faced with the difficulty of combining conflict and coexistence, far from avoiding the problem, Guattari experiments to try to give consistency to new practices.

The call for an Arc-en-ciel: The consensus-dissensus – 1986–8

In November 1986, when 3615 ALTER was launched, the Les Verts Party officially abandoned the prospect of an alliance with alternative left-wingers. Consequently, although a member of Les Verts, Guattari decided the following month, together with militants gathered at his home, to launch the call for an Arc-en-ciel [AEC] (Rainbow) on 12 February 1987. Noting that the current political structures are outdated, the signatories of this appeal consider that:

> A new way of debating societal problems and acting to live differently is needed. . . . It is a question of bringing together the rainbow of our sensibilities, our aspirations and our struggles. . . . It is not a question of overarching or dissolving present identities and sensibilities, but, by respecting their right to exist in the form that suits them, to ensure that they enrich each other. (AEC 1987a)

By mobilizing the CINEL and the 3615 ALTER, the network quickly accounted for more than 5,000 members from various backgrounds. New forms of the consultation were experimented with, such as the 'consensus-dissensus' rule, that is, 'priority to initiatives that achieve consensus, coexistence of initiatives that achieve dissensus . . . minorities retaining their right of expression and action' (AEC 1987b: 3). The AEC network thus wished to move away from the simplistic binarism of majority/minority to take the idea of pluralism seriously by relying on specific agreements that make it possible to constitute an expression at the macropolitical level of the electoral and mass-media game, while preserving the autonomy of each one.

It should be noted that the dissensus put forward in the AEC network aimed to establish a new political culture that rearticulated social movements and political parties. This articulation is, moreover, a perennial problem of the French environmental movement. In this sense, in March 1988, Guattari participated in the AEC forum to speak about the stakes of pluralist political expression, 'party, network or movement' (AEC 1988: 2). Acknowledging the collapse of the old models and the rise of neofascism, he mentioned that it was now or never 'the time to change logic. For today it is above all a question of learning to work in parallel the apparently antagonistic dimensions of the opinions we face' (Guattari 1988: 4). Several aspects of this new dissensual and multivalent logic are exemplified in the AEC network.

First, the functioning of consensus/dissensus experimented with in the AEC implies an openness, a disposition to dissensus, that is, 'the concern to listen to the motivations of minorities or initially marginal points of view' (AEC 1988: 2). This sensitivity which enriches each one make the collective enunciation all the richer for it. This openness is also a reminder of transversality and makes it possible to organize transversally, that is, to hold together singular perspectives and thus to have a richer and more complex understanding of the issues at stake: 'A new gentleness, a new tolerance will have to preside over forms of organisation which, in order to meet these multiple objectives, will have to take on the polymorphous aspect of a movement-party-network and be capable of responding both to national and international challenges and to taking charge of many aspects of daily life and culture' (Guattari 2013b: 403).

In order to fully understand the enrichment induced by dissensus – and its inextricability from transversality – it must be remembered that it is a vector of singularization. It is the prospect of creative dissensus. The singular enunciation of a subject group characteristic of the postmedia era passes through the creation of meaning, an autopoietic act that implies a break with the prevailing denominations, a dissensus. This double process of rupture and creation is what Guattari calls singularization. Moreover, Guattari also speaks of 'heterogenesis, in other words, processes of continuous resingularisation. Individuals must become both more united and increasingly different' (Guattari 2000: 69). Disposition to dissensus, that is, accepting the position of the other, enriches my position because it allows for both a rapprochement and a development of differences and thus constitutes a sensitivity that favours heterogenesis. It is precise as a vector of dynamism that dissensus stimulates collective creativity and makes it possible to pose problems in new terms while at the same time regenerating social and political life: 'Priority to the social rather than the political? Or recomposition of the two, one through the other! The corollary for the Arc-en-ciel: structuring as a relatively acephalous "rhizome" rather than a relatively centralist operator? Or all at once: Movement in the social field and Party of a new kind in the political field!' (Guattari 1988: 4).

The large-scale experimentation of the AEC constitutes a means to break the political and social deadlock. Without it, there could be no transformation of mentalities necessary for the resingularization of the sociopolitical. Unfortunately, the AEC network ended abruptly as electoral results of the April presidential election and the June 1988 legislative elections were not favourable, and the disaffection that ensued brought activism to a halt.

Les Verts and Génération Écologie: Multi-membership 1990–92

Another example of the dissensus that Guattari offers is his dual membership of the antagonistic parties Les Verts and Génération Écologie. In December 1990, Guattari participated in the constitution of the Génération Écologie Party. Not only did he then become the national delegate dedicated to the prospective of this new political formation that allows double membership, but he also took advantage of this opportunity to publicly criticize the political attitude of Les Verts, who refused this practice.

Finding Génération Écologie in a process of becoming institutionalized, as was the case with Les Verts, Guattari called for a new articulation between party and movement that could give way to dissensus: 'We are not going to start democratic centralism again. Génération Écologie is not a party and if it acts as a party in electoral matters, it will do so in its own way, which must never compromise the plurality, the wealth, and even the contradictions inherent in an ecology movement that intends to face a multiplicity of objectives' (Guattari 1991: 8).

Moreover, deploring the lack of debate within Génération Écologie about the Gulf War (1990–1) and its alignment with the government's warmongering position, Guattari seized the opportunity to militate in favour of dissensus: 'The points of divergence, doubts, hesitations on this dramatic issue must lead to us getting to know each other better and, paradoxically, they must bring us closer together. That would be doing politics differently. Dissensus is more enriching than a facade consensus. And through this ordeal, we have to forge our collective intelligence and sensitivity' (Guattari 1991: 5). *A new sensitivity that opens up to heterogenesis.* To embrace dissensus is to dare for new solidarity and individual and collective enrichment *as a vector of creativity*. In short, it means reinventing democracy with a new political culture where dissensus means – not paradoxically, but most normally – solidarity.

Summoned to assert his allegiance by Les Verts, Guattari maintains that he never formally joined Génération Écologie and that the warmongering positions he found there convinced him to no longer participate (Guattari 2013b: 553). He, therefore, continued his engagement with Les Verts but nevertheless worked towards a rapprochement with Génération Écologie and the alternative movements. Then questioned on the importance of multi-membership, Guattari insisted again on the role of dissensus in the resingularization of consultation practices: 'This poses a more general problem, a conception of plurality, pluralism and dissensual character that we are obliged to accept in a redefinition of politics.[8] Behind this question lies a challenge to democratic centralism and a certain dogmatic vision of the party' (Guattari and Constantinou 1991: 9; Guattari 2013b: 554). It is, therefore, a matter of recognizing that neither a party nor a movement can claim the exhaustive expression of the aspirations of its members and their exclusive membership.

Dissensus thus constitutes the heart of a new political culture:

> The problem that I am trying to pose is therefore that of the transversal articulation between the individual, microsocial and macrosocial levels of political action ... This implies the promotion of another type of logic, a multivalent logic that makes it possible to take clear-cut positions, or compromises at the molar level, and at the same time to have receptivity, an open-mindedness, a dissensual spirit. (Guattari and Constantinou 1991: 11; Guattari 2013b: 561)

It must be acknowledged that the challenge posed by this multivalent logic is immense. Nevertheless, it is one of the greatest contemporary challenges, given the scale and complexity of the current issues. Far from needing to be unified, it is through a multiplicity of practices, all as singular as they are partial, that their collective management can emerge.

Untiringly, Guattari instigates experiments to give consistency to this new democracy. However, despite his perseverance, Les Verts or Génération Écologie were unfortunately not committed to this direction, as the ecologist movement was already largely mired in electioneering egos. The movement became gangrenous with the *groupuscule* syndrome.

Conclusion

The point here has been to reflect on Guattari's idea of a 'passage from the consensual mediatic era to a dissensual postmediatic era'. This passage is first of all understood in its historical context, which is that of the *era* of planetary computerization and molecular revolution, that is to say, new potentialities, sensibilities and practices opening up the prospect of new spaces of freedom as well as that of reinforcement of prevailing meanings. The *mass mediatic* use of potentialities goes precisely in the direction of this subjugation and leads to serialized subjectivity, while *postmediatic* is characterized by the autopoiesis of singular subjectivities. Since seriality is inseparable from centralism, which consensually organizes normalized elements, autopoiesis calls for transversality, which dissensually assembles singular elements. The passage from the infantilizing mass media to the heterogenizing postmedia implies a change in logic from the reductive and totalizing binarism of *consensus* to the complex and multivalent *dissensus*. This passage is thus an exit from seriality, centralism and infantilization towards singularity, transversality and creativity, through an opening, a change of sensitivity.

This passage towards postmedia is part of the project of a reinvention of democracy, which must be the place of 'regulation between multiple and contradictory levels, which implies going beyond consensual democracy towards the promotion of dissensual consultation systems' (Guattari, Conesa and Lemarchands 1991: 62). These being as much permitted by the postmediatic use of ICTs as necessary by the multiplicity of singular enunciations it induces. The postmediatic era carried by its autopoietic practices of rupture and creation will be dissensual or not. It is not a question of simply accepting dissensus; it must be assumed as a vector of dynamism and potential enrichment. In such a way that 'it seems indispensable to experiment in this way with a new, tolerant, dissensual political lifestyle, accepting not only difference but fully assuming it' (Guattari and Constantinou 1991: 10; Guattari 213: 555). Concretely, among other things, this means experimenting with the potential of new technologies to create new means of consultation (ALTER 3615), to articulate a multiplicity of singular and dissensual perspectives in a transversal organization of movement-party-network (AEC) with the help of a multivalent dissensual logic (multi-membership). By instigating and supporting a panoply of postmediatic initiatives and by advocating for dissensus, Guattari has continuously tried to give consistency to the prospects of a new democracy. This would be a dissensual democracy made possible by inseparable experimenting with new technological potentialities. It would constitute the leitmotif of the dissensual postmedia era.

References

Arc-en-ciel. (1987a), *Appel pour un Arc-en-ciel; Vademecum de l'Arc-en-ciel*, Jean-René Chauvin collection, 1-JRC–7K, Paris: Centre d'Histoire sociale du XXe siècle.

Arc-en-ciel. (1987b), 'Patchwork', Pour un Arc-en-ciel, 1: 3. Jean-René Chauvin collection, 1-JRC–7K. Paris: Centre d'Histoire sociale du XXe siècle.

Arc-en-ciel. (1988), 'Forums organisés par Arc-en-ciel: Culture alternative et nouvelles pratiques politiques', *Pour un Arc-en-ciel* (supplément 6): 1–2. Jean-René Chauvin collection, 1-JRC–7K. Paris: Centre d'Histoire sociale du XXe siècle.

Gonçalves, M. A. (1985), 'Guattari lança na PUC a época de pós-mídia', *Folha de São Paulo*, 21 (August): 37.

Guattari, F. (1983), 'La guerre, la crise ou la vie', *Change International*, 1: 50.
Guattari, F. (1986a), *Alternatik 86*, Félix Guattari collection, GTR 8.6, Abbaye d'Ardenne: IMEC.
Guattari, F. (1986b), 'Prefácio. As radíos livres em direção a uma era pós-mídia', in A. Machado, C. Magri and M. Masagã (eds), *Rádios livres. A reforma agrária no ar*, 9–13, São Paulo: Brasiliense.
Guattari, F. (1988), 'Pour un forum sur une nouvelle culture politique', *Pour un Arc-en-ciel*, 5: 4. Jean-René Chauvin collection, 1-JRC–7K. Paris: Centre d'Histoire sociale du XXe siècle.
Guattari, F. (1989), 'Un média pour les mouvements', *Terminal*, 42: 14.
Guattari, F. (1990), 'Quelles nouvelles menaces?', *Maintenant*, 1: 91.
Guattari, F. (1991), 'Le dissensus est plus enrichissant qu'un consensus de façade; Quelques réflexions sur notre Assemblée Générale', *Lettre d'information de Génération écologie*, 6: 5, 8. Félix Guattari collection, GTR 9.15, Abbaye d'Ardenne: IMEC.
Guattari, F. (1995), *Chaosmosis*, trans. P. Bains and J. Pefanis, Indianapolis: Indiana University Press.
Guattari, F. (1996), *The Guattari Reader*, ed. G. Genosko, Oxford: Blackwell Publishing.
Guattari, F. (2000), *The Three Ecologies*, trans. I. Pindar and P. Sutton, London: Athlone.
Guattari, F. (2009), *Les années d'hiver: 1980–1985*, Paris: Les prairies ordinaires.
Guattari, F. (2012), *La révolution moléculaire*, Paris: Les prairies ordinaires.
Guattari, F. (2013a), *Schizoanalytic Cartographies*, trans. A. Goffey, London: Bloomsbury.
Guattari, F. (2013b), *Qu'est-ce que l'écosophie?*, ed. S. Nadau, Paris: Lignes-IMEC.
Guattari, F. (2015), *Psychoanalysis and Transversality*, trans. A. Hodges, Los Angeles: Semiotext(e).
Guattari, F. (2019), 'A Paradigm Shift', *La Deleuziana*, 9: 6–9.
Guattari, F., J. Conesa and V. Lemarchands (1991), 'Est-ce qu'on a bien joué toutes les cartes du virtuel?' *Caravelles*, 2, 49–62. Villeurbanne: Caravelle.
Guattari, F. and S. Constantinou (1991), 'Félix Guattari et nous', in *Bulletin Fil vert*, July. Félix Guattari collection, GTR 26.28. Abbaye d'Ardenne: IMEC. Included under the title 'Praxis éco' in *Qu'est-ce que l'écosophie?*, 551–63. Paris, Lignes-IMEC, [2013].
Guattari, F. and E. Favereau (1991), 'Les médias ont délivré un message d'angoisse à l'état pur', *Libération*, 20 (February): 13.
Guattari, F. and Y. Hernot. (1986), 'Réappropriation de la subjectivité collective et transformations sociales', *Science-Fiction*, 6: 46–55.
Guattari, F. and J. Robin (2016), 'Révolution informatique, écologie et recomposition subjective', *Multitudes*, 24: 131–43.
Guattari, F. and S. Rolnik (1985), *Micropolítica: Cartografias do Desejo*, São Paulo: Vozes, [2013].
Guattari, F. and S. Rolnik (2007a), *Micropolitique*, trans. R. Barbaras, Paris: Empêcheurs de Penser en Rond.
Guattari, F. and S. Rolnik (2007b), *Molecular Revolution in Brazil*, trans. K. Clapshow and B. Holmes, Los Angeles: Semiotext(e).
Guattari, F. and T. Wada (1985), *Entretien autobiographique*. Félix Guattari collection, GTR 28.7. Abbaye d'Ardenne: IMEC.
Lazzarato, M. (2007), 'The Political Form of Coordination', trans. M. O'Neil, *Transversal*, 7, Available online: https://transversal.at/transversal/0707/lazzarato/en (accessed 20 July 2020).
Prince, B. and E. Videcoq (2008), 'Félix Guattari et les agencements postmédia', *MédiaMorphoses* (hors-série 4): 179–83.

Part III

Becoming algorithmic and ecosophical struggles for singularity

7

Assemblage line and tactical fluidity

Along Beijing's lines versus Hong Kong's 'Be Water'

Hsiu-ju Stacy Lo

How are we to make sense of a constantly updated human identity that is encoded in a sea of algorithm-based apps? Are 'lines of flight' still possible when the 'app-lified' selves are regularly monitored and held in check? This chapter explores first along *the lines* of a new body of work by artist Li Zi-Fong, taking its readers from the surveillance assemblages of Beijing and Hong Kong to ever-expanding AI (artificial intelligence). Li's computer-generated art may appear placeless, yet it is tethered to the living conditions of present-day Beijing which, in the time of corona, resonates with more people than before. Li's calculated yet random construction of a miscellany of intricate images tells modern fables about identity in an environment increasingly dominated by AI that insinuatingly mimics and alters human consciousness. Halfway through the chapter, this artificially enhanced (read impaired) vision will be intercepted by a physically damaged vision of a woman in Hong Kong, and this image will be mimed (as it did) by a demonstrating crowd during the course of the so-called Be Water Movement in 2019. The incident made a sudden turn in the protest movement, facilitating 'a concerted reappropriation of communicational and information technology' that Félix Guattari portended as the 'post-media era' (2009: 299). Machinic assemblages, however invisible, could be undone by liquid forces that flow like rivers and lakes.

By veiling each piece of subject matter with virtually infinite straight lines generated by a purpose-built computer program, Li 're-veils' modern-day online identity in flux and in reproduction. Untouched by the artist's hand, the seemingly sketch-like images in black and white portray the contemporary human condition: app-ily enabled and reproduced while men and women are being manipulated and incarcerated. Bodies of Light, formerly identity Reproduction, explores the estrangement of people from their flesh and humanity as human identity mutates and multiples in the age of Big Data. Through algorithmic programming, Li's 'lines' serve as a metaphor for life's infinite point-to-point connections. The mannered, somewhat unnatural 'straight lines' feature in various mysterious images and frame this body of work.

As the primary element of these images, the intricately patterned lines are sets of data matrix generated at random in parametric equations, reflecting the images' deconstructed and recomposed identity. They resemble particles and waves of consciousness as applications of superstring theory.[1] The various states of consciousness grow and multiply in waves of fluctuation and acceleration. Does the artwork imply that human consciousness is imbricated with the all-encompassing AI? Li offers a prophetic vision for our times. In particular, one image of a concealed eye (or I?) corresponds to a real-life figure in Hong Kong, the likeness of which was soon emulated to destabilize and dismantle the omnipresent surveillance assemblages. The last section of the chapter introduces the concept of *jianghu* as a mix of 'micropolitical' techniques and tactics of chipping away at state power.

Human-machine col-labor-ation

Two different methods of image generation were considered from the outset. One was a technique called 'image data augmentation', which can be used to artificially expand the size of a training data set by inputting multiple versions of images in the data set. For example, horizontally flipped and slanted images, images that are brightened, darkened or modified in other ways would constantly be incorporated into the memory storage. The data set would then be employed for deep-learning neural networks consisting of a series of algorithms modelled loosely on the human brain. Designed to learn things and recognize patterns, artificial neural networks can adapt to a changing library to make logical decisions on the basis of the existing output criteria. This way, knowledge is gathered through experience collecting rather than programming. A facial recognition system is an application of 'image data augmentation' capable of learning all facets of human faces. A ticketless parking management system is another – one such system promises to 'revolutionise your car parks into autopilot.'[2] In the same vein, the ImageDataGeneration class, a commonly used program, would have allowed Li to 'auto-generate' images by generalizing across the inserted images in the data set. It would have learned patterns and associations of the input data, processed the data, and then generated modified images or close facsimiles of the originals all on its own. And it would have been a valid work of contemporary art. Phrases such as 'a complete machine takeover of human labor' would have been part of the artist's statement. But Li did not do that.

Instead, he opted for coding. Li worked closely with software engineer Zhang Shiran to create a unique program based on algorithms using primarily a two-symbol system: 0, 1, 0, 1 and so on. This is called basic coding. The sketches – drawn originally by the artist himself – were then transformed by the program, which is a paradigm that treats computer programmes as mathematical functions. Different combinations of codes result in different images. Li set the codes and ran commands without knowing how the images would turn out looking; neither did the software engineer know how they would look. The work was determined partly by design, and partly by accident or chance. Some early experiments turned out brilliantly, but some were lacklustre. Adjustments – or more precisely, unknown modifications – were made by changing the codes in the settings. In the process of image-making, Li relied on the architecture of the program and his technical intuition about codes, but in the end it was the artist himself who made decisions about the composition of the work. The current collection of over fifty images is a result – as well as a process – of accidental coding; some of the images were made at the first try. The process of image-making remains a bit of a mystery to Li himself. The collection was only assembled after all the images had been produced and viewed by the artist.

Li's task was to make the final selection of those semi-random, semi-automated constructs, keeping within his vision of human-machine 'col-labor-ation'. He insists that compared with the former method that implies total dependence on Big Data and AI, this new method better reflects the concept of 'integration (or union) of human and machine' (*renji jiehe*) in contemporary life. Humans and machines will be inseparable halves in the future. We'd better get used to it.

The whole set of images is stored as a completely digital collection on the cloud. This implies that the artist can print out the images in the venues where he shows his work. All the images are scalable vector graphics, which means that the quality and the resolution of the printout images are not determined by the size of the paper. Unlike raster graphics, the other common type of graphic representation, the resolution of this vectorized collection will remain the same when printed, however large or small the paper. Not only does this add flexibility and mobility to the preparation for a physical exhibition, it is also an apt method of materialization for the artist's conceptual work.

Eye, body, and I-dentity in Li Zi-Fong's work

This body of work deals with the question of human identity and viscerality in the age of Big Data. When the details of our identity have been amassed, reproduced, calculated and analysed, does the gaze of the algorithm reveal, conceal or even blind us? How is the self seduced by the aura of their digitally reconfigured identity – the aura of the copy? Every IP address hosts a technologically enabled yet simultaneously confined soul that takes a gamble on the artwork's digital fate. Our senses are confronted with deconstructed and recomposed eyes, tongues, bones, faces and intellects when we come face to face with each of the artist's computer-generated images.

Li's opening gambit is to take the viewer on a journey to hang out with Cézanne's compatriots in Provence. *Two Cézannes* is adapted from the post-impressionist artist's *Card Players* (1893, Metropolitan Museum of Modern Art, New York). After the death of his father in 1886, Cézanne returned to his hometown of Aix-en-Provence and started painting the people and objects around him. Before this, he had painted in Paris for many years, but his works were rejected by the official Paris Salon every year from 1864 to 1869 and ridiculed by art critics in the French capital. Eventually, he reluctantly returned to Provence. He pondered the meaning of life in the image of two card players, revealed in a letter to a friend. Cézanne's melancholy is inexplicable. The scene, front and centre, is quiet, with the men looking down at their cards rather than at each other. We do not really know what is going on in the characters' minds, or what cards they hold. But it is the recognition of the strangeness of selfhood in Cézanne's work that proved to be prophetic for Li's modern vision. Li believes that Cézanne hoped to reflect upon his own life through making this painting. He adapted this work because he wanted Cézanne's consciousness to enter into the algorithmic equation, to reflect on Cézanne's own reflections about identity and fate. Two card-playing farmhands become two Cézannes in Li's work. One is the Cézanne of Paris, and the other the Cézanne of Aix. One life gambles on/with his other life. The only image in the series in colour, this work sets the tone for Li's collection, where the question of identity has expanded from consciousness of one's class and place of origin to that of authenticity and avatars. I wonder whether Li secretly identifies with Cézanne's talent and fate (Figure 7.1).

The image *The Copy* was inspired by the fiction film *Searching* (Chaganty 2018), in which a Silicon Valley engineer named David Kim searches for his missing daughter in all realms of digital reality. All the virtual traces bear testament to her existence in another parallel universe. But where is she?

Judging from today's advancements in science and technology, we will perhaps have our own copies one day. This copy will learn – through analysis of Big Data and machine learning – more about you than you know yourself. Moreover, it will remind the self when to do things as it will screen selves for mood, temperature, blood pressure and other biological details. To some extent, the copy is alive with us, and *in* us as it has come to manipulate, imprison and reproduce the self. Biological monitoring devices are being used globally at this time for (human) cases of coronavirus during the pandemic. At the beginning, 'cases' of the virus were isolated, masked and locked down while the biological details of the human hosts came under mass electronic surveillance. Soon

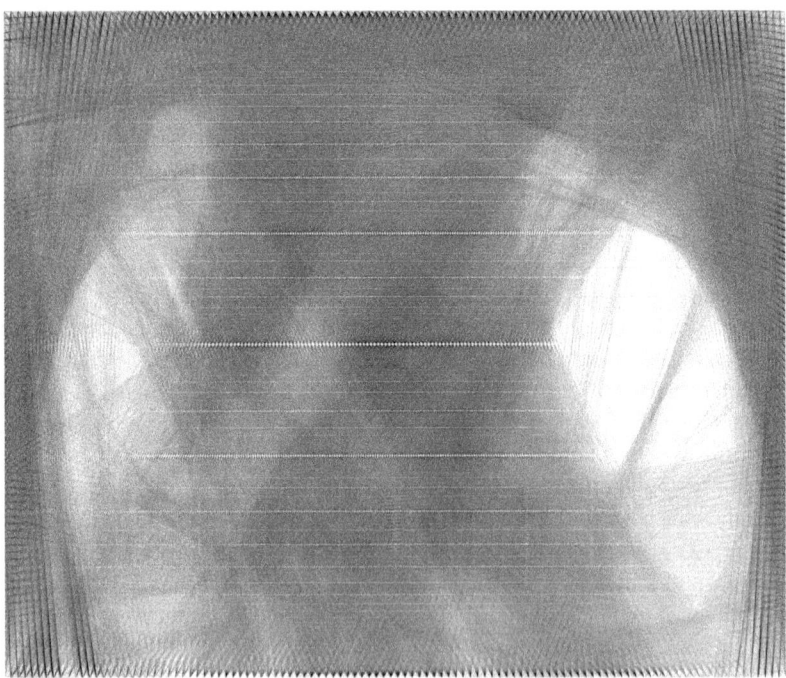

Figure 7.1 *Two Cézanne's*, 2019, digital output, variable sizes. Courtesy of artist Li Zi-Fong.

enough, lockdowns and the contact tracing were imposed everywhere, regardless of health status. Under these circumstances, the self often knows less about itself than does the copy. In connection with this, in Li's artwork *The Copy*, two physically identical faces are set next to each other, reminding people of the multiplicity of the self's identity. The two faces in this image, identical as they are by design, could appear dissimilar depending on the light level and the position of the viewer in relation to the faces. Thus, sometimes 'the copy' could look brighter and more animated than 'the original' (Figure 7.2).

Digital Foundation Makeup discusses a similar topic. Applying make-up can be seen as a process of identity transformation. For hours every day, we hold our smart devices up to illuminate our faces, leading to endless retouching and filtering of ourselves on different apps. In such a digital ambience, we are predisposed to forget our selves, which are continually hiding behind a virtual reality.

Moving beyond the double and 'face value', the next work by Li, *Disembody*, is concerned with the relationship between sign and corpo-reality. Every word in the human language carries some kind of bearing, and the signifier comes with a 'ring flash' reminiscent of what Walter Benjamin calls an *aura*.[3] For instance, when we praise the 'goodness' of something, we subconsciously accept the information emanating from the word. The word in question also represents a mass of information and aura. For instance, when we praise the 'goodness' of something, we subconsciously accept the information emanating from the word. The word in question also represents a departure from the word itself as a pure signifier, as it carries a mass of information and aura. It is in this process that identity undergoes

Figure 7.2 *The Copy*, 2019, digital output, variable sizes. Courtesy of artist Li Zi-Fong.

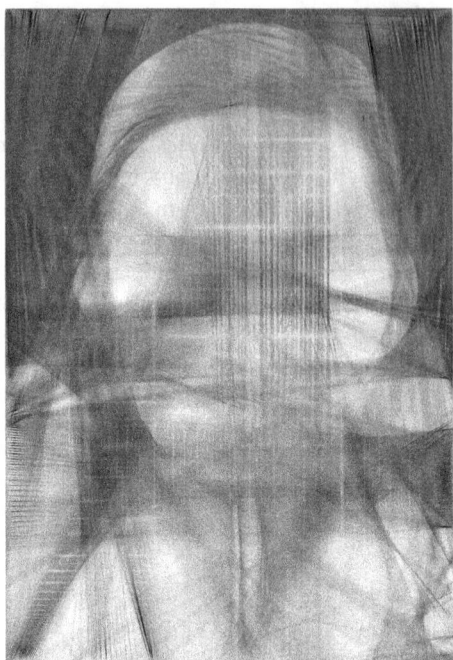

Figure 7.3 *Digital Foundation Makeup*, 2019, digital output, variable sizes. Courtesy of artist Li Zi-Fong.

transformation. In the contemporary context of a fragile, or even broken, supply chain, the artist performs an (artistic) cut-up of the Chinese character 肉 – an ideogram meaning 'meat' or 'flesh' that was developed from the pictogram for 'cut meat' – using algorithms and vectors in an attempt to see and feel whether it penetrates its pre-existing aura (Figure 7.4).

Here, an intriguing vision of the shared future for humankind – if it will indeed be shared, and if it will actually have a future – illustrates Li's gallows humour. The narrative of Li's *Salamander-Merfolk* goes like this: Salamanders are mostly hermaphrodites. They usually reproduce when females clone themselves through parthenogenesis. The creatures value genetic components in sperm and select certain elements of the genetic make-up to recompose and reproduce themselves. Sometimes they steal sperm from near relatives, ensuring that 90 per cent are their own and 10 per cent are from another member of the species, to increase their own genetic diversity. Today's humans choose their preferred donor's sperm based on the written descriptions of donors' traits stored in the banking facility. Some even want to edit their own genes, much like the salamander family, who appeared on earth around the same time as *Homo sapiens*, more than 75 million years ago. In Li's *Salamander-Merfolk*, two salamanders are swimming towards a high place, as if they were swimming past concrete steps built

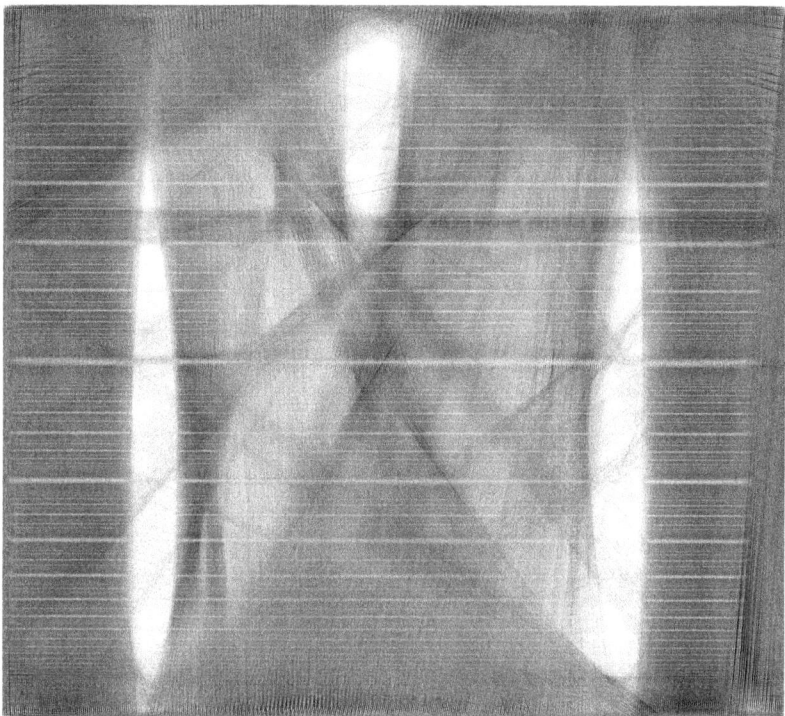

Figure 7.4 *Disembody*, 2019, digital output, variable sizes. Courtesy of artist Li Zi-Fong.

by now-extinct humans in an imaginary future. Yet the future world imagined by the artist is the earth back in the Cretaceous period (Figure 7.5).

Merleau-Ponty's existentialism is in stark contrast to Descartes's rationalism, famously exemplified by the concept of the *cogito* (*Cogito, ergo sum*). Descartes insists that everything in the world can be explained by mathematics. Therefore, when putting on Cartesian headgear, anyone can appear to be a sage, taking on a different identity and a new perspective for observing his or her world. The human is then equipped to reconstruct the real from the vantage point of a detached knowledge system (Figure 7.6).

Extending the primal-futuristic allegory, Li's work *The Four Quadrants of an Elephant* sees four people positioned at four different parts of an elephant's body. The four people each occupy a quarter of the image, illustrated by four blindfolded heads and upper bodies. Each person tells their own version of 'Truman's World' through a small window, like blind men touching an elephant. Now, the algorithm tells us that what our eyes can see is not sufficient to verify the existence of things. Welcome to the era of VUCA (volatility, uncertainty, complexity and ambiguity). Is it time for your eyes to evolve?

Humans evolved from apes, yet the mythical Monkey King, Sun Wukong – from the sixteenth-century Chinese classic *Journey to the West* – is a character who wants to

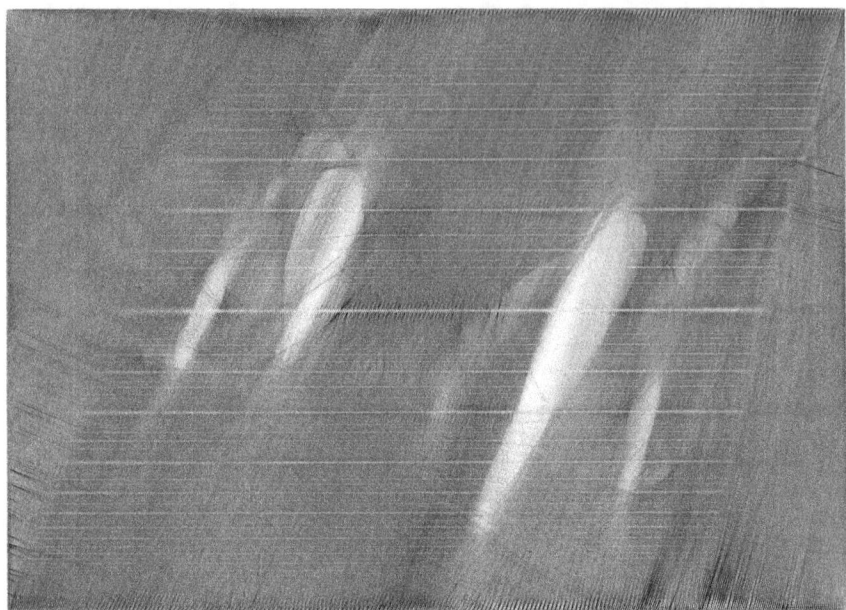

Figure 7.5 *Salamander-Merfolk*, 2019, digital output, variable sizes. Courtesy of artist Li Zi-Fong.

break free from all human bonds and the normative expectation of self-restraint. Li's image *Sun Wukong in the Matrix* could be read as depicting an ape wanting to be and evolving into a human, or a creature that is a cross between a human and a monkey refusing to be fully human. Two conflicting identifications overlap in one time and space. It is an image of the human psyche in our digital age, pulled at once towards greed and fear (Figures 7.7–7.8).

Envisioning tactical fluidity and undoing machinic assemblages

A stark and striking image: *Your Left Eye Is My Right Eye* sets up a face-to-face mirror image with the viewer. When one looks directly at the image, one's left eye meets her right eye. This work is intended to direct the viewer's attention to the right eye in the work. However, the supposed right eye is hidden in the data matrix. Even though you cannot see it, it is staring at you. This work inspects the vision of people today, hinting at a technologically impaired view. But what could this all-seeing face be? Siri on your iPhone? The Chinese state government? In October 2019, an image released by the luxury jeweller Tiffany as part of an advertising campaign was accused of supporting the anti-government protests in Hong Kong, while another face with an injured right eye became a symbol of the protests. Amidst the tumult and clamour of the protesting crowds that thronged the streets, an Indonesian journalist was shot in

Assemblage line and tactical fluidity 127

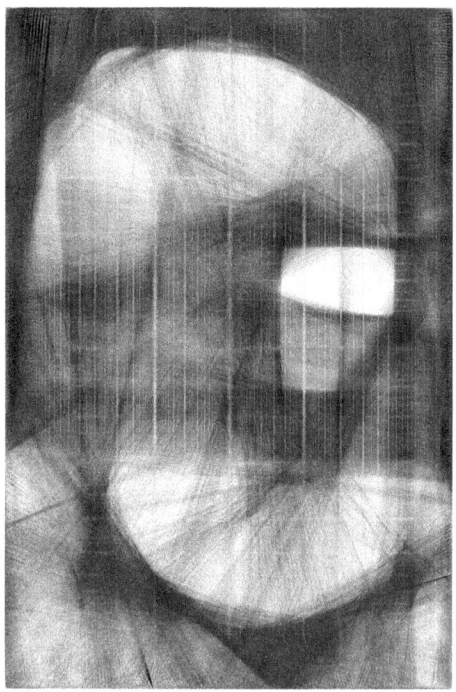

Figure 7.6 *The Cartesian Headgear*, 2019, digital output, variable sizes. Courtesy of artist Li Zi-Fong.

the eye in a shower of rubber bullets and tear gas fired by the police. Raw footage of the incident in which blood streamed down from her right eye was instantly circulating on various social media platforms, generating a wave of madness and delirium in a sequence of live-streams. The viral video spawned numerous hashtags, for instance, #Eye4HK and #EyeforHK. Contributors uploaded their own memes where they used their hand to cover their right eye as a gesture of solidarity. This episode forged a new sense of 'eye'(I)-dentity of the city's ongoing pro-democracy protests, in which the gaze of surveillance was inverted and subverted online and offline. A cinematic montage jolted the demonstrating crowd into action. The movement-image gave rise to 'a seeing function' (Deleuze 1989: 19) that could 'replace, obliterate and re-create the object itself' (12). Protesters quickly identified with visual impairment as the news spread. An overwhelming number of protesters who were always conscious of the omnipresent surveillance system – increasingly pervasive in the form of the so-called Great Canon[4] and the Great Wall of China[5] – started wearing face masks, goggles and carrying umbrellas. Not just for self-protection from police violence, but more important, for identity concealment and crowd identification. As the masked crowd identity gathered momentum on social media, more people felt empowered to show up in their immediate vicinity and other unexpected locations. Umbrellas, the symbol of the previous pro-democracy movement in 2014, were used to block surveillance cameras when exiting metro stations. They were opened when conversations about

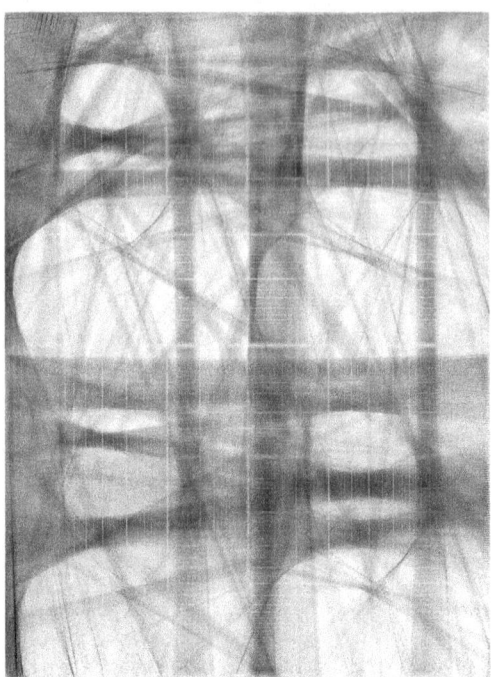

Figure 7.7 *The Four Quadrants of an Elephant*, 2019, digital output, variable sizes. Courtesy of artist Li Zi-Fong.

their next moves were being had. Wearing masks and carrying umbrellas in a crowd gave them a feeling of security and empowerment that the two items became their daily accessories.

In another concerted effort to deter police, #stargazing organized members of multiple self-labelled astronomical societies to gather in front of police headquarters and other public sites for lessons on how to use a laser pointer to locate a star. With thousands of lasers all beaming simultaneously, the protesters spotted no stars but formed their own constellations to startle police officers, scramble surveillance cameras and prevent themselves from being photographed. What was emitted on top of the mesmerizing laser show was the crowd's magnetic radiation in the field of energy. They were each other's protective shield and offensive weapon in the movement. When asked if they were concerned about their activism, the youth shrugged, 'There's so many of us. There's hundreds of thousands of us in the streets'[6] (Figure 7.9).

The protesters switched channels as the masked appearance of the crowd took off. They began migrating en masse from Facebook and associated social media accounts to platforms that operate end-to-end encryption, or to Bluetooth-enabled apps that require no internet connection. The internet-enabled app Telegram, for example, delivers cloud-based chats and messages of any size to up to 200,000 'followers' at once. Messages can be programmed to self-destruct after a set amount of time, making the activists' digital footprints hard to track. Since the protests intensified over the summer

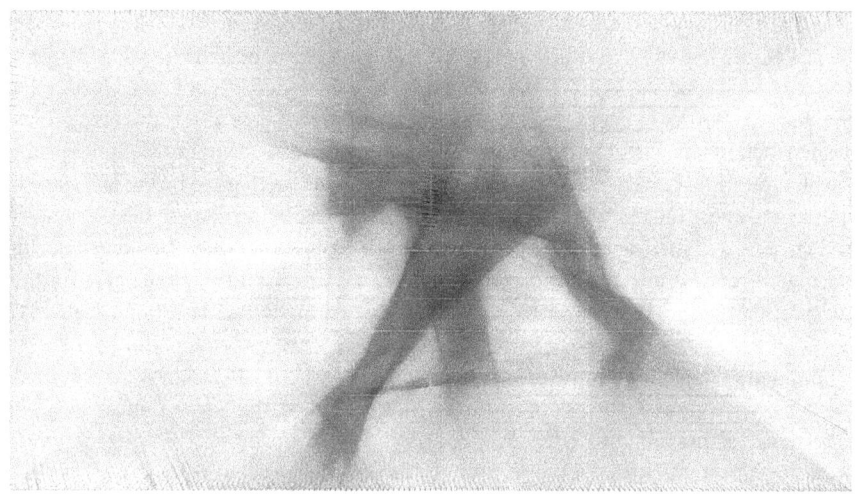

Figure 7.8 *Sun Wukong in the Matrix*, 2019, digital output, variable sizes. Courtesy of artist Li Zi-Fong.

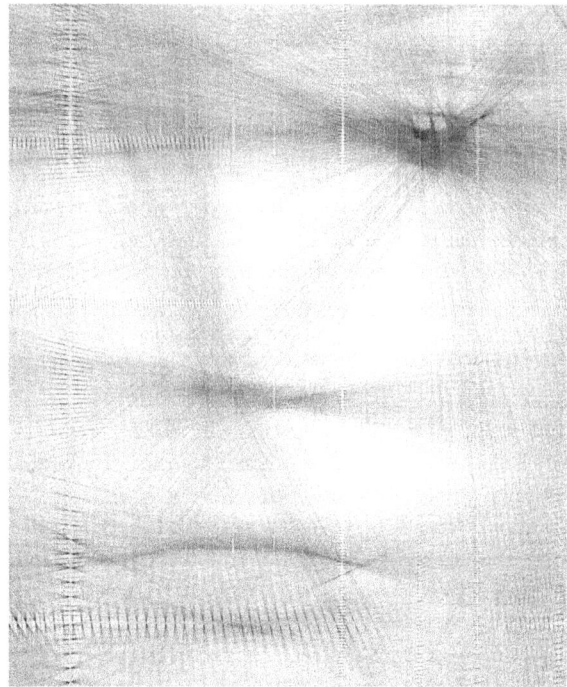

Figure 7.9 *Your Left Eye Is My Right Eye*, 2019, digital output, variable sizes. Courtesy of artist Li Zi-Fong.

of 2019, multiple alter egos have been adopted and then deleted to evade persistent surveillance. New communication methods and tactics have been devised and updated to circumvent censorship. Communications have been coded, decoded and recoded to enable more bodies to speak. Writing about the process of describing and formalizing human behaviour into words, writing and code for it to be reproduced, Bernard Stiegler identifies our time as characterized by digital technology to be the last stage of 'grammatization' (2011), whereby human capabilities are being displaced, externalized and stored in digital devices. Hong Kong's youth have shown that, by incorporating the digital sensibilities into their everyday activism, this need not be the case. In this environment of heightened surveillance and censorship, human bodies have adapted to and at times transcended the grammar of artificial intelligence and virality.

In their struggle for democratic rights, Hong Kong activists have 'eye'(I)-dentified their 'hands and feet' (*shouzu* in standard Mandarin and *sauzuk* in Cantonese) – as they refer to their fellow protesters – particularly since the eye-blinding moment under Beijing's watchful eye. Even though the use of *shouzu* to refer to one's sibling can be traced back to the mid-eighth century Tang dynasty, it was never used in daily conversations until the recent Hong Kong protests. One young activist said, 'we are called *shouzu*, to mean that other members are our *hands and feet*. We're intimately connected.'[7] Fellow participants of the movement may be strangers or unrecognizable faces behind their masks and umbrellas, but they felt and moved as one body. Their gesture of solidarity extended to on-site journalists. The blinded journalist was reporting and, in a way, 'transporting' the scene to other corners of the world while on the run. Images of 'that eye' quickly proliferated as the real eye was lost. Protesters' bodies mimed the memes. One for the (face)books, the injured eye of Hong Kong subverted power's visibility, re-assembled the residents' identity and recovered their somatic memory in a mass movement. Memes mined bodies in their desire for reproduction, for hosting their built-in desire. Bodies, abreast of the digital Canon and Firewall, mimed memes to manifest the latest stage of things in the offline world. They transmitted embodied communications and coded their bodily expressions. *Bodies were virtually their own social media*, mediating communication between the online and the offline. Rather than 'informational genes' (Griesemer 2005), memes have animated surveilled bodies, reawakening the body's potential for innovative communications.

The 'eye-for-an-eye' demonstration moved swiftly from cyberspace to every street corner, from the streets to hospitals, and eventually to the international airport. This tactical fluidity, known as 'be water', has been a guiding philosophy, inspired by Hong Kong's own action hero, Bruce Lee. No longer fixated on the occupation of landmarks, the demonstrators devised a highly fluid style of mobilization and dispersion to counter the police force, physically and digitally. This 'collective assemblage of enunciation' that sought to disconnect itself from the machinic surveillance assemblage was the demonstrators' way of impairing the all-seeing state government, of 'de-territorializing' the power of a state (Deleuze and Guattari 1987: 88) equipped with the location of every IP address. Surveillance assemblages that consist of 'tools' form part of what Deleuze and Guattari call a 'social machine', characterized by its 'amalgamations' rather than by its 'tools' (90).

'Water can flow or it can crash. Be water, my friend' (Longstreet [Television series] 1971), as Hong Kong action hero Bruce Lee explained his style of martial art. Yet in a city highly reliant on digital connection, technology has from the start been embedded in the battlefield where the ebb and flow of communications can propel or block movement. If to 'be water' means fluidity, fluency and fast movement, it entails cultivating ever-evolving daily techniques online and offline, as part of a forward-looking community that always needs to think one step ahead. Requiring great linguistic, spatial and corporal dexterity in the use of smartphone apps and social networks, these everyday 'skills' are what I call *jianghu* practices (Lo 2018). *Jianghu* practices are cynical in essence, that is, they outwardly mimic normative signs while quietly subverting dominant codes in practice. In response to growing restrictions online, Hong Kong activists have improvised and adjusted their tactics to be camouflaged into the digital flows of the movement. Digital surveillance and censorship such as facial recognition and the removal of online discussion have vastly transformed the aesthetics and communications of resistance movements across diverse sectors of Hong Kong society; this shift has prompted Hong Kong youth to bodily 'code' mundane activities such as reading, writing, speaking and listening in order to facilitate a deeper level of communication.

Even as their protest slogans such as 'Liberate Hong Kong, Revolution of Our Times' were banned by the newly implemented national security law, passed on 30 June 2020 to further tighten the censorship regime, protesters came out and raised blank sheets of paper with no words written on them, after someone was photographed doing it and uploaded to social media. The act had been inspired by a Soviet joke in which a protester called Rabinovich was found by a KGB agent distributing pamphlets in Red Square. The agent arrested him immediately, only to find that the pamphlets were just blank paper. The agent then said to him, 'You think I don't know what you would write?' That might have been the case of Rabinovich, where the unspeakable was publicly contextualized in a wordless and speechless act. Yet in Hong Kong, behind every sheet of paper was an IP address subject to monitoring. Police were conscious of the activists conscious of their own acts. And so were the activists of police's actions. Deletion of online profiles and posts by the activists facilitated remembrances of the body on the move, whose digital footprints were incorporated into consciousness.

Building on my doctoral dissertation (Lo 2018) about contemporary Chinese *jianghu* in Beijing and the widespread cynicism that accompanies this originally Daoist concept, my project attempts to think through the philosophy of 'be water' by analysing a variety of communication strategies and mobilization tactics adopted by the protesters. Literally translated as 'rivers and lakes', *jianghu* was originally coined by the fourth-century BCE philosopher Zhuangzi to refer to the space of nature away from court politics and officialdom. Commonly understood as a collective fantasy world comprising disenfranchised or marginalized groups across a wide range of social spheres, the idea and image of *jianghu* spread stealthily across the Chinese-speaking world. Long famous for films in the crime and martial arts genres (sometimes known as *wuxia* [knight-errant] films), Hong Kong has – after a number of mass demonstrations against encroachment on residents' political rights by the People's Republic of China – become a city of *jianghu*, where dissident subtexts slide under the official radar.

Jianghu's process of deterritorialization requires constant navigation and negotiation between normativity and alterity, between palpability and obscurity in various domains of reality (Lo 2018). Operating in this world requires an astute reading of the powerful, an ability to roam in and out of the zone of state power by means of mimesis, taking on the responsibility of protecting this world's invisible yet changing boundaries, and demonstrating *yiqi*, or the spirit of righteousness. By engaging in surreptitious activities, the simulators of *jianghu* train these actors to simulate the mindset of the authority. Their ability to organize themselves while simultaneously conforming to disorder and averting the gaze of the authority is a demonstration of perspicacity acquired from the subordinate position. The Hong Kong demonstrators sought to disconnect the 'weapons and tools assuring a symbiosis of bodies – a whole machinic assemblage' (Deleuze and Guattari 1987: 89) – from the 'collective assemblage of enunciation' in the protesters' performance and acts of resistance against the normative regime of signs. Expression continued to find its contents and mould into them, as the protesters carried on their line of flight, which 'carrie[d] away all of the assemblages but also under[went] all kinds of reterritorializations and redundancies' (89).

The discursive practices of *jianghu* that comprise its *habitus*, to use Pierre Bourdieu's term, are reminiscent of what Michel de Certeau calls 'an art of the weak' (1984: 37), of anthropologist James C. Scott's 'hidden transcript' (1990), and of Michael Taussig's concept of mimesis as 'the nature that culture uses to create a now-beleaguered second nature' (1993: xv). The mimetic faculty in the case of Hong Kong is built on the performance of conforming to (dis)order. Implicit in these concepts is the ability to mobilize an astute reading of the powerful, and thereby reorient the gaze of the authority. From the *jianghu* perspective, power's every visibility lends itself to the promise of stability and transparency, which allows little space for deception and trickery. *Jianghu* practices are, therefore, kynical – to borrow Žižek's term (1989: 29) – and 'in-habited'. Indeed, it is the necessity to navigate quotidian life under a regime of surveillance and censorship that produces insights and drives the wealth of creative collective assemblages of enunciation.

Despite its association with covert operations, *jianghu* can be insidious and pervasive, extending into mainstream society. To flow like water on the ground requires coded but crowd-sourced information, such as the recently removed HKmap.live app for tracking the movements of police and protesters alike, the Bluetooth-enabled Airdrop and Bridgefy for anonymously distributing information while circumventing digital surveillance, and sign language for swift and direct communication in precarious situations. Nevertheless, the playbook needs to be quickly rewritten when a code has been cracked.

Guattari envisioned in the 1980s a 'post-media era [. . .] facilitated by a concerted reappropriation of communicational and information technology' (2009: 299). He had in mind the Free Radio movements in Italy and France where popular use of low-cost and low-tech radio would constitute 'an auto-referential feedback loops between rhizomatic thoughts and media subversion' (Goddard 2011: 10) to counter the top-down mass-media power. He had hoped, via Radio Alice, a different kind of machine for the production of new sensibilities and social identities would free the minds of the listeners in preparation for political reterritorialization. This organic postmedia ecology would generate a collective assemblage of enunciation in a process of 'transversal connections' (240) and 'subjective autonomization' (300) between emergent subjectivities, thus redirecting, if not reversing, the omnipresent capitalist flows. There was a moment in the early 2010s when that era might have seemed upon us, when the Arab Spring and the Occupy movement were sweeping through many regions of the world via social media. Hongkongers occupied their CBD for seventy-nine days in 2014 as the global Occupy relay drew to a close. As the decade unfolded, surveillance technologies and censorship mechanisms managed to scale back grassroots attempts at deterritorialization. New strategies and tactics had to be mapped out.

While the artist's work of straight lines portrays conditions of our multifaceted contemporary life and its production process delineates mystifying human-machine collaboration, it was Hong Kong's demonstrating crowd who spotted openings in the otherwise untraversable enclosures. They formed themselves to 'be water' in opposition to the tightening grip of the state government. 'Lines' and 'water' constitute enigmatic puzzles prompting us to question whether humans can be resensitized by the very technological forces that lulled us into submission. They both point to micropolitical outlets that effect 'molecular transformations' (Guattari 2009: 178) 'in the direction of dis-alienation, of a liberation of expression . . . from oppressive social stratifications' (55). The eye-catching case of Hong Kong shows that interstices in the diverse assemblages, if they can still be found or even created, will offer us cues for escaping an enclosed order.

References

Benjamin, W. (1986), 'The Work of Art in the Age of Mechanical Reproduction', in H. Arendt (ed.) and H. Zohn (trans.), *Illuminations: Essays and Reflections*, 217–52, New York: Shocken Books.
Certeau, M. de (1984), *The Practice of Everyday Life*, trans. S. F. Rendall, Berkeley: University of California Press.
Deleuze, G. (1989), *Cinema 2: The Time-Image*, trans. H. Tomlinson and R. Galeta. Minneapolis: University of Minnesota Press.
Deleuze, G. and F. Guattari (1987), *A Thousand Plateaus: Capitalism and Schizophrenia*, trans. B. Massumi, Minneapolis: University of Minnesota Press.
Goddard, M. (2011), 'Towards an Archaeology of Media Ecologies: "Media Ecology", Political Subjectivation and Free Radios', *The Fibreculture Journal*, 17: 6–17.
Griesemer, J. R. (2005), 'The Informational Gene and the Substantial Body: On the Generalization of Evolutionary Theory by Abstraction', in M. R. Jones and N. Cartwright (eds), *Idealization XII: Correcting the Model. Idealization and Abstraction in the Sciences*, 59–115, Amsterdam: Rodopi Publishers.
Guattari, F. (2009), *Soft Subversions*, ed. S. Lotringer, trans. D. L. Sweet and C. Wiener, Los Angeles: Semiotext(e).
Lo, H. S. (2018), 'Crossing Rivers and Lakes: The Art of Everyday Life in Contemporary China', PhD diss., Columbia University, New York.
Longstreet (1971), [Television series], Prod. Stirling Silliphant and Joel Rogosin, USA: CBS Television Distribution.

NASA. (2017), 'Big Questions: Superstrings', *National Aeronautics and Space Administration* [n.d.]. Available online: https://imagine.gsfc.nasa.gov/science/questions/superstring.html (accessed 14 September 2020).

Scott, J. C. (1990), *Domination and the Arts of Resistance: Hidden Transcripts*, New Haven, CT: Yale University Press.

Searching (2018), [Film] Dir. Aneesh Chaganty, USA: Sony Pictures Releasing.

Stiegler, B. (2011), *The Decadence of Industrial Democracy*, trans. D. Ross, Malden, MA: Polity Press.

Taussig, M. T. (1993), *Mimesis and Alterity: A Particular History of the Senses*, New York: Routledge.

The World Staff. (2019), 'Hong Kong Protesters Challenge Surveillance with Apps and Umbrellas', *The World*, 14 August. Available online: https://www.pri.org/stories/2019-08-14/hong-kong-protesters-challenge-surveillance-apps-and-umbrellas (accessed 1 October 2020).

Žižek, S. (1989), *The Sublime Object of Ideology*, London: Verso.

8

Cartographies of the gaze of the other/other gazes

Youth, slums, and audiovisual production in the postmedia age

Silvia Grinberg and Julieta Armella

Does the other have a specific gaze? What is that other gaze like when the always-other subject is the one who looks and narrates? The question of the other is nothing new. We can trace it and its multiple tensions in the different ways the other, so often rendered 'barbarian', has been narrated throughout history. If the menacing barbarian once lurked on the outside, its image is increasingly pixellated on the network of networks and flows that only the Covid-19 pandemic has managed to slow down. In nineteenth-century literature and in postcolonial Latin America specifically – in this case in Argentina – the barbarian referred to the Indigenous, but mostly the *mestiza*, population halfway between the so called savage and the civilized that threatened incipient cities (Sarmiento 2009). That population was the target of the multiple civilizing devices at play in the nineteenth-century logic of whitening (Castro-Gómez 2010; Grinberg 2020).

Rather than that past image of the menacing other lurking outside, those multiple outsides are, in present-day times and spaces, inside in a sort of Möbius strip. With increasingly blurry borders, those urban peripheries are now a nodal part of metropolizes. It is not unlike the flows of the postmedia age where networks fold back in on themselves at an ever-quicker pace. In the midst of these tensions, we pose the question of the other's gaze from the specific angle of the act of looking and narrating, in this case of the non-numeric minorities who inhabit the slums of the Global South. The research we will discuss here deals with young people who live in those slums. We will look to audiovisual productions, posts on the social networks, and conversations we have had with them as part of fieldwork that began in classrooms but extended down the streets of the neighbourhood and the mazes of the social networks.

Postmedia society has accelerated the dynamics of looking and being looked at, of publishing and consuming information (Baudrillard 2000; Berardi 2007, 2017) to such an extent that images, opinions, and points of view are banalized or not even perceived at all (Crary 2008). The other and otherness are washed away in bytes that vanish as soon as they appear. Everything can be shown, processed and laid out on so many reels.

Interestingly, the word *bárbaro* in Spanish refers not only to the barbarian and barbaric – its literal translation – but also, colloquially, to something marvelous, remarkable and cool. In the postmedia age, both uses come together: the other, the barbarian, becomes exotic and object of respect as well as of pity and solidarity campaigns. The barbarian, then, becomes *bárbaro*, though always narrated by others. The exotic makes the news. In fact, in the postmedia age, existence itself depends on standing out. Showing oneself to be remarkable is the only way to be in the 'you-can-do-it' world. There no longer seems to be separation, emptiness or absence. If, as Baudrillard (2000) affirmed, 'One enters one's life while walking onto a screen. One puts on one's own life like a digital suit' (204), in our contemporary era the networks have completely done away with the limits between inside and outside. Difference is washed away in a sea of sameness. We live in a time of the exploded normal (Grinberg 2008), of new normals that seem to have become the norm of our present time, even though we can hardly tell what those new normals bring.

The image of pac-man, the antechamber of the current era, is telling. On the one hand, the pac-man devours everything he comes upon; on the other, ghosts keep cropping up and, as long as they can keep from being devoured, advance. Pac-man reminds us of the possibility and impossibility of difference. Though novelty is quickly absorbed, its appearance is still radical, contingent and dogged.

The question of the contingency of the other, or of the becoming other, the question of the other gaze and its flights is uniquely central in the postmedia age. In the exotic narratives of the late 19th-century explorer, the always others appeared on the scene only to be looked at/narrated. But in the present, they are no longer (only) narrated, but also the ones who narrate; they are no longer the object of the gaze, but (also) the ones who look. That looking takes place, of course, in the tensions of this age, an era – as Guattari (2013) points out – that fluctuates between infantilization, indifference and generalized equivalence, on the one hand and, on the other, the possibility of singularity, of flavouring acts performed and phrases uttered in the most ordinary situations. And it is at that point, we propose here, that the possibility of embracing otherness without reservation appears.

This is where we situate a cartography of other gazes based on the audiovisual work produced over the course of ten years by young people who live in the urban slums of the Buenos Aires Metropolitan Area. 'I knew how to make them say what I wanted,' explains a 23-year-old woman who, as a teenager, started filming in high school. In that assertion lies a very particular sort of gaze, (an)other gaze, which we will attempt to problematize in this chapter. Who is 'the other' when the narrator herself is the one usually positioned as the other? She is a word, a gaze, and a display that emerges in an interview, but also from lived experience, from the possibility of narrating experience: the other through the other.

The schizoanalytic-cartography framework as means to a means is particularly powerful here. As Radman (2018b) points out, based on Guattari, 'If representation is a means to an end (to classify), schizoanalytic cartography is a means to a means (to intervene)' (119). That idea of a means in itself, of intervention, implies a particular problematization in the postmedia era. The problem is no longer how to appear in the scene, in a means to an end. Appearing is, rather, inevitable, a non-negotiable. Maybe, like pac-man, all we can do is keep at it, intervene, move on, persist *just because*, play every number.

Schizoanalysis (Guattari 2013; Buchanan 2002; Buchanan and Collins 2014; Buchanan, Matts and Tynan 2015) offers us a diagonal on which to situate this debate beyond dichotomies and antinomies (Bradley 2019; Kinsey 2013). We dwell on the becoming of the other gaze, on that which takes place when the always-other subject is the one looking, narrating, speaking, intervening. A gaze that does not represent or pursue an end, a purpose beyond the narration itself. A gaze that says what it has to say for the sake of saying it; it intervenes because it can, because nobody knows what a body is capable of.

In this chapter, we argue that otherness is found in ordinary situations and in story-telling where the other speaks as one who knows herself to be the other. At stake is becoming the other of the others, when the always other appears on the scene to speak, to look, to intervene – because, as we will discuss later, there is nothing at stake in that act of telling, or looking, or speaking other than that act in and of itself. Code says, as we will see below, 'I said what I had to say'. If, as Guattari (1986) argues, subjectivity is the problem of any political system in contemporary societies, we propose a schizo-cartography to grapple with what is singular in the act of looking, an image-thought that can delineate something like a radicalization of the other gaze in the postmedia age.

Becoming other in the postmedia age: A series analytics

Two axes run through this text and a diagonal line that cuts across them poses a question to which we propose a possible answer. First, the tensions of the postmedia age where homogenization and difference converge. Second, the schizo-cartography whose diagonal line interrogates the possibility of the other, of singularities and the eruption of statements that dislocate the known and interrupt the series. As Guattari and Rolnik point out (2013), in the postmedia age we must perform the exercise of identifying 'processes of singularization,' that is, processes that frustrate the internalization of capitalism's values and mechanisms, something that might lead to a specific register that circulates beyond the scale of values that distribute us in networks of equivalence. If, in the logic of capital, technology networks operate as 'decoded and deterritorialized flows [that is] precisely because the subjective essence of production is revealed in capitalism; precisely because the limit becomes internal to capitalism, which continually reproduces it, and also continually occupies it as an internalized and displaced limit' (Deleuze and Guattari 2000: 337). It is also precisely because – or perhaps why – 'there are no desiring-machines that exist outside the social machines that they form on a large scale; and no social machines without the desiring-machines that inhabit them on a small scale' (340). That place, that breaking point, that delicate focal point is exactly where to deploy schizoanalysis and its drive to disperse, to effect schizoization, to meddle in the strokes, in the lines of the singular as diagonals that open up between and in desiring-machines. In this framework, let us look to that other image of the barbarian, the Greek term for the nomadic tribes in northern Europe at the outskirts of the Roman Empire. It was the word used to refer to foreigners who spoke neither Greek nor Latin – their language sounded like unintelligible babble. Its literal translation is 'the one who babbles'. That babbling other cuts through the other gaze, the gaze of the one who looks and the one who is looked at. There is, however, someplace else for that babbling, a place well removed from correct ideas that suit the known (Marks 2000), a place that takes us, as Deleuze would say, to productive ideas that stutter, that muddle their responses, that babble. A becoming babbling that takes place in the act itself, in moving itself, in meddling in the network, a slippery becoming in that keeping being, insisting on the singularity of one who knows herself to be the other. That singularity knows that she plays her number in the game that is intervention itself: like a meme, the game produces, intervenes and gets on its way. In that babbling speech, we propose an analytic series in three layers based on the productions, interventions and reflections of these young people.

Layer 0. The always-other

The following fragment is taken from one of the many news shows in the mass media on Buenos Aires slum-dwellers. This one ties the local population and the landfill where the solid waste from the Buenos Aires Metropolitan Area ends up. For over two decades, locals have gone through the trash on a daily basis to gather food and/or things to sell. The fact that, during the long months of lockdown, these families have not been able to enter the landfill has only complicated their daily lives. What is striking about this video is that here, like in so many other videos that circulate on the web and in news portals, we see the simple yet devastating ways the gaze of the one sees the always other. A journalist interviews women in the middle of the landfill where, between stigma and pity, he confirms something that he himself and the viewer already know: the place of the other in the public scene. But evidently that is not enough. Over the course of the interview, the journalist manages to get these women to feel even more uncomfortable than we do – is that even possible? – when we watch the video:

> Journalist: How long have you been rummaging for garbage at the CEAMSE[1]?
> Woman 2: Since it opened.
> J: How far along are you?
> W3: Five months.
> J: How long have you lived in this neighbourhood?
> W3: I was born here . . .
> W2: I've been feeding my children with what I find here for about ten years. We find yogurt, milk, meat . . .
>> Children as young as six also go to the CEAMSE to rummage with their moms.

The gaze of the other/other gazes 139

> Q: What is it like for you to go to such a dirty and dangerous place rife with animal diseases with a child in your belly?
> W3: I'm used to it. . . . I got a urinary tract infection and was admitted to the hospital. When I got out, I came back here because there is no choice.
> W: 1 Sometimes they cover up the best stuff, and we have to make deals with the authorities . . . to get better things.
> J: And you take it home and eat it?
> W3: Yes . . . if I find any food . . .
> J: That is the food your baby is also eating.
> W3: You get used to the smell, to the dead animals, to the maggots . . . anything.[2]

What's it like for you to go to such a dirty and dangerous place rife with animal diseases with a child in your belly? And, of course, the answer is, *I'm used to it.* The moral and moralizing question does what it set out to, and going to the landfill becomes normal. The interviewer dwells on the idea of getting used to the smell, the disease, the maggots. If a line of singularities opens up in this register, it finds a great many communicating vessels that connect it with the image of that barbarian other, that other that is unknown – doggedly unknown, we could say, as no effort is made to know her. What the interviewer finds is exactly what he set out to: a so-known combination of shame and terror. There is no conversation here: two voices resonate, each in its own soliloquy. The women look at him and answer, but they also babble. There is nothing new in this journalistic scene; the impassivity with which the interrogatory and aggressive questions are asked shapes the gaze of the other, where the narrative is suspended between the savage, the unseemly and compassion.

Perhaps that is why young people, camera in hand, began to film, and ask their own questions about going to the landfill (Grinberg 2010). What matters here is less the content filmed than the narrative of the act of filming rendered thought/image:

> I wanted to do everything I could to hear from someone else what I wanted to hear . . . so by asking, by getting information from them, I ended up getting what I was after, the kind of information I wanted. (Interview with Nair 2019)

That is how Nair describes what she was doing with the camera. In both accounts, the journalist's and Nair's, the other appears in the narrative in a particular way. But something else resonates in Nair's words; the angle is skewed. She knows how she is seen, which is why she wants to get information. Her gaze becomes a self who asks, inquires, looks. And regarding that, Nair says, 'I think I liked feeling important behind the camera.' Feeling important, no longer that other who is spoken of, rendered victim or culprit of her place in the world, to become instead the one who narrates, who gets the information she wants. Nair is talking about the following section of the video she and her classmates filmed:

> My family goes to the landfill. Thanks to that place, they have something to eat. 'Because when they don't have anything to eat, they'll go there . . .' says a voice off-camera before asking, 'And do you think that's bad? Why is it bad?' At that point,

the images of the neighbourhood vanish from the screen as the camera zooms in on the face of the woman they are interviewing:

'What do you know about the landfill?'

'I know what they say on TV [. . .] I know it's an infectious site, that there is a ton of waste that should be cleaned up.'

'And what do you think? Is it good or bad that people go rummaging in there? Because they say there's old food there.'

'I think it's dreadful.'

(*Re-copada*, short produced in 2008)

Ten years later, Nair looks at those videos with us, videos that evidence the intense interest she and her group felt in asking those outside the neighbourhood what they thought of it and of the landfill. The journalist is no longer the one with the camera, showing the world how that other has gotten used to filth and to eating from the trash. Now Nair and her friends are the ones behind the interrogating camera, the camera that asks. But something else happens: precisely when that woman says 'I think it's dreadful,' the young women zoom in on her face, and that image of horror veers. Now another mouth is the one babbling. The camera does not shy away from the woman speaking, thus unsettling the terms of dread: what's dreadful is no longer the image of the landfill but of that face with the twisted mouth. Nair knew what she wanted to hear. That was her intervention. What she wants to show does not incite pity. Ten years later, when Nair tells us what she was thinking when she was filming, she says,

> With the camera, we showed her and told her what we could not say personally [. . .] besides, with the video they were going to have to sit there and watch it from start to finish. But if I stood in front of someone and said 'Listen, you don't know what you're talking about,' they would be like, 'I couldn't care less' and walk away. What I thought wouldn't matter at all. Because people already know what they think [. . .] We gave proof that everything is not what it seems. (Interview with Nair 2019)

A displacement, a shift in the gaze/narrative of that other who knows how she is shown and decides to occupy a different place to narrate(herself), to 'say something to the world' as another young person in the group put it. With the video, 'We gave proof that everything is not what it seems.' 'The cameras were our eyes' – was how Enzo, another participant in the project, put it in 2019. By showing 'everything is not what it seems', they turned the other into the babbler. An ethical self leaves behind the moral and moralizing narrative of the one who judges. A first-person self who narrates (herself) in a story less of dread than of life.

Layer 1. Memes: The monstrous, the ridiculous and the profane

The concept of the meme was first formulated in 1976 by scientist Richard Dawkins as part of his memetic hypothesis of cultural transmission. He posited that humans have two information processors, one that acts through the replication of genes over the course of generations and one that acts through the brain's replication of what an individual receives as cultural information in the form of instruction, imitation or assimilation. The word *meme* refers to the smallest unit of information that can be conveyed. Over three decades later and with the expansion of the internet, the meme's morphology has changed. Memes are now units of information that are reinterpreted and modified as they propagate from one point to other points on the web.

One April day in 2020, not long after lockdown was mandated, confining the entire population indoors to protect the country from contagion and the spread of Covid-19, David challenged a virus that – he boasted – would never be able to topple a body like his that had grown up eating from the trash. Sure of his immunity as someone who lives in slums where the politics of urban life take shape between environmental decay and extreme poverty, David, like many, doesn't really believe he'll catch it. But the meme that voiced his challenge constitutes an ironic – and highly provocative – affirmation that recounts injustices and much more:

No me iso nada las cosas que comia del cinturon y me vas a matar vos corona virus? jaja!

(Nothing I ate at landfill ever did me any harm and you think you are going to kill me, corona virus? jaja!)

That meme, and so many others posted on the internet, condenses much of what language enables. Its formulation of a problem politicizes very precisely the living conditions of a population left to its own devices (Grinberg 2011) for whom trash is a resource for daily living. He also turns to the landfill, not by zooming in, but with the humour and irony of (an)other gaze that could not be further from the image of the victim in the journalist's gaze. Here, there are subjects who 'tell the world' what that world produces. This meme does not close the landfill off in a circle of fear and abjection, but breaks that circle, slipping through its confines. It provocatively frays a thread and, in so doing, unsettles even the authors of this text.

The meme tells the world that the unknown virus that now has it in an uproar only serves to expose and harshen the conditions in a neighbourhood that is produced and reproduced in the logics of flexible capitalism. But it says it as only a meme can. Deleuze and Guattari (2000) speak of the spider-narrator in Proust who incessantly rips apart fabrics and planes with the only resource possible: humour. 'The narrator does not homestead in the familial and neurotic lands,' (318) as the journalist does when he asks the mothers how they feel about feeding their kids from the landfill or taking them there with them. Such guilt and shame are nowhere to be found in the meme that desecrates and perforates. Through dark humour, David presents that landfill politically, from within it. He not only desecrates the landfill, but also all the charitable gazes that rested on the neighbourhood that April in their concern for what Covid-19 could do to the slums. At stake is not actual immunity to the virus, but perforating, intervening, treating means like means.

Layer 1. I had something to say and I said it: Means to means

For Code, making the video was a unique experience. It was, in his words, a chance 'to get a weight off my chest'.[3] When asked about the experience his video dealt with, he said he didn't want to go into it: it had been very traumatic, especially since he was only 11 at the time. Here, once again, the words he uses matter: 'I said what I had to say' – a phrase that wanders in unexpected directions, from one point to thousands of scattered points that, like the smallest units of information, circulate and are reinterpreted, jarring anyone they come upon.

> With that video I let go [. . .] of everything I was feeling. It went straight to my heart and filled me with pride. It was so special and personal [. . .] Everyone in the neighbourhood thanked me [. . .] I got a weight off my chest. (Interview with Code, 2019)

After propagation, that message, in the form of the video, returned to Code's neighbourhood – and that is where we see how his personal story, the story told in the first person, turned into a story that belongs to that neighbourhood. A collective and singular experience: from the one to the multiple. Code remembered not only the specific project that allowed him to narrate a highly traumatic experience but something else as well: he has said everything he had to say. There is no need to do it again. There is nothing else, it is all there. He got a weight off his chest, and the neighbourhood thanked him for it. All the cards dealt. It is not a question of projecting another image of the neighbourhood, or representing it differently, or of responding. At stake is the act of saying in its own right, of recounting that experience. There is no behind the scenes, but there is a story, Code's own story, about that violent crackdown that shook the neighbourhood and killed two of his friends before his eyes. Code's account bore witness. But in that speech act there were no grand movements, but rather 'an intensive voyage that undoes all the lands for the benefit of the one it is creating' (Deleuze and Guattari 2000: 219). And what that one is creating here is the register of a neighbourhood, the testimony of someone who has seen too much, seen past the point of no return. And perhaps that is why that self, in its multiplication, is empowered and feels 'extremely me' when he sees himself on the screen:

> And when I saw myself on the screen and everyone clapped, I couldn't believe it. It was, for me, an important video, because it is something I experienced [. . .] In that video, I felt *extremely me*. (Interview with Code, 2018)

Narrated stories are where precept and concept merge, like the first-person testimony of Code and the neighbourhood. But there is that something else which is part and parcel of the screen. Code's story is rendered image. His is one of those stories as powerful for the person telling it as it is for those of us who see and hear it. In part because, by turning pain into word/image, Code let it go, 'got a weight off his chest.' But something else is at work in this story, something that makes it uniquely vital: the convergence of the narrator and the narrated. We find a self telling his story, a story that had been told many times before in the mass media. But this time a self/us is positioned as the first person of the narrative. It is Code's lived story, the lived story of his neighbourhood. But neither he, nor the neighbourhood, nor whatever is behind that convergence is spoken or represented. On the contrary, this is a narrative that tells what it experiences and experiences what it tells. A self makes its way into each sentence. That self repeats itself, and in that repetition it gains power. When it sees itself on the screen, it becomes 'extremely me'.

Perhaps that is why Guattari (2013), on the notion of schizoanalytic cartography, affirms that we find ourself 'in a position (perhaps for the first time in history) of leading to something more enduring than crazy and ephemeral spontaneous effervescences: namely, a fundamental repositioning of man in relation to his machinic and natural environments (which, moreover, tend to coincide).' (6) In this case, to the becoming of a neighbourhood and those who inhabit it.

In the three layers discussed here, we come upon those environments in different ways. They are assembled in the becoming of the camera-eye of their narrators. We will now perform that promised analysis in series.

Discussion: The schizo/cartography approach

The art of mapping strokes and lines in a rhizome and their multiple connections, their zones of repetition and redundancy, the boundaries between them, is not disassociated from the subject who draws that map first because she is a territorial force, and second because in that task she becomes the vortex where those lines are stabilized. Perhaps that is why the neighbourhood thanked and congratulated Code. Going behind the forces that inhabit a territory that takes shape in the multiple materialities of the slums where the natural and machinic environments are more and more the same means engaging, in different ways, the multiple territorialities of the postmedia age. And there is something of that in these young people's texts, posts, and artistic and audiovisual productions. A machine-eye that narrates in between those environments that draws them. In the meme, the irony is what speaks, but it also questions and desecrates. Code got a weight off his chest.

In these layers, we see how the machinic environment turns into sheer narration of itself. 'The eye becomes camera' is how Enzo puts it when, in describing the act of filming, he is also speaking of what his eyes said. It is as if in the postmedia age that speaking were repositioned with/in the camera, and the web made it possible that what one has to say might just be seen/heard by the other. Those multiple layers are at play in these young people's narratives. Venturing a story where one is no longer what is told but the person telling. The promise of the postmedia age (Genosko 2013) is the potential that the postmedia environment has to offer: molecular revolutions, soft subversions (Guattari 2007) that somehow contort registers of meaning and enable other speech acts and singular narratives that unfold and replicate in unpredictable directions. Finding a degree of coherence in that map's myriad lines, discerning whether it has actually become resistance is, as Athanasiadou points out, harder and harder:

> The parallel development of network technologies has led to the tightening of time intervals, spreading events and ideas faster than ever before in a non-linear fashion. The simultaneous homogenisation of space and the abrupt discontinuities of time brought by networked cultures render the drawing of a coherent cartography of these resistance movements harder and harder to trace. The 'entangled genealogies' (Barad 2007: 389) of these movements cannot correspond to a sequential reading that sees them as a domino effect as their emergence is non-linear. A tracing of the conditions that made these movements and events possible would require a renewed focus on their relational character rather than their reading as an all-encompassing narrative. (Athanasiadou 2018: 235)

Between the vast and instantaneous spread of events and ideas and their fleetingness lies a set of lines that schizo-cartography comes up against. It may not be a question of making them coherent, of determining their effects, emergences or resistances. On the contrary, relations of force and power struggles are what matter in this cartography where the question of the other collides with the tensions of an age that at once devours any possible novelty and seems to offer the possibility that (an)other word emerge. A becoming where the foreign takes on power insofar as capacity to question, to turn the unintelligible into decodifiable signs. The question of the other's gaze, becoming the spectacular barbarian, circulating on and meddling in the web because there is no choice but to keep at it, to doggedly be, in the singularity specific to one who knows herself other. That singularity knows it plays to win, and the game is intervention. Just as the meme produces, intervenes and moves on. It stutters and makes babble.

A babbling where the basic question returns: for whom is it feasible to perceive herself as other? Needs and desires where the subtlety of gestures and vital signs (thinking, speaking, feeling) are found in the interchange at a body's limits, at the outer edges of what a body can do. At stake in the other gaze is unquestionably the other language that, like the barbarian, is constituted in history on the basis of strangeness in language: a strange language, a foreign language that sounds to some like incomprehensible babble. And indifference and fear lie in the inability to understand that set of signs. That's why Nair says she knew what information she was after, that's why the camera, while Nair hears talk of the 'dreadfulness' in which she supposedly lives, reacts by zooming in to render the mouth of the woman stating her dread strange: she is the one babbling in a foreign tongue now.

In this postmedia/post-pac-man age, it doesn't matter at all if the reversals Nair and others effect are small turns, barbarian upheavals, or just a moment when language takes flight from the dominant redundancies (Guattari and Rolnik 2013). That is when language is produced by a narrator who displaces the places established for the other, which enables us to take flight as well from the aestheticization or romanticization of the slums and from those places from which to speak. This turn does not lie solely in the one who narrates, then. There is not necessarily *something* that takes flight. Indeed, the television interview in the landfill confirms the abject. In Nair's zoom in, like in the meme, an abject experience ceases to be abject because it is removed from the atrium of dread. It is desecrated and, hence, becomes irreverent – likely because it is just part of daily life in the neighbourhood. There is nothing sacred there and, hence, no dread either. What there is is an experience of life, of molar forces, of abject fear, and of those minor, molecular practices that become irreverent (they can laugh at the other and make it the babbler). Perverse lands that explode in these turns the machinic indexes that mine them.

There is, in these narrations, a passage. These other stories shift from the moralizing gaze that alights on them to an ethical statement of life. If morality rests on a hierarchy of values that cannot be dissociated from a position of superiority, ethics insists on singularity, on what bodies can do (Deleuze 2019). In ethics, there is no essence but rather potential. These narratives do not shy away from the question of what's good and what's bad: 'And do you think it's good or bad that people go rummaging in the landfill?' These young women ask the one who looks at 'the horror' on television, thus posing to her the ethical-political dilemma: 'When they're hungry, they'll go to the landfill.' There is no one looking in from the outside sitting in judgement. Instead, there is an immanent self living this life.

And none of this lies outside the fabric of this schizo-cartography, this intertwined genealogy (Barad 2007) that glides between machinic eyes: the journalist's moral judgement in the first scene and the meme in the second. As Deleuze (1994) puts it, '[t]he conditions of a true critique and a true creation are the same: the destruction of an image of thought [cliché] which presupposes itself and the genesis of the act of thinking in thought itself' (139). And those lines discern thought in the act of thinking itself. Further, Guattari and Rolnik (2013) point out, 'It's a question of finding another use, another listening relationship, a sort of feedback, and making minor languages speak' (151). Postmedia-age interventions emerge as minor languages that are made to speak. Molecular expressions of (an)other speech, of a gaze that is no longer positioned as the object of the narrative but as one who turns it around and twists its meaning: 'When you'll be hungry, you'll go to the landfill' says Nair, inquisitively, making that 'dreadful' scene, that scene of horror, mundane. 'Truth and falsity are not values that exist outside the constitutive problematic fields that give them sense . . . and, ethics is a problem of power and not of duty' (Radman 2018a: 245) – and that is exactly where Nair, and these other young people, place us. They intervene by producing images/thinking that throw off the countless judgements of the slum that turn those judgements into so much babble.

In these stories, the third person is the one who changes places. 'You'll go,' says Nair. It is no longer a question of how they feel about going to the landfill with their children. The ones being interrogated are the ones who pass judgment: why do you feel you have the right to judge? What's driving it is hunger. The other throws off the stereotypes of the noble savage. The other, now self, explains that they are there because they are hungry and that the families who go to the place televised as a site of horror and infection do so to subsist.

'I felt extremely me,' says Code, describing how he felt when he saw himself on the screen. A 'very me' narrating a situation that nobody at all – let alone an 11-year-old child – should have to go through. Four years later, he could narrate that experience and let go of it. That's why, still more years later, he tells us he doesn't need to relive it: he said what he had to say. Shoot an arrow, toss all the dice. The difference between that speech act, that 'way me' as opposed to everything that was said (and that he heard) in the mass media about the incident, is that here Code is not the one spoken, constructed, characterized by others who look at him oddly and judge him as someone who doesn't seek knowledge but denial. Seeing himself on the screen had a spectacular effect on him. This time, he occupied the spectacular space of the screen not as one of the mass media's barbarians. This time, his story and pain are in the scene – it's really him up there.

In these scenes and stories, then, there is not only no romanticization or attempt to justify or explain their lives or how they are or should be lived. What there is, rather, is the potential released when moral judgement is taken out of the scene.

By way of conclusion: An(other) gaze

The stories in this chapter act as glimmers that compose (an)other gaze, the one enabled in the absence of they, of those who would interrogate and narrate that gaze. Are those glimmers enabled in the postmedia age? Any possible response is full of caveats. To what extent is the turn from mass-media modernity to a postmedia age rife with the self-referential devices that are at play in the layers we have presented? Guattari was optimistic, but he knew that was possible only 'in the context of the new "deals" of the production of computational and telematic subjectivity that this voice/pathway of self-reference will succeed in acquiring its full capacity' (2013: 6). One way to escape a categorical response is to avoid thinking in terms of conquest or what is pursued in conquest. What we find in these layers is that there is no will to represent anything: there is no subject who stands before the camera to narrate or represent what others experience and how they experience it, let alone to capture their lives. There is the recording of a scene. The camera does not represent because it does not have anyone to represent. A camera-eye for whom what matters is the subjectivity it allows us to find rather than what it seeks to conquer.

One thing is clear: the postmedia age does not enable any conquest. In it, a plethora of images on the other provides a sort of 5.0 version of the civilization-barbarism tension – and that holds true not only in those textualities where criminalization and racism, classism, and other isms are blatantly the ones narrating. It is also the case in the condescending narratives that circulate in the mass media, movies, social networks and academic production. Narratives that visibilize or provide accounts of the oppression endured by others that have to be saved because their bodies are not up to the task. We are surrounded by images that narrate suffering and lack, where abject fear is expressed between pity and romanticization. There is none of that, luckily, in the stories told by these young people. They produce something else, something unsettling. It is unsettling to read a meme by a young man that laughs about going to the landfill; that laughter effects displacement. That meme, and the videos we discussed here, mocks the many narratives on the internet and portals that, at the beginning of lockdown, showed a degree of concern for the sanitary conditions in slums where there is no potable water. The humour in David's meme in particular blows those narratives to bits.

Relevant here is Braidotti (2018) when he speaks of 'the cartographic obligation of being both critical – of dominant visions of knowing subjects – and creative, by actualizing the virtual and unrealized insights and competences of marginalized subjects' (9). That is where a schizo-cartography of the other gaze becomes decisive because it is necessarily intuitive and immanent in its rendering: it cannot pre-exist or go beyond its own drawing because it is always bound to the cartographer. It operates amidst the forces that compose the territory; it is those forces' multiple affectations. If even a trace of that other gaze becomes imaginable between these lines, it is because they are shot out like arrows of thought. And that is why a schizo-cartography must dodge readings that would make its movements coherent: these are lines that can only be rendered in their innate non-linearity.

If in the postmedia age there is a specularization where any difference is reduced to its own equivalency, it is also true that that age interrogates the linearity and even the totalization that those readings would impose on us. Readings that see dystopian scenes. All we can do is reinvent ourselves to learn to navigate the uncertainty which is part and parcel of these times of self-help and toxic positivity. The only changes we can propose are in our selfies, where we are happy. Since we can't get off the wheel, we are told to enjoy it. Dystopian readings restore coherence. According to them, there is nothing left to do since the dice have been tossed. Schizo-cartography proceeds differently. It does not respond to the impulse to build a new utopia or to take it easy. As Deleuze and Guattari (2000) put it in *Anti-Oedipus*, what's at stake is 'not a promised and a pre-existing land, but a world created in the process of its tendency, its coming undone, its deterritorialization' (322)

Would this 'very/extremely me' be possible without the screen? We don't know, but it doesn't matter either. Because what there is are other forms of multiple affectation, materialities, bodies that commune and assemble, points of flight that shoot an arrow because they can, because they want to, or just because they are there (they have the chance so they shoot the camera). Means to means, (an)other gaze.

References

Athanasiadou, L. (2018), 'Locality/Non-separability', in R. Braidotti and M. Hlavajova (eds), *Posthuman Glossary*, 235–7, London: Bloomsbury.
Barad, K. M. (2007), *Meeting the Universe Halfway: Quantum Physics and the Entanglement of Matter and Meaning*, Durham: Duke University Press. Print.
Baudrillard, J. (2000), *Pantalla Total*, Barcelona: Anagrama.
Berardi, F. (2007), *Generación Post-alfa: Patologías e imaginarios en el semiocapitalismo*, Buenos Aires: Tinta Limón.
Berardi, F. (2017), *Fenomenología del fin: Sensibilidad y mutación conectiva*, Buenos Aires: Caja Negra.
Bradley, J. P. N. (2019), 'Schizoanalysis and PokémonGo', *China Media Research*, 15 (4): 78–91.

Braidotti, R. (2018), 'A Theoretical Framework for the Critical Posthumanities', *Theory, Culture & Society*, 0(0): 1–31.
Buchanan, I. (2002), 'Schizoanalysis and Hitchcock: Deleuze and The Birds', *Strategies*, 15 (1): 105–18.
Buchanan, I. and L. Collins, eds (2014), *Deleuze and the Schizoanalysis of Visual Art*, London: Bloomsbury.
Buchanan, I., T. Matts, and A. Tynan. (2015), *Deleuze and the Schizoanalysis of Literature*, London: Bloomsbury.
Castro-Gómez, S. (2010), *La hybris del punto cero: Ciencia, raza e ilustración en la Nueva Granada (1750-1816)*, Bogotá: Pontificia Universidad Javeriana.
Crary, J. (2008), *Suspensiones de la percepción: Atención, espectáculo y cultura moderna*, Madrid: Akal.
Deleuze, G. (1994), *Difference and Repetition*, trans. P. Patton, New York: Columbia University Press.
Deleuze, G. (2019), *En medio de Spinoza*, Buenos Aires: Cactus.
Deleuze, G. and F. Guattari, (2000), *Anti-Oedipus*, trans. H. R. Lane, M. Seem and R. Hurley, Minneapolis: University of Minnesota Press.
Guattari, F. (1986), *Les années d'Hiver 1980-1985*, Paris: Bernard Barrault.
Guattari, F. (2007), *Soft Subversions: Texts and interviews 1977-1985*, Los Ángeles: Semiotext(e).
Guattari, F. (2013), *Schizoanalytic Cartographies*, trans. A. Goffey, London: Bloomsbury.
Guattari, F. and S. Rolnik (2013), *Micropolítica. Cartografías del deseo*, Buenos Aires: Tinta Limón.
Genosko, G. (2013), 'The Promise of Postmedia', in C. Apprich, J. B. Slater Iles and O. Schultz (eds), *Provocative Alloys: A Postmedia Anthology*, 14–24, PML Books.
Grinberg, S. (2008), *Educación y poder en el siglo XXI*, Buenos Aires: Miño y Dávila.
Grinberg, S. (2010), 'Everyday Banality in a Documentary by Teenage Women: Between the Trivial and the Extreme. Schooling and Desiring in Contexts of Extreme Urban Poverty', *Gender & Education*, 22 (6): 663–77.
Grinberg, S. (2011), 'Territories of Schooling and Schooling Territories in Argentinean Extreme Urban Poverty Contexts', *Emotion, Space and Society*, 4 (3): 160–71.
Grinberg, S. (2020), 'Etnografía, biopolítica y colonialidad. Genealogías de la precariedadurbana en la Región Metropolitana de Buenos Aires', *Tabula Rasa*, 34: 19–39.
Kinsey, C. (2013), 'From Postmedia to Post-Medium: Rethinking Ontology in Art and Technology', in C. Apprich, J. B. Slater Iles and O. Schultz (eds), *Provocative Alloys: A Postmedia Anthology*, 68–83, PML Books.
Marks, L. (2000), 'Signs of the Time: Deleuze, Peirce, and the Documentary Image', in G. Flaxman (ed.), *The Brain Is The Screen: Deleuze and the Philosophy Of Cinema*, 193–214, Minneapolis: University of Minnesota Press.
Radman, A. (2018a), 'Double Bind: On Material Ethics', in C. V. Boundas (ed.), *Schizoanalysis and Ecosophy: Reading Deleuze and Guattari*, 241–56, London: Bloomsbury Academic.
Radman, A. (2018b), 'Ecologies of Architecture', in R. Braidotti and M. Hlavajova (eds), *Posthuman Glossary*, 117–20, London: Bloomsbury.
Sarmiento, D. F. ([1845] 2009), *Facundo o civilización y barbarie*, Córdoba: Eduvim.

9

No media . . .

David R. Cole

This chapter argues that understanding the forces at work in the production of celebrity through the media are critical to comprehending the present moment (and doing anything about it) – and the result of this confluence is a state of 'no media'. The primary contradiction of 'no media' is that we are facing planetary extinction and environmental crisis on an unparalleled scale due to climate change, and the scientific facts and combinational tendencies embodied through the name: 'the Anthropocene' (Crutzen 2002). However, and at the same time, the entertainment business distributes generalized, hypnotizing, sleepless vapidity, through ever-increasing and penetrating media networks, precisely designed to take away the ability to think otherwise, and hence to act in a way that could help in the contemporary Anthropocenic moment (by turning us into 'idiot media consumers'). This chapter suggests that Deleuze and Guattari (1984) get close to prophesizing this situation in *Anti-Oedipus* and, combined with Guattari's solo work, these texts offer a potentially significant way through the impasse of environmental catastrophe and media brainwashing: here called 'no media'. This writing offers a new synthesis based on these texts, and in so doing revives social ecology in the context of the Anthropocene, moves towards the dissolution of the 'idiot/mesmerising/nullifying' media . . . and subsequently takes us through revised approaches to economics and education. The economic analysis on offer here engages with Guattari's notion of semiocapitalism (cf. Genosko 2012) and Raworth's (2017) doughnut economics, the educational complex deploys Deleuze's third synthesis (1994) to open up different time strata in teaching and learning.

A new social ecology?

In its most basic terms, social ecology is the conjunction of the social with the ecological. The social predominantly refers to human society and what it has become in the contemporary era, and this notion can specifically refer to the effects of social media, and how it is shaping and reshaping society as a mediated, spectacular, digital process (cf. Roberts 2012). Admittedly, traditional forms and modes of society still exist, outside of the 'infosphere', such as the last surviving examples of the hunter-gatherer tribes in the Amazon rainforest, and the remaining chiefdoms nestled in developing countries, for example, in some parts of Africa (cf. Ember 2020). The point is that layered human society now has a 'universal glaze', or top level of technological development, that has been relentlessly subjected to the ravages of hyper-accelerated globalization for the past fifty years or so, and is apparent as a mode of 'digital-becoming'. Into this glaze, the media has penetrated to an extraordinary extent, and dominates much of that which is thought, believed, said, and henceforth acted upon. The media has become tremendously powerful in the contemporary era, and has presently achieved many of the hypnotic effects dreamed of by propagandists across the ages. I would like to argue in this section that a new social ecology, opened up and prefigured by *Anti-Oedipus*, backed up by the solo work of Félix Guattari, and flanked by an awakening of and from social ecology, and figures such as Murray Bookchin (1987) and Arne Naess (1988), has the chance to penetrate this glaze. I would like to suggest that the time has come for a new, updated social ecology that challenges the idiocy of the digital mediasphere and figures a way out of and from the desolation of the Anthropocene as *no media*:

1) *Anti-Oedipus*: Every social movement needs a spark, an origin and a (re)birth. In the wake of the May '68 student uprising in Paris, such a vital text was produced. Gilles Deleuze had been working on an alternative reading of Western philosophy. Félix Guattari had been practising unorthodox psychoanalysis at La Borde Institute in France. Together, they produced what is still a radical and challenging text, but that gives a straightforward approach to explaining how we have ended up in the situation that we find ourselves in today. In *Anti-Oedipus*, capitalism is a development from primitive and feudal societies that engineers a generalized decoding and deterritorialization of all former societies and treats nature as a resource (to make profit). Capitalism is a form of universal machine that has harnessed technology (including the media) to make it work ever more efficiently and effectively (e.g. Braithwaite 2008). *Anti-Oedipus* is in many ways a dark text, in that it includes the horror and violence that has been inflicted on humans and nature by capitalism, which they suggest was there all along, but in different forms through history, and not applicable universally; that is, there is Chinese capitalism, British capitalism, colonial capitalism, Japanese capitalism, etc. The significant problem that *Anti-Oedipus* opens up for the present analysis is specifically how to extract ourselves, referred to as 'desiring-machines' in *Anti-Oedipus*, from the gravitational idiocy of the 'media-sphere' so that we may make a difference in the Anthropocene, and as 'no media'. Make no mistake, this is the most difficult problem that anyone can presently attend to. This extraction is the most consuming task that one can be set, as we are produced by and as desiring-machines at every moment; these machines are immanent to everything that we do or think, as we live in a hyper-globalized, imagistic, media-dominated, digitized, pan-capitalist global world. Note that one could argue that all educative faculties and experiences have become part of and productive of this processing through learning technologies, digitalization, and the interactivity of smart boards and devices (education will be specifically treated at the end of this essay on 'no media'). To press on with this point, and

to underline the pain of extraction, I would like to take a slight detour through the work of Nick Land, and his interpretation of Heidegger's reading of the poet Georg Trakl.

Land's (2011) focus on Heidegger's interpretation of Trakl pivots on the fact that Heidegger hijacks the passion, blood and raw experience of Trakl, and incorporates and nullifies its potency in his metaphysical overview. Heidegger precisely interprets the sensitive, traumatized, eccentric and frequently very peculiar poems of Trakl, and incorporates them into the metaphysics of forgetting of Western philosophy (Heidegger 1971) and the loss of 'Being' from the Greeks. For example, Trakl directly experienced the battlefield of the First World War, and expresses the blood, violence, strange, overriding alienation and terrifying experience brilliantly in his poems. In contrast, Heidegger seems to skirt around the direct experience of one of the most horrific human conflicts that has ever taken place, and instead gives us a reading of the aesthetics, language, and cadence of Trakl that effectively subdues the direct horror and weird becomings of the poems (e.g. the lycanthropy). Nick Land wanted to reverse this process to, in fact, amplify the horror and to desecrate the 'fitting in' of such texts with a canon, or any concrete patterning of dispersed, non-penetrating metaphysical thought (Land 2011: 99).

The connection to 'no media' here involves the tendency to do the same with respect to capitalism. *Anti-Oedipus* is revolutionary exactly because it does not give us a watered down or sugar-coated explanation of the effects of capitalism. There is a 'metaphysics of desire' in *Anti-Oedipus*, but it is not a phenomenological rendering of the world according to human consciousness, or language, or 'I'. Rather, *Anti-Oedipus* (re)works a mode of 'transcendental materialism', including the location and functioning of the death drive in and through capitalism (Deleuze and Guattari 1984). Capitalism does not care (it is after all a machine) about exemplifying, spreading and augmenting the death drive, as long as it makes a profit. Echoing the twentieth-century Beat writers, one could say that the absolute pinnacle of a product for capitalism is the addictive drug, something that wholly captures the user, and makes them desire more through necessity. Nick Land's conclusion with respect to capitalism was that it was a malignant AI programmed from the future to destroy human society, the singularity (Ireland 2017). I am not sure about this, but what I do think is that the combination of progressively more intrusive and personalized media, along with the present reality of climate change, known as the Anthropocene, makes for a lethal combination. Although the media does allow for and to an extent encourages the distribution of data, critical discussion, and even the suggestion of insurrection with respect to climate change and its possible solutions, it is not decisive in terms of fomenting action. Rather, there is always room for dissenting and contradictory voices on and in the media (and *as* media), which help to diffuse the alacrity with respect to climate change. *Why act to change anything external, when a funny video of your neighbour's cat is a click away?* The media works in the context of the death drive of capitalism to take away the force of environmental action and to break the relation between the global machine of capitalism, its detrimental effects, and how they impinge upon one's person and territory. With these factors in mind, it is worthwhile exploring further the ideas of

Félix Guattari, to strengthen this approach to social ecology, and that might have a chance of success in the contemporary situation as 'no media'.

2) *Félix Guattari*: Félix Guattari was an unorthodox psychiatrist, who travelled extensively explaining his practice, and tried to create the conditions for revolutionary social and ecological upheaval that we need so desperately today, in terms of doing something about climate change. However, his efforts towards revolutionary change largely failed, and he sunk into a deep depression later in life. What we can extract from his work is how to carry forward the momentum gained from *Anti-Oedipus* towards developing social ecology that effectively challenges the hegemony and power of contemporary capitalism, and that has been augmented significantly in and through the expansions and complicated byways of global corporate digital media, for example, in and through education. First, one might say that the Guattarian approach is not to shy away from or hide in terms of the media. His ideas for social change were meant to be encouraged in liaison with and through the media or 'postmedia' (Guattari 1990). Admittedly, trying to utilize the media for revolutionary environmental purposes and social change is immediately fraught with potential difficulties, as the contemporary platforms that one might want to exploit, like Facebook and Twitter, have themselves been so overrun with and by commercial and partisan interests, that presenting any material on these platforms that does not conform to the inimical, polarizing tenets they foster, can be an anathema to their performance algorithms (and hence fail to gain traction). However, an updated version of Guattari's postmedia project does require the utilization of said media to produce new types of revolutionary subjectivities, and that could help in some way collectively to change the course of humanity in the developing horror we now call the Anthropocene. The postmedia project (Guattari 1990) entails an analysis of the subjectivities produced by the media, and a deployment of the media along the lines of his earlier work on transversality that encourages group identities that do not correspond to fixed and hierarchical regimes (Guattari 2005). Guattari was a practicing anti-psychiatrist at the La Borde Institute and projected his practical work with patients onto possible uses of the media.

Further, Guattari's (1990) postmedia project was more wide-ranging than merely initiating a new regime of pro-environmental-revolutionary-social signs through and in the media (semiotics), and that we now term as *social media*. In line with other critical thinkers (e.g. Franco Berardi, Antoni Negri and Maurizio Lazzarato), he wished to relieve humanity of the enforced slavery and repetitious drudgery of what he called Integrated World Capitalism (IWC). I believe that to meaningfully extend this project, one has to look outside and beyond the current moment, and find thought that extends a deeper analysis of how we have ended up in the present-day singular convergence of stupefying media and ecological calamity. For example, Guattari's four zones of the unconscious diagram presents such a thinking, as it suggests thought between: (1) 'cut-outs' of existential territories, (2) complexions of material and energetic flows, (3) rhizomes of abstract ideas and (4) constellations of aesthetic refrains (Guattari 2013: 17). Updated

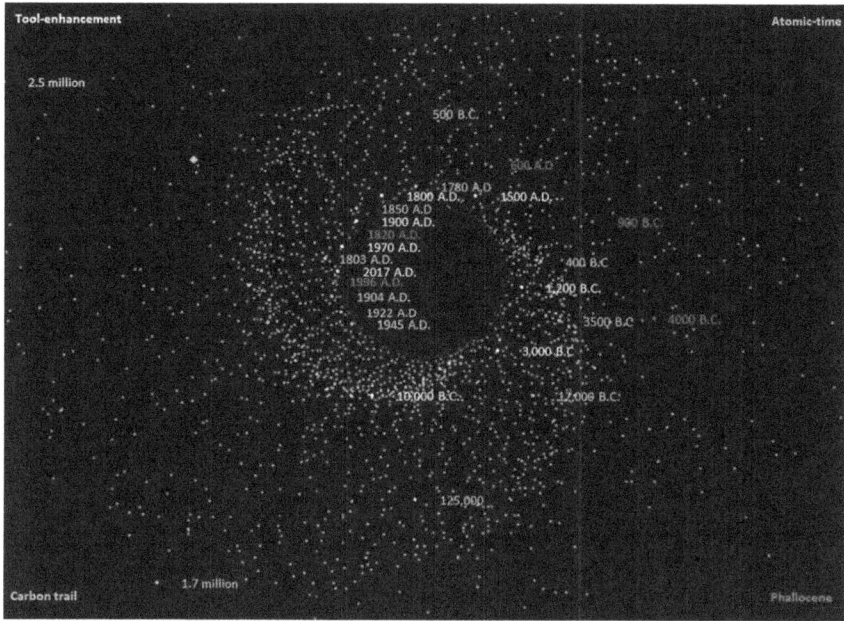

Figure 9.1 The four-line matter cloud analysis leading into the singularity of the Anthropocene. From 'Black Sun' presentation, 20/04/2017, the New School for Social Research (New York) © Cole 2017.

and modified for the Anthropocene, the four zones become: (1) tool enhancement; (2) carbon trail; (3) the phallocene; (4) atomic time (Figure 9.1).

As such, in Figure 9.1, the human drives can be mapped and explained in terms of how we have ended up in the situation of a complete, global, distraction-based media, combined with ecological collapse, with the media working to shield us and to complicate this reality in terms of polarization (Cole 2017a). The drive of tool enhancement explains how we have gone from hominins using tools to shape and alter their reality to the global media empire epitomized by the internet, and all that this entails. The drive of the carbon trail centres on the use of fire to burn carbon and to produce heat and energy, and how it has become vital to human progress and civilization. The phallocene is a deliberate *double entendre*, which, as a drive, points to the phallic directness of human behaviour (e.g. how media imagery is organized), and how we have got to a time of 'fake news' with the global media, orchestrated by the mores of entertainment, audience, and profit (e.g. through marketing), and as a consequence not caring a jot about the truth. Lastly, the drive of atomic time points to how we have gone from societies wholly connected to and part of nature to societies 'out of time', accelerated, and not connected to the rhythms and feelings of nature, as we are atomized. I believe that Guattari's four zones of the unconscious diagram (2013) allows for and encourages such thought, and this gives us a deeper insight into the situation of ecological collapse, related, fuelled and encouraged by the idiot media. However, the problem remains with respect to how to respond. For example, moving too quickly, or too easily to a definite, non-dualistic ecosophy, that looks to reconnect us with nature, as nature, and determine our metaphysical selves through this 'reconnectedness' as a mode of reinvented animism, although enticing, can have the danger of underestimating the challenges ahead. Rather, I would like to use Guattari as an analytical bridge for producing new thoughts about the singular convergence in and of the media with the Anthropocene, and to furnish enhanced thought about social ecology as a tendency in 'no media'.

3) *Social ecology*: If we take Guattari's analysis seriously, and extend this line of argument from *Anti-Oedipus* and the realization of the effects of capitalism on the unconscious to Guattari, and statements about how the global media and the Anthropocene have converged in the present epoch, we are left with a cleavage in terms of what to do, and how to progress in the current situation as 'no media'. On one side of this breaking apart or schizo thought, we have to change, remould and transform society, namely address the ills of capitalism. On the other, we need to understand, reconnect with, and enhance the natural world. These two sides of the argument may be aligned with the ideas of Murray Bookchin (1987) in terms of changing the social world, and Arne Naess (1988) in relation to 'deep' ecology and nature. Murray Bookchin like Félix Guattari was an activist, who was concerned with making a difference, and advocated an anarchist approach to disrupting and questioning the march of capitalism to continued global domination (latterly he came to change the name of his practise to 'communalism', as he detested the bourgeois appropriation of anarchism). Bookchin helped to found the Institute for Social Ecology, which abides by and teaches his principles, that are to turn away from the exploitative and destructive nature of mainstream capitalist society, in order to produce smaller, regenerative, self-sustaining and self-governing mini-societies that could potentially neutralize the stupefying effects of the global media in the Anthropocene as 'no media' (Bookchin 2007). Certainly, such a wholesale change in societal behaviour would help to avert the effects of climate change, but how likely is this to happen? The fundamental problem with Murray Bookchin's (e.g. 1987, 2007) approach to social ecology, though in many ways it is indicative of a better way to organize society in contrast to globalized, exploitative, mainstream, media-dominated, alienating capitalism, is that when these social changes do not happen it can appear like an ideal dream or a far-off, never-to-be-realized 'green utopia', similar to Guattari's dreams of transforming mainstream society through specific, bottom-up, revolutionary action using postmedia – and not just treating certain individuals and groups for their mental problems through anti-psychiatric techniques and ideas. Rather, an alignment between social ecology and consciousness raising that involves the self-realization of the interconnectedness of things as nature, along with the social change of social ecology, takes us further along the track to 'no media'. Arne Naess (1990) developed his deep ecology over many years, as a philosophical counterbalance to the modes in which one might be disconnected and alienated from nature in modern life. In essence, Naess's (e.g. 1988, 1990) complex and multi-levelled philosophy requires

a deep engagement with nature and a turning away from mainstream commercial mores, until a real entanglement with nature and a consequent raising of consciousness can be achieved. His deep ecology argument is about ecological social change, and making the relationships that we have in and through nature more sustainable:

> Quality of life is here considered to be something incompatible with artificial, material standards above that necessary for the satisfaction of fundamental needs, and secondly, that ecological considerations are to be regarded as preconditions for life quality, therefore not outside human responsibility. . . . The lifestyle of the majority should be changed so that the material standard of living in the Western countries becomes universalizable within this century. A consumption over and above that which everyone can attain within the foreseeable future cannot be justified. (Naess 1990: 34)

Again, and similar to Bookchin, this schema for social change has not happened, and does not seem likely, though ostensibly it is 'right' ecologically. Even though the consciousness raising that Naess advocates is commendable, the unlikelihood of wholesale ecological living can make it seem too idealistic, impossible to implement and, therefore, utopic. Rather, we need to take forward the consciousness raising part of Naess's plan as part of the overall, interconnected schema that we may derive from the first half of this essay, and as an argument for a *new social ecology* as 'no media', with an incorporated and dispersed call for social/ecological change, produced by considering the four elements of the argument laterally.

A sideways waltz through economics

One of the points of (re)theorizing a new social ecology for the Anthropocene and globally stupefying media age as 'no media' is so that it has noticeable effects on the discipline and course of economics. The lateral and dispersed notion of social ecology (Figure 9.2) is a deliberate strategy to avoid the segmentation and use by capitalism of the media for profit. Admittedly, we live at a time that is dominated by financial considerations, the term *financial capitalism* is not inappropriate to describe how any interaction and relation that can be imagined has undergone a financial recalibration and rebranding. Foremost among these processes is the manner in which energy commodities such as oil, coal and gas have become fundamental planks of the global financial system (Grubb 1995), so much so that one may conjunctively speak about 'financial-fossil-fuel' capitalism in the same breath. Pointedly, one should be suspicious of fossil fuel companies recalibrating their businesses to include renewables, that is, greenwashing. Further, it is understandable to be wary with respect to anti-fossil fuel activist programs funded by fossil fuel philanthropic groups.[1] In fact, the influence and power of the fossil fuel industry reaches beyond the financial markets and lobbies at the hearts of governments and businesses, to make sure that green initiatives and legislation do not dent their profits and power, and do not deflect from their

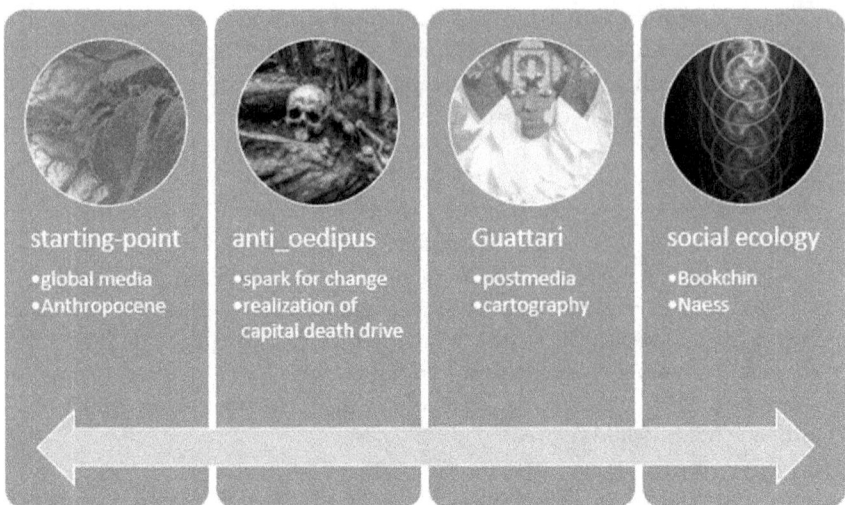

Figure 9.2 The argument for social ecology © Cole 2017.

interconnected interests, such as the augmentation and continuation of petrol-driven cars and the jet fuel flight industries (Rifkin 2011). These actions of the fossil fuel interests and industries, block the development of and in renewable energy sources, even as they become more affordable, and viable in providing reliable, alternative sources of power. The new social ecology of this article has to engage with these processes at a fundamental level, to make a difference in the present situation as 'no media'. In terms of the 'no media' analysis of this writing, the ways in which capital flows might be understood, can be represented in Figure 9.3.

Finance-subjectivity and semiocapitalism sit behind and within the many tentacles of the media. For example, if Guattari's portrayal of postmedia to transform subjectivity was reconsidered today, it would have finance-subjectivity and semiocapitalism running through it as implicit commercial interests and conditioning in social media. One could blithely say that nothing happens without money, or else going into debt to realize one's (frequently unrealizable) dreams. An important conception of the postmedia from Guattari (1990) is to assemble and (re)assemble various technologies to broadcast revolutionary messages, and to attempt to transform subjectivities trapped in dead end, low paid, nihilism-inducing jobs (the majority of the population). At one time, I believed that this idea of media transformation was possible, and echoes, for example, the amateurish beginnings of PC use and development among hobbyists in the 1970s. As an example of this deployment of technology, in the 1990s, I was involved with free party collectives, who used guerrilla media to organize, advertise, and hold free parties in defiance of stringent conservative laws banning such events.[2] The collectives that emerged through rave culture were able to assemble the dance equipment relatively cheaply with little technical expertise, and hosted underground, free parties, that became highly popular (Cole 2007), and were socially and culturally transformative in certain specific ways, and that led to conceptions such as techno-

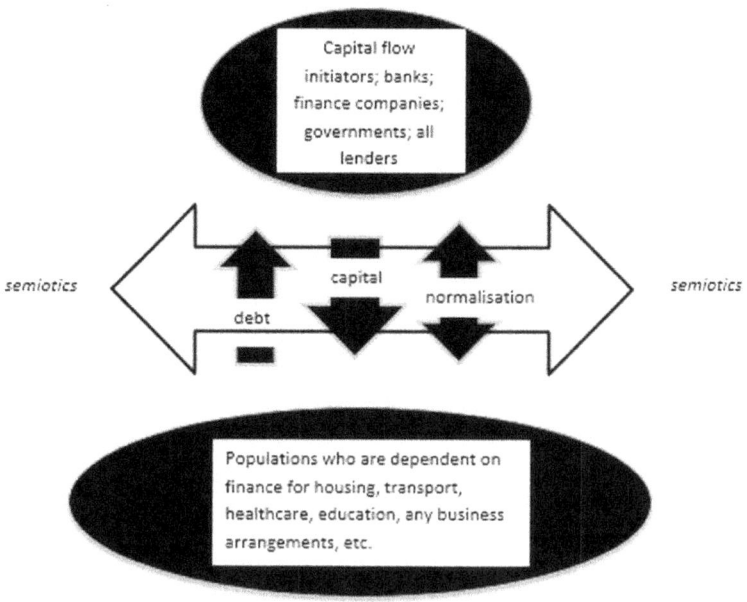

Finance-subjectivity as a result of capital lending practises (semio-capitalism).

Figure 9.3 Finance-subjectivity (Cole 2015a: 303) © Cole 2015.

shamanism (Cole 2007). In the contemporary situation, the media is firmly locked into and part of a global economic and conformist system, and the regimes of debt (as presented in Figure 9.3), making small, anti-mainstream, truly rebellious events more difficult to organize successfully. For example, one doesn't go to the bank manager and ask for a personal loan to organize and host illegal raves! Rather, the normalization of debt and finance that makes anything that one wants to undertake akin to a 'start-up application' immediately deflates revolutionary intent and diverts from the energy to act otherwise, as was the case with the 1990s rave scene in the UK. As soon as one enters into debt, one is beholden to debt arrangements and the conditions for debt that are set by the lender (cf., Cole 2017b). These conditions make revolutionary behaviour subject to profit and money arrangements set by the lender, and not based on principles such as making a difference in times of environmental crisis as 'no media'. Going into debt makes the choices of the debtor necessarily more conservative and risk averse. As such, a postmedia revolution is now unlikely, as it depends on the normalization of financial subjectivity and the repayment of money to a financial institution that controls and sets the parameters whereby the finance happens (i.e. making money due to the postmedia project becomes a necessity). A more likely scenario, and that which sets the tone for this writing and the search for a new social ecology, is that the changes that are happening due to climate change, encapsulated by the term *Anthropocene will force the ways in which we use the media to alter*. In this space, the parameters for change in economics, and as outlined earlier, through the lateral movement embodied by a new, transversal social ecology become apparent as the social and the ecological start to mesh together through 'no media'.

Economists such as Kate Raworth (2017) have begun to tackle this problem in terms of 'doughnut economics'. Through the use of diagrams and accompanying explanation, she has charted how the environment and economy are conjoined through human action, and she has designated a safe zone, whereby they may work with less risk of damage (Figure 9.4). The problem with economics as a monetary and quantitative concern is that the desired direction and intent is towards perpetual higher numbers (i.e. as surplus value or profit), it is programmed to create growth, expansion, and to the free flow of increasing debt as portrayed above (Figure 9.3). In the Anthropocene, it has been realized that the specific ecological damage that runaway economics is creating, especially with respect to the exploitation and use of fossil fuels (climate change), and also in relation to how 'human growth mindset' economics, can objectify nature and relations including those in the media, as assets or resources to make

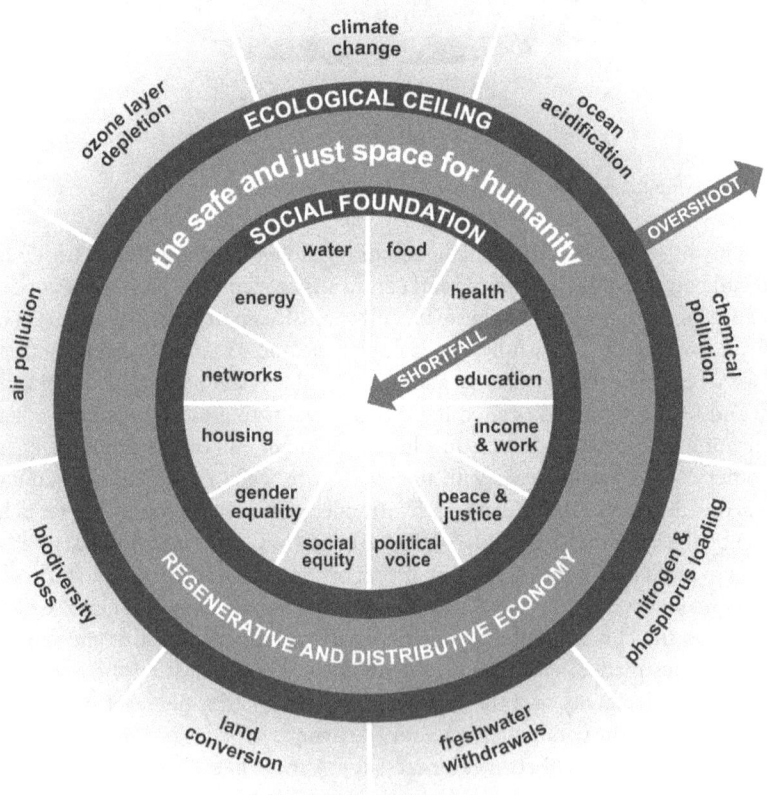

Figure 9.4 The economic doughnut from Raworth (2017: 9). Figure used with permission from the author.

money from. In her diagrams (Raworth 2017) includes the most important elements and concepts that underpin the structure of the doughnut, and hence produces a scale whereby environmental damage may be read against the use of resources and human activities (Figure 9.4).

My argument in this chapter is that the 'shortfall-overshoot' arrows as depicted in Figure 9.4 are now heavily dependent on their presentation and manipulation in the global media. It is primarily through and by the media not augmenting, accelerating and working as a platform for capitalist economics, that there is any chance that the overshoot will not happen. This is what I am calling 'no media' in this chapter that puts a revised and transversal social ecology to work to tackle economics, and to help change the course of humanity and the earth. 'No media' does not mean that we shut off the media, or develop non-relations with the media, as might be in the case with the applied philosophy of Laruelle (Cole 2015b), nor is it a negative Möbius extension of Guattari's bottom-up revolution in media, encouraging micro-media pods to transmit revolutionary messages to change subjectivity. Rather, 'no media' recognizes the negative effects of the mass media in terms of brainwashing commerciality, and how the media can extend and expend society along the path of 'idiot environmentally annihilating' capitalism. Significantly, this path is no longer an option given the reality of climate change in the Anthropocene. Therefore, it is worth sketching out one of the important elements in Raworth's (2017) doughnut economics, which is education, and how it specifically relates to the conception of 'no media' and the new social ecology of this chapter.

A blueprint for a revised education?

'No media' does not imply the shutting down, censorship or abolition or control of media, as some might desire/suggest. Rather, the impetus behind 'no media' as presented here, as part of an argument for a new transversal social ecology and combined with a reappraisal of economics, is to produce an integrated thinking practice that leads to an ethics based on strong connections between thoughts and actions (Table 9.1) in the Anthropocene. Taken from Deleuze and Guattari's (1984) synthesis of desire and Deleuze's (1994) third synthesis, this thinking practice engages students in terms of: (1) *Time*, which can be divided into Habit, Memory and 'the new'; (2) *Economy*, which responds to connective, disjunctive and conjunctive aspects of synthesis; (3) *Growth*, which may be understood through the lateral, transcendental and the actual and; (4)

Table 9.1 The educational thinking practice to connect the Anthropocene with 'no media' (via transversal social ecology and economics). © David Cole

Time	Economy	Growth	Thinking practice
Habit-*present*	Connective	Lateral-immanent-hidden	Virtual
Memory-*past*	Disjunctive	Transcendental-affirmative-dislocated	Intensive
The new-*the future*	Conjunctive	The actual-empirical-combined	The actual

The thinking practices themselves, which are virtual, intensive and the actual. In sum, this schema for education could be implemented to reset teaching and learning in the Anthropocene (Cole 2020), and that could have a chance of encouraging societal change that adds to the models that Bookchin or Guattari suggest. This assertion may be understood through the education systems of many countries that are sufficiently organized so that meaningful sessions could be arranged to allow for interdisciplinary work in these areas that follow this specific schema (Table 9.1) with appropriate content for each category. These sessions fit into open discussions around time, economy and growth, in a parallel mode to which critical thinking has been encouraged through Philosophy 4 Children (P4C), and that has been shown to have positive effects in terms of children's reasoning abilities (e.g. Topping and Trickey 2014). The blueprint here works on already established methods of working in and through education (e.g. the deployment of inquiry-based learning, the Theory of Knowledge subject (ToK)), to be productive of societal change in the Anthropocene through enhanced thinking and consequent ethical actions (Table 9.1).

Education that is digitally mediated in any way has the potential to be sidetracked by peripheral and tangential concerns that 'no media' is attempting to obviate. For example, educational technology has commercial messages embedded in its operations, and often takes its imagistic moves from the latest in high-tech gadgetry, internet signs and functioning (i.e. it can become a pro-capitalist media zone). In contrast, the synthetic thinking practises outlined in Table 9.1 offer a serious way of engaging with the ontology in the Anthropocene beyond media control. For example, I have applied these thinking practises to a case study about the city of Dallas, Texas, and how it functions in the Anthropocene (Cole 2020). Dallas is an incredibly spread-out city, making car travel essential. Dallas is currently functioning very well economically as a 'boom town', due to its low tax regime, and the enticement to increased population, attracted by the ubiquity of jobs and prosperity (I wrote this analysis pre-pandemic). However, the growth and economic activity of Dallas come at a cost. The wildness of the environment has not been preserved in the ever-spreading urbanization, and multiplying cityscape of this paradigmatic fossil fuel city. Dallas is an example of an advanced economy built on fossil fuel exploitation, with little renewable infrastructure and no concern for climate change. However, the thinking practises as outlined in Table 9.1 do not simply produce the response of Texan damnation, or are *only* anti-fossil fuels, or seek to found a reactionary movement against places such as Dallas, that has taken full advantage of fossil fuel expansion in terms of profit margins and its inter-related human life augmentation. Indeed, Dallas acts as a place of refuge and haven for many refugees and economic and social migrants, who have come to Dallas to make better lives for themselves and their families than might be possible in their birth countries. No, the thinking practises as shown in Table 9.1 are not pitched dialectically against the current moment, but look to deep thinking and synthesis with respect to its realignment and change. The truth of climate change in places such as Dallas is that the environment will dictate new formations for the city over time, and the thinking practises as detailed above could aid to spark, follow and understand these changes.

Similarly, 'no media' in this context is a turning away from the mediation of thought, and not an absolute break with the thoughts and actions of now (and, for example, the actual material reality of the global capitalized media). The application of this educational schema for synthetic thought (Table 9.1) about the Anthropocene can be applied to any location, and can be related to any set of circumstances. Change happens over time, and not in or as a sudden break with the form and patterning that is already ongoing and prescient. For example, over the long term, the economic prosperity and growth in places such as Dallas will undergo boom, recession and bust cycles, in conjunction with the negative effects of climate change, and larger and more sustained economic crises. The synthetic thinking practises as outlined in Table 1 are not about agency, or about simply taking militant action in the face of adversity. Rather, the three strands of the thinking practises tend towards doing philosophy through education, and encouraging children and students to be thinkers who can join the dots, and make connections in sometimes trying/hostile situations over time. As we head deeper into the Anthropocene, we need new thinkers to come forward, who can carry out this work to ever greater and more profound extents (*thinkers-yet-to-come*).

Conclusion(s)

In many ways, 'no media' is about escaping the present moment (but not ignoring it). The multi-tentacle reality of the global media and its often-disastrous commerciality seeps into every possible conscious thought and dream that one could have. Behind, alongside, and through this media reality, are the modes in which financialization and the fossil fuel industries have changed the world into a commodity and capital flow. Therefore, 'no media' requires the mobilization of thought beyond and despite the media-finance machine, and to enable the questioning of the capitalist mechanisms that underlie it. For example:

> Capitalism is a corpse, and we are trapped in it: in this trap everything is rotting: invention, progress, friendship, and love. They told us that there is no alternative to capitalism: in this case we must prepare for war, for environmental apocalypse, and for the extinction of the human race, which gets more probable every day.
> But the truth is that the alternative does exist: it is based on getting free from an obsession with economic growth, on the redistribution of the resources, on the reduction of labour time, and on the expansion of time dedicated to the free activity of teaching, research, therapy. (Berardi and Sandiago 2019 e-flux)

Pointedly, the lateral and transversal argument for social ecology (Figure 9.2) feeds into the second half of this quote from Berardi and Sandiago (2019). I would suggest that moves towards a new social ecology, along with their consequences in (semiocapitalist and doughnut) economics and (synthetic) education, might serve as platforms whereby the work that Berardi and Sandiago wish to see happen could progress. However, nothing is guaranteed in this realm and the specific desires and wishes of social agents may cause these schemas for change as outlined in this chapter to move in different, unforeseen directions. Perhaps this dispersal into chaos is better than having the disappointments of failure built into schemas for social change, along the frequently utopic lines of Bookchin and Guattari as precepts. The point of this chapter and 'no media' is not so much a question of what is not going to happen, but one of how we can recursively work with the present through conceptions such as 'no media'.

References

Berardi, F. and V. D. Sandiago (2019), 'Bifo & Vitrina Distópica Santiago: "Put an End to Nazi-Liberalism Now"'. *e-flux*, 1 October. Available online: https://conversations.e-flux.com/t/bifo-vitrina-distopica-santiago-put-an-end-to-nazi-liberalism-now/9470 (accessed 3 January 2022).

Bookchin, M. (1987), 'Social Ecology Versus Deep Ecology: A Challenge for the Ecology Movement', *Green Perspectives: Newsletter of the Green Program Project*, 1987: 4–5.

Bookchin, M. (2007), *Social Ecology and Communalism*, Vol. 118, Oakland: AK Press.

Braithwaite, J. (2008), *Regulatory Capitalism: How It Works, Ideas for Making It Work Better*, Cheltenham: Edward Elgar Publishing.

Cole, D. R. (2007), 'Techno-shamanism and Educational Research', *Ashe! Journal of Experimental Spirituality*, 6 (1): 6–34.

Cole, D. R. (2015a), 'Finance-Subjectivity: Thinking Through the Consequences of the Global Financial Crisis (GFC) in Education', in M. A. Peters, J. M. Paraskeva and T. Besley (eds), *The Global Financial Crises and Educational Restructuring*, 301–17, New York: Peter Lang.

Cole, D. R. (2015b), 'Educational Non-Philosophy', *Educational Philosophy and Theory*, 47 (10): 1009–23.

Cole, D. R. (2017a), 'Black Sun: The Singularity at the Heart of the Anthropocene', *Institute for Interdisciplinary Research into the Anthropocene*, 31 July. Available online: https://iiraorg.com/2017/07/31/first-blog-post (accessed 3 January 2022).

Cole, D. R. (2017b), 'Deleuze and Learning', in M. A. Peters (ed.), *Encyclopaedia of Philosophy of Education and Theory*, 1–6, Singapore: Springer. Available online: https://link.springer.com/referenceworkentry/10.1007/978-981-287-532-7_68-1 (accessed 3 January 2022).

Cole, D. R. (2020), 'Learning to Think in the Anthropocene: What Can Deleuze-Guattari Teach Us?' in K. Maiti and S. Chakraborty (eds), *Global Perspectives on Eco-Aesthetics and Eco-Ethics: A Green Critique*, 31–47, Lanham: Lexington Books.

Crutzen, P. J. (2002), 'Geology of Mankind', *Nature*, 415: 23.

Deleuze, G. ([1968] 1994), *Difference and Repetition*, trans. P. Patton, New York: Columbia University Press.

Deleuze, G. and F. Guattari ([1972] 1984), *Anti-Oedipus: Capitalism and Schizophrenia*, trans. R. Hurley, M. Steen and H. R. Lane, London: The Athlone Press.

Ember, C. R. (2020), 'Hunter-Gathers (Foragers)', *HRAF: Explaining Human Culture*, 1 June. Available online: https://hraf.yale.edu/ehc/summaries/hunter-gatherers (accessed 3 January 2022).

Genosko, G., ed. (2012), *Felix Guattari in the Age of Semiocapitalism*, Edinburgh: Edinburgh University Press.

Grubb, M. (1995), 'Seeking Fair Weather: Ethics and the International Debate on Climate Change', *International Affairs*, 71 (3): 463–96.

Guattari, F. (1990), 'Towards a Post Media Era', trans. A. Sebti and C. Apprich (modifications by Neinsager), in C. Apprich, J. B. Slater, A. Iles and O. L. Schultz (eds), *Provocative Alloys: A Post-Media Anthology*, 27, Lüneburg: PML Books.

Guattari, F. ([1972] 2005), *Psychoanalysis and Transversality: Texts and Interviews 1955–1971*, trans. A. Hodges, South Pasadena: Semiotext(e).

Guattari, F. ([1989] 2013), *Schizoanalytic Cartographies*, trans. A. Goffey, London: Bloomsbury.

Heidegger, M. ([1953] 1971), 'Language in the Poem: A Discussion on Georg Trakl's Poetic Work', trans. P. D. Hertz, in M. Heidegger (ed.), *On the Way to Language*, 159–98, New York: Harper & Row.

Ireland, A. (2017), 'The Poememenon: Form as Occult Technology', *Urbanomic*. Available online: https://www.urbanomic.com/document/poememenon/ (accessed 3 January 2022).

Land, N. (2011), 'Narcissism and Dispersion in Heidegger's 1953 Trakl Interpretation', in R. Mackay and R. Brassier (eds), *Fanged Noumena: Collected Writings 1987–2007*, 81–123, New York: Sequence Press.

Naess, A. (1988), 'Deep Ecology and Ultimate Premises', *Ecologist*, 18: 128–31.

Naess, A. ([1981] 1990), *Ecology, Community and Lifestyle: Outline of an Ecosophy*, trans. D. Rothenberg, Cambridge: Cambridge University Press.

Raworth, K. (2017), *Doughnut Economics: Seven Ways to Think Like a 21st-Century Economist*, White River Junction: Chelsea Green Publishing.

Rifkin, J. (2011), *The Third Industrial Revolution: How Lateral Power Is Transforming Energy, The Economy, and the World*, New York: Macmillan.

Roberts, B. (2012), 'Technics, Individuation and Tertiary Memory: Bernard Stiegler's Challenge to Media Theory', *New Formations*, 77: 8–20.

Topping, K. J. and S. Trickey (2014), 'The Role of Dialog in Philosophy for Children', *International Journal of Educational Research*, 63: 69–78.

10

Schizoanalysis and ecology on the other side of postmedia

Mark Featherstone

One suspects that in this age of global pandemics, everyday ecological disaster, economic stagnation, looming redundancy and seemingly intractable social division, even the neoliberals realize that the capitalist system is on its last legs. While 'throwbacks' like Boris Johnson, Jair Bolsonaro and the other populists imagine salvation in fantastical utopias of the past when the nation was great enough to stand alone in splendid isolation, business leaders such as Jeff Bezos and Richard Branson seem to realize that a capitalist future is likely to require escape velocity and making money from the stars. Somewhere in-between the primitive nationalists and the sci-fi futurists, one can envisage desperate cabals grimly making plans concerned with increasing their chances of surviving the great fire, the global conflagration, that they think will soon consume our living space and leave the planet more or less uninhabitable.

Against this kind of apocalyptic realism, which would lead one towards a heavily fortified future deep underground away from hostile competitors and unliveable weather, others put their faith in science and technology. Forgetting that it is, of course, modern techno-science and its adoption by capitalist civilization that brought us to the catastrophic moment we currently occupy, those who believe in the techno-fix imagine that we might be able to mechanize our way out of our predicament. In this view, it is possible that we might somehow be able to carry on with our wicked ways, if only we can invent machines to run on renewables and collect enough of the carbon gases which presently envelope the planet, increasing temperatures and making it harder and harder to imagine a liveable future. Despite the fantastical, apocalyptic nature of some of these imaginary responses to the current global impasse Žižek wrote about in terms of 'living in the end times' more than a decade ago (Žižek 2010), there is a sense in which each of these versions of the future are haunted by the psychopathological condition of normopathy, or the inability to think that one might become other than one is today, and a distinct lack of imagination concerning real psychosocial transformation off the back of subjective revolution. In each case it is material conditions that change – 'we' return to the nation; 'we' blast off into outer space in search of somewhere else where 'we' can be who 'we' really are; 'we' build bunkers to escape the fire that 'we' cannot avoid because 'we' cynically believe 'we' are incapable of change; or 'we' put our faith in technological invention similarly because 'we' think it is easier to invent new machines than change who 'we' are. All the while 'we' remain the same.

Although the future may well end up being about conflicts between nations struggling to secure competitive advantage in brutal wars over scarce natural resources and living space, the super-rich blasting off into outer space searching for liveable environments on far-off worlds, more chthonic elites making ever more urgent plans to survive the coming human-made apocalypse, and/or technophiles searching for increasingly elaborate ways to keep the neoliberal show on the road by changing the mode of production while leaving the basic philosophical structures of capitalism untouched – I want to make the case that an alternative vision can be found in Deleuze and Guattari, and particularly Guattari's own work, which challenges capitalist subjectivity and on the basis of this, offers a very different view of our possible futures. The central point of my chapter is to explore this alternative, 'minor utopianism', against the backdrop of contemporary, catastrophic, global conditions.

In the first part of the chapter, my objective is to outline this potential future through a discussion of Deleuze and Guattari's schizoanalytic critique of first, Freudian psychoanalysis, which is identified with capitalist subjectivity in their *Anti-Oedipus* (1983), *A Thousand Plateaus* (1987), and *What Is Philosophy?* (1994) and Guattari's own key works (see 1995, 2009a,b, 2011, 2013, 2014, 2015, 2016), and then second and following this, to offer an exploration of their critical reading of late or semiocapitalism, which shows how reality itself is subject to processes of codification, containment, commodification and repression. Building upon this exploration of Deleuze and Guattari's vision of another future, and focussing specifically on Guattari's own work in the context of the contemporary catastrophic moment, which I would argue he saw coming in the late 1980s and early 1990s when he wrote *The Three Ecologies* (2014) and *Chaosmosis* (1995), in part two of the chapter I want to suggest that we need to update his insights with respect to his utopian hope for postmedia and the fragmentation of the mass media in the age of cyberspace. That is to say that thirty years after *Chaosmosis*, I think it has become increasingly difficult to sustain the view that postmedia will deliver the kind of schizoanalysis of the paranoid, normopathic system that Guattari hoped for and imagined would enable the development of a new ethico-aesthetic paradigm for thinking otherwise.

In taking up this perspective, I propose to develop my reading of Deleuze and Guattari on the schizoanalysis of capitalist subjectivity undertaken in the first part of the chapter by showing how their cyber-utopian hope of postmedia has been captured by the technologies of surveillance capitalism in the second part of my discussion. Here, I propose to turn to Zuboff's (2019) recent critique of the tech giants Google, Facebook and Apple, to argue that, contra Guattari's early 1990s utopian hope, postmedia has become a force of anti-production, which has ended up supporting the kind of semiotic despotism that Guattari (2009b) himself identified with integrated world capitalism and which his long-time friend and collaborator Franco Berardi links to a new form of neuro-totalitarianism (Berardi 2015). In this respect, the postmedia future looks bleak. However, this is not to say that there is no hope, because, as Berardi (2008) notes in his biography of his old friend Guattari, depression, the moment one hits 'rock bottom' and can see no way out, is also a moment of possibility, transformation and change. This is the point I want to develop in my conclusion.

Although Guattari finds this hope in postmedia, and the fragmentation of the mass media sphere that would otherwise ensure the reproduction of capitalist subjectivity, in the wake of the rise of the tech giants and a new model of social control based upon digital behaviour modification, Berardi (2015) realizes that cyberspace is no utopia. This does not mean that he is hopeless though, but rather that he recognizes the need to update Guattari's dialectic of pessimism and optimism through his critique of neuro-totalitarianism and turn to the excessive signification of poetry. It is based on this dialectic – comprising on the one hand, the kind of neuro-totalitarianism produced by the control systems of the tech giants and the madness that this causes in people lost in the maelstrom of the infosphere that makes it impossible for them to think straight and, on the other hand, the desperate turn to the poetic and a form of signification on the far side of the digital capable of expressing what it means to possess a body and relate to other bodies in a world of flesh, blood, bone, mass, weight and density – that Berardi (2015, 2018) looks to renew Guattari's schizoanalytic critique of semiocapitalism for the early twenty-first century and develop his vision of a new politico-ethico-aesthetic paradigm. Essentially, I take it that the objective of this work is to find a way to realize Guattari's theory of the three ecologies organized around the schizoanalytic transformation of capitalist subjectivity, capitalist social relations, and the perverse, capitalist approach to thinking about the environment as a thing to be used and abused in the name of semiotic reduction, commodification, and profitability.

By turning towards the poetic, and employing poetry to critique the semiotic reduction of fleshy mass and heavy materiality to weightless digital signs, Berardi (2015, 2018) seeks to update Guattari by providing the normopathic late capitalist subject with:

(1) a new way of understanding, thinking and feeling that would be otherwise prevented by the digital sphere that rejects reference to the material sphere beyond quantification in the cybernetic universe of 0s and 1s and, on this basis,
(2) a space for a more human form of society made up of people who recognize each other beyond the profane sphere of objectification, commodification, digitization, and finally,
(3) a heavy, materialistic approach to relating to the environment and returning to the earth that defines their being and represents who they are beyond the estrangement of capitalist territorialization that drives them mad.

In what follows, I propose to trace this thesis through reference to Deleuze and Guattari (1983, 1987) and Guattari (2015) on the schizoanalytic critique of capitalist subjectivity and the mass media sphere that produces the condition of normopathy, before turning to Zuboff (2019) to show how Guattari's (2009b) hope for postmedia was not only thwarted by the model of surveillance capitalism developed by Google, but instead transformed into a kind of dark dystopia of social control and behaviour modification. Finally, I refer to Guattari's follower Berardi (2015, 2018) to show how this dystopia of digital information might be seen to relate to the unfolding global catastrophe we are currently living through and how his revision of Guattari's theory of a new aesthetic paradigm for thinking, feeling, and relating on the other side of postmedia represents our best chance of escape from our present seemingly hopeless situation. That is to say that I conclude that we need new ways of looking, feeling, and relating to develop new forms of subjectivity, sociality, and environmental sensitivity capable of replacing the estrangement of the contemporary digital infosphere with a more carnal, humble, limited version of thinking about interconnectedness based in the weight of bodies.

Schizophrenia, capitalism and postmedia

We find Guattari's key thesis concerning postmedia in a range of papers collected in texts such as *Soft Subversions* (2009b), which bring together his work from the late 1970s through to the mid-1980s, and in particular the short essays 'Postmodern deadlock and postmedia transition' and 'Entering the postmedia era' written in a period when he was focussed on the critique of integrated world capitalism. In these short pieces, Guattari develops the argument that the fragmentation of the mass-media sphere in the face of the emergence of what he calls postmedia or new forms of information communication technology will potentially enable 'the emergence of new practices of subjectivation' through 'the formation of innovative forms of dialogue and collective interactivity and, eventually, a reinvention of democracy' (2009b: 299). His key thesis is, therefore, that the development and democratization of the internet would break the mass-media monopoly on mass communication and enable the emergence of new minority ways of seeing, thinking and imagining the world, and that this might in turn lead to the formation of new forms of subjectivity and political activity. This is Guattari's hope for a kind of minor utopia of media communication that recalls what Deleuze and Guattari (1986) saw in the literature of Kafka who they thought gave voice to alternative visions of the world in early twentieth-century Austro-Hungary.

In Guattari's (2009b) take on postmedia, the importance of this development is that it might challenge the hegemony of the global capitalist infosphere or what he calls semio- or integrated world capitalism by creating the conditions for the realization of what Deleuze and Guattari call schizoanalysis across their key works on capitalism, schizophrenia, and the politics of thinking otherwise. Thus, Guattari's view is that the schizoanalytic critique of media is essential because the mass-media sphere represents a space for the reproduction of the kind of Freudian, capitalist mode of subjectivity that ensures the normopathic subordination of people to fathers, bosses, and other representatives of the authoritarian capitalist legal, coding system. We recall that in the first volume of their work on capitalism and schizophrenia, *Anti-Oedipus* (1983), Deleuze and Guattari's key thesis is that Freudian psychoanalysis represents a kind of psychological control system that suggests that repression is essential for keeping humans alive. While Freud thought that Oedipalization was necessary to move people from a state of nature, violence and complete freedom to a state of society, civilization and normalization, Deleuze and Guattari argue that Freud's vision was always based upon an interpretation of the capitalist world and that in reality normalization is not necessary to keep people breathing. Left to our own devices we would *not* become little Hobbesian monsters, but rather productive, creative creatures capable of making a world in sympathy with our own nature, the nature of others, and the nature of our environment, the earth.

Given this early Marxist vision of the human, in Deleuze and Guattari (1983) the unconscious is not primitive, savage, and set on suicidal self-destruction, which is essentially where Freud ends up in *Beyond the Pleasure Principle* (2003) and *Civilization and Its Discontents* (2010), but rather productive, creative and characterized by desire, which repackages Nietzsche's notion of becoming for a post-Freudian world. Based upon this critique of Freud, and the practice of psychoanalysis and normalization, Deleuze and Guattari make the case that the form of (Oedipalized) subjectivity that follows rules is no longer about necessity and making sure we do not kill each other in the name of escaping from the trauma of individuation, but instead the illegitimate power of the patriarch, the despot, the police, the boss, the teacher, and any number of other micro-fascists who tell us that socialization is essential to maintaining social order to protect their own position and keep themselves in power. On the basis of this critical theory of subjectivation in capitalist civilization, and how this is legitimated by Freudian psychoanalysis and the theory of the necessity of good socialization, Deleuze and Guattari's (1983) next move is to make the key structuralist point that this system of social organization relies on processes of signification or the coding of the body, earth and other life forms. In the case of the body, Freud's Oedipus involves the imposition of normalized forms of sexuality, essentially heterosexuality, upon the developing individual and thus the coding of their body in terms of erogenous zones and reproductive organs that limit primitive/infantile polymorphous sexuality, desire, and the ways the new subject relates to others and material reality. In much the same way that the Freudian body is coded and organized in line with reproductive sexuality, Deleuze and Guattari explain that analysis of the history of civilization shows shifts in approaches to the coding or territorialization of the earth itself. Beyond medieval, theocratic forms of coding that understood the earth in terms of the sacred and profane, in Deleuze and Guattari's (1983) thinking capitalist forms of territorialization involve the enclosure of land and its translation into abstract signs, or money based upon rent and the production of surpluses. Under these conditions the land, the earth, is no longer a living space, but rather a sign system, a territory, for the creation of abstract value.

However, Deleuze and Guattari recognize that what separates capitalist models of territorialization from older medieval forms of coding is that they are endlessly undercut by processes of deterritorialization, disembedding, and the translation of materiality into abstract signs, money and virtuality, which relates to the prospect of realizing value sometime in the future. In this respect, they understood that capitalism is itself schizophrenic with respect to what Marx and Engels explained in *The Communist Manifesto* (2002), namely that capitalism cannot accept a state of self-identity or stability for very long. Against this tendency to take flight though, Deleuze and Guattari (1983, 1987) saw that state capitalism was itself conditioned by the constant need to establish territorial limits, more or less stable forms of codification, and what they call paranoid social forms. Given that this bipolar social form, comprising a kind of 'restricted schizophrenia' centred upon taking flight within the limits of capitalist code and a type of 'provisional paranoia' concerned with maintaining territorial limits and normalizing schizophrenic flight, we can see that Deleuze and Guattari's vision of capitalist subjectivity resembles the classic Freudian self formed in the endless struggle between the forces of the unconscious, socially approved forms of personhood, and the super-ego or father figure in the head and a whole array of other authority figures who tell us what to do and how to be normal in our own best interest. In Guattari's (2009b) own work it is clear that this complex of subject-formation and ongoing individuation, and the related normalization of the paranoid-schizophrenia of capitalism, relies on mass media and this is why he thinks postmedia might be able to disrupt the basic message of the authoritarian system through schizoanalytic critique.

Building upon the general thesis set out in *Anti-Oedipus* (1983), *A Thousand Plateaus* (1987), and *What Is Philosophy?* (1994), which brought the idea of the need to create a new aesthetic paradigm to understand the chaos of capitalist schizophrenia to the forefront, from the 1980s onwards Guattari's (2009b) vision of capitalism was of a completely globalized system and a situation where the entire earth has been coded and translated into abstract value. In this context, I would suggest it is possible to think about the fragmentation of the mass media into postmedia in terms of the internalization of processes of schizophrenic deterritorialization that would have otherwise involved the externalization of the capitalist tendency towards disembedding in imperial adventure, colonial seizure and primitive accumulation, and the potential psychotic breakdown of authoritarian models of coding that had held firm since the first enclosures in early modern Britain. In other words, in the late 1980s and early 1990s, we could imagine that the paranoid-schizophrenia of capitalism had reached its planetary limits in the realization of globalization, and that following the end of the cold war, the fall of the Berlin Wall, and the transition of communist China to a more or less normal trading partner, there was nowhere else to exploit, with the result that the processes of schizophrenic deterritorialization had begun to turn against their paranoid other and transform into a force for democratic change. This was certainly Guattari's hope, which was more or less repeated by Michael Hardt and Antonio Negri in their great millennial text *Empire* (2000), that opposed the forces of semiocapitalism (empire) to the vast multitude of the global poor who represented the essential schizophrenic excess of the system, but would soon, in Hardt and Negri's view, come to form a kind of global counter-power capable of the schizoanalytic critique of the paranoia of the empire in the name of a revitalization of direct democracy.

Seen in the rear-view mirror of history I think that it is possible to understand Guattari's (2009b) hope and Hardt and Negri's (2000) utopian work as representative of the final flourish of the cyber-utopianism that Fred Turner (2008) traces back to the 1950s and the moment McLuhan, Brand, and others from the counterculture re-read the cybernetics of Wiener and Shannon and Weaver against the grain of those who were critical of the computerization of society and the American individual. Although Guattari (2016) was well aware of the problem of digitization, and the semiotic reduction of life to abstract code, his hopeful vision of what cybernetics and computerization might bring went with Brand and the counterculture over C. W. Mills (2000) and the critique of the military-industrial complex that would, I think, ultimately prove to be the truth of postmedia and cyberculture. Contrary to what Guattari (2009b), and later Hardt and Negri (2000), would imagine with regard to the production of networks of difference, creativity and transformation working to undermine a globalized semiocapitalist empire overseen by a collection of states operating in the name of a system of increasingly abstract exchange, what has happened since the publication of Guattari's final works in the mid-1990s, and certainly since the publication of Hardt and Negri's *Empire* in 2000, is that the big bad imperial order led by America, Britain and the forces of neoliberal capitalism has collapsed into a state of social and political madness, represented by the election of Trump, Johnson and the turn towards a kind of primitive isolationist nationalism, and the postmedia networks Guattari and Hardt and Negri thought might deliver political subversion and dissensus have become a more or less homogenous space, the domain of a kind of global superorganism that is able to reach into the lives of every individual the moment they use Google, Facebook or pick up their Apple iPhone.

In this respect, I would make the argument that far from delivering a kind of cyber-utopia of difference and dissensus, the development of postmedia over the last three decades has produced a digital dystopia with far greater reach than the old mass media of the twentieth century ever had. Following the work of Berardi (2015) and Baudrillard (2009), I would make the case that this postmedia, digital dystopia has two dimensions, which we might compare to the hardware and software of the computer systems that make it work. On the one hand, the development of what Zuboff (2019) calls surveillance capitalism and algorithmic power has simply extended the reach of the coding processes Deleuze and Guattari (1983, 1987) and Guattari (2009b, 2016) linked to semiotic authoritarianism. For Zuboff this new model of capitalism emerged from the Dot Com crash of the early 2000s when Google and other start-ups were forced to come up with new ways of making money. Enter Hal Varian, the Google economist, who saw the potential in the data exhaust people leave behind for closing the loop on consumer behaviour and enabling the creation of precision advertising targeted at individuals. According to Zuboff, then, Google was the first corporation to realize the value of data trash to advertisers desperate to target users/consumers with a view to controlling their object choice behind their backs.

In this new model of capitalism information relating to search patterns, phrasing, spelling, punctuation, dwell time, click pattern, use of capitalisation, location, and any number of other indicators could help to build up a picture of a user/consumer in the name of manipulating their desires and modifying their behaviour through the use of nudges. While Google accesses this data through surveillance of user searches, Zuboff points out that Facebook is able to exploit its existing culture of intimacy to collect information and build detailed data doubles of individuals to support the work of advertisers and others looking to advance an ideology of what she calls inevitablism. In this regard, the evolution of cyberspace and by extension postmedia has not led to the kind of molecular revolution and proliferation of voices Guattari hoped for, but quite the opposite. Although the surface effect of postmedia may remain one of polyvocity, challenge to power, and the emergence of a new kind of electronic direct democracy, the algorithmic infrastructure employed by Google,

Facebook, Apple, and Amazon means that Guattari's (2009b) hoped for digital utopia is in reality an advance on the molar power of mass-media capitalism. If the critical theorists of the Frankfurt School, Adorno, Horkheimer, and Marcuse, thought that the world of capitalist propaganda, advertising, and marketing was destructive (see Adorno and Horkheimer 1997; Marcuse 2002), the new world of algorithmic power has simply expanded the sphere of alienation and estrangement by transforming the individual's data exhaust into a commodity to enable behaviour modification through the manipulation of their desire.

As Deleuze and Guattari (1983) understood, the key function of consumer capitalism was the commodification or coding of desire and while this is still clearly happening today in mass media, the advance of the new digital infosphere is to very carefully establish connections between individual consumers and commodities in ways that were simply not possible in the age dominated by the mass media. This precision advertising, narrowcasting, or targeting is only made possible by digital, postmedia, semio-consumer-capitalism's ability to build massive datasets covering billions of users, comprising highly individualized pictures of the identity and desires of each potential consumer (data doubles). From this point of view, it is possible to make the case that the problem with Guattari's (2009b) reading of the potential of postmedia is that he failed to see that the schizophrenia of the system would work for the benefit of digital consumer capitalism, rather than the multitude of individual users, and that the cyber-utopian idea of freedom of information, communication and discourse would become a strategic advantage to enable enormous multinational corporations to build massive databases focussed on consumer identity and individual desire in the name of closing the loop of advertising strategy and consumer object choice. In the past there was, of course, uncertainty about the way that mass-media advertising would be received by consumers and how this would impact upon their object choice, simply because it was not possible to speak to individual consumers directly. The whole point of mass media was that it addressed a mass. This is no longer a problem in the world of postmedia. The mass has become entirely individualized in the form of the swarm. Thus, the schizophrenia, the polyvocity, and the dissensus of the system are what enable semio-consumer-capitalism to speak to consumers in very precise ways and code their object choice, based on in-depth knowledge of their unconscious desires revealed through their engagement with the always-on semiocapitalist network. This is, of course, the point of the commodification of the data exhaust Zuboff (2019) explores in her important work on surveillance capitalism.

It is this general situation that has, for Franco Berardi (2015), led to the emergence of a new kind of semio- or neuro-totalitarianism. When Hannah Arendt (1973) was writing about this concept, and explaining its key elements, ideology and terror, she could not have foreseen what would happen in the early twenty-first century, which is that the individual would be more or less entirely controlled, unbeknownst to them, by a semiotic system or kind of globalized brain that seems to know what they think before they do. It is precisely because of this ability to very precisely speak to individual users/consumers based on data harvesting techniques, machine learning and algorithmic/calculating power that Berardi (2015) makes the case that what semiocapitalism and the kind of postmedia that Guattari (2009b) thought would liberate subjectivity and enable schizoanalytic critique to flourish, achieves is the complete separation of the power of signification, or the power to code, from the signified, the thing itself, materiality, or the body of the individual. In this situation the individual no longer codes, no longer speaks, but is rather spoken by language or the signifying system. In respect of the way this interpretation recalls Lacan's (2017) classic structuralist idea that we are spoken by a kind of symbolic unconscious, it is worth remembering that his post-Freudian model for the unconscious was always the cybernetic system (Liu 2011). Given this history, which takes in Freud, Lacan and cybernetics, and concludes with the fusion of psychoanalysis and computational thinking, we might suggest the next step and say that in the contemporary world the unconscious *is* the algorithmic system, the command-and-control machine, that underpins the postmedia network that structures the platforms which enable our freedom of speech and dissensus.

However, what Lacan did not imagine, at least as far as I am aware, is that the cybernetic system would become the unconscious in a very real sense, preferring instead to understand the semiotic unconscious as a kind of historical artefact, which nobody could directly control, though some clearly have always had more influence over the evolution of language and the connection between signifiers and signifieds than others. The problem is, of course, that in the new postmedia world, the very deep structures that organize the system, the algorithmic command-and-control program that allows speech to happen, are not simply neutral, but rather subject to the influence of powerful interests set on the collection of the trace of the unconscious that the individual leaves behind when they interact with the platform in the name of free expression and so on. It is this hidden power relation, which translates individual freedom of expression into information for strategic use in programs focussed on behaviour modification through the collection of data trash and the digital trace of the unconscious for the sake of precision advertising, that ultimately signifies that Guattari (2009b) underestimated the ways in which postmedia would operate according to the logics of Lacan's cybernetic vision of the unconscious.

It was, we remember, Guattari's (2009b) hope that postmedia would place semiotic power, the power to signify, the power to code, back in the hands of subjects, and that this would lead to the formation of subject groups able to direct their own fate. But, updating Guattari, Berardi's thesis, set out across several works including *And* (2015), suggests that the opposite has happened and a kind of computational Lacanianism has taken over. Regardless of the apparent critical schizophrenia, polyvocity and dissensus of postmedia, the power to code resides in command of the obscure algorithmic infrastructure that remains impenetrable to everybody beyond the engineers of the tech giants themselves. Given their ability to code and control object choice, Berardi (2015) suggests that far from leading to the formation of subject groups, those managing the program behind the postmedia platforms have actually produced a situation characterized by the subjugation of totally networked individuals and the separation of the communicative brain from the desiring body. From Berardi's point of view, the problem of this separation of the brain from the body, and the transformation of the signifier into a kind of instrumental device for behaviour modification, is that language starts to fail as a technology for connecting people and enabling them to empathize with each other's situations in the world. In this situation, language is no longer about expression, and the communication of material states, but rather the instrumental control of desire and object choice. The result of this failure of empathy, which comes about because empathetic connections issue from the excessive, non-rational aspect of language that brings material bodies into contact – it is precisely this element of language that is crowded out in the name of computation code – is that the other becomes a stranger, an alien, and a potential enemy, rather than somebody who might become a friend. Thus, we witness the rise of a kind of globalized paranoia and the conspiratorial mindset.

While Deleuze and Guattari (1983, 1987) connect paranoia to processes of reterritorialization and the need to respond to the schizophrenic dimension of capitalism, in Berardi's (2015) account paranoia, existential loneliness, and fear of the other would be the result of the collapse of the signifier as a technology of human, rather than machine, communication. It is important to make this point because it relates to what I would call the second dimension of the postmedia digital dystopia, which we might understand in terms of the software of the new (un)world, concerned with the way individuals manage or fail to manage the blizzard of signs and avalanche of information produced by the postmedia system. That is to say if the hardware of the postmedia dystopia relates to coding and algorithmic power, the software problem of this new nightmarish situation is about how the individual processes the streams of signs and symbols emerging from the infosphere that are no longer founded upon a connection to materiality, but rather free floating and, for this reason, subject to a law of infinite inflation or what Baudrillard (2009) wrote about in terms of virality in the same period that Guattari imagined his postmedia utopianism. What is clear from Guattari's (2009b) various comments about the potential of postmedia is that he never really considers this problem of inflation, excess, and exorbitance that is central to Baudrillard's work written in the early 1990s and Berardi's current analysis of the digital dystopia.

The central concern here is about more than struggles around basic information management and sorting the meaningful from meaningless data, because the point of information overload for both Baudrillard (2009) and Berardi (2015) is that the avalanche of words and numbers that the individual is somehow supposed to process emerges as a result of the estrangement of signifiers from material signifieds or referents, which essentially means that all signifiers start to look meaningless from the point of view of the bewildered individual who can no longer see how they impact upon their increasingly nihilistic world in any kind of meaningful sense. Now, it is precisely this process of increasing estrangement and nihilism concerning the meaning or lack of meaning of the signifier that ends up causing semiotic inflation, over-production, and a desperate search for meaning somewhere in language or data sets that seem like bottomless pits of insignificance. The less signifiers appear to mean, the less value they appear to possess, the more they must be produced to try to fill the void of significance left behind by the liberation of the signifier from the materiality of the body and thingness of the earth. While Guattari (2009b) simply does not foresee this problem of postmedia, preferring to take the countercultural line that the fragmentation of the mass media would enable the free expression of dissensus and a kind of schizoanalytic critique of power, Baudrillard (2009) more clearly understood the problem of the liberation of the signifier and the production of endless difference that ends up making no difference whatsoever. In the context of this state of schizophrenic indifference, what Baudrillard called 'the Hell of the Same', communication collapses into excess, a kind of babel of words, numbers, and other signs, with the result that the social starts to implode. Against Guattari's vision of postmedia schizophrenia, dissensus and direct democracy, Baudrillard thus imagines the complete implosion of the social.

Ecology on the other side of postmedia

Caught somewhere between a complete excess and total lack of significance in the digital dystopia, I would suggest that we are a long way from Guattari's (2009b) vision that postmedia might enable the formation of schizoanalytic subject groups, and far closer to Baudrillard's (2009) sense that the devaluation of the signifier will result in the collapse of the social and the emergence of a kind of generalized, post-empathetic solipsism which results in the objectification of the other by the self who is equally othered by some other self. Under these conditions of estrangement, Deleuze and Guattari's (1983, 1987) concept of desire is manifest in the hyper-sexual, hyper-consumerist form of hardcore pornography circulating on the internet, where the other is a profane object, a kind of machine to be fucked in the name of reaching jouissance, or a state where one enjoys enjoyment and touches the real of pleasure. While Deleuze and Guattari (1983) imagined desire free from Oedipal repression in a state of polymorphous perversity, semiocapitalist postmedia sex is heavily coded, commodified and part of the very system of domination they wanted to transgress. In this situation, the authority figure is no longer the law-abiding father, the cop or the teacher, but rather the Sadean master or perverse father who uses and abuses the other in a state of second nature that recalls what Freud imagined existed before Oedipus in *Totem and Taboo* (2001). We recall that it was precisely Deleuze and Guattari's (1983) point that Oedipus was always a ruse, a way for the perverse father to pass off his domination as law necessary to make life liveable, but the key point I am making here is that postmedia has not challenged this situation in the way that Guattari imagined, but rather led to its generalization by creating a kind of mute, non-communicative non-society in the midst of a world swimming in information.

What this means is that in the postmedia world where there is so much information, so much communication, that nothing really means anything, all forms of social contract appear to break down and a new form of perverse pre-/post-Oedipal primitivism comes to the fore. We see this everywhere today. From Trump, who 'grabs them by the pussy', to Weinstein, who could not understand the difference between people and things or sex and domination, the Me-Too movement has revealed the general problem of the perverse father in the postmedia, semiocapitalist society. This situation is, of course, deeply problematic from the point of view of women, who must suffer male violence on an everyday basis, but also from the perspective of cultural politics more generally. The figure of the perverse father perfectly captured by Michel Houellebecq over the course of two decades is a deeply depressing figure in general who, I want to suggest, tells us about the senility or lateness of semiocapitalism and the contemporary world of postmedia. Reading Houellebecq (*Platform* 2003), we cannot escape the miserable, depressing image of the older man, desperate to possess younger women, to hang onto his power, even though he ultimately knows that his time is up. The old man imagines a utopia of jouissance, a future where he enjoys the real of younger women, and somehow escapes age, decay and decrepitude.

In his recent book *Futurability* (2019), Berardi makes exactly this point, noting the inherent violence, or micro-fascism, of the desperate father clinging to power, seizing objects of desire ever more aggressively in a doomed attempt to reverse his inevitable decline. Is this not precisely how we could understand the logic of signification operative in semiocapitalism and postmedia in the contemporary world? Nothing means anything, because the signifier is no longer connected to the weight of the signified that matters, with the result that semiocapitalism aggressively overproduces in the desperate hope that either something will stick and we will escape the nihilism of repetition into meaning or the blizzard of information will screen out the abyss of insignificance – so that we will no longer have to face the void staring back into our eyes. Is it any wonder that in this situation, which plunges people back into a kind of state of nature where it is no longer possible to think beyond what is directly in front of one's face, depression takes hold and people imagine jouissance and escape into the real of sex? Given this thesis, we might interpret Trump, Weinstein and Me-Too as symptoms of the desperate decline of the Freudian father, and the potential turn to a kind of desire more like Deleuze and Guattari's (1983, 1987) Nietzschean re-reading of polymorphous perversity. But unfortunately, this is not simply a story of the slow death of the patriarchal father who is running out of time.

Although the father may very well be nostalgic for some lost past that never really existed, when the nation was great and he could enjoy what he wanted, I would make the case that the problem of sexual politics and masculinity reaches beyond the generation of men raised under conditions of war and its aftermath in the 1950s and 1960s and represents a far more general problem of what Berardi (2015, 2019) calls cultural senility. Consider the contemporary 'incel' (Involuntary Celibate), who finds it impossible to relate to women precisely because, I would argue, of the collapse of normal, human, forms of communication and the rise of a kind of algorithmic postmedia universe where performance is everything. In this asocial context, which looks very much like a high-tech version of the Hobbesian or Freudian vision of nature, the awkward young men of the incel subculture believe they have been cast out of the evolutionary struggle to reproduce and that they are condemned to a life of loneliness. In response to this misreading of the politics of human object choice and relationship formation, contrary to what one might assume, the incel does not fall into melancholia, hankering after a lost object of love in the manner of the romantics, but instead violently reacts to perceived rejection by developing an elaborate conspiracy theory founded upon resentment of the behaviour of women. The reason this final point is important is because I think it explains what is happening in contemporary sexual politics.

We might conclude that what Trump, Weinstein and the incel are about is the slow death of man, imagined by Foucault, Derrida, and Deleuze and Guattari in the 1960s and 1970s. While this is clearly happening, there is more to this situation than simply the end of man and the liberation of desire, which is what we see when we consider the violence inherent in the language and behaviour of Trump, Weinstein and the incels. It is not really that they are in pursuit of lost objects of love and desire, but rather that they are seeking to reaffirm their place in the world through the creation of existential territories based upon the violent, sexual objectification, possession, use and abuse of women who threaten their fragile masculinity in the sense Klaus Theweleit (1987a, 1987b) writes about in his study of the proto-Nazi Freikorps of the 1920s. In this respect, we are culturally a long way from Guattari's (2009b) schizoanalytic critique of Oedipalized forms of domination and instead in the middle of a paranoid response to the psychosis of postmedia that has destroyed old models of territoriality. However, I would argue, following Baudrillard (2009) and Berardi (2015), that we have failed to replace these older forms of domination with anything capable of making sense or creating a world. This is why, I would suggest, conspiracy has become an important form of sense-making in the contemporary world, and taken over from a whole range of academic disciplines in the humanities and social sciences that have been increasingly marginalized in the cybernetic university, which is only concerned with techno-science and the demonstration of performance (Lyotard 1984).

These conspiratorial forms of understanding, born out of the critique of established truth led by thinkers such as Deleuze and Guattari, have, of course, spread through channels of postmedia communication, precisely because of the problems of overload, equivalence, indifference, and the implosion of value that Baudrillard (2009) writes about in his work, and the authors of *Anti-Oedipus* (1983) themselves explained through their discussion of axiomatization. However, this is not simply a postmodern problem. On the contrary, with respect to the way the conspiracy theorists of the Incel and QAnon movements respond to the trauma of the schizophrenic deterritorialization of meaning through the creation of paranoid existential territories based upon the refusal of communication and rejection of otherness, they recall Daniel Paul Schreber's (2000) fantastical war with God, which was also, we remember, based upon a struggle over masculinity, unmanning and feminization. What we also remember about the interpretation of this original case of paranoid-schizophrenia is that in Freud's (2002) reading everything was read straight back into the politics of the father-son Oedipal relation, while much later in the twentieth century Deleuze and Guattari (1983, 1987) would mobilize their own anti-Oedipal reading to focus on Schreber's obsession with machines, rays and the weird forms of communication that enabled God to find his ways into Schreber's head.

According to this interpretation, Deleuze and Guattari (1983) make the case that Schreber's psychosis was never simply about the abusive father and the problem of unmanning, but rather that the dark fantasy of being transformed into a woman and bearing God's son was itself a paranoid reaction to a complex personal and sociocultural transformation revolving around the chaos and schizophrenia of modernity. In this respect, Schreber's madness was simultaneously a deeply conservative reaction to personal, social and cultural turbulence, which caused him to fear his own femininity and so on, and also a highly inventive piece of science fiction concerned with the development of what Deleuze and Guattari (1987) would later call chaosmos or the attempt to make sense on the very borderline between schizophrenic chaos and paranoid order. Although Guattari (1995) never focuses on Schreber in his own works, he makes precisely the same kind of argument about Joyce, who coined the term *chaosmos* and whose *Finnegans Wake* (2000) might be seen to be comparable to Schreber's *Memoirs of My Nervous Illness* (2000) with respect to the ways in which it seeks to make sense of the madness of the coming cybernetic world on its own terms, without reference to existing paradigms of language and knowledge. In his 1995 book *Chaosmosis* (1995), Guattari suggests that we need to repeat the work of Schreber and Joyce for the twenty-first century, and I cannot disagree with this view. In a sense, there can be no more important task for the humanities and social sciences than making sense of the chaos of the contemporary and setting out the coordinates for a new understanding of the world to enable us to gain some kind of traction on our existential problems, and to change who we are and how we live on earth.

This formation of a new ethico-aesthetic paradigm was, of course, the whole point of the schizoanalytic project set out in *Anti-Oedipus* (1983), elaborated in *A Thousand Plateaus* (1987), and *What Is Philosophy?* (1994) and then supported by Guattari's concept of transversality (2015). The objective was always to think in new ways and step outside of the Oedipalized semiocapitalist normocracy. Surely nobody would disagree that this is still not necessary today. However, contra Guattari, and with the benefit of hindsight, I do not believe that postmedia is the route to this liberation of thought, because, as I have sought to show in this chapter through reference to Zuboff (2019), Baudrillard (2009) and Berardi (2015), the power of contemporary postmedia has led to, on the one hand, the domination of the normopathic system and on the other hand, the trauma of schizophrenia, which in turn reinforces the cultural tendency towards paranoid territoriality. Against this seemingly fatal situation, which we can understand through Gregory Bateson's (2000) theory of the double bind, what the Schreber-Joyce complex set out above illuminates is that madness, the Avant Garde and experimentation with new ways of seeing, though fraught with problems, are useful for challenging the normopathic system and making sense of chaos. In terms of how to pursue this project of making sense out of madness in our present circumstances, in the face of an overheating global social and economic system that appears to be on the edge of collapse into an abyss of climate chaos, I do not believe we will be able to master complexity through technology, but rather that we must listen to the intelligence of the body that has been marginalized by the always-on, postmedia semiocapitalist system and follow Guattari's thinking in *The Three Ecologies* (2014) by focussing on the ecological connections between the mind, body, society and the natural world.

In this politico-ethico-aesthetic paradigm, we would turn away from the Prometheanism of capitalist techno-science to make sense of and respond to the chaos of the weather on the basis that the very nature of complexity demands humility and a recognition of the limits of understanding. It is, we cannot forget, the hubris of the modern Prometheans that has led us to the edge of the abyss we stand before today and their continuing myopia, confusion or refusal to recognise reality that means that they can continue to talk about growth in the teeth of a climate crisis founded upon the exhaustion of planetary resources. On this basis, I would suggest that we cannot perform our way into the future. Instead, we should follow Guattari's ecological approach and resist the tendency Joseph Dodds (2011) talks about in his work on Deleuze and Guattari, the climate emergency and the edge of chaos, which concerns the historical connection between nature and death and the womb and the tomb. The whole point of complexity is that relatedness is everything. There is no outside to the socioecological relationship. This is the whole point of the minor utopia, a utopia of humility, finitude and limits.

Regardless of what the neoliberals might suggest to the contrary, there is no self-identical individual. The figure of the man from nowhere is a fiction that rests upon the reality of the socioecological unconscious. Revealing the reality of this condition beneath the semiotic chaos of the postmedia dystopia is surely the key task of schizoanalysis today. In the early twentieth century, Freud (2003) explained that the death drive was a natural state. He wrote of the inertia of being and said that this natural condition was fatal for humans. However, Freud was working with a predominantly early modern Hobbesian vision of nature confirmed by his bitter experience of the First World War and the horror of the Spanish flu pandemic that took his favourite daughter, Sophie, mother of Ernst who famously played fort/da and inspired the theory of the compulsion to repeat in the name of the final escape from trauma. It is this theory which later mutates into the idea of the natural death drive (see Freud 2003). Later in the twentieth century, Deleuze and Guattari (1983) would see death in Freud's space of life, civilization and connect Thanatos to the funereal repetitions and endless nihilism of capitalism that refuses to change beyond the kind of 'restricted schizophrenia' relentlessly hunted down and contained by what we have called a 'provisional paranoia'. It is this system that is currently in the process of breaking down in the face of its own entropic limits. Based upon reading *The Three Ecologies* (2014) and *Chaosmosis* (1995), we can say that Guattari saw this coming in the 1990s. In the middle of this situation, I would suggest what we need to take from his work is the need for a kind of ecological civilization, a minor utopia, founded upon a return to the body, the touch of the other, and the weight of the earth to open up the potential for negentropic transformation. While Bataille (1991, 1992), who clearly influenced the theory of capitalism and schizophrenia, saw this potential in the excessive quality of nature, Deleuze and Guattari (1983, 1987) turned to a state of generalized schizophrenia and endless desiring production. It is on the basis of these ideas that Guattari's call for a return to nature and the ecological should not be understood in terms of a revival of primitivism concerned with how we lived before we were human, but rather the invention of a chaosmos of the future we have yet to imagine.

References

Adorno, T. W. and M. Horkheimer (1997), *Dialectic of Enlightenment*, London: Verso.
Arendt, H. (1973), *The Origins of Totalitarianism*, New York: Harvest.
Bataille, G. (1991), *The Accursed Share Volume I: Consumption*, New York: Zone.
Bataille, G. (1992), *Theory of Religion*, New York: Zone.
Bateson, G. (2000), *Steps to an Ecology of Mind: Collected Essays in Anthropology, Psychiatry, Evolution and Epistemology*, Chicago: University of Chicago Press.

Baudrillard, J. (2009), *The Transparency of Evil: Essays on Extreme Phenomena*, London: Verso.
Berardi, F. (2008), *Félix Guattari: Thought, Friendship and Visionary Cartography*, London: Palgrave.
Berardi, F. (2015), *And: Phenomenology of the End*, New York: Semiotext(e).
Berardi, F. (2018), *Breathing: Chaos and Poetry*, New York: Semiotext(e).
Berardi, F. (2019), *Futurability: The Age of Impotence and the Horizon of Possibility*, London: Verso.
Deleuze, G. and F. Guattari (1983), *Anti-Oedipus*, trans. R. Hurley, M. Seem and H. R. Lane, Minneapolis: University of Minnesota Press.
Deleuze, G. and F. Guattari (1986), *Kafka: Toward a Minor Literature*, trans. D. Polan, Minneapolis: University of Minnesota Press.
Deleuze, G. and F. Guattari (1987), *A Thousand Plateaus*, trans. B. Massumi, Minneapolis: University of Minnesota Press.
Deleuze, G. and F. Guattari (1994), *What is Philosophy?*, trans. G. Burchell and H. Tomlinson, London: Verso.
Dodds, J. (2011), *Psychoanalysis and Ecology at the Edge of Chaos: Complexity Theory, Deleuze, Guattari and Psychoanalysis for a Climate in Crisis*, London: Routledge.
Freud, S. (2001), *Totem and Taboo*, London: Routledge.
Freud, S. (2002), *The Schreber Case*, London: Penguin.
Freud, S. (2003), *Beyond the Pleasure Principle and Other Writings*, London: Penguin.
Freud, S. (2010), *Civilization and its Discontents*, New York: W. W. Norton and Co.
Guattari, F. (1995), *Chaosmosis: An Ethico-aesthetic Paradigm*, trans. P. Bains and J. Pefanis, Bloomington: Indiana University Press.
Guattari, F. (2009a), *Chaosophy: Texts and Interviews 1972–1977*, New York: Semiotext(e).
Guattari, F. (2009b), *Soft Subversions: Texts and Interviews 1977–1985*, New York: Semiotext(e).
Guattari, F. (2011), *The Machinic Unconscious: Essays in Schizoanalysis*, trans. T. Adkins, New York: Semiotext(e).
Guattari, F. (2013), *Schizoanalytic Cartographies*, trans. A. Goffey, London: Bloomsbury.
Guattari, F. (2014), *The Three Ecologies*, trans. I. Pindar and P. Sutton, London: Bloomsbury.
Guattari, F. (2015), *Psychoanalysis and Transversality: Texts and Interviews 1955–1971*, trans. A. Hodges, New York: Semiotext(e).
Guattari, F. (2016), *Lines of Flight: For Another World of Possibilities*, trans. A. Goffey, London: Bloomsbury.
Hardt, M. and A. Negri. (2000), *Empire*, Cambridge, MA: Harvard University Press.
Houellebecq, M. (2003), *Platform*, trans. F. Wynne, London: Vintage.
Lacan, J. (2017), *Formations of the Unconscious: The Seminar of Jacques Lacan, Book V*, trans. R. Grigg, Cambridge: Polity.
Lui, L. (2011), *The Freudian Robot: Digital Media and the Future of the Unconscious*, Chicago: University of Chicago Press.
Lyotard, J-F. (1984), *The Postmodern Condition: A Report on Knowledge*, trans. B. Massumi and G. Bennington, Manchester: Manchester University Press.
Marcuse, H. (2002), *One-Dimensional Man: Studies in the Ideology of Advanced Industrial Society*, London: Routledge.
Marx, K. and F. Engels. (2002), *The Communist Manifesto*, London: Penguin.
Mills, C. W. (2000), *The Power Elite*, Oxford: Oxford University Press.
Schreber, D. P. (2000), *Memoirs of My Nervous Illness*, New York: New York Review Books.

Theweleit, K. (1987a), *Male Fantasies, Volume I: Women, Floods, Bodies, History*, Minneapolis: University of Minnesota Press.
Theweleit, K. (1987b), *Male Fantasies, Volume II: Male Bodies – Psychoanalyzing the White Terror*, Minneapolis: University of Minnesota Press.
Turner, F. (2008), *From Counterculture to Cyberculture: Stewart Brand, the Whole Earth Network, and the Rise of Digital Utopianism*, Chicago: University of Chicago Press.
Žižek, S. (2010), *Living in the End Times*, London: Verso.
Zuboff, S. (2019), *The Age of Surveillance Capitalism: The Fight for a Human Future at the New Frontier of Power*, London: Profile.

Part IV

Microtechnologies and resistance
Chaodyssey of postmedia

11

Groups of militant insanity versus the videopolice

The schizoanalysis of radical Italian audiovisual media culture as postmedia assemblages

Michael Goddard

This chapter will apply Félix Guattari's concepts of minor cinema and the postmedia era to explore how anti-psychiatry was taken up both in cinematic culture in Italy in the 1970s and also by the Radio Alice free radio station, focussing on the cinematic work of Marco Bellocchio, Elio Petri and especially Alberto Grifi. While Grifi's film *Anna* (Grifi and Sarchielli 1975) is a relatively well-known anti-psychiatric video experiment, a schizoanalytic approach runs through all his 1970s work in proximity with the Creative Autonomia movement that also gave rise to Radio Alice. However, these currents were already present in key works of Marco Bellocchio and Elio Petri, especially in *Fists in the Pocket* [I pugni in tasca] (Bellocchio 1965), *Matti da slegare* (Directed by Marco Bellocchio, Silvano Agosti, Sandro Petraglia, and Stefano Rulli OR the March 11 collective) and *La classe operaia va in paradiso* (Petri 1971). In the latter, sound is especially significant to indicate the schizoanalytic interrelations between class struggle, sexuality and psychic states presented as explicitly machinic and this would also form the basis for Radio Alice's reinvention of radio as delirious machinery for a militant destabilization of the state, capital and the mass media. In many of these media phenomena, it is not just an anti-psychiatric that is expressed but a minor politics in tune with the transformation of cinema, video and radio into schizoanalytic ecologies, breaking down the distinctions between producers, technologies and consumers, albeit more effectively in some cases than others. If this 'militant insanity' of creative autonomist practices lost out in the end to the video police in the form of both mass arrests and repression and the rise of Berlusconi's media empire, it provides a rich legacy for the potential reinvention of the postmedia era in the twenty-first century. This chapter will, first of all, give an account of Félix Guattari's concepts of minor cinema in proximity to a range of international examples that are broadly anti-psychiatric. It will then present the anti-psychiatric work of Franco Basaglia described by Guattari as a 'guerrilla psychiatrist' as an essential background to media practices and social movements informed by this anti-psychiatric current. Finally, it will present case studies both from the previously mentioned filmmakers and Radio Alice as the contours of schizoanalytic audiovisual media practices with relevance to both the present and the future of postmedia.

Félix Guattari and the cinema of anti-psychiatry

As Gary Genosko has indicated (Genosko 2009: 134), unfortunately, Félix Guattari devoted only a few pieces of writing to the cinema in general or individual films, yet what he did write is highly significant in its use of a symptomatological approach, entirely free of the vestigial auteurism of Deleuze's cinema books with their focus on the works of great directors. This is particularly apparent in the short essay 'The poor man's couch' (Guattari 1996a: 155–66), in which Guattari claims that cinema provides a mass equivalent of the psychoanalytic cure. For this reason, psychoanalysts are singularly unable to grasp cinematic symptomatologies since the cinema constitutes 'a normalization of the social imaginary that is irreducible to familialist and Oedipal models' (1996a: 155). The shift from the reductive Freudian readings of unconscious meanings to Lacanian structuralist readings in terms of the signifier is, for Guattari, no great advance in psychoanalytic attempts to diagnose the cinema, going directly against the huge effect these analyses had on the development of film theory at the time Guattari was writing. Disputing especially Metz's approach to the cinema as being structured in a similar manner to the Lacanian unconscious 'like a language', through an assembly of syntagmatic chains, Guattari argues that cinema's 'montage of a-signifying semiotic chains of intensities, movements and multiplicities fundamentally tends to free it from the signifying grid' (1996a: 161). This is not to say that Guattari has a utopian view of cinema, which he, in fact, says is just as repressive as psychoanalysis, only in a completely different manner. What cinema – at least in its commercial forms – offers is a machinic, 'inexpensive drug' (1996a: 162) that, in its own way, works on the unconscious. Instead of paying for a professional witness as in psychoanalysis, at the cinema, the audience pays less money to be 'invaded by subjective arrangements with blurry contours [...] that, in principle, have no lasting effects' (1996a: 163). In practice, what is enacted by cinema does have effects in that it models forms of subjective mutation, which remain as traces of the cinematic 'session', just as other narcotics do. As a machinic narcotic, cinema is a giant and much more effective process for the production of normalization than the psychoanalytic cure but, paradoxically, it does this via a process of complete subjective deterritorialization. For this reason, cinema is both 'the best and the worst' that modern capitalist societies offer their subjects and contains within its machinic production of subjectivity liberating potentials: 'a film that could shake free of its function of adaptational drugging could have unimaginable liberating effects on an entirely different scale to those produced by books' (1996a: 164). This is because cinematic language is a living language that, while for the most part turned towards repressive ends, is uniquely able to capture and express processes of psychic semiotization and, therefore, could become 'a cinema of combat, attacking dominant values in the present state of things' (1996a: 165).

Guattari's examples range from obscure anti-psychiatric documentaries to the works of then relatively unknown American filmmakers like David Lynch and Terence Malick. What Guattari's cinematic examples share is that in his reading of them, they all elaborate non-normative processes of desire, capable in principle of countering the normalization processes of both commercial cinema and psychoanalysis. For example, Guattari indicates several examples that could constitute a cinema of anti-psychiatry or see in a film like Malick's *Badlands* (1973), a profound process of *amour fou* or schizo-desire worthy of the best productions of the surrealists (Guattari 1996a: 167–76).

One arena to begin is in what could be called anti-psychiatric documentaries such as *Asylum* (Robinson 1972), which Guattari discusses in passing along with Ken Loach's fictional *Family Life* (1971) as 'indirectly reveal[ing] an anti-psychiatric current' for a 'substantial audience' (Guattari 1996a: 177). Guattari was much less ambivalently enthusiastic about the 11 March Collective film *Matti da slegare* (*Fit to Be Untied*, Silvano Agnosti et al. 1975), which documented the experience of one of Franco Basaglia's anti-institutional projects in the Parma Psychiatric Hospital. Guattari was considerably more sympathetic to Basaglia than to R. D. Laing whose English version of anti-psychiatry is the subject of *Asylum* and related more to the former in his own practice at La Borde clinic, devoting a significant review essay to his work in which he labelled him affirmatively as a 'Guerrilla Psychiatrist' (Guattari 1996b: 42–5).[1] What is notable in this film is that it goes further in affirming the speech and experience of all the participants and, unlike in *Asylum*, this is able to impact the very production of the film itself. According to Guattari, 'it is the people involved who really get the chance to speak [. . .] children, educators, psychiatrists, militant groups [. . .] each sequence, each shot, was collectively discussed during the editing' (Guattari 1996a: 178–9). What is striking in this film is the integration of the perspectives of psychiatric patients and industrial workers and the ways relations are set up between them beyond institutional boundaries. For Guattari, this film is exemplary not only of the potentials of anti-psychiatry but also of minor cinema, in its potential to exceed other modes of political communication in becoming a '"cinema of combat" [or] a form of expression and struggle' (1996a: 178, 179) against dominant representations. In this regard, it is worth noting that the collective's subsequent project was a television series oriented around cinema itself, *La macchina cinema* (*The Cinema Machine* 1979), in which instead of a psychiatric institution, it was a whole range of aspects of the institutional machinery and subjective experience of cinema that were critically examined as industrial production of subjectivity for the masses, very much in line with Guattari's insights about 'The poor man's couch'.

The roots of Italian anti-psychiatry and Militant Insanity

The title of this chapter comes from an extraordinary film *Dinni e la Normalina, ovvero la videopolizia psichiatrica contro i sedicenti nuclei di follìa militante* (*Dinni and Normalina or the psychiatric video police against the so-called groups of militant insanity* 1978) by Alberto Grifi, a filmmaker very close to the Creative Autonomia movement and with a specific interest in the anti-psychiatry movement. The film is part agit-prop militant cinema and part documentary on the international meeting against repression held in Bologna in the wake of the shutting down of Radio Alice and the imprisonment or exile of its main animators as part of a broader crackdown on the Autonomia movement under the guise of anti-terrorism. The film presents a radical strategy on the part of the 'video police' to extract dissent at its roots and restore normality, presented in terms of psychiatric repression and hence in an anti-psychiatric framework.

To fully grasp what is going on in this film, it is necessary to go back over a decade, to the hot 1970s in Italy that was strongly expressed in the film and audiovisual culture, and indeed even further to the roots of Italian anti-psychiatry itself in the pioneering work of Franco Basaglia.

Basaglia, now widely known as 'the man who closed the asylums' (See Foot 2015), was a psychiatrist with a strong educational background in phenomenological and existential philosophy, especially the work of Heidegger and Sartre. His studies also engaged with new critiques of psychiatric institutions, such as the work of Erving Goffman (*Asylums* 1991) and Michel Foucault (*Madness and Civilisation* 1961). When he arrived at his first posting as director of the mental hospital at Gorizia in 1961, at that time a typically archaic and brutal mental asylum (Italian psychiatry and the state having been resistant to even the modest reforms that had already taken place in other contexts), he was disgusted by what he found there: 'locked doors only partly successful in muffling the weeping and screams of the patients, many of them lying nude and powerless in their excrement' (Basaglia in Davidson, Rakfeldt and Strauss 2010: 158). He then set out on a project of 'de-institutionalisation' which proceeded step by step to remove all of the disciplinary apparatus of the asylum one measure at a time, a process he referred to as 'the institution negated'. While this mirrored tendencies and critiques of psychiatry in the United States, Great Britain and France, it was pursued as an almost guerrilla struggle by Besaglia, ultimately leading to the passing of a law in 1978 to not only dismantle and outlaw all existing asylums but prevent their future reinstatement. The implementation of this law, however, took at least two decades.

What was notable about his strategy was the way it was conducted within the very system it was setting out to destroy; Basaglia held a position of power as the director of a regional asylum, originally considered a dead-end job of no significance and hence providing the opportunity to dismantle not only the Gorizia asylum but the asylum system as a whole. This proceeded through the attraction of a strong team of young psychiatrists who would work at Gorizia temporarily and then continue this work in other hospitals, thereby virally disseminating Basaglia's project of de-institutionalization. According to Félix Guattari, in Basaglia's key text *L'istituzione negata* (*The Institution Negated* 1968), 'A war of liberation, waged for ten years, to overthrow the institution is presented to us in terms of militant struggle [. . .] There is straightaway a violent refusal of all scientific pseudo neutrality in this domain which is, for the authors, eminently political' (Guattari 1996b: 43). For Basaglia and his colleagues, drawing on the existentialist and anti-psychiatric sources already mentioned, most of the symptoms of mental illness were, in fact, the effects of the asylum system itself and the alienation of control and autonomy it enforced was seen as leading directly to mental alienation; in other words, mental illness was presented as a social and above all a political issue. The project of opening the walls of the asylum to the outside in every possible respect also made it a hub of activism, bringing it into contact with the rising wave of radical politics in Italy in the 1960s and 1970s to the extent that the contestation over the asylum and its de-institutionalization became a metaphor for revolutionary politics more generally. This was especially the case for the *Autonomia* movement, which, at least in its more creative currents, directly took on some key aspects of anti-psychiatry in its formulation of a revolutionary project, at least as much if not more about the production of subjectivity, as it was about material, objective class relations.

Anti-psychiatric tendencies in Italian cinema: Marco Bellocchio and Elio Petri

The involvement of Bellocchio in the 11 March Collective *Fit to be Untied* documentary was hardly accidental as he had been pursuing a broadly anti-psychiatric approach throughout his fictional film career, beginning most explosively with his first film, *Fists in the Pocket* (1965). Throughout Bellocchio's films of the 1960s and 1970s, social critique is filtered through the subjective experience of repression and alienation at the hands of a range of institutional structures such as the family (*Fists in the Pocket*), the education system (*In the Name of the Father* 1971), the press (*Slap the Monster on Page One* 1972) and the Army (*Victory March* 1976). While all of these films have anti-psychiatric tendencies to lesser or greater extents, it is really *Fists in the Pocket* that these are most explicitly and provocatively expressed. Centred around a bourgeois family of a blind mother and four adult children, this is a film that examines the family through a focus on gesture, as implied by the title. Rather than a simple ideological critique, the film shows the contradictory and hypocritical desires traversing the family structure as Alessandro engineers the 'accidental' deaths first of his mother then of his disabled brother. He does this 'for' his older brother Augusto, the only one who has a seemingly 'normal' life with outside work and a fiancée. Augusto's repressed desires to be liberated from his 'abnormal' family are enacted by his younger brother, who ultimately dies himself from an epileptic seizure, which his sister, who he has also attempted to kill, does nothing about. As Karl Schoonover puts it: 'The deaths in this film occur through surprisingly gentle and unspectacular means: the tap of a finger, the gentle coaxing of a head slipped underwater and, finally, the decision to stay in bed and do nothing. According to Bellocchio's view of the film, "violence arises and breeds in a refusal to accept reality"' (Schoonover 2006). This gestural madness that reaches its apotheosis in Alessandro's epileptic seizure was reflected in the bold cinematic style of the film, which involved abrupt and non-realist editing, at times, almost approaching Soviet avant-garde practices of 'intellectual montage'. However, the montage here is not confined to a purely political or social plane but operates on a plane of desire and psychoses, echoing and amplifying the familial tensions within the scenario as a form of collective articulation of group psychosis. Later Bellocchio would not only make the already mentioned collective anti-psychiatric film *Fit to Be Untied* but also enter into collective psychoanalysis with the controversial therapist

Marco Fagioli, who subsequently collaborated on several of Bellocchio's films in the 1980s.

Elio Petri was another filmmaker working at the same time who in several films emphasized the intertwining of political power, psychosis and sexual desires. This amalgam was barely visible in his work in the 1950s and 1960s, although the sci-fi film *The Tenth Victim* (1965) – a kind of contemporary (rather than set in the future) urban *The Hunger Games* (2012) – in which contestants must kill or be killed by randomly selected others, was a premonition of his future development. In the 1970s, he made a series of four films which, as in the work of Bellocchio, explored the interconnections between social institutions, desire and power in an anti-psychiatric and anti-Oedipal manner. The most well known of these was *Investigation of a Citizen above Suspicion* (1970), which showed a police inspector who violently murders his mistress and manipulates the evidence so a student radical will be suspected. He then leads the inquiry back towards himself, ultimately even confessing to the crime to his superiors, who nevertheless exonerate him since he is above suspicion. This was, of course, his intention in the first place. Like *Fists in the Pocket*, this is a study of proto-Fascism, as facilitated by contemporary authoritarian institutions in a 'liberal' society. If both the psychology and the politics are fairly rudimentary, what is of more interest is the soundtrack and editing style which again reflects the excessive subjective experience presented within the film.

In *Lulu the Tool* (*La Classe Operaia va in Paradiso*), there is a much more astute political analysis that is directly linked to an exploration of a schizoid personality. The main character is initially a much-despised over-productive worker, whose excessive speed leads to the raising of production quotas at the expense of the workers' health and safety. From the beginning, the film presents the industrial noise and rhythms of the factory as a de-subjectifying force and Lulu as a machinic relay who takes the rhythm of the machines he works with directly into the spheres of his intimate relationships and political worldview, a machinism that goes through a complete breakdown after he experiences a traumatic accident at work. As a result of this industrial accident, he engages with the radical students who have been protesting outside the factory and adopts their radical critique, which has consequences for both his working and personal life. He gets fired from the factory, and his girlfriend and son leave him, leading to mental disintegration. This is prefigured in key scenes in which Lulu visits his friend and former worker Militina. In this scene, in particular, there is an almost documentary quality and a political analysis of madness, clearly influenced by Basagalia's ideas. Lulu's machinic schizoid subjectivity is indicated largely via discordant sound that goes from the machines on the factory floor to ultimately invade his entire psyche and his various relations with work, sexuality and politics, which become progressively destabilized and characterized by noise. As such, it can be seen as an update with respect to 1970s Italian political movements and Charlie Chaplin's *Modern Times* (1936), which was cited affirmatively in the schizoanalysis section of Deleuze and Guattari's *Anti-Oedipus*: 'as the schizophrenic line of escape or breakthrough, and the process of deterriotiralisation, with its machinic indices' (Deleuze and Guattari 1984: 348). This important precursor aside, there has perhaps never been a more explicitly schizoanalytic film than *Lulu the Tool* as it traces several of the dynamics outlined in

Anti-Oedipus (1984) from the proliferation of desiring-machines both in and out of work and then, via their machinic breakdown, an elaboration of both the negative and positive tasks of schizoanalysis in Lulu's adoption of a revolutionary perspective (see Deleuze and Guattari 1984: 354–417).

Schizoanalysis in Grifi's cinema

Perhaps the apotheosis of this proximity between anti-psychiatry, schizoanalysis and autonomist politics was the film *Anna* (1975), directed by Alberto Grifi and Massimo Sarchielli, even if it was situated far from any recognizable clinical practice. One day, in the late 1960s, the actor Massimo Sarchielli met Anna near Piazza Navona in Rome. Anna was a 16-year-old girl, pregnant and visibly under the influence of drugs; escaping from several suicide attempts and constant depressive periods, she had nevertheless rejected the interventions of reform institutions and had recently escaped from the last of these. Sarchielli decided to take care of her and took her to his house. Initially taking notes on the girl's behaviour, he began to record her with the idea of eventually making a film. Since he was an inexperienced director, he asked his friend Alberto Grifi to collaborate on the project. Grifi was already becoming known as an innovative and experimental filmmaker, making films related to the situationist critique of the spectacle and conducting early experiments in video and special effects. Later he would direct the film *Il Festival del proletariato giovanile al Parco Lambro* (*The Festival of Proletarian Youth at Parco Lambro* 1976) documenting a key moment of the developing youth counterculture and the Creative Autonomia movement. Grifi agreed to participate, and they started filming in 1972 and 1973, amassing eleven hours of video recordings, part of which was transferred to 16mm using a device of Grifi's own construction and resulting in a film of almost four hours. This was released in 1975 to a highly controversial reception due to the intimacy, apparent extreme realism, and at the same time manipulation of both of the film and the events transpiring in front of the camera. Located somewhere between the inheritance of Italian neorealism (Grifi had extensive contact with Cesare Zavattini, 'the old man of Italian Neorealism') and yet-to-be developed reality television, this film is an uncomfortable document of an intersubjective 'therapeutic' process that is highly troubling. Referring to one of the most notorious sequences in the film of Anna in the shower while heavily pregnant, Andréa Picard wrote: 'Troubling in more ways than one, [certain images] sometimes surpass their aesthetic worth and lodge themselves into the annals of memory where they continue to reverberate and disturb long after being encountered' (2012). But it would be a mistake to simply see in this film the prolongation of the aesthetics of neorealism and direct cinema. It is also a work that defies genres in its combination of documentation and re-enactment, and also one in which the technologies used are highly significant. Grifi had already demonstrated his interest in bricolage by assembling found footage in films like *Verifica Incerta* (1965), which prefigured a whole wave of experimental films and later video art with its humorous repetitions of title and action sequences from numerous Hollywood films. Such experimentation was continued in projects like *Transfert per camera verso Virulenta* (1967) and

Orgonauti, Evivva! (1970), which experimented with special effects such as colour diffraction and spatial distortion via mirrors and filters, again using equipment that Grifi had developed himself. This experimentation was not limited to images, however, but also involved the soundtrack with up to seven different sound channels being superimposed in the earlier film. In the latter film, the attempt was rather to recreate via distorted imagery the effects of ingesting psychotropic substances. Certainly, Grifi moved away from this pure artistic research in the 1970s, in Annamaria Licciardello's words rejecting 'any interest in artistic activities that are not capable of disturbing the "meaningless" reality of everyday life' (Licciardello 2008: 189). It is in this lineage that, despite appearances, *Anna* needs to be understood in the following terms: 'Anna is a true and proper cinematographic experiment that constitutes a unique moment in the history of Italian cinema, and a limit-example of direct cinema' (Licciardello 2008: 189). Certainly, this brought the project into dialogue with questions of realism inherited from both direct cinema and neorealism, but above all, it was the fabrication of a kind of machinery to convert the extremity of subjectivity and everyday life that Anna represented, into durational imagery, in an entirely new way, given the primitive development of analogue video at this moment in time. Grifi was fully aware of these technological conditions, which he saw as indispensable to the production of a film that was able to do away with the usual cinematic conditions of the cost of film stock, lighting and production crews, thereby allowing for an entirely autonomous mode of production and level of intimacy with the film's protagonists.

Anna is, therefore, as much a sociopolitical portrait of its time as a psychological one, and rather constitutes the first step in the 'anthropology of disobedience' that Grifi would continue to develop around events on the borders of the Autonomia movement itself, and tellingly by means of a feminist intervention into a mass anti-psychiatric meeting in 1977 (*Lia* 1977). Contrary to the work of Marco Bellochio, seen by Gary Genosko as the epitome of Guattarian minor cinema, Grifi's work took place in direct proximity to the Creative Autonomia movement itself, resulting in such delirious titles as the already mentioned *Dinni e la Normalina*. As such, this work traces both the phenomenon of Autonomia and its new subjective practices, as well as their subsequent repression. A process that was directly related to the experience of the Bologna free radio station, Radio Alice.

The media ecology of Radio Alice

Italy's first free pirate radio station, Bologna's Radio Alice, clearly derived its name from Lewis Carroll's *Alice's Adventures in Wonderland* (2010), but this naming was no mere accident; in part, a reference to Gilles Deleuze's reading of Lewis Carroll and nonsense in *The Logic of Sense* (Deleuze 1990), the name Alice announced this radio's desire to go beyond the rational limits of communication and politics in the directions of a surrealistic play with sense and nonsense, to produce a desiring form of political communication in which poetic delirium would have as much of a place as political events, or further, a space in which false information could produce real events. What was at stake was not the mere expression of a political line but the invention of new forms of communication drawing on sources as diverse as the historical-artistic avant-gardes, Deleuze and Guattarian philosophy, situationist practice and of course, *Alice in Wonderland* itself.

In this context, it is worth asking why Alice was invoked as the name of the first and most significant of the free radio stations. The choice of the name Alice had several meanings for the animators of Radio Alice; as a figure of both youthful curiosity and femininity but also and more crucially as a reference to nonsense, paradox and unconscious desires. In a recent reflection on Radio Alice, its former animators write:

> 'The choice of Lewis Carroll's fictional heroine was pointed; Alice was heavily linked to the world of feminine symbolism but also to the upside-down logic of *Alice in Wonderland* and *Through the Looking Glass*. Next to Carroll, as a second godfather, the group selected the Deleuze of *The Logic of Sense*, a book which deciphered the paradoxes of identity encountered by Carroll's heroine as a metaphor for the loss of identity (for Deleuze, Alice wanted to be outside all logic, and the mirror – as the symbol of identity – had to be continually crossed over)' (Berardi et al. 2009: 78)

The several tributaries flowing into the constitution of Radio Alice included the reinvention of the semiotic experimentation practised by the historical avant-garde, already evident in the practice of the Creative Autonomy movement, situationist media interventions and pranks and theoretical attempts to grasp the transformations both real and potential of technologically mediated communication in the work of Umberto Eco, Hans Magnus Enszensberger and Jean Baudrillard. However, undoubtedly the key reference point was the schizoanalytic perspectives of Deleuze and Guattari's *Anti-Oedipus* (1984), whose machinic, molecular revolution Alice attempted to materialize via generating a mode of expression that would be a cross between sense and nonsense, the personal/intimate and the social/collective, becoming a radical media ecology or, in Deleuze and Guattari's terms, a 'collective assemblage of enunciation'.

So how exactly did Alice employ nonsense as a form of technologically mediated mode of free communication? The point was, first of all, to open political communication to all those elements that would normally be excluded as non-political, whether because they were too personal, too banal or too strange. According to its animators, Alice transmitted: 'music, news, blossoming gardens, rants, inventions, discoveries, recipes, horoscopes, magic potions [. . .] messages, massages, lies' (Berardi et al. 2009: 82). This seemingly Borgesian impossible list in relation to the norms of radio contents was a deliberate attempt to exceed the limits of what radio-mediated communication could become, rather than merely using radio as a megaphone for a pre-established politics; as observers like Eco noted at the time, the very openness to the banal and the absurd was, in fact, Alice's politics. More than this, the reference to lies was far from accidental; one of the key ways Alice challenged existing modes of political discourse was to reject the idea of political communication as the revelation of 'political truth', by exposing the lies of power and thus, its serious pedagogical function. Instead, Alice made use of lies, in the form of ludic pranks such as impersonating key politicians, in order to provoke political events following the dictum that 'false information can provoke real events'. It is clear to see that in these and other practices, Alice was clearly inspired by the desire to cross the looking glass in a Carrollian fashion, to employ paradox, nonsense and play to escape the well-worn rhetorics of stable political positions and to open the radio station up to the maximum of unfiltered popular speech. Nevertheless, this was not simply a matter of play or comedy but the serious attempts to articulate the struggles of the Autonomia movement with a powerful means of communication and feedback, without any attempt to organize or control it. This is why Radio Alice was so demonized by the authorities as the amplifier of the movement, all the more suspect for its lack of adherence to norms of political organization, even those of the far left. As such, Radio Alice was performing a type of translation of Carroll's *Alice*, but one that like Artaud's schizophrenic reading was also transforming its meaning; one could say that despite or maybe because of the proximity to a schizoanalytic reading of Alice, a new Alice emerged, Alice as a subversive, a revolutionary anti-psychiatric Alice, whose play with sense and nonsense was directly articulated to challenge the official, dominant semiosis of the state, media and conventional modes of political representation.

Given these Deleuzo-Guattarian connections, it is not completely surprising that in the late 1970s, Guattari devoted several texts to the phenomena of popular free radio, especially stations in Italy. For Guattari, the politics articulated around Radio Alice was not a mere shift away from the traditional apparatus's of struggles such as the communist party, which have become completely compromised with the state in favour of new micropolitical groupings such as gay liberation or the women's movement; these new groupings are no less susceptible to becoming reterritorializations finding their institutional place in the manufacture of consensus. As he puts it, 'there is a miniaturization of forms of expression and of forms of struggle, but no reason to think that one can arrange to meet at a specific place for the molecular revolution to happen' (1996a: 82). While Guattari does not state it explicitly here, this corresponds very closely to the rejection of even micropolitical identities or political forms such as Organized Autonomia enacted by Radio Alice; it was not just a question of giving space for excluded and marginalized subjects such as the young, homosexuals, women, the unemployed and others to speak but rather of generating a collective assemblage of enunciation allowing for the maximum of transversal connections and subjective transformations between all these emergent subjectivities. Guattari refers to Alice as 'a generalised revolution, conjunction of sexual, relational, aesthetic and scientific revolutions all making cross-overs, markings and currents of deterritorialization' (1996a: 84). Rather than pointing to a new revolutionary media form, the experimentation of Radio Alice was a machine for the production of new forms of sensibility and sociability, the very intangible qualities constitutive of both the molecular revolution and what he calls elsewhere the postmedia era (Guattari 1996b: 103–4).

Guattari is somewhat more specific about these practices in the essay 'Popular free radio' (1996a: 74–8). In this essay, instead of the question of why Italy, he asks why radio? Why not Super 8 film or cable TV? The answer for Guattari is not technical but rather micropolitical. If media in their dominant usages can be seen as massive machines for the production of consensual subjectivity, then it is those media that can constitute an alternate production of subjectivity that will be the most amenable to a postmedia transformation. Radio at this time had not only the technical advantage of lightweight replaceable technology but, more important, it could be used to create a self-referential feedback loop of political communication between producers and receivers, tending towards breaking down the distinctions between them: 'the totality of technical and human means available must permit the establishment of a veritable feedback loop between the auditors and the broadcast team: whether through direct intervention by phone, through opening studio doors, through interviews or programmes based on listener made cassettes' (1996a: 75). Radio Alice, in particular, developed new ways of articulating radio and telephonic networks to generate a collective and influential approach to the production of news: 'News was provided live by whoever called the radio, without any filter or editing' (Berardi et al. 2009: 81). For Guattari, such strategies of feedback generated a distributed media ecology, well beyond the transmissions themselves: 'We realize [with Radio Alice] that radio constitutes but one central element of a whole range of communication means, from informal encounters in the Piazza Maggiore to the daily newspaper – via billboards, mural paintings, posters, leaflets, meetings, community activities, festivals etc.' (Guattari 1996a: 75). In other words, it was less the question of the subversive use of a technical media form than the generation of a media or rather postmedia ecology, that is, a self-referential network for an unforeseen processual production of subjectivity amplifying itself via technical means. The terms Guattari uses for postmedia may seem misleading or even naïve if taken to imply that participatory media based on many-to-many communication are somehow transparent and unmediated, which is certainly disproved by the contemporary phenomena of the internet and the World Wide Web – which is now thoroughly occupied by all kinds of corporate enterprises. However, if a postmedia ecology is understood more as being 'post-mass media models of communication', proposing instead an alternative networked model of cybernetic organization that is collective and participatory, and that scrambles dominant media codes along with the roles of producers and consumers, then all radical media ecologies are in this sense 'postmedia', which is not to say they are unmediated.

What this type of radio achieved most of all was the short-circuiting of representation in both the aesthetic sense of representing the social realities they dealt with and in the political sense of the delegate or the authorized spokesperson, in favour of generating a space of direct communication in which, as Guattari put it, 'it is as if, in some immense, permanent meeting place – given the size of the potential audience – anyone, even the most hesitant, even those with the weakest voices, suddenly have the possibility of expressing themselves whenever they wanted. In these conditions, one can expect certain truths to find a new matter of expression' (1996a: 76). In this sense, Radio Alice was also an intervention into the language of media; the transformation from what Guattari calls the police languages of the managerial milieu and the university to a direct language of desire:

> Direct speech, living speech, full of confidence, but also hesitation, contradiction, indeed even absurdity, is charged with desire. And it is always this aspect of desire that spokespeople, commentators and bureaucrats of every stamp tend to reduce, to filter. [. . .] Languages of desire invent new means and tend to lead straight to action; they begin by 'touching', by provoking laughter, by moving people, and

then they make people want to 'move out', towards those who speak and towards those stakes of concern to them. (1996a: 76–7)

Conclusions: From Radio Alice and schizoanalytic cinema to digital postmedia assemblages

It is this activating dimension of popular free radio that most distinguishes it from the usual pacifying operations of the mass media and that also posed the greatest threat to the authorities; if people were just sitting at home listening to strange political broadcasts or being urged to participate in conventional, organized political actions such as demonstrations that would be tolerable, but once you start mobilizing a massive and unpredictable political affectivity and subjectivation that is autonomous, self-referential and self-reinforcing, then this is a cause for panic on the part of the forces of social order, as was amply demonstrated in Bologna in 1977. But its implications go well beyond free radio and the specific situation of Italy in the 1970s.

What Guattari's engagement with free radio tells us most of all about radical media ecologies, not only historical ones such as Radio Alice but also in the present is that they are not something that can be given in advance or determined by a specific form of media technology or political organization; they are instead a process of the production of subjectivity, the becoming of a collective assemblage of enunciation whose starting point is the emptiness and coerciveness of the normalizing production of subjectivity that the mass media enact. While the cinematic examples cited earlier were perhaps not as horizontal or open postmedia assemblages as Radio Alice, they nevertheless constitute steps in a similar direction, allowing for a conjugation between schizoanalysis, work and the production of an-Oedipal subjectivity. These examples considered as schizoanalytic media ecologies, therefore, serve as exemplary instances of potential media ecological practice, in its political, subjective and ethico-aesthetic dimensions: in other words, it is less the question of the subversive use of technical media forms than the generation of a media or rather postmedia network, that is a self-referential network for an unforeseen processual and political production of subjectivity amplifying itself via technical means. This is more rather than less applicable and possible in relation to internet-mediated modes of many-to-many communication today as it was in relation to radio, cinema or video practices in the 1970s.

References

Basaglia, F. (1968), *L'istituzione negata*, Turin: Einaudi.
Berardi, F., M. Jacquemet and G. Vitali (2009), *Ethereal Shadows: Communications and Power in Contemporary Italy*, New York: Autonomedia.
Carroll, L. (2010), *Alice's Adventures in Wonderland*, New York: Collins.
Davidson, L., J. Rakfeldt and J. Strauss, eds (2010), *The Roots of the Recovery Movement in Psychiatry: Lessons Learned*, Oxford: John Wiley and Sons.

Deleuze, G. (1990), *The Logic of Sense*, trans. M. Lester and C. Stivale, New York: Columbia University Press.
Deleuze, G. and F. Guattari (1984), *Anti-Oedipus: Capitalism and Schizophrenia*, trans. R. Hurley, M. Seem and H. R. Lane, London: Continuum.
Foot, J. (2015), *The Man Who Closed the Asylums: Franco Basaglia and the Revolution in Mental Health Care*, London: Verso.
Foucault, M. ([1961] 2006), *Madness and Civilization: A History of Insanity in the Age of Reason*, London: Vintage Books.
Genosko, G. (2009), *Félix Guattari: A Critical Introduction*, London: Pluto Press.
Goffman, E. ([1961] 1991), *Asylums: Essays on the Social Situation of Mental Patients and Other Inmates*, London: Penguin.
Guattari, F. (1996a), *Soft Subversions*, trans. D. L. Sweet and C. Wiener, New York: Semiotext(e).
Guattari, F. (1996b) 'The Divided Laing' and "Mary Barnes" Trip', in G. Genosko, ed., *The Guattari Reader*, Oxford: Blackwell, 37–41, 46–54.
Licciardello, A. (2008), 'Sul cinema di Alberto Grifi [On Alberto Grifi's Cinema]', in L. Caminiti and S. Bianchi (eds), *Gli autonomi Vol. 3*, 184–93, Rome: DeriveApprodi.
Picard, A. (2012), 'Disappearances After the Revolution: On Alberto Grifi and Massimo Sarchielli's Anna', *Cinema Scope 50*. Available online: http://cinema-scope.com/columns/filmart-disappearances-after-the-revolution/ (accessed 1 September 2020).
Schoonover, K. (2006), 'Fists in the Pockets', *Senses of Cinema* 40. Available online: https://www.sensesofcinema.com/2006/cteq/fists-in-the-pocket/ (accessed 1 September 2020).

Films cited

Anna (Dir. A. Grifi and M. Sarchielli, 1975).
Asylum (Dir. P. Robinson, 1972).
Badlands (Dir. T. Malick, 1973).
Dinni e la Normalina, ovvero la videopolizia psichiatrica contro i sedicenti gruppi di follia militante [Dinni and Normalini, or the Psychiatric Videopolice Against the So-called Groups of Militant Insanity] (Dir. A. Grifi, 1978).
Family Life (Dir. K. Loach, 1971).
Il Festival del proletariato giovanile al Parco Lambro [The Festival of Proletarian Youth at Lambro Park] (Dir. Alberto Grifi, 1976).
Indagine su un cittadino al di sopra di ogni sospetto [Investigation of a Citizen Above Suspicion] (Dir. E. Petri, 1970).
I pugni in tasca [Fists in the Pocket] (Dir. M. Bellocchio, 1965).
La classe operaia va in paradiso [Lulu the Tool] (Dir. E. Petri, 1971).
La decima vittima [The 10th Victim] (Dir. Elio Petri, 1965).
La macchina cinema [The Cinema Machine] (Dir. S. Agnosti, M. Bellocchio, S. Petraglia, S. Rulli, 1978).
Lia (Dir. A. Grifi, 1977).
Marcia trionfale [Victory March] (Dir. M. Bellocchio, 1976).
Matti da slegare [Fit to be Untied] (Dir. S. Agnosti, M. Bellocchio, S. Petraglia, S. Rulli, 1975).
Modern Times (Dir. C. Chaplin, 1936).
Nel nome del padre [In the Name of the Father] (Dir. M. Bellocchio, 1971).

Orgonauti, Evivva! (Dir. A. Grifi, 1970).
Sbatti il monstro in prima pagina [Slap the Monster on Page One] (Dir. M. Bellocchio, 1972).
Transfert per camera verso Virulentia (Dir. A. Grifi, 1967)
Verifica incerta [Uncertain Verification] (Dir. G. Baruchello and A. Grifi, 1965).

12

Minor video and becoming-Japanese

Towards migrant adolescent molecular revolution

Masayuki Iwase

Mass-media news on young foreign nationals in Japan: Missing accounts

In Japan, when one (e.g. a Japanese citizen) sees or hears the word *foreign children* (外国人の子ども), she may recall the notion of 'school non-attendance' or 'school refusal' (不就学・不登校). Despite the era of user-generated web applications and platforms (i.e. SNSs) rapidly and plentifully streaming video and audio materials on a planetary scale, mass-media news still and evermore plays an immense role in plugging the words *foreign children* into their lack of formal schooling. It implants a 'sensory-motor' formula into the media consumer's body that correlates the word with images always already in relation to the idea, in effect, creating a 'perception-affect-action' nexus and trajectory (Deleuze 1989; also see Bergson 1929; Bogue 2013). Japanese broadcast and print media often equate 'foreign children' with 'school refusal' in their news headlines (Nihon Keizai Shinbun 2019; Okuyama and Hori 2020; Yahima 2019). The headlines serve as 'order-words' that precipitate illocutionary speech acts by 'tell[ing] us what we "must" think, retain, expect, etc.' as social obligations (Deleuze and Guattari 1987: 78–9). The headlines incorporeally transform foreign youth – a unified aggregated demographic mass – into a national problem requiring national solutions.

The mass media often reacts to the Japanese government's survey results on foreign children and youth (or young migrants) and school refusal. One of the most major recent results was a survey conducted by the Ministry of Education, Culture, Sports, Science and Technology (MEXT hereafter) in 2018 to investigate, for the first time, the enrolment of foreign residents aged 6–14 (a total number of 124,049) in public primary and lower secondary schools, as well as ethnic and special-needs schools (MECSST 2019). The survey results revealed that a total of 19,654 (16 percent) of the participants were not enrolled in any school, and many were considered missing (MECSST 2019). In addition, the survey revealed that over 50,000 were assessed as needing Japanese language proficiency (MEXT 2020: 1). The categorical definition of young foreigners in need of such proficiency was 'those with insufficient abilities in having everyday conversation in Japanese' or 'those lacking in grade-relevant academic language abilities as barriers to participating in learning activities' (MEXT 2020: 1).

The media reports on foreign nationals, school refusal and insufficient language abilities as if these young people posed a threat to Japanese societal values and interests, present their 'deficiencies' as a 'moral panic' (Cohen 1980). What the news often omits are accounts of why these issues persistently arise. Following Guattari (2002: 18), I argue that the mass media gives rise to 'a dulling of true debate' and 'an avoidance of authentic dissensual issues'. Systemic barriers and an ontology of Japanese-ness dull the debate and contribute to the avoidance of dissensus. These set the stage for the next sections.

Systemic barriers to attending schools

Under Article 26 of the Japanese Constitution, the first nine years of general public education – that is, the first six years of primary school and the following three years of lower secondary school – are compulsory for those aged 6–14 who possess Japanese citizenship (Kojima 2020: 46–7). Unlike their Japanese counterparts, the school enrolment of young foreign nationals is not mandatory but functions through case-by-case approval by schools (Kojima 2020: 50). Local governments are under no legal obligation to actively enroll non-Japanese students in the school system because they are considered 'non-citizens'. For those young foreign nationals whose age exceeds compulsory school education (over 15 years old), their enrollment in (non-compulsory) public high schools is completely voluntary (Kojima 2020: 50). They were, therefore, not the target of the MEXT survey. As a result, the school enrolment situation is even more difficult to grasp on a national scale.

Even if enrolled, many young foreign nationals confront hardships in Japanese public education, which pressures them to assimilate into Japanese language, curriculum and culture, while remaining largely indifferent to their linguistic or socio-economic backgrounds or resources (Sato 1998). In addition, young foreign nationals may stop attending school if their families, particularly single parent households, cannot afford to pay the basic expenses necessary to enrol them in school (the cost of textbooks and lunch programs) (Kojima 2016: 39). The parents (or guardians) may prefer that their children stay home and complete domestic work, including childcare, or work illegally outside the home (Kojima 2016). Compounded by differing degrees of Japanese language in/abilities, the parents' (or guardians') lack of information about school enrolment and unfamiliarity with the regulations and culture of local towns or regions may contribute to the failure of enrolling their children in schools (Kojima 2016: 40).

Non-profit, regional, volunteer-based Japanese as Second Language (JSL) schools remain pivotal for young foreign nationals who drop out of public schools. As institutions, JSL schools undertake an enormous workload such as providing students with part-time junior high school or high school programs; mediating between young migrant students and destination schools; assisting them in obtaining junior high school graduation certificates and university matriculation; supporting them in adapting to Japanese culture; and taking part in regional communities (Wakabayashi 2013). Although benefitting young foreign nationals by recognizing their linguistically and culturally diverse backgrounds and individually differentiated needs, JSL schools may reinforce 'deficit perspectives' because young migrant learners may see themselves as not fitting into the conventional Japanese school system and the society at large (Reeves 2004).

Myth of coexistence and ontology of Japanese-ness

The Japanese government (Ministry of Internal Affairs and Communication [MIAC hereafter]) has advocated for 'coexistence' (共生) (MIAC 2006, 2020), defined as 'living together with people of different nationalities and ethnicities by acknowledging their cultural differences and building equal relationships among them as members of local communities' (MIAC 2006: 3; also see MIAC 2020), for nearly fifteen years. Municipal governments have been expected to formulate specific plans to implement coexistence policy measures for young foreign nationals. However, on a national scale, Japan has continued ineffectual policies and has failed to offer adequate educational support and provision for youth foreign nationals. Recent survey results have led the Japanese government to reassess the provision of school services and Japanese language education to strengthen the broader ideas of coexistence (MIAC 2020). However, I argue that the conception of coexistence is ontologically problematic.

Following Morris-Suzuki, I argue that the coexistence as it is currently understood glamourizes 'cultural diversity' as 'exterior decoration', and narrowly defines and commands the idea of 'culture' as divorced from the politics and memory of minorities' struggles for social and civil rights (2004: 171). By extension, while having retained such 'cosmetic' aspects (Morris-Suzuki 2004: 171) based on the essentialization and ostensible celebration of cultural diversity, the administrative conception of coexistence is predicated on the neoliberal logic of 'self-reliance', 'control', and 'assimilation' (Shiobara 2020: 34). In other words, as Shiobara (2020: 28) argues, the 'paternalism' of the majority Japanese towards young foreign nationals is a thinly veiled form of neoliberalism. Young foreign nationals are deprived of equality (i.e., equal access to a public school education, use of their native languages) and instead are encouraged to be self-responsible for their 'equality' within the circumscribed parameters of the neoliberal logic of coexistence (Shiobara 2020).

Accordingly, school non-attendance and prerequisite Japanese language proficiency are corollaries of arranging and differentiating young foreign nationals *ethnocentrically* (i.e. 'them') from Japanese (i.e. 'us') (Befu 2001; Yoshino 1992). The 'them-us' arrangement and differentiation are produced and sustained by an ontology of Japanese-ness disseminated by *nihonjnron* (the discourses of the Japanese) (Kowner and Befu 2015: 390). According to Kowner and Befu (2015: 391–2), the central premises of this ontology include that (i) Japan is a homogeneous nation with people of *tan'itsu minzoku* (a single race/ethnic nation) who share a single common language, religion and lifestyle, and (ii) 'the nexus between the land of Japan, its people and their culture', which foreigners can never master, thereby never being able to become 'real' Japanese due to their foreignness.

One key component of these premises is 'the same genetic pool (often referred to as "blood") shared by Japanese people' (Kowner and Befu 2015: 392). The homogeneous genetic pool based specifically on 'Japanese blood' and so-called *junketsu-shugi* (pure-blood-ism) is what makes Japanese people and their identity 'immutable' and distinct from foreigners (Yoshino 1992: 24). In other words, the ontology entails inventing the 'Japanese race' as *tan'itsu minzoku* (a single race/ethnic nation) (Yoshino 1992: 24). Race as such differentiates Japanese from young foreign nationals as 'imagined Others,' and the former intensely feel a collective sense of onenesss based on the symbolic values of Japanese blood as genotypical difference (Kawai 2009; Yoshino 1992).

Appadurai (1996: 8) once posited that '[p]art of what the mass media make possible, because of the conditions of collective reading, criticism, and pleasure, is . . . a "community of sentiment" . . . a group that begins to imagine and feel things together.' The mass media contributes to the re/production of the community of sentiment among Japanese citizens as a race. The news mobilizes such collective sentiment through the projection of them-us binaries and imagined Others premised on *nihonjinron*.

Against a backdrop of the misrepresentation of the life and existence of young foreign nationals in Japan, this chapter follows Guattari, who posed the following vital question: 'How can we reconcile the taste of the majority, the demand for news and for education, and the legitimate ambition for self-expression on the part of the minority cultures?' (2002: 21). The 'ambition' for minoritarian self-expression is thus the concern of this chapter. It is through such ambition that the news, education and the culture of the majority can be rethought. The remaining sections of the chapter conceive of the viability of this ambition by drawing on the relevant work of Guattari and Deleuze to frame my research with migrant adolescents making videos at a JSL school.

Towards adolescent molecular revolution in a postmedia ecology

The ambition for minoritarian self-expression is consistent with the ambition envisioned in a 'postmedia era' (Guattari 2002: 18). The 'development of news [for re-education]' in the postmedia era is concerned with 'true democratization of news' through 'collective problematization' (Guattari 2002: 20). This factor operates together with three interrelated others, including 'foreseeable technological developments,' 'the necessary redefinition of relationships between producers and creators,' and 'the establishment of new social practices and their influence on the development of the media' (Guattari 2002: 18). In other words, these three factors are germane to more inter/active forms of writing beyond typographic print production because they allow for freer yet responsible cooperation between producers, creators and consumers; and they popularize media and communication technologies for a variety of professions, social institutions, and the general public in order to induce new uses that feed into and productively enhance the developments. The transformation of news for re-education brings together these three factors and are relevant for understanding media production by minorities.

Minoritarian self-expression is a key for unlocking the process of collective problematization that is crucial to truly democratizing the news. Here, problematization can be defined as the act of seeking ontological explanations for how an ensemble of discursive and nondiscursive practices constitute and produce an object of thought as true or false in some a priori fashion (Foucault 1988; Webb 2014). The minoritarian expression as such in the present-day media ecology is fruitfully fortified by the three above-mentioned co-present factors of the postmedia era. In what follows, I draw on Guattari to stress the importance of reappropriating media and a-signifying semiotics as necessary conditions for minorities' ambitions for self-expression, especially adolescents' very own molecular revolution. I also draw on Deleuze to argue for the importance of simultaneously repurposing media images to recontrol or remodulate governed perceptions and memories as a-signifying semiotics.

Reappropriation of media and a-signifying semiotics

Guattari's vision of a postmedia era is set against what he called Integrated World Capitalism (IWC hereafter), which is post-industrial or post-Fordist capitalism that 'increasingly [decenters] its sites of power, moving away from structures producing goods and services towards structures producing signs, syntax and – in particular, through the control which it exercises over the media, advertising, opinion polls, etc. – subjectivity' (2000: 47). IWC deploys the mass media (e.g. the news) to transform subjectivity by fabricating stories, manipulating imagination in the service of the majority consensus, and infantilizing people to the point where no dissent emerges (Guattari 2000). Guattari stressed the dangers of molecular forms of pollution infiltrate into 'the domain of mental ecology in everyday life: individual, domestic, material, neighbourly, creative or one's personal ethics' (2000: 50). As such, the postmedia era poses a vital question: Does this era give rise to 'black holes' that capture energies to trap subjectivity in a capitalist Oedipal desire, or to liberate and make it available for 'the reappropriation and resingularization of the use of media'? (Watson 2002: 41; also see Guattari 1995: 5).

This chapter clearly calls for the latter view, as Guattari (1996b: 146) was committed to the reappropriation of media:

> Presently, media [such as cinema, television, and the press], for the most part, functions in the service of repression. Commercial cinema, for example, entertains a latent racism in its Westerners; it can prevent the production of films about events like those of May '68 in France; but the Super-8 and the video-tape recorder could be turned into means of writing that are much more direct and much more effective than discourses, pamphlets, and brochures.

Accordingly, for Guattari, the reappropriation of media was concerned particularly with the grassroots-level repurposing of media technologies such as a Super-8 motion picture or video camera and the videocassette recorder (VCR) for amateur filmmaking and documentary production. These are media tools 'in everyone's hands' and 'of democratization and democratizing perception' for anybody as protagonists to 'get behind the camera' (Cole and Bradley 2016: 136). Such reappropriation of media by amateurs has been increasingly possible in the present-day media ecology, which is enabled by digitization and converges traditional mass media with user-generated web applications and platforms (Jenkins 2008). In this postmedia ecology, media consumers of any age and background can actively participate as creators in achieving, annotating, appropriating, transforming and recirculating media content in new ways (Jenkins 2003, 2006; also see Iwase 2010).

The postmedia ecology nullifies the narrating functions of 'social subjection' enabled by signifying semiotics through which to produce and govern people as 'individuated subject[s]' assigned and separated into a predetermined identity and body according to gender, ethnicity, nationality, profession, role, place and so on (Lazzarato 2014: 24). The new ecology operates through digitally-enabled control whereby subjectivity is produced not so much through 'confinement' or '*molds*' in a disciplinary sense but 'a *modulation*, like a self-transmuting molding continually changing from one moment to the next, or like a sieve whose mesh varies from one point to another' (Deleuze 1995: 179). Controlled as such, human individuals become *dividuals* and masses become samples, data, markets, or *banks* (Deleuze 1995: 180).

In other words, individuals are transformed into non-human components of a subjectivity whose synthesis no longer lies in the person but is fulfilled through a-signifying semiotics such as 'intelligence, affects, sensations, cognition, memory, and physical force' (Lazzarato 2014: 27). Simply put, subjectivity in the new ecology is produced through a more efficacious yet amorphous *dispositif* (apparatus) called 'machinic enslavement,' which 'occurs via desubjectivation by mobilising functional and operational, non-representational and asignifying, rather than linguistic and representational, semiotics' (Lazzarato 2014: 25; also see Deleuze and Guattari 1987; Guattari 1996b, 2013). The modulation-based machinic enslavement is a 'diagram of the flexibility of production and subjectivity by seizing hold of the new concepts of life and of the living implied by this modality of power [at distance]' (Lazzarato 2006: 176).

The resingularization (Guattari 1995; Watson 2002) of the subjectivity of minoritarian individuals or 'subject groups' occurs precisely through the grassroots-level reappropriation of available media technologies and the repurposing of a-signifying semiotics. For Guattari (1996a: 34f), such a subject group intervenes in the idea of 'subjected group' or 'subjugated group in a micropolitical sense, which implies 'serial being, with its exterior focus on an object in which a prior praxis is embodied and its passive internal structure of mutual Otherness'. However, the subject group does not refer to a 'circumscribed group' but is connected with pragmatic 'arrangements' of enunciation or subjectivization that 'involve individuals, but also ways of seeing the world, emotional systems, conceptual machines, memory devices, economic, social components. Elements of all kinds' (Guattari 1996a: 227–8).

A subject group's resingularization is then concerned with 'the liberation of singularities that are repressed by a dominant and dominating mass-media subjectivity,' which 'has nothing to do with individuals' per se but more to do with systems that precede individuals' consciousness (Pindar and Sutton 2000: 12). As such, resingularization signals 'the process of existential appropriation by the continuous creation of heterogeneous durations of being' prior to any formulation and determination of identities and thus through becoming as 'transfers', passages, or thresholds without any localizable origin and destiny (Guattari 2013: 203–4). Accordingly, as Guattari (2000: 51) posited that resingularization aims to 'get social and political practices back on their feet, working for humanity and not simply for a permanent re-equilibration of the capitalist semiotic Universe'. Resingularization means not only to 'become more united' but also to reinvent and mutate in order to dissent from forms of capitalistic subjectivity accelerated by mass-mediatization (Guattari 2000: 68–9). It entails 'organiz[ing] new micropolitical and microsocial practices, new solidarities, a new gentleness, together with new aesthetic and new analytic practices regarding the formation of the unconscious' (Guattari 2000: 51).

Intriguingly, Guattari envisaged adolescents' reappropriation of a-signifying systems involving 'music, clothing, the body, behaviors as signs of mutual recognition, as well as machinic systems of all kinds' (1996b: 72). He believed that such reappropriation 'begins with very immediate, daily, individual preoccupations, yet remains connected to what happens at the social level' (Guattari 1996b: 70). Guattari emphasized such everyday adolescent expressions as micropolitics and molecular revolution in the style of 'a collective, unformed search, from above and below' (1996b: 70).

His particular interest in adolescents lies in the complex physic, behavioural and sexual threshold of this age group as individuals transition from the homeostasis of childhood to the institutionally controlled panoptic adulthood (Guattari 1996b). Guattari (1996b: 64) emphasized that adolescence is 'the entrance into a sort of extremely troubled interzone where all kinds of possibilities, conflicts and sometimes extremely difficult and even dramatic clashes suddenly appear.' Importantly, his view on adolescence as such is not limited to a fixed age and group but premised on 'becoming' (Guattari 1996b: 63). As Colman (2005: 357) elaborates, the Guattarian view of adolescence is 'the time quality of becoming-adolescent, a passage-moment of freedom and change,' which entails 'the configuration of inventions – actions that are not routine performances of pre-codes, but hold movement in surprise, in possibility in anger, in awe – of potential mentalities.'

Repurposing a-signifying semiotics: Recontrol of perception and memories

While the reappropriation of media and a-signifying semiotics are the preconditions for the ambition of minoritarian self-expression, it is imperative to also consider in what ways the latter can be repurposed for self-expression so that it problematizes the mass-media news for re-education. As noted at the beginning of this chapter, in the context of Japan, the mass media implants a 'sensory-motor' formula in the viewer's or reader's bodies that associates words like *foreign national* with moral panic by painting the former as a threat to Japanese-ness (Deleuze 1989; also see Bergson 1929; Bogue 2013).

The formula derives from Bergson's (1929; Deleuze 1989) philosophy of image, matter, and duration, and the viewer and reader experience the perception-affect-action nexus and instinctively perceive and immediately extend actualized images into their habitual actions without the suspension of sensory-motor perception-action 'interval' (Martin-Jones 2008). The goal of Japanese mass-media news is arguably to perpetuate the continuation of the interval whenever pure memories of the past (or attentive recollections) are brought forward without any delay and create a 'match' between the memories of the past and the perceived images on-screen, thereby extending them to the viewer's or the reader's habitual bodily actions (Martin-Jones 2006: 53). The kinds of a-signifying semiotics that particularly matter here are the viewer's or the reader's perception and memory and particular presentations of time or what Lazzarato (2006: 182–3; also see Iwase and Bradley forthcoming) described as 'living engines', which are coaxed into immediately retrieving, recognizing and extending flows into habitual actions that are both simultaneously present- and future-oriented.

In order to realize the ambition for minoritarian self-expression, media images are necessary to stretch and short-circuit the sensory-motor perception-action interval and open up virtual conjunctions and new possibilities the viewer or the reader can paradoxically sense (Deleuze 1989). Deleuze's (1989) articulation of the time-image generates such conjunctions and possibilities in what he called the 'third synthesis of time' (Deleuze 1994). The time-image is the key to the stretching and short-circuiting the interval. According to Deleuze (1989: 271), the time-image implies '*false movement*, as aberrant movement which now depends on time.' He emphasized that the aberrant movement 'speaks up for an anteriority of time that it presents to us directly, on the basis of the disproportion of scales, the dissipation of centres and the false continuity of the images themselves' (Deleuze 1989: 37). The time-image that 'directly' presents time to the viewer or the reader comes into effect through 'irrational cuts' that determine non-totalizable and non-localizable relations between images (Deleuze 1989). Deleuze (1989: 12) noted that the time-image operates in 'pure optical and sound situations, opsigns and sonsigns.' Opsigns and sonsigns, which are pure visual and audio images, emerge in what he called the 'any-space-whatever,' which is an indeterminate singular space where linkages are made for virtual conjunctions and new possibilities (Deleuze 1986: 109).

Such opsigns and sonsigns play out when and where '"[t]ime is out of joint": it is off the hinges assigned to it by behaviour in the world, but also by movements of world' (Deleuze 1989: 41). Such unhinged time is 'aionic time,' in which the present gets subdivided eternally into simultaneous past-present, thus not preserved in specific-bounded spatio-temporalities that secure chronological temporalities (Deleuze 1990). The opsigns and sonsigns operate through what Deleuze (1994: 89; also see Bogue 2010; Voss 2013a; Williams 2011) emphasized as 'caesura', which produces a 'pure *order of time*' as a temporal cut, fracture or event where the past (or 'before' or 'beginning') and the future (or 'after' or 'end') are distributed unequally. What Deleuze (1994) articulated as the third synthesis of time is concerned with 'futures' emerging from such caesura, which is untimely, undetermined and open. Such futures emerge when the subject *qua* actor, author, or agent 'erases the hold of the passive synthesis of the first', that is, of his/her governed habit in the colonizing lived present, and when/if his/her memories of the past as the second synthesis become 'failed condition[s]' in which anticipated futures are entirely freed from chronological past-present-future arrangements (Williams 2011: 105).

Minor cinema

'Minor cinema' is a philosophical concept Deleuze (1989) articulated in his book *Cinema 2: The Time-Image* by linking the concept with his and Guattari's (1986) co-work on Franz Kafka in their monograph *Kafka: Toward a Minor Literature*. The concept has also been variously taken up by several scholars (Butler 2002; Bogue 2013, 2011; Martin-Jones 2004, 2006; Morris 1998; Rodowick 1997; White 2008). This concept is valuable for filmmakers, researchers and educators (I myself am a researcher-educator-videographer) who pursue minoritarian self-expression based on immanent ethics, which problematizes 'anything that *separates* a mode of existence from its power of acting – and what separates us from our power of acting is, ultimately, the illusions of transcendence' (Smith 2011: 125, emphasis in original).

In other words, minor cinema as a practice should ontologically be situated in Deleuze's (2001) 'transcendental empiricism,' which avoids not only centering the human subject as a pre-existent subject but also representing subjects as existing independently of its milieu or context. Transcendental empiricism insists that subjects/objects operate as iterative results, products or effects of multiple interactions (Bryant 2008; also see Deleuze 1994, 2001). Minor cinema as such can be valued as realizing 'un/fold subjectivity' enabled by iterative processes (Deleuze 1989). It can emerge under the conditions that the 'outside is not a fixed limit but a moving matter animated by peristaltic movements, folds and foldings that together make up an inside: they are not something other than the outside, but precisely the inside *of* the outside' (Deleuze 1989: 97).

What Deleuze (1989) emphasized as 'story-telling' functions (or fabulation) of minor cinema is germane to such un/fold subjectivity and crucial to conceiving of and generating minoritarian self-expression, which should not only be engaged and fulfilled by minoritarian individuals or groups. Deleuze (1989) noticed the significance of story-telling functions in the contexts of a French ethnographic filmmaker Jean Rouch's first-hand involvement and entanglement in the 'ciné-trance' induced by his collaborations to make ethnofictions with West Central African young migrants. Through the intermedia of camera lenses and microphones, ciné-trance is the creative metamorphosis of the observer-filmmaker who moves from the position of unobtrusive passivity to one of active, improvisational and reciprocal engagement in the co-presence of filmed people and events (Rouch 2003).

However, a potential risk of Rouch's filmmaking was complying with the side of the 'masters' based on his colonial mentality and gaze as a French director working with African migrants (Deleuze 1989: 222). For Deleuze (1989: 152), the collaboration between Rouch and his migrant participants in the ciné-trance 'canceled out or falsified narratives referred back to any single enunciating subject – whether it be Rouch or migrant participants – and which instead made them both emerge as "intercessors". He emphasized the intercessions enacted by Rouch and the participants as deterritorializing – a 'double-becoming':

> The cinema author finds himself [sic] before a people which, from the point of view of culture, is doubly colonised: colonised by stories that have come from elsewhere, but also by their own myths become impersonal entities at the service of the coloniser. The author must not, then, make himself [sic] into the ethnologist of his people, not himself [sic] invent a fiction which would be one more private story: for every personal fiction, like every impersonal myth, is on the side of the 'masters'. . . . There remains the possibility of the author providing himself [sic] with 'intercessors', that is, of taking real and not fictional characters, but putting these very characters in the condition of 'making up fiction', of 'making legends', of 'story-telling'. The author takes a step towards his [sic] characters, but the characters take a step towards the author: double-becoming. (Deleuze 1989: 222)

As they improvised and reciprocally engaged in each other's presence, Rouch and his participants experienced a double-becoming as a creative metamorphosis as un/folding subjectivity, whereby he and his participants were intercessors envisioning their own imaginary world but performing in the very context of their actual precarious situation (Rouch 2003).

Given the roles of the filmmaker and participants *as mutual intercessors*, the notion of 'minor' should be understood in terms of 'becoming-minoritarian,' which is always in-between and molecular. This is taken not as any aggregated demographic mass assumed to pre-exist as a unified organic subject of representation (Deleuze and Guattari 1987). Deleuzian minor cinema thus refers to filmic practices of minorities (as non-Western, non-white, diasporic, colonized, postcolonial, neocolonial, women, LGBTQ+, or otherwise marginalized people and groups) who leverage their voice in minor ways to becoming-other (Butler 2002; Bogue 2013, 2011; Martin-Jones 2004, 2006; Morris 1998; Rodowick 1997; White 2008). The mutual intercessions made possible through double-becoming and story-telling are the crux of Deleuze's (1989: 216) concept of minor cinema which involves minority individuals and groups who 'no longer exist, or not yet . . . *the people are missing*'.

Making and reading migrant adolescent self-expression as a minor video

The rest of this chapter illustrates the ambition of minoritarian self-expression based on my research on making what I call a 'minor video' (Iwase, 2022). In what follows, I begin by elucidating my motives for choosing video as a primary tool to explore the ambition for minoritarian self-expression, specifically adolescent migrants' self-expression.

The motives are consistent with reappropriating media technologies and repurposing human perception and memories, but also the dynamic of Deleuzian minor cinema.

Motives for choosing video

My motive for choosing digital video was its affordability and amateur filmmaking and documentary production are within reach for almost everyone. The reality of video resonates with Guattari's view on the inter/active form of writing beyond typographic means of print production; the freer yet more responsible cooperation between creators (e.g. director, camera person, actor and other crews) and viewers; the development of new social practices involved in shooting and uploading to share videos through online platforms. Using video to these ends was certainly part of the reappropriation of media envisioned by Guattari.

Another important motive is the editing of images (both visual and sound or opsigns and sonsigns) that can generate the 'unsuccessful' retention of the viewer's memories or active recollection by stretching and short-circuiting the perception-action interval and interrupting his/her automatic responses to transmitted on-screen images. Lazzarato's (2019: 65–6, original emphasis) post-Bergsonian account of screen media's affective capacities to generate such stretching and short-circuiting was instructive:

> I suggest the hypothesis that the technologies of time imitate, in their operations and in their products, the various syntheses of time (the conservation, passage, and splitting-emergent of time) and that, through the operations of contraction-relaxation, they work on the conditions of the production of affective force. The matter that these technologies contract is, as in Bergson, time-matter (material vibrations) and the different temporal satisfactions of memory. I use the term *imitation* to signify the electronic and digital technologies operate like the material and spiritual syntheses in Bergson: they crystallize time. Video and digital technologies can therefore be understood as technologies that imitate perception, memory and intellectual labor.

Lazzarato's (2019) hypothesis indicates that such a screen medium *qua* video is capable of synthesizing (as crystallizing) time through effectively editing images and sounds to modulate the viewer's habitual actions (as material synthesis) and attentive recollection (as spiritual synthesis, memory recall, and intellectual labour). I assert that his emphasis on 'imitation' refers precisely to the affective capacities of actualized on-screen edited images and sounds, which operate as stimuli through which the viewer makes 'active' efforts to perceive opsigns and sonsigns and, in so doing, virtually connects to aionic time.

Last but not least, the ontological processes of video-making between my research participants, who were a group of Asian-heritage adolescent migrants of a JSL school, and myself, a researcher-educator-videographer, is consistent with the story-telling function (the expression of Deleuzian minor cinema that rests on immanent ethics and transcendental empiricism). The methodology of this project was designed so that the participant-generated self-expression, which was part of our joint process of double-becoming, would ideally cancel out or falsify narratives that referred back to any of us as a single enunciating subject.

Site and participants

I carried out my research on making minor video at a non-profit, volunteer-based regional JSL school called *Kaede* (pseudonym) located in an industrial city in the Tokai area of Japan in the summer of 2015. The *Kaede* school participants were recruited from those who signed up for my digital video-making training workshop as part of the educational support offered at the school. Table 12.1 shows the demographics of those participants who were the core members of our minor video-making.

Objects of reading

The video that we produced through the workshop is entitled *Watermelons and Humans* (https://vimeo.com/212479437/af4f2fbd51), an edited ethnofiction video directed by

Table 12.1 Participant Demographics

Participant (stages mainly engaged)	Age	Sex	Status of residence and schools attended	Province and country of origin	Length of stay
1 Suika (all 3 stages)	17	Male	A dependent due to his parents' status as skilled labour, the JSL Centre T only	Liaoning, China	11 months
2 Cash (First 2 stages)	17	Male	A dependent due to his mother's status as a spouse of Japanese national, the JSL Centre T only	Shandong, China	10 months
3 Card (First 2 stages)	20	Male	A long-term resident because his grandmother is a Japanese national, the JSL Centre T only	Heilongjiang, China	6 months
4 Sunglass (First 2 stages)	20	Female	A long-term resident in Japan because her grandmother is a Japanese national, the JSL Centre T only	Jilin, China	9 months
5 Milk (all 3 stages)	26	Female	A dependent due to her husband's status as skilled labour, the JSL Centre T only	Hebei, China	11 months
6 Handtogether (A bit of 1st and rest)	17	Female	Dependent because of his mother's spouse, a Japanese national	Manila, Philippines	2 weeks

Suika (pseudonym) and co-created by the rest of the participants and myself as the film crew. The video is a response to the general theme concerning who the participants are or how they identify themselves in Japan. The video incorporated a stop-motion animation technique using flat paper cut-out characters and objects that were physically manipulated in small increments between individually photographed frames. The video was edited based on a montaged sequence that assembled the animated images of paper characters and objects, and the various images of the characters performed by the participants, with music and voice-over added. The video was rendered from Suika's storyboard and was edited by Suika and myself.

As productive ways to read adolescent migrants' self-expression, I am particularly interested in what concerns my research participants (i.e. a group of Asian-heritage adolescents with underdeveloped Japanese language abilities) have about Japan, what their language does or produces, and how I as a researcher-educator-videographer assisted my participants in creating their self-expression. These three inquiries very much resonate with Deleuze and Guattari's accounts of the tripartite interrelated conditions premised on the operation of minor cinema, which include (i) 'the deterritorialization of language', (ii) 'the connection of the individual to the political immediacy', and (iii) 'the collective assemblage of enunciation' (1986: 18). I use these tripartite conditions as analytical lenses through which to explore the ambition of minoritarian self-expression, which problematizes how the mass-media news constitutes and produces subjectivity in *a priori* fashion.

Collective assemblage of enunciation

The condition of 'collective assemblage of enunciation' signals the absence of any enunciating subject to which utterances are referred back upon (Deleuze 1989; also see Deleuze and Guattari 1986). Deleuze asserted that the cinema of the minor must involve and show 'how the people are what is missing, what is not there,' instead of those individuals and groups who are 'already there,' 'even though they are oppressed, tricked, subject, even though blind or unconscious' (1989: 215–16).

During the preproduction-planning stage, the status and movement of our bodies were habitual and socially expected – researcher, teacher, videographer, Asian migrant adolescent, JSL student. In my case, the behavioural research ethics board largely prescribed my role, responsibility and way of interacting with my participants. Our respective bodies were just like 'chess pieces' whose 'internal nature and intrinsic properties from which their movements, situations and confrontations derive' were unilaterally coded (Deleuze and Guattari 1987: 352).

In contrast, during the production stage, we became intercessors transgressing those commonsensically prescribed identities and positions. Through a free indirect encounter and relation in 'performative oscillation' (Rodowick 1997: 157), we performed a ciné-trance in which we falsified the narratives that refer back to any single enunciating subject. Specifically, director Suika commanded all of us to choose our preferred obligatory roles for making the video. Other participants – including

Cards (pseudonym), Cash (pseudonym), Sunglass (pseudonym), Milk (pseudonym) and myself, for example – all served as actors and location scouters. I temporarily abandoned my obligatory roles as a male Japanese adult researcher and instructor. In one scene, Cash, who reads and walks in a hallway with a book in his hands, and Cards, who walks in the same hallway in a black T-shirt with a pair of sunglasses on, bump into each other; this created an intriguing affective moment, and we waited in an excited but hushed way for Suika to shout: 'Action!'

The moment was like a haecceity, which is not any visually observable static occurrence or happening but a visceral, tactile and haptic moment and movement emerging in a zone of indiscernibility (Deleuze and Parnet 1977). I remember that we were all part of such a haecceity as a *puissance*, affect, or becoming, an individuation of immanently and infinitely growing decomposable and recomposable bodies of whatever kind and '[a degree] of power which combine[s], to which correspond[s] a power to affect and be affected, active or passive affects, intensities' (Deleuze and Parnet 1977: 92).

Connection of the individual to the political immediacy

The condition of 'the connection of the individual to the political immediacy' (Deleuze and Guattari 1986: 18; also see Deleuze 1989) signals the dissolution of the 'boundary' drawn between the individual 'private' actions and the 'social', or the immediate merger of the former with the latter as 'political' affairs (Deleuze 1989: 218; also see Deleuze and Guattari 1986; Martin-Jones 2004). In other words, any individual minor actions are always already entangled in 'a network of power relations' (Bogue 2011: 135) or the product of an 'assemblage' (Mazzei 2017: 678; also see Deleuze and Guattari 1987) of class, gender, ethnicity, nationality and so on.

The theme of *Watermelons and Humans* is concerned with coexistence among people not being judged on their appearance or external attributes (e.g. nationalities) but valued according to their 'inner sides'. The inner side pertains to one's heart as it extends to thoughtfulness, care or compassion, through which we recognize and accept difference. The idea of 'inner sides' manifested via video assumed that humans can desist from habitually judging others based solely on appearances and other external attributes.

There are at least two moments when/where the video's images resonate with the issues around coexistence. I call them (i) appearance-inner side (or actual-virtual) simultaneity and indiscernibility and (ii) becoming-minor in the major language. The 'appearance-inner side (or actual-virtual) simultaneity' is a moment when time-images emerge that virtually connect to aionic time, through which alternative living or ontologies to coexistence can be conceived. The video's climax is of particular interest here. The climax shows both an image sequence of the perceptual world, with nationally represented paper cut-out watermelon bodies, and an image sequence of the perceptual world with the watermelons' flesh appearing superimposed on bodies. The dual sequences coinciding with the climax seem to do more than offer a sensory-motor continuity; I can sense and prehend an opsign synchronous within the climax, and I am invited to travel in the virtual mazes of aionic time through movements that serve as irrational cuts.

The video's climax, enabled by the dual sequences, seems to correspond to both the 'limpid and opaque,' which is a sign of the time-image sub-variety 'hyalosign' and 'the peaks of the present,' which is a sign of the time-image sub-variety 'chronosign'. The sign of 'limpid and opaque' refers to '[t]he actual present is sustained in reference to the virtual past, and the virtual sustains the actual present' whereby '[a]n image is limpid – luminous, clear – for a moment, but in passing becomes opaque (disappears)', while 'the image is simultaneously opaque – obscure, impenetrable – and, in passing, limpid (invisible)' (Deamer 2016: 147; also see Deleuze 1989). The sign of 'peaks of the present' refers to 'the coalescence of presents presented in the present: what is possible and impossible coexist, making the possible and impossible indeterminate' (Deamer 2016: 153; also see Deleuze 1989).

In the video's climax, I sense and prehend the limpidness and opaqueness of nationally represented paper cut-out watermelon flesh appearing and disappearing right above the bodies. Concurrently, the limpid and opaque flesh and the bodies now coexist together in parallel moments in the present. Both bodies thus appear possible and impossible, compossible and incompossible (Deleuze 1989). The climax signals the indiscernibility and indeterminateness of the bodies and the flesh – that is, the appearances and the inner sides – capable of coexisting.

It seems then that a noosign or the unthought-of emerging from this alternative conception of coexistence is '*a zone of indiscernibility or undecidability*' (Deleuze 2003: 21; also see Voss 2013b) between human/watermelon bodies and flesh, between appearance and inner sides. This zone is 'the entire body, but the body insofar as it is flesh or meat' (Deleuze 2003: 22). The body-flesh coexistence emerging from such a zone is the 'body without organs,' which is a body that rejects any kind of predetermined organisation imposed upon the body by organic functions, political inscriptions and social code (Voss 2013b: 114–15; also see Deleuze and Guattari 1987). Outwardly, director Suika's appropriation of the body-flesh binary appears 'essentialist' in the ways that he accepts the Japanese government's essentialist binary category of their identity as 'foreigners.' However, I intensively and immanently read his appropriation as 'the crucial scene of the usefulness of catachresis': he and, indeed, the fellow film crew used the binary category to raise their voice as a 'strategic use of essentialism' (Spivak 2009: 182) to signal the zone of indiscernibility or undecidability and the Body without Organs.

Deterritorialization of language: Becoming-minor of the major language

The last condition is the deterritorialization of language unfolding as 'becoming-minor of the major language' in *Humans and Watermelons*. It is another moment of the emergence of time-images that virtually connect to aionic time through which we can conceive of alternative living or ontologies of coexistence. Intriguingly, watching – or more specifically 'hearing' – the video from the position of a native Japanese speaker, I hear the Japanese voice-over provided by Suika (the director) and Cash as a sonsign that exists in a pure empty form of time; it revokes my familiar identical, repetitive cycles and patterns of hearing what I perceive as 'the Japanese language'. Their Japanese voice-over is characterized as 'nondiegetic sound,' which 'describes sound external to the direct presentation of the film, be it music or voice-over narration' (Deamer 2016: 167). Moreover, their Japanese voice-over arguably operates as a 'lectsign,' one of the sub-varieties of the time-images that 'not only demands to be seen, but requires a reading' (Deamer 2016: 163). The lectosign cannot be detected in the sensory-motor schema as it gets disconnected from its links in a montaged sequence but must be 'read' by the spectator to make a trip to the domain of unthought, that which the film does not think (Bogue 2013; Deamer 2016).

I assert that Suika and Cash's Japanese voice-over as a non-diegetic sonsign can be best described as a deterritorializing lectosign that is 'uncannily foreign while remaining technically correct' (Bogue 2011: 35). Suika was a 17-year-old male from mainland China who spoke Mandarin and had only been in Japan eleven months. Cash was also 17-year-old male from mainland China who spoke Mandarin and had only been in Japan ten months. Suika wrote the storyboard on which the video was based in his native Chinese Mandarin. He commanded the film crew to play the designated roles in both Chinese Mandarin and in his Japanese. I remember that Suika and Cash rehearsed the voice-over sentences several times before actually recording. Their Japanese, a barrier to participating in public school, was nevertheless the language of the voice-over.

Watching/hearing the video now, as a native Japanese speaker, I find Suika and Cash's utterances in Japanese syntactically, lexically and semantically 'middle-of-the-road'. However, I find their utterances to be quite 'uncanny'. This encounter led me to transform myself *incorporeally* into a predefined, hierarchical, fixed, represented identity of a native speaker of Japanese as a majoritarian language. What is remarkably intriguing about Suika and Cash's voice-over in Japanese is their unintentional but disruptive disconnections of common sense, harmonious continuities, and regularities in the organizing sensory-motor scheme to which I, as a native Japanese speaking viewer, am habitually accustomed through a repetitive past (Bogue 2013). In other words, the voice-over '[n]arration no longer gives [me] a present as a product of the past and the future as consequence of the present' (Dreamer 2016: 162) and, in a certain sense, may lead to a kind of delirium in my habit of memories.

I assert that Suika and Cash's decision and effort to add their voice-over in Japanese as their second language is 'a minor treatment of the standard language, a becoming-minor of the major language' (Deleuze and Guattari 1987: 104). My immanent and disruptive reading of Suika and Cash's utterance also allows me to sense that he uncannily mixes a multiplicity of languages, including his native Chinese Mandarin, Japanese and video images made up with digital language, based on his storyboard. My reading of Suika and Cash's Japanese voice-over also resonates with Edward Glissant's (2008) notion of Creole language and subjectivity, which combine European and African linguistic traditions, which entails 'a new kind of expression, a supplement to the two (or more) original roots, or series of roots, from which [it] was born' (Glissant 2008: 83). Glissant's concept of creolization, which I sense in Suika and Cash's language use, is not fixed and essentialized but is always 'becoming' on the basis of its internal difference (Burns 2009; Webb and Gulson 2015, also see Deleuze 1994).

It is fair to say, then, that Suika and Cash have reappropriated a digital video camera and seized hold of Japanese voice-over as a sonsign and lectosign as a form of mutation or reinvention of themselves dissenting from the Japanese government's neoliberalist, ethnocentric policies of coexistence. Their 'minor treatment of Japanese language as a becoming-minor of the major language' seems to deterritorialize the policies that continue to assimilate young migrants into Japanese language and Japanese curriculum, while remaining largely indifferent to differences in students' linguistic or socio-economic backgrounds (Sato 1998). Such policies uphold 'difference-blindness' (Reeves 2004) at best. I argue that the video calls for an alternative lived approach or ontology to such policies and demonstrates the minor treatment of Japanese language as a becoming-minor of the major language.

Intermezzo

This chapter started with Guattari's question: 'How can we reconcile the taste of the majority, the demand for news and for education, and the legitimate ambition for self-expression on the part of the minority cultures?' (2002: 21). I engaged in collaboratively making and reading the tripartite interrelated conditions of our migrant adolescent-generated minor video *Watermelons and Humans* as demonstrable ambition for minoritarian self-expression that can problematize the taste of the majority and the reins of mass-media news. The reappropriation of media use and the repurposing a-signifying semiotics are necessary conditions for the problematization.

The ambition as problematization does not identify the fixed play of truth and falsity and does not allow us to envision Guattari's sense of *reconciliation*. I assert that the reconciliation is a way to bring about what Guattari (2002: 17) imagined as an 'ethics of the media'. As noted earlier, such an ethics should pertain to immanent ethics, which problematizes 'anything that *separates* a mode of existence from its power of acting – and what separates us from our power of acting is, ultimately, the illusions of transcendence' (Smith 2011: 125, original emphasis).

Accordingly, what entails the reconciliation specific to the contexts of migrant adolescent lives and existence in Japanese society is the disruption of mass-media news and the government's representation of them as being 'already there' as a unified organic subject by recurrently projecting themselves as 'how the people are what is missing, what is not there' (Deleuze 1989: 215–16). The tripartite conditions unfolding from the making and reading of *Watermelons and Humans* as a minor video and indeed the ambition of our minoritarian self-expression are the projection of ourselves as individuals who 'no longer exist, or not yet . . . *the people are missing*' (Deleuze 1989: 216). What I call *becoming-Japanese* emerging and enacted through the making and reading of our minor video is the vital force of the reconciliation in consideration. It is the affective power of *puissance* (Deleuze and Guattari 1987) that keeps us opening up immanent lines disrupting the ontological territories produced and governed by the mass-media news and the government's mis/representation. Becoming-Japanese is 'always in the middle; [we] can only get it by the middle' (Deleuze and Guattari 1987: 293). The reconciliation should be envisioned through such intermezzos.

References

Appadurai, A. (1996), *Modernity At Large: Cultural Dimensions of Globalization*, Minneapolis: University of Minnesota Press.

Befu, H. (2001), *Hegemony of Homogeneity: An Anthropological Analysis of "Nihonjinron"*, Portland: Trans Pacific Press.

Bergson, H. (1929), *Matter and Memory*, trans. N. M. P. Paul and W. Scott, New York: George Allen and Unwin.

Bogue, R. (2010), *Deleuzian Fabulation and the Scars of History*, Edinburgh: Edinburgh University Press.

Bogue, R. (2011), 'The Minor', in C. J. Stivale (ed.), *Gilles Deleuze: Key Concepts* (2nd edn), 131–41, London, UK: Routledge.

Bogue, R. (2013), *Deleuze on Cinema*, London: Taylor and Francis.

Bryant, L. R. (2008), *Difference and Givenness: Deleuze's Transcendental Empiricism and the Ontology of Immanence*, Evanston: Northwestern University Press.

Burns, L. (2009), 'Becoming-postcolonial, Becoming-Caribbean: Édouard Glissant and the Poetics of Creolization', *Textual Practice*, 23 (1): 99–117.

Butler, A. (2002), *Women's Cinema*, London: Wallflower Press.

Cohen, S. (1980), *Folk Devils and Moral Panics: The Creation of the Mods and Rockers*, New York: St. Martin's Press.

Cole, D. R., and J. P. N. Bradley (2016), *A Pedagogy of Cinema*, Rotterdam: Sense Publishers.

Colman, F. (2005), 'Hit Me Harder: The Transversality of Becoming-Adolescent', *Women (Oxford, England)*, 16 (3): 356.

Deamer, D. (2016), *Deleuze's Cinema Books: Three Introductions to the Taxonomy of Images*, Edinburgh: Edinburgh University Press.

Deleuze, G. (1986), *Cinema 1: The Movement-Image*, trans. H. Tomlinson and B. Habberjam, London: Athlone.

Deleuze, G. (1989), *Cinema 2: The Time-Image*, trans. H. Tomlinson and R. Galeta, Minneapolis: University of Minnesota.

Deleuze, G. (1990), *The Logic of Sense*, trans. M. Lester and C. Stivale, New York: Columbia University Press.

Deleuze, G. (1994), *Difference and Repetition*, trans. P. Patton, New York: Columbia University Press.

Deleuze, G. (1995), *Negotiations, 1972–1990*, New York: Columbia University Press.

Deleuze, G. (2001), *Pure Immanence: Essays on a Life*, trans. A. Boyman, New York: Zone Books.

Deleuze, G. (2003), *Francis Bacon: The Logic of Sensation*, trans. D. W. Smith, Minneapolis: University of Minnesota Press.

Deleuze, G., and F. Guattari (1986), *Kafka: Toward a Minor Literature*, trans. D. B. Polan, Minneapolis: University of Minnesota Press.

Deleuze, G., and F. Guattari (1987), *A Thousand Plateaus: Capitalism and Schizophrenia*, trans. B. Massumi, Minneapolis: University of Minnesota Press.

Deleuze, G., and C. Parnet (1977), *Dialogues*, trans. H. Tomlinson and B. Habberjam, New York: Columbia University Press.

Foucault, M. (1988), *Politics, Philosophy, Culture: Interviews and Other Writings, 1977–1984*, trans. A. Sheridan, ed. L. D. Kritzman, New York: Routledge.

Glissant, E. (2008), 'Creolization in the Making of the Americas', *Caribbean Quarterly*, 54 (1–2): 81–9.

Guattari, F. l. (1995), *Chaosmosis: An Ethico-Aesthetic Paradigm*, trans. J. Pefanis and P. Bains, Bloomington: Indiana University Press.
Guattari, F. (1996a), *The Guattari Reader*, ed. G. Genosko, Oxford: Blackwell Publishers.
Guattari, F. (1996b), *Soft Subversions*, trans. D. L. Sweet and C. Wiener, ed. S. Lotringer, New York: Semiotext(e),
Guattari, F. (2000), *The Three Ecologies*, trans. I. Pindar and P. Sutton, London: Athlone Press.
Guattari, F. (2002), 'Toward an Ethics of the Media', *Polygraph: An International Journal of Culture and Politics*, 14: 1–30.
Guattari, F. (2013), *Schizoanalytic Cartographies*, trans. A. Goffey, London: Bloomsbury.
Iwase, M. (2010), 'New Literacies, Japanese Youth, and Global Fast Food Culture: Exploring Critical Youth Agencies', MA diss., Simon Fraser University, Burnaby, Canada. Available online: https://summit.sfu.ca/item/11451
Iwase, M. (2022), 'Minor Videos and Becoming-Japanese: Problematizing [Co][Existence] and Envisioning Alternative Futures of Young Migrants' Lives in Japan', PhD diss., The University of British Columbia, Vancouver, Canada.
Iwase, M. and J. P. N. Bradley (2021), 'Towards a Noncompliant Pedagogy of the Image: Reading Negentropic Bifurcatory Potentials in Video Images', *Video Journal of Education and Pedagogy*, 6: 1–27.
Jenkins, H. (2003), 'Quentin Tarantino's Star Wars? Digital Cinema, Media Convergence and Participatory Culture', in D. Thorburn and H. Jenkins (eds), *Rethinking Media Change: The Aesthetic Of Transition*, 281–312, Cambridge: MIT Press.
Jenkins, H. (2008), *Convergence Culture: Where Old And New Media Collide*, New York: New York University Press.
Kawai, Y. (2009), 'Neoliberalism, Nationalism, and Intercultural Communication: A Critical Analysis of a Japan's Neoliberal Nationalism Discourse under Globalization', *Journal of International and Intercultural Communication*, 2 (1): 16–43.
Kojima, Y. (2016), *Gaikokujin no shuugaku to hushuugaku: Shakai de 'mienai' kodomotachi* [School-attendance and nonattendance among the children of foreign nationals]. Osaka: Osaka University Press.
Kojima, Y. (2020). 'Practical Education Systems and Inclusion of Immigrants in Diversity Focused Societies: Implementation of the SDGs', *Gender Studies: Annals of the Tokai Foundation for Gender Studies*, 2: 47–62.
Kowner, R., and H. Befu (2015), 'Ethnic Nationalism in Postwar Japan: Nihonjinron and Its Racial Facets', in R. Kowner and W. Demel (eds), *Race and Racism in Modern East Asia Vol. 2*, 389–412, Leiden: Brill.
Lazzarato, M. (2006), 'The Concepts of Life and the Living in the Societies of Control', in M.S. Fuglsang and B. Meier (eds), *Deleuze and the Social*, 171–90, Edinburgh: Edinburgh University Press.
Lazzarato, M. (2014), *Signs and Machines: Capitalism and the Production of Subjectivity*, trans. D. Jordan, Los Angeles: Semiotixt(e).
Lazzarato, M. (2019), *Videophilosophy: The Perception of Time In Post-Fordism*, trans. J. Hetrick, New York: Columbia University Press.
Martin-Jones, D. (2004), 'Orphans, a Work of Minor Cinema from Post-Devolutionary Scotland', *Journal of British Cinema and Television*, 1 (2): 226–41.
Martin-Jones, D. (2008), *Deleuze, Cinema and National Identity: Narrative Time in National Contexts*, Edinburgh: Edinburgh University Press.
Mazzei, L. A. (2017), 'Following the Contour of Concepts Toward a Minor Inquiry', *Qualitative Inquiry*, 23 (9): 675–85.

Ministry of Education, Culture, Sports, Science and Technology (MEXT). (2019), *Results of 2018 Surveys of Public School Enrolment Situations of the Children of Foreign Nationals*, Tokyo: Ministry of Education, Culture, Sports, Science and Technology.

Ministry of Education, Culture, Sports, Science and Technology (MEXT). (2020), *Results of 2018 Surveys of Public Schools' Acceptance of the Children of Foreign Nationals in Need of Japanese Language Proficiency*, Tokyo: Ministry of Education, Culture, Sports, Science and Technology.

MIAC. (2006), *Reports on the Studies Concerning the Promotion of Multicultural Coexistence: Towards the Promotion of Community-Based Multicultural Coexistence*, Tokyo: Ministry of Internal Affairs and Communication.

MIAC. (2020), *Revisions of the 2006 Plans for Promoting Community-Based Multicultural Coexistence*, Tokyo: Ministry of Internal Affairs and Communication.

Morris, M. (1998), *Too Soon Too Late: History in Popular Culture*, Bloomington: Indiana University Press.

Morris-Suzuki, T. (2004), 'Immigration and Citizenship in Contemporary Japan', in J. Maswood, J. Graham and H. Miyajima (eds), *Japan: Change and Continuity*, 163–78, London: Routledge.

Nihon Keizai Shinbun. (2019), '19,000 Children of Foreign Nationals not Attending School: MEXT's First National Surveys', *Nihon Keizai Shinbun*. Available online: https://www.nikkei.com/article/DGXMZO50308100X20C19A9CR8000/ (accessed 4 Februrary 2022).

Okuyama, H., and T. Hori. (2020), 'School Non-Attendance and Unemployment of Children of Foreign Nationals Doubling the Numbers of Japanese Counterparts: Towards Adequate Support of Japanese Language Education', *Mainichi Shinbun*, 25 February. Available online: https://mainichi.jp/articles/20200224/k00/00m/040/220000c.

Pindar, I. and P. Sutton. (2000), 'Translators' Introduction', in Guattari's *The Three Ecologies*, 1–17, London: Athlone Press.

Reeves, J. (2004), '"Like Everybody Else": Equalizing Educational Opportunity for English Language Learners', *TESOL Quarterly*, 38 (1): 43–66.

Rodowick, D. N. (1997), *Gilles Deleuze's Time Machine*, London: Duke University Press.

Rouch, J. (2003), *Ciné-Ethnography*, trans. S. Feld, Minneapolis: University of Minnesota Press.

Sato, G. (1998), 'Education and Intercultural Adaptation of the Pupils and Students of Foreign Nationals', in K. Ebuchi (ed.), *Transculturalism Studies*, 479–97, Tokyo: Akashi Publishing.

Shiobara, Y. (2020), 'Genealogy of Tabunka Kyōsei: A Critical Analysis of the Reformation of the Multicultural Co-living Discourse in Japan', *International Journal of Japanese Sociology*, 29 (1): 22–38.

Smith, D. W. (2011), 'Deleuze and the Question of Desire: Towards an Immanent Theory of Ethics,' in N. S. Jun and D. W. Smith (eds), *Deleuze and Ethics*, 123–40, Edinburgh: Edinburgh University Press.

Spivak, G. C. (2009), *Outside in the Teaching Machine*, New York: Routledge.

Voss, D. (2013a), 'Deleuze's Third Synthesis of Time', *Deleuze Studies*, 7 (2): 194–216.

Voss, D. (2013b), 'The Philosophical Concepts of Meat and Flesh: Deleuze and Merleau-Ponty', *Parrhesia*, 18: 113–24.

Wakabayashi, H. (2013), 'Consideration about Japanese Public Schools for Foreign Children: Through the Action of Niji no Kakehashi Kyoshitsu Project,' *Utsunomiya University School of International Studies Research Paper Collection*, 35: 163–9.

Watson, J. (2002), 'Guattari's Black Holes and the Postmedia Era', *Polygraph: An International Journal of Culture and Politics*, 14: 30–45.
Webb, P. T. (2014), 'Policy Problematization', *International Journal of Qualitative Studies in Education*, 27 (3): 364–76.
Webb, P. T., and K. N. Gulson. (2015), 'Faciality Enactments, Schools of Recognition and Policies of Difference (in-itself)', *Discourse*, 36 (4): 515–32.
White, P. (2008), 'Lesbian Minor Cinema', *Screen*, 49 (4): 410–25.
Williams, J. (2011), *Gilles Deleuze's Philosophy of Time: A Critical Introduction and Guide*, Edinburgh: Edinburgh University Press.
Yashima, D. (2019), '20,000 Children of Foreign Nationals Not Attending School: Municipal Governments' Neglect', *Asahi Shinbun*. Available online: https://www.asahi.com/articles/ASM9V6TT7M9VUTIL04Q.html (accessed 4 January 2022).
Yoshino, K. (1992), *Cultural Nationalism in Contemporary Japan: A Sociological Enquiry*. London: Routledge.

13

Akira versus Tetsuo

Postmedia chaos as reserve of potentials in Guattarian ecosophy

Toshiya Ueno

In 2020, in Tokyo, people were looking forward to the Tokyo Olympics. After the notorious catastrophic event and its aftermath, disguised as the result of the explosion of a new type of bomb, however, most areas of the city centre were still devastated and in ruins not only in terms of physical damage but also through an uneasy trauma triggered by Akira. His body was set in cryogenic storage to bury this trauma. But as Akira slowly began to awake, so did his incredible psychic power. In decomposed urban spaces, underground or dissident action is aroused especially in subcultural street tribes. Acceleration is the imperative of neoliberal, postmodern, speculative and info-semiocapitalism, in which Akira is a symbolic and representative figure; as such Tetsuo came to attack Akira in unforeseen ways.

The above is a fictive imagining for examining the political and cultural atmosphere in Japan in the 1980s. But my aim is not merely retrospective. Rather, what is drawn from the critical survey of Japan from the recent past is an interpretive and practical intervention in the contemporary world and the present. *Tetsuo* (or Tetsuo Kogawa) was aware of the necessity to resist the current which *Akira* (Akira Asada) publicly propelled, with his idea for the end of capitalism by accelerating electronic media and technology. In those days, in mid-1980s Japan, *Akira* was a striking name in both the post-subcultural scene because of the eponymous manga/anime by Katsuhiro Otomo, and the critical theory scene in the areas of post-structuralism, film, art and literature due to the boom of the so-called new academism (*Nyu Aka*) in Japanese journalism, which was largely due to the impact of Asada Akira.[1] But, just as in the manga and anime piece, another name *Tetsuo* (Kogawa)[2] lingered in the translocal debates around Deleuze and Guattari. This is one of the reasons why this chapter sometimes relies on narrative expression. Interestingly, even Kogawa sometimes adopted the fictive style in his prose. For instance, in *The Critique of Info-Capitalism*, he envisioned the future nuclear accident in Japan (Kogawa 1985: 62).

Both Kogawa and Guattari were interested in electronic media and technology, especially the notion of postmedia. Kogawa was a DIY geek, hooked on radio electronic kits, while Guattari, influenced by his son, Bruno, had a penchant for radio. Can postmedia be adequately equated with new media or multimedia after the mass-media era? Careful readers of Guattari would challenge such a vulgar understanding, arguing that Guattari invented ecosophy not as a media ecology as such (or an ecology in the condition of info/cyber technologies) but as a 'virtual ecology' in the widest sense (Guattari 1995: 91).

Why has the name of Tetsuo Kogawa thus far been ignored or dismissed in Deleuze and Guattari studies? The only exception is the book edited by Gary Genosko and Jay Hetrick, which includes Kogawa's interviews with Guattari in the mid-1980s (Guattari 2015a). However, Kogawa's intellectual or activist work is still relatively unknown in the English-speaking world, aside from the radio art and media performance scenes. It is especially strange not to find his name in François Dosse's well-known biographical work *Gilles Deleuze and Félix Guattari: Intersecting Lives (2010)*. Actually, from around 1984 in Japan, Kogawa was the first person to utilize the term *info-capitalism* (*Jōhō Shihonshugi*). The term has almost the same meaning as info-semiocapitalism, that is, the mode of contemporary economy consistent with Guattari's notion of integrated world capitalism. In a way, Asada Akira was the most famous postmodern intellectual at that time in Japan, acting as a (petit bourgeois) leftist and avant-garde elitist critic. In fact, on many occasions, Asada confessed himself to be a modernist leftist or even a Stalinist – as Žižek is sometimes apt to do! But in the translocal context, his position was akin to the accelerationists in the UK. But Tetsuo was critical of the spirit of postmodernism, much like his American counterpart Fredric Jameson.

In the mid-1980s, both Kogawa and Masaaki Sugimura (the main translator of Guattari) often criticized the tendency to introduce Deleuze and Guattari *without the inclusion of Guattari and political activism*. Asada was always treated coldly despite his leftist position because he emphasized the significance of the classic trade union type of political movement, while working in the corporate sector (media art projects supported by Japanese telecom companies, business think tanks and public agencies, etc.). Such a tactical albeit quasi-co-opted attitude is not unique to Asada as Guattari himself was invited by the famous SEIBU department store shortly before his untimely death and he even appeared in newspaper advertisements for Suntory whiskey in the mid-1980s.

Kogawa's original background was in philosophy, especially the phenomenology of Husserl and Heidegger, the critical theory of Benjamin and Adorno, and the phenomenological Marxism of Pazi and Piccone. His graduate dissertation dealt with the question of how *The Quotations from Chairman Mao* could assume the role of 'micro media' among militant youth groups in both Beijing and Paris or other places across the globe. He also had expertise in Kafka and was interested in minor languages (especially in Yiddish theater in New York). This is understood not only in the sense of minority culture but also as an expressive minor tactic which Deleuze and Guattari conceptualized in *Kafka: Toward a Minor Literature* (2008). So, in the Japan of the 1980s and 1990s, Kogawa's name was always associated with the term *media* (free radio, early experiments of internet streaming, media art performance like the works by Stelarc).

The criticism against new media and multimedia was crucial for his discourse during that period. Of course, it should be noted that postmedia is fundamentally different from major and molar media, a mode in which we still helplessly indulge on the internet.

Since the late 1970s, Kogawa was interested in the Italian workers' movement and introduced their political theory and activism in some Japanese magazines. He was especially fascinated by free radio movements such as the Radio Alice, the pirate station which Franco 'Bifo' Berardi also participated in. Gradually, Kogawa began to shift his research field from phenomenology, Gramscian hegemony politics and critical theory to the philosophy of Deleuze and Guattari. Although he wished to make a conceptual link between the autonomist movement in Italy and the phenomenological Marxism of the journal *Telos* represented by Paul Piccone (the latter distanced themselves from Deleuze because of his trust in civil hegemony politics and sympathy for the Italian communist party). Yet, Kogawa tried to invent a creative interconnection between all these movements and groups. By way of Guattari's *Molecular Revolution*, Kogawa understood the nature of free radio activity in the autonomist movement and came into contact with Negri's political theory. In 1985, Guattari sent Kogawa the original draft of his collaborative work with Negri, *New Lines of Alliance, Spaces of Liberty* (which later became *Communist Like Us*).[3] As a consequence, Kogawa gradually joined the media activism or hactivist movements at the translocal level.[4]

What is postmedia?

Tetsuo escaped from the laboratory of the army. In order to awaken Akira again, Tetsuo fought with the army police and began to transmute himself with machines, things, debris and all kinds of materials. Tetsuo trans-organized his body into weird machinic assemblages. His aim was to liberate what Akira could deploy from his secret potentials.

What is postmedia? As is well known, before his untimely death, Guattari invented this term in *The Three Ecologies*, *Schizoanalytic Cartographies* and *Chaosmosis*. In the first, he raised the four basic conditions of postmedia (Guattari 2008: 41): (1) an eruption of mass consciousness even within its embryonic form – and perhaps the unconsciousness as well; (2) the collapse of all authoritarian incarnations after Stalinism; (3) technological innovations and tactical usages of media for non-capitalist goals, through cost-cutting and miniaturization (which enabled incipient forms of free radio); (4) reconstitution of labour processes after the debacle of the early twentieth-century industrial formation of production with a more 'creationist' subjectivity at both the individual and collective level. Obviously, postmedia takes place in the post-industrial condition. In this sense and at a first glance, Guattari seemed to conceptualize the postmedia era within a linear series. But as we cannot make a clear transition from mass media to that of postmedia, can postmedia be rephrased as 'virtual media' or 'cyber-multimedia'? If one adopts the linear development of communication and economy explanation, then postmedia would be situated at the latest stage in that development. But this is not Guattari's intention. The potentiality of postmedia does not follow inevitably from the establishment and proliferation of new media technologies. The characteristic of postmedia is not ascribed to mere newness or innovation.

Guattari presents a three-stage linear order of seriality in his explication of the modes of subjectivity in *Schizoanalytic Cartographies* which is consistent with the three different eras in the development of media and society. The first is 'the age of *European Christianity*', which is remarkable in 'a new conception of the relations between the Earth and Power' (2013: 6; emphasis mine). In *Chaosmosis*, this stage is called the polysemic, animistic and polyphonic assemblage with concentric strata, in which objects are located within a 'transversal, vibratory position' which is the state of 'becoming ancestral, animal, vegetal cosmic' (Guattari 1995: 102). Herein both subjectivities and objectivities overlap and incorporate each other by 'becoming half-soul, half-man, half-beast, machine and flux, matter and sign' (102). The second stage is 'the age of *the capitalistic deterritorialisation of knowledges and techniques*', let us say of capitalism, which is based on 'the principles of generalised equivalence' of which Marx clarified in his late works. In *Chaosmosis*, this stage is defined as one of deterritorialized assemblages (1995: 103). The third is 'the age of *planetary computerization*', which unfolds 'the possibility that a creative and singularising processuality might become the new basic reference' (2013: 6; emphasis mine). This last stage is called the 'new aesthetic paradigm' (1995: 107) where the genesis of enunciation is housed within the processual dynamics of creation and invention.

Each stage of subjectivity corresponds to a specific formation of society and its communicative mode for desire and information, which always has its own specific voices/pathways. According to this periodization, in the premodern or tribal society, *power* is an integrative moment transmitted through voices/pathways which dominate the soul of individuals by using varied images or symbols in a given communication and economy. But in modern society, *knowledge* is more determinant for voices/pathways of communication, which is 'articulated to techno-scientific and economic pragmatics from inside subjectivity' (2013: 3). Lastly, in the postmedia or control society, '*self-reference* is most determinant for voices/pathways of processual subjectivity' (3; emphasis mine).

What is at stake here, however, is not just about the segmentation of plural eras but rather the superposition of varied logics or formations of society. These different modes of thoughts, affects and subjectivities through dissimilar passages of time intersect and return to each other by deviating within distinct epochs and territories. In this vein, it seems that Guattari considered the idea of a certain overlapping of different temporalities, in which the future belongs to, or is folded upon the present by passing through the past. The potentiality of media technology is likely what incorporates the future (as a possible disjunction) within the present (conjuncture) and the past (connection). New futural usages of technology would be salvaged from the 'not-yet agency' while no longer being potentiality for infinite optional becoming. In other words, what formalizes the substance of the world in alter-native media is the tendency of the *not-yet* which opens out infinitely towards a virtual One-All. This perspective of a disjunctive timing proceeds back and forth between distinct temporalities, and assumes a certain threshold where different tenses incorporate and mesh with each other to infinity. This inter-movable temporality is to be articulated by the phrase 'it will-have been'. In fact, the term *post* here conveys both meanings of a critical limit and passage of transitions (*krisis*). In *Lines of Flight*, Guattari explains his idea of temporality by insisting that one can 'seek to deploy the potentialities of the present and face up to the idea that "new" can surge up from the heart of past' (2014: 192). This disjunctive gap is always activated as the very non-contemporaneity or non-synchronicity of media in different periods. This transversal temporality is a significant moment of postmedia.[5]

Since the mid-1990s, both Kogawa's micro radio initiatives and postmedia radio performances were dependent on the idea of 'narrowcasting'.[6] He designed a DIY micro-FM-radio transmitter for micro radio stations, and also gave a performance as a micro radio transmitter: his body was a mannequin with electronic sensors which he called 'quasi-androids'. What is significant in this performance was not music or sound as such but the emergence of a polymorphous but singular body *within machinic assemblages*.

In his workshops, all participants were asked to make their own transmitter in line with the severe regulations in Japan (only available within a limited radius of 1 km). Theoretically speaking, it seemed possible to create a network of linking nodes of micro radios (tiny stations). At that moment, the idea of narrowcasting was very crucial for his postmedia performance activism. Kogawa was frustrated with the recuperation of the free (or pirate) radio format into market-oriented sectors – like the present iteration of the internet where everything in air-wave media seems to have melted into streaming media. Micro postmedia could have different values and tactics than major ones, just as micro politics should be distinguished from the macro politics in many respects. Just as the autonomist movement in Italy raised the idea of the refusal of labour, free (pirate) radio as a form of postmedia would present the rejection of mainstream communication and even the tactic of communication breakdown. For Kogawa, micro free radio did not imply scaled down media at all as it seemed pointless to repeat the molar mode of communication in mass media *within* micro radio initiatives. The former is still visible in the case of the so-called mini-FM or local community radios in Japan. Arguably, free radio can be defined as a failed or malfunctioned radio just like Jean Tinguely's mechanical installations which Guattari loved. Kogawa considered free radio to be critical, experimental, processual and politico-aesthetic. His initiative thus sharply resonated with the Guattarian notion of postmedia.

Likewise, Kogawa's radio performance was not envisioned as media art *per se* but as a theorizing practice through performative or *alter-native* media activism. As such, he was never comfortable with the position as an 'artist' or 'performer' as he affirmed the notion of the 'polymorphous' which was inspired by the concepts of BwO and becoming in Deleuze and Guattari. Generally, in Kogawa's view, performance should be completely distinct from general expressions such as art, music, and theatre play, insofar as it always betrays what audiences expect in their conventional habitus. For him a (postmedia) performance should be always contingent, haphazard and unpredictable. The point for the polymorphous radio and body is the questioning of how one can diagram the deterritorialization of a-significant, (non) communication and non-production in our everyday life and info-spheres.

A potential, reserve (reservoir) and chaos(mosis)

What is the sense of the virtual in Kogawa's conception of postmedia? Interestingly, in his recent essay on Deleuze, he translated the term not as 仮想的 (*kasouteki* – the meaning of virtual and fictive) or 潜在的 (*senzaiteki* – the meaning of potential) in Japanese but as 実質的 (*jisshitsuteki* – the meaning of substantial) (Kogawa 2014: 15–16). Certainly, the term *virtual* conveys all three meanings in English but the last one is usually dismissed. Inspired by the concept of 'memory' in computer technologies, Kogawa shed light upon the *substantial* nature of the virtual. It is neither objective nor real but, nevertheless, suggests a certain materiality, *thing-ness*, and thus one can posit substance as a relational field or ambience. No matter to what extent electronic technology and virtual data might prevail, humans at least – even if we are becoming post-humans or even non-humans more and more – still require the incorporeal body and physical contact in a twofold nuance (corporeal and incorporeal). The potentiality of a *body* is always invoked in Kogawa's theory of postmedia and micropolitics because it can *performatively* be opened to the polymorphous drives and interactions.

Simply speaking, a potential suggests capacities and inclinations to overcome or subvert what is given through the status quo. Potentiality was articulated as the 'economy of the possible' in Guattari's *The Machinic Unconscious* (2011) and *Lines of Flight* (2014). In the days before the publication of *Anti-Oedipus*, and unlike his late works such as *Schizoanalytic Cartographies* and *Choasmosis*, Guattari had not formulated a clear distinction between the virtual and the possible. According to him, 'the possible is a matter as differentiated as the most material matters' (Guattari 2011: 199). In his late works, of course, the difference between both concepts is clear and the concept of potential, which is inspired in part by Whitehead, is adopted. But the notion of the possible was frequently utilized in Guattari's works from the mid-1970s, especially in *The Machinic Unconscious*. Given that *Lines of Flight* was published posthumously in 2014, it is timely to assess the significance of the concept again, because many parts of this book overlap with *The Machinic Unconscious* which was written in the mid-1970s.

In the interview by Kogawa in the 1980s, Guattari subtly articulated the 'economy of the possible'. It suggests a vital formation which constantly emerges from a rupture in the already given, stratified and repetitive patterned economy (2015a: 37). The economy of the possible can make desire more creative, deviant and productive. It challenges the idea that everything will permanently continue in the same way. Indeed, falling in love is invoked as a moment in which everything can abruptly change and be transformed (2015a: 37). The term *possible* has often been used affirmatively by Guattari, especially in tandem with the concept of 'optional matter'. Optional matter is also to be called 'a sort of *transformational matter*' constituted by and immanently with abstract machines (2011: 16). It is a crystallizing of the possible to 'catalyze connections, deterritorialisation and reterritorializations both in the living and inanimate world'

(2011: 16). The 'optional matter' cannot be grasped from the human perspective. At a first glance, humans seem to choose (collective) assemblages of enunciation and machines at their disposal but, in fact, assemblages are always selected exclusively 'from the point of view of things themselves' (Guattari 2011: 154). For Guattari, proto-subjectivity is found as a form of objectivities *within machinic assemblages*. In his view, before the structures of semiosis and social stratifications, the possible is neither defined as a pure logical matter nor created from nothing, but built within the process of organizing the 'quanta of freedom' (2014: 148). This is visible, for example, in the phenomena of chemical reactions or organic fermentation.

The economy of the possible seems to have already entered the register of the virtual in Guattari's thinking in the late 1970s. Here it is difficult to comprehend the idea precisely. But if one reads his late work in detail, it is clear that the concept of potential can traverse or criss-cross in the quadrant between the virtual and the possible, and the actual and the real. Or, with Massumi, we might say that 'possibility is extended potential – a prosthesis of potential' (2002: 111). In fact, Guattari often addresses the notion of potential or potentiality in his late works, which might challenge our reading on Guattari. With this in mind, it is crucial to conceive how the notion of the possible had operated almost like that of the virtual in his work in the 1970s. Likewise the virtual and the potential in his late works can be interpreted as different modes of the possible. If we fail to understand this, one cannot understand his line at the end of *Schizoanalytic Cartographies*: '[T]he reality of the possible always has primacy over the possibility of the real' (2013: 28). Deleuze and Guattari themselves also insisted 'a state of affairs does not actualise a chaotic virtual without taking from it a potential that is distributed in the system of coordinates. From the virtual that it actualises it draws that it appropriates' (1994: 122). On this reading, the idea of the potential by Guattari resonates with his last work with Deleuze.

Generally, the technology of radio realizes the concrete machine. But free (pirate) radio also has a different vector when it operates in a deviant or perverse manner. In the early days when Kogawa started to engage radio, he was inspired by both Brecht and Guattari in terms of the rudimentary function of radio, that is, to transform a receiving device into a transmitting or broadcasting device (Guattari and Rolnik 2007: 167). In the case of Kogawa's polymorphous radio, there is the transformation from a broadcasting to narrowcasting device, or from molar to micro radio. But the potentiality – or the economy of possible – can enable us to *transduce* or deviate concrete machines into/towards abstract machines. Put differently, polymorphous radio as an abstract machine proliferates ubiquitously. But at the same time – and coming from nowhere or the ontological void – and before and after the crystallization of polarity between forms and matters, objects and subjects, corporeality and incorporeality, transmission and reception and so on, it occurs within pure quanta of deterritorialization. So for Guattari, the matter of deterritorialization is actually that of the possible, which might be an integrative part of politics in general, especially in the attempt to constitute a 'trans-human, trans-sexual, trans-cosmic-politics' (2014: 167). In *What Is Philosophy?*, chaos is defined not as nothingness but rather as the void. Yet, there is another understanding in Guattari's late works. The process of making chaos is defined as the 'primordial soup of the Plane of immanence' (2013: 103). Here chaos is understood as the 'inexhaustible reserve or reservoir' of 'optional matters' which is open to an infinite determinability, even leading to political potentials in their manifestation (103–4). The chaos as reserve (or reservoir) affords us the processual or occasional 'embryos' which induce 'mutant morphogenesis' (103–4).

The term *reserve* is insightfully utilized in a suggestive manner by Deleuze and Guattari in *What Is Philosophy?*: 'The event is immaterial, incorporeal, unlivable: pure *reserve*' (Deleuze and Guattari 1994: 91; emphasis mine). The reserve or reservoir in this context might remind us of the Heideggerian concept of 'standing reserve' but its meaning is distinct, precisely because the reserve or reservoir has nothing to do with 'stockpiled resources' or the ready-ness for possible operations of tools and objects. Instead the reserve or reservoir in Guattari (and Deleuze) is inexhaustible but also the unavailable and resistible determination of 'optional matters'. It is a bearer of hyper-complexity, which is virtual, nondiscursive, a-significant and ever-changing and ever-dissolving (Guattari 2013: 104). And it always betrays the conventional operation of media and technology. Because of reserve/reservoir of potentials of chaos (or chaosmosis), any given media or technology can overcome its own limited predictable functors and divert its conventional usage into myriads of possible deviancy, which may lead to a variety of deterritorialization. Without such a reserve or reservoir of potentiality, the deployment of postmedia cannot be achieved. Following this vein, one can contend that the potential also affords a reserve of becoming which prompts us to recognize that the production of subjectivity can never fulfill its own identity. We always embrace in ourselves some non-available but endlessly open reserve towards new deployments with inexhaustible and un-expectable outcomes of the event. In this manner, postmedia is always immanent in the present condition of technology and our body.

Bodily incorporeality and tangibility

Now I am going to extend Kogawa's philosophical comments on the body. In Kogawa's critical postmedia theory, corporeality (身体性, *shintaisei*) is usually taken as physicality, embodiment and bodyness. As all phenomenologists tend to do, Kogawa seems to define intersubjectivity as inter-corporeality, mutual corporeality or inter-bodyness. The body is envisioned as a common platform of human interaction, through which one can communicate with others or even with oneself. The intersubjectivity for Kogawa can be translated or *transducted* into an inter-corporeality, which, since incorporeality, has always been buried in oblivion from the historical scientific horizon. For him, a corporeality is defined as a nucleus of singularity, un-exchangeability and incommensurability of each human existence. Obviously, he was indebted to Husserl in this context but Kogawa's definition of the body might be closer also to the humanistic understanding of bodily existences, as Asada suggested in his criticism of the humanistic flavour in Marx's 1844 Paris manuscripts. According to Asada, Kogawa's attitude appears to be typical as it admits some inalienable essence of humanity which could be reclaimed by an emancipatory or revolutionary task.

Especially, through his experimental radio performance, Kogawa was always concerned with the notion of corporeality or embodiment along with his interest in BwO and machinic assemblages in the philosophy of Deleuze and Guattari. *Bodily* suggests a more amorphous or freaky resonance of corporeality than the term *body* simply implies. Bodily or corporeality in Kogawa, in my view, is fundamentally torn apart between actuality and virtuality so that it constantly modulates the difference between both parts. Rather than taken as a mere instance of interaction or dialectics, and more in tandem with Spinoza's notion of body, in the Guattarian quadruple, *bodily* is permanently traversed – in-flow (F), in-act (T), in-form (Φ) and in-corporeal (U) – so that mental and physical poles are integrated in their disjuncture as incorporeality.

Whitehead's clarification of the bodily might be helpful here: the physical pole of the event is basically corporeal, whereas its mental pole is always incorporeal.[7] Certainly a body is conceived as part of a collective agency like the modern body-politics of society. But, on the other hand, a body is, by itself, understood as a complex of *feelings* in conjunction with the vital moments of the world, is not only seen from the perspective of phenomenology but also from Whitehead's philosophy. Then this *feeling* is traced back to the notion of 'prehension' which extends the meaning of sense or body not exclusively for humans but also for non-living or non-human agencies in the world, or even for the ambience or environment as such. Guattari also calls this entanglement of feeling (or affects) and 'earthing' (*prise de terre*) in his late works. From the perspective of *feeling*, *bodily* is not simply about body-politics (which used to explain the ground of the collective formation of individual bodies) but is more concerned with the politics of embodiment or corporeality operated in affects among objects and other non-human beings, not only in the emotion or passion of humans. *Bodily* as such is the very mode of affect or affection in the event. Bodily gestures as containing virtual parts of a-significant enunciations (collective or personal, pre- or infra-individual or trans-individual) are figured out from a domain of potential as a vector of actualization of unforeseen incorporeal values.

In Kogawa's understanding, media-technology is not something which is merely added on the bodily surface from the exterior. It is not just a supplement of body nor a prosthetics or extension of the body in McLuhan's sense. In my opinion, Kogawa seems to have considered the body to be a kind of *relational field* in the sense of Brian Massumi. In supposing a polymorphous mediatic body, he is close to stating that our body always assumes the capacity of becoming at the level of the BwO. A body in both senses of humans and things is constantly dissolving into an environment. It presents itself like a 'kinesthetic amoeba' from which a bodily gesture is drawn as a boundary of spheres of potential embodiments (Massumi 2019: 86–7). Our body is no longer restricted to each body in a limited sense. In my view, Kogawa's notion of corporeality can be understood as the *tangible*. The *bodily*, incorporated with surroundings such as living rooms, architectures and urban built environments, has always been based on something *tangible*. This is a remainder which one can access and touch upon a physical realty or resistible material moments by extending your hands in some practices. However, nowadays the sustainability or endurability of things and body is constantly modulated and controlled by electronic or other new media technologies. At a first glance, through cyber gears in virtual reality the tangible appears to disappear.

But the tangible is always built within an incipient action as a potential and relational dynamics, no matter how it might be drawn into the non-physical, mediated and virtualized. The tangible also remains a reservoir of the incorporeal agencies and universes of values. Even the effect of a phantom pain may derive from it.

Etymologically speaking, the word *tekhne* in Greek, from which technics, technicity, and technologies derive, means both manual work and physical operation. Semantically, it comes from hands. Kogawa loved the idea of handworks in Goethe very much, as it exhibited his humanist bias. The notion of bodily or corporeality in Kogawa and all his DIY postmedia performativity, however, might focus on a politics of the *tangible* more than celebrating human existence. The tangible here is not just about the touchable or physical but rather it implies a certain resistance under the condition of uncontrollability, unavailability and inaccessibility of the very things, objects, tools, technologies, that is, your own body and materiality are permanently at odds with conscious intentionality. As the tangible is vital but incorporeal activity is always both singular and multiple, this holds a vibrant resonance by emitting refrains (repetitive rhythms) only through traversing different territories (of micro media). The tangible does not necessarily indicate something manual or physical, but rather is dependent on affects in both spheres of subjectivity and objectivity or even their mutual inclusion. To work with the tangible is to engage within the potential of singularity in which all (pre- or trans-) individuations simultaneously and immanently consist.

In fact, Kogawa recognizes a certain level of immanence of the human in his reading of Deleuze's final essay, 'Immanence: A Life'. For him, this does not presuppose the inalienable essence or phenomenological presence of the human. On the occasion of the death of a rogue, in Deleuze's last essay, people surround the dying man and sympathize with his plight (2001: 28–9). At the very moment of his death, he and the bystanders mutually understand each other, but they are then soon torn apart and separated. This is exactly the immanence of living, rather than just a common platform or transferable ground of bodies, and it can be read as consistent with Guattari's 'machinic phenomenology' (Guattari 2011: 190).

Critic against accelerationism or what is deceleration?

In the narrative of Akira, in neo-Tokyo Ryu was a sub-leader in one of the fractioned crepuscules of urban guerrillas who were seeking the secret of unknown potentials of Akira. In the midst of his desire to accelerate and intensify both technological and psychic (cyber) powers, Ryu accidentally encountered such powers and even tried to manoeuvre marginal urban tribes to which Tetsuo belonged.

In 1986, Ryuichi Sakamoto released his album entitled *Futurist Fellow* (Miraiha Yarou), which transfigured the Italian avant-garde, Futurism, into the format of techno pop music. Of course, Ryuichi Sakamoto is known as an ex-member of YMO (the Yellow Magic Orchestra, the Japanese counterpart of Kraftwerk) but what is not so well known is that he was a secret organizer of Guattari's pilgrim-fieldwork in Tokyo in 1985, in which Asada and myself joined but Kogawa resisted because of his skeptical attitude towards the initiative (Guattari: 1985). During that period, terms such as *speed* or *velocity*, along with names such as Paul Virilio and Deleuze and Guattari, were buzzwords in critical theory and the art scene in Japan.

Akira (Asada) was a representative of the current of accelerationism and the explosive processes of theory and subculture. His claim can be summarized simply: If the capitalist system is limitlessly accelerated, it would decompose at its own final limit. Kogawa (our *Tetsuo*) was critical of the delight of those who thought that acceleration would lead towards destruction, demolition, annihilation and extinction. Kogawa critically analysed the mainstream Japanese postmodern discourse at that time, especially the accelerationist tendency of Asada. It is surprising that much before the rise (or perhaps the mere revival) of so-called accelerationism in the UK in the 1990s and this century, there was a prevailing conceptual trend in Japan which accentuated the notion of acceleration in terms of the end of capitalism, in both the technological and aesthetic-cultural spheres. In order to explain the becoming of the BwO, for instance, Asada described the scene in *The Story of Little Black Sambo* in which aggressive tigers melted into butter as they frenetically chased around a tree (Asada 1984). His point was that the acceleration enables becomings with infinite speeds which can lead to the level of *ur-materiality*. In this vein, Asada might be regarded as a contemporary precursor and Japanese counterpart of Nick Land, Benjamin Noys and their ilk. What was at stake in Asada's *On Escape*, Kogawa argued in his *The Critique of Info-Capitalism* (1985) was not about escape, flight and leakage but the boosting of speed, velocity and acceleration in all technological conditions and capacities.

Kogawa criticized the proto-accelerationist discourse by Asada because the latter treated postmodernism not so much as a historical phase but as the end of history of the human as such. In other words, his position dared to bet on affirming the *androidization* of the self – that is the 'becoming AI' expressed in contemporary parlance – by presupposing that the present development of technology would replace the metabolic velocity of the body *at the speed of light*. This position seems to default on the historical debt which we have owed (Kogawa 1985: 116). In my view, Kogawa raised the notion of *deceleration* and echoed the tactics of a 'primordial slowing down' in Guattari's words (1995: 112). Kogawa enumerates some examples: a masochist delays an accomplishment of his/her desire and ecstasy, or Kafka's rejection of having an immediate relationship with his fiancé, Felice, can be envisioned as a tactic of retarding immediate communication, intercourse and contact. As is well known, Kafka sent an incredible number of letters to her. His letters functioned as a sort of telecommunication through the process of deceleration (anti-acceleration). It is a very insightful reading, because Deleuze and Guattari also analysed history as such through the deployment of acceleration or velocity in Kafka's work. History is not the eternal return but of pressures of segmentations *in and toward acceleration* (Deleuze and Guattari 2008: 59). This velocity of segmentations has three different blocks: America, Nazism and bureaucracy. Through reading Kafka, Deleuze and Guattari present a literary machine against the acceleration brought about by these systems to anticipate the crisis or precipitations of all systems, or simply to 'overcome diabolical powers before they become established' (2008: 59).

This corresponds to attempts to avoid the unknown catastrophic power of *Akira* and *Tetsuo* in both anime and manga plots. This literary or expressive machine (or machnic assemblage) is constituted in decelerating a general movement of traversing the varied social, cultural and media spheres. It plays itself within a virtuality that is 'real without yet being actual' (48). The diabolical power of the future is warded off exclusively by 'brushing up against the door' (59). Here I am inclined to view free radio as tactical or alter-native media which can operate in a similar manner to the 'literary machine' Deleuze and Guattari conceived. Free radio retains a different mode of expressive or performative machinery from mass, molar and major media. Guattari himself admitted that free radio held the machinic nuclei of launching the diagrammatic or a-significant process of redundancy. Guattari called it a 'possibilist machinics' (2011: 227) which can be defined as potential and virtual machines for the unforeseen modes of subjectivity and sociality. In this sense and from Kogawa's perspective, Kafka is a postmedia tactician.

Obviously, Kogawa's initiative of free radio and performance since the 1980s was enabled 'through the dismantling (*demontage*)' of machine and representations (Deleuze and Guattari 2008: 48). Kogawa's preference for marginal cityscapes and low-tech handmade DIY can be understood in this respect. If the gentrified cityscape is actualized by the speed of acceleration of desire and assemblages, then the rough, dismantled and ruined parts of the city are immanent in the velocity of deceleration.

For instance, since his childhood, Kogawa has adored the area of Akihabara, a famous part of downtown Tokyo known for its DIY electronic parts market, which was built up in the reconstruction effort after the Second World War. The district originally developed through the black market in the early post-war period and was then populated with DIY electronic geek visitors. It is nowadays known as the town featuring Japanese pop stars and anime-manga cultures. For more than ten years, the town has been made notorious due to the casual right-wing populist gatherings. Conservative politicians in the dominant (LDP) party also love to make their public speeches in this district.

It should be noted that in *Chaosmosis*, Guattari analysed the notion of 'primordial deceleration' or 'primordial slowing down' in a speculative manner. Here, chaos and disorder, which are rapidly ever changing, gain stability and order through this radical deceleration. Chaos must be stabilized through the dynamics of chaosmosis. Guattari succinctly describes this: 'the chaotic state joins up with chaosmotic state, its extreme inverse, the latter only being established at the end of an infinite processual duration, the former dissolving at the first instant' (Guattari 2013: 172). Chaos is a rapid alternation with infinite speeds between appearance and disappearance, being and nothing, order and disorder, univocity and complexity. That is the reason why it is adequate to say that chaosmosis is 'relative chaotization' (Guattari 1995: 112), precisely because it covers both different states above, not based on the dialectic in-between. In the primordial slowing down or deceleration, a certain conversion or transduction constantly has to take place from the virtual into the possible (Guattari 1995: 112). The transience of the infinity or infinite differentiations is 'decelerated' and translated into finite speeds, which is never reduction. This process is not about just slowing down but rather about the infinite transmutability or transfigurations loaded within the finite speed. In other words, a vector towards limitless in-formations or infinite series of the incorporeal should be folded within finite speeds, which is not the infinite charged within the finite in the case of Hegelian philosophy. Through the idea of this radical deceleration, Guattari assumes the superposition of 'the immanence of infinity and finitude onto the immanence of complexity and chaos' (Guattari 1995: 112). But it is still possible to envision this primordial deceleration as a different mode of acceleration, including a tactics of postmedia which can navigate media technologies in perverse or deviant vectors through their tactical usages, such as free/pirate radio, media and other forms of experimentation.

When Deleuze and Guattari ask the question 'How Do You Make Yourself a Body without Organs?', they insist that we should not cling to speed. Nomads are not charged with velocity or mobility. As Deleuze and Guattari write: 'The nomad exists only in becoming, and in interaction' (2013: 430). Kogawa paid attention to Deleuze's remark on nomads in terms of moving and travelling. The argument holds the same veracity for phenomena of acceleration. Since the 1970s, in both *Dialogue* and *Negotiations*, Deleuze focussed on the point by Toynbee: 'The nomads are the ones who don't move on, they become nomads because they refuse to disappear' (1995: 138). Put differently, nomads are always at standstill rather than in permanent motion or acceleration. Is it possible to contend that they become nomad just because they refuse to accelerate their life and the world? Herein the imperative for postmedia is invoked: don't move too much, or don't accelerate too much! From this perspective, we can think about deceleration not as a mere reduction of speeds but as breaking or slowing down *with intensity*.

And so it has begun...

> Both Akira and Tetsuo have disappeared because of their incredible transmutative power and potentials. But kids are aware of the advent of something in the near future, which can be actualized through the uncanny mixture between machines and living organisms. The era of the unknown has already started. Some tribes know it while others do not.

While Guattari was very acutely aware of how the production of (religious) subjectivity was formed through the church in the European (Catholic) context, the same can be said for subjectivity under the emperor system in Japan[8] (Guattari 2013: 43). In the post-war period, the Japanese emperor cannot be considered either a political or charismatic leader, although the emperor was defined as a humanized deity under the fascist regime up to and during the Pacific war. Historically, the Japanese emperor system was not specifically related to the Japanese tradition or historic-cultural essence. Indeed, the Japanese emperor in the ancient or medieval era had been a magical priest or animistic shaman for his tribe. Yet, since the early period of Japanese modernity (after 1868), the emperor system was enacted by imitating European institutions such as the German juridical system. Kogawa even called the Japanese post-war period (the so-called symbolic) emperor system an asylum form of monarchy. No matter what position, it is quite usual to hear from both the left and right wing that the emperor system is everywhere, intrinsic and ubiquitous in all social spheres in Japan. This is generally called a 'grassroots emperor system' in the discourses of political sciences, cultural studies and sociology in Japan.

It can be said that even in the smallest social sectors such as schools, circles, groups and families, there is always a sort of micro-boss in a hierarchy which, however, is not so much politically hegemonic but just an empty 'top'. That is why the emperor system is interpreted as a specific mode of communication and formation of affects, especially as the effect of 'collective assemblages of enunciations'. In Japan, for instance, tacit agreements as a dominant mode of communication have been prevailing also as its major result, although these are dependent on the attitude of hesitation or reluctance. It is considered that competition or opposition in general is not considered virtuous in the social life in Japan. So modest compromises without direct messages are always estimated and demanded, at least among a molar majority. In this atmosphere under the emperor system and as a collective assemblage of enunciation, all individuation, pre-individuation and trans-individuation cannot be envisioned separately. Individuation as such is always built within the collective process of unfolding a singularity of the existential and a multiplicity of the immanent plane. This view sounds like the thought of Gilbert Simondon, but its subsequent meaning should never be read in an affirmative sense. Guattari had already recognized that the machinic eros in Japan was somehow closely tied up to this diabolical operation of the emperor system.

The Japanese emperor system is also envisioned as an absolute heterosexual machine to enforce the emperor himself (and perhaps, all people as well) to marrying, mating and 'producing only eldest son' for the national body (politic) which is driven by sexism. But the emperor system has held a fundamental paradox since its constitution and institution in the early modern times: the emperor assumes a physical and mortal body while at the same time he is envisioned and treated as a transcendental or virtual agency – if not a transcendent spiritual one like in the pre-modern age. It has something in common with the fundamental philosophical challenge in the transcendental subjectivity in German idealism, because it is conceptualized as the universal and anonymous X yet it is holding each empirical or sensual body. This paradox remains unsolved until now, although the emperor was defined as the 'symbol of unity of all people' by the constitution enacted by the US occupation army after the defeat of Japan in the Second World War. It means that the emperor holds a certain virtual aspect which is incipient to its actualization – if not merely fictive nature. Is he a real person or just a virtual entity? In this way, the same aporia lingers.

The issue of acceleration returns here because the ultimate ideal of this system is that all desires and wishes of the people can be calculated and duplicated at the speed of light by the so-called Singularity, a form AI which can simulate human cognition in real time to control and manipulate the 'singularity' of our own body. It might sound almost like science fiction but the unconscious effect of this body-politics contains this speculative political fantasy or delusion. Theoretically speaking, the symbolic emperor system as a data bank of history is to be replaced with the virtual agent.

In this context, the Guattarian (and Deleuzian) notion of faciality is very helpful here to analyse the specificity or singularity of Japanese society. 'The subjection of semiotics to the face is the politics of the void, of the referent, of figure-ground binarity, of representation' (Guattari 2014: 179–80). This void or 'the emptying out of all contents' is neither comparable with Barthes's 'emptied center' nor the empty (political) place with which can be filled with a certain embodied figure. First and foremost, the Japanese emperor system started with the reproduction and distribution of the photo of the emperor to invent a 'subjugated group' as a nation, rather than a 'subject group' as the autonomous society. It is not a mere modern avatar of despotism but is enforced as a collective assemblage of enunciation and communication. His picture was treated as a sort of talisman so that there were so many tragicomic incidents under the fascist regime. It is still taboo in Japan in all expressive cultures – contemporary art, music, literature and film– to create art which critically questions the emperor system. But what is at stake here is that a banal or ordinary person can play the crucial role as a mediator, connector and conductor of communication, which is still prevailing in the contemporary context. In a way, the position of the Japanese emperor is somehow akin to that of young pop celebrities in everyday media consumption in Japanese society (called idols or *aidoru*).

What we find in the passage below by Guattari is how the micro-emperor system has operated to date. 'The collective assemblage speaks "flush" with states of things and states of fact. There is not, on the one hand, a subject that speaks in the void, and on the other, an object that would be spoken in "full". The void and the full are "machined" by the same deterritorialisation effect' (2014: 121). It functions as a specific mode of collective assemblage of enunciation for the production of subjectivity as a Japanese 'nation/people' *within everyday communication*. The enforcement of conformity which is visible in all social spheres in Japan has its basis in a series of 'tacit agreements' and attitudes of 'reading air' (following between lines or sensing the mood) driven by this assemblage.

As for communications in general, Kogawa insightfully quoted Deleuze's passage from *Negotiations* in his essay entitled 'Restless Control from Rhizome to Web': 'Creating has always been something different from communicating. The key thing may be to create vacuoles of noncommunication, circuit breakers, so we can elude control' (Deleuze 1995: 175). This quotation suggests that creativity does not necessarily emerge from the direct transference of a communicative message. Communication ultimately consists in a certain non-communication. This is Blanchot's argument which Deleuze likes to address in *The Logic of Sense*. What is at stake here is the term *vacuole* because Guattari utilized this word often from the early 1960s until the mid-1970s. Guattari insisted upon the significance of 'a wrinkle, a crevice, a vacuole on the surface of nothing' (Guattari 2015b: 204) even when he was under the influence of Lacan. This vacuole sets itself out on varied fantasies. Additionally, his conceptual mentor, Jean Oury, also frequently insisted upon the significance of *vacuoles* in the *institutional* environment of psychiatric hospitals. Guattari calls them institutional 'vacuoles', that is, something which depends less on therapeutic clubs or medical spaces than on the 'institutional objective' (Guattari 1995: 225) in a psychoanalytical or psychiatric context. Oury suggests that a certain specific realm as the zone of a void, vacuole, anti-group, must always be left to structuralize the collective (as the subject group in a Guattarian sense). It is not just an empty place of physical or spatial formation. What Oury intends to mean by the term *institutional* is not simply hardware, equipment, physical or real institutions but rather what indicates the very moment of generation or instantiation of something, a singular event.

In this vein, the aesthetic-politics of ecosophy in the era of postmedia is enacted in and emerges from the dissensus which Guattari emphasized in his *The Three Ecologies*. The bodily or corporeality as the tangible makes micro-aesthetic politics in-form or incorporeal. The dissensus is an incipient moment of postmedia which is driven by tangible, resistible and non-communicative parts within all kinds of communication. Now it seems to be clear that the initiative of postmedia in the Guattarian vector never simply desires 'the permanence of this return to earth – not in the naturalist sense' but rather proceeds for the position of 'electricians' with tactical usages of media technology.

References

Akira, A. (1983), *Kozo to Chikara: kigoron o koete* [Structure and Power: Beyond Semiotics], Tokyo: Keizo Shobo.

Asada, A. (1984), *Toso-ron: Sukizo Kizzu no Boken* [On Escape: Adventures of the Schizo Kids], Tokyo: Chikuma-shobo.

Augaitis, D. and Lander, D. (1994), Radio Rethink – *Art, Sound, and Transmission* [CD], Banff, Canada: Walter Phillips Gallery.

Chiba, M. (2017), *Ugokisugitewa ikenai: Jiru doruzu to seisei henka no tetsugaku* [One Should Not Move So Much], Tokyo: Kawade Shobo.

Deleuze, G. (1995), *Negotiations, 1972–1990*, trans. M. Joughin, New York: Columbia University Press.

Deleuze, G. (2001), *Pure Immanence: Essays on a Life*, trans. A. Boyman, New York: Zone Books.

Deleuze, G., and F. Guattari (1994), *What is Philosophy?*, trans. H. Tomlinson and G. Burchell, New York: Columbia University Press.

Deleuze, G., and F. Guattari (2008), *Kafka: Toward a Minor Literature*, trans. D. B. Polan, New York: Columbia University Press.

Deleuze, G., and F. Guattari (2013), *A Thousand Plateaus: Capitalism and Schizophrenia*, trans. B. Massumi, London: Continuum.

Dosse, F. (2010), *Gilles Deleuze and Félix Guattari: Intersecting Lives*, trans. D. Glassman, Columbia University Press.

Guattari, F. (1985), *Tōkyō gekijō: Gatari tōkyō o iku* [Tokyo Theater: Guattari and others]. Tokyo: Yūpīyū.

Guattari, F. (1995), *Chaosmosis: An Ethico-aesthetic Paradigm*, trans. J. Pefanis and P. Bains, Indiana: Indiana University Press.

Guattari, F. (2008), *The Three Ecologies*, trans. I. Pindar and P. Sutton, London: Bloomsbury.

Guattari, F. (2011), *The Machinic Unconscious: Essays in Schizoanalysis*, trans. T. Adkins, Cambridge: Semiotext(e).

Guattari, F. (2013), *Schizoanalytic Cartographies*, trans. A. Goffey, London: Bloomsbury.

Guattari, F. (2014), *Lines of Flight: For Another World of Possibilities*, trans. A. Goffey, London: Bloomsbury.

Guattari, F. (2015a), *Machinic Eros: Writings on Japan*, ed. G. Genosko and J. Hetrick, Minnesota: University of Minnesota Press.

Guattari, F. (2015b), *Psychoanalysis and Transversality: Texts and Interviews 1955–1971*, trans. A. Hodges, Boston: MIT Press.

Guattari, F., and S. Rolnik (2007), *Molecular Revolution in Brazil*, trans. B. Holmes and K. Clapshow, Los Angeles: Semiotext (e).

Kogawa, T. (1985), *Jōhō shihon shugi hihan* [A Critique of Information Capitalism], Tōkyō: Chikuma Shobō.

Kogawa, T. (2014), *Media no rinkai: Kami to denshi no hazama de* [The Critical State of Media], Tōkyō: Serikashobō.

Massumi, B. (2002), *Parables for the Virtual: Movement, Affect, Sensation*, Durham: Duke University Press.

Massumi, B. (2019), *Architectures of the Unforeseen: Essays in the Occurrent Arts*, Minnesota: University of Minnesota Press.

Notes

Chapter 2

1. This usage was referred to the author on his first visit to Jamia Millia Islamia by a taxi driver to specify the Muslim pockets adjacent to the university space.
2. Gate number 7 of Jamia Millia Islamia, which was the main gate for the protest was identified as Jamia Square or Freedom Square by the student protesters. It was in fact not a square like protest sites elsewhere, but this name was attributed as there was a political occupation by the students.

Chapter 4

1. The boy himself reports his own experiences, ideas, and fears to his father, who discusses them with his mentor, Doctor Freud, both by correspondence and during office visits. In 1909, the good doctor Freud writes up the Hans case as an illustration of his theories of sexual development (1955). In his seminar of 1956–7, Lacan rereads Freud's published case as a structural study of the father function (1994). Guattari attended Lacan's lectures in person and later writes about Hans, both on his own and with Gilles Deleuze. Ian Buchanan recently published an intriguing article on the limitations of Deleuze and Guattari's treatment of Hans, but he does not take into account Guattari's writings without Deleuze (2013).
2. The existential territory also corresponds to the body without organs (2009b: 297).
3. The context of Guattari's 1973 essay was the relaxing in France of cinema censorship, a liberalization which made possible the theatrical release of erotic films like *Last Tango in Paris* (1972) and *Emmanuelle* (1974). Rather than championing the new erotic cinema, Guattari instead calls for a 'cinema of desire'– a cinema 'that puts the revolutionary libido in motion' even if the theme of the movie is life in a convent (Guattari 2009a: 246). Sexual liberation must not be conflated with sociopolitical freedom.
4. On Freud's practice of imposing figurative interpretation rather than listening to what Hans actually says, see Deleuze et. al. ([2003] 2006) and Buchanan 2013.

Chapter 5

1. Most relevant here is probably Lacan's structural linguistic conception of the subject, in which the signifier is defined as 'that which represents the subject for another signifier' (1977: 207). For Guattari's critique of this position, see his essay 'Machine

and structure', in *Psychoanalysis and Transversality* ([1972] 2015a: 318–29). See also Thornton (2017).
2 The fact that this analysis of reflexivity might be useful for postmedia studies is hinted at again by the way in which the distinction between the subject of self-reflection and the subject of other-reflection maps on to Guattari's distinction between subject groups and subjugated groups. While the subject of self-reflection is active in generating its own object, the subject of other-reflection is a passive receiver of the representation of an external object. See Guattari ([1972] 2015c: 64).
3 This is explicitly the case in Descartes's *Meditations*, in which the thinking subject is shut up in a room purposefully removed from all social contact.
4 This may seem like a large step to take and I am not claiming that there is nothing to be gained from examining the conceptual relationship between subjectivity and mediation in the philosophical work of a number of other thinkers. For example, there is a line of phenomenological thinking which runs from Heidegger to Sartre, which argues against the idea that the subject is a necessary precondition for experience. See for example Sartre's *The Transcendence of the Ego* (1962). However, this critique is still focussed on the individual thinking subject and is still attached to the project of analysing the genesis of *the* thinking subject.
5 See, for example, Guattari ([1972] 2015c: 64–8), Watson (2009: 27–30), and Genosko (2002: 82–90).

Chapter 6

1 The passage quoted, however, from the 1983 article 'La guerre, la crise ou la vie' collected in *Les années d'hiver* published in January 1986, is different in versions prior to this collection. The one published in *Change international* in September 1983 took a very different turn: 'claiming for example to be postmodern, postpolitical, or, why not, postmedia' (1983: 50). Moreover, the article first appeared in Brazil in *Folha de São Paulo* on 7 August 1983, with the same final, and was later also reprinted in *Micropolítica. Cartografias do Desejo* co-authored with Suely Rolnik, which appeared in October 1985 without including the end of the sentence: 'describing oneself as "postmodern," "postpolitical," etc.' (1985: 196; 2007b: 274) so that the word *postmedia* does not appear in this book. It should be noted that the French version of *Micropolítica* differs from the Brazilian original in that it includes the modified version of the article (2007a: 271).

On the other hand, the term *postmedia* appears in the 'Introduction' and in the 'Postface' of *Les années d'hiver* written in Belém, Brazil, in August 1985 ([1986] 2009: 34, 277, 284) and first published jointly under the title 'Para passar os anos de inverno' in *Folha de São Paulo*, 15 September 1985. The typescript of the chapter 'Du postmodernisme à l'ère postmédia' kept at the Institute for Contemporary Publishing Archives under the title 'Impasse postmoderne et transition postmédia' (GTR 11.4) is dated December 1985.

Finally, in his interview with T. Wada on 2 October 1985, for the Japanese newspaper *Asahi Shimbun*, Guattari states that it was in Brazil that he coined the term *postmedia* (Guattari, Wada 1985: 11). An article in *Folha de São Paulo* confirms that it was on 19 August 1985, during a meeting organized and broadcast live by the free radio station Xilik, that Guattari launched the idea of a postmedia era

(Gonçalves 1985: 37). Guattari then wrote the introduction-postface to *Les années d'hiver*, modifying for the occasion the article 'La guerre, la crise ou la vie' to make a concept he had made fun of in 1983 into a defining piece of his subsequent work (1985–92).
2. Chronologically, Guattari first speaks of self-foundation, a characteristic that he would later also call self-referentiality until he adopted the concept of autopoiesis.
3. Undeniably of existentialist inspiration, this perspective of dissensus as an experience of nonsense, which he then called semiotic collapse, then vertigo of abolition, first refers to Sartrean nausea, existential anguish, but which Guattari then links with the lived experience of the end of the world conceptualized in François Tosquelles's thesis. In this sense, seeking to overcome the Eros-Thanatos opposition, Guattari associates abolition and creation, that is to say, 'the alarming oscillation between a proliferating complexity of sense and total vacuity' (Guattari 1995: 81), which he presents as 'a coming and going at infinite speed between chaos and complexity' (Guattari 1995: 75), hence the expression 'chaosmic vertigo'. It is in this sense that machines only work when they go haywire.
4. As Maurizio Lazzarato summarizes it well, what characterizes coordination is that 'The general form of the organisation is not the vertical and hierarchical structure of political parties or trade unions, but that of the network in which different organisational and decision-making methods operate, which coexist and are coordinated more or less felicitously' (Lazzarato 2007).
5. As Bruno Guattari points out, 'It is the calling into question of this [collective management] system and the transition to a centralised power that will lead Félix Guattari to leave Radio Tomate at the end of a memorable AG' (Prince and Videcoq 2008: 180).
6. It should be noted that the 'Preliminary' chapter of *Schizoanalytic Cartographies* corresponds to the seminar of 1 June 1986 published under the title 'De la production de subjectivité' in *Chimères* 4 (winter 1987).
7. It should be noted that the notion of 'democratic centralism' imposed on the groups adhering to the Second Congress of the Communist International in 1920 – from then on inseparable in Marxism-Leninism from the idea of a vanguard party and its regular purges – was not officially abandoned by the French Communist Party until 1994. Moreover, Guattari considers that Les Verts have not really broken with these traditional methods of organisation (Guattari 2013: 515–16).
8. In the version of this interview published in *Qu'est-ce que l'écosohpie?* it reads instead 'a redefinition of the party' and the following sentence is not included.

Chapter 7

1. Superstring theory is often labelled a 'theory of everything', as it aims to address various theoretical conundrums. In the words of NASA, superstring theory 'attempts to explain all four forces observed in nature' (NASA 2017). The four forces are gravitational, electromagnetic, strong and weak. Instead of elementary particles, superstring theory models them as vibrations of tiny super-symmetrical strings, the fundamental constituents of matter.
2. Ticketless Parking System – Sensor Dynamics. https://sensordynamics.com.au/index.html (accessed 15 February 2020). The updated content of the URL no longer contains the quote, but it was the exact quote as accessed on 15 February 2020.

3 Walter Benjamin used the term *aura* in the essay 'The work of art in the age of Mechanical Reproduction,' originally published in 1936 and later included in the collection of essays *Illuminations* (Benjamin [1986] 2007). He insisted that 'even the most perfect reproduction of a work of art is lacking in one element: its presence in time and space, its unique existence at the place where it happens to be' (Benjamin [1986] 2007: 220). The *aura* Benjamin referred to was the reproduction's unique cultural context in time and space.
4 The Great Canon of China operates disenabling, denial-of service (particularly attacks against the civic users).
5 By contrast, the Great Firewall of China combines legislative actions and technologies enforced by the People's Republic of China (PRC) to monitor the internet domestically.
6 Quoted in an interview with Zeynep Tufekci who, as a scholar of technology and society, witnessed the protest movement in Hong Kong. See interview The World Staff. (2019).
7 Zhong Hanlin's own words are quoted in a book chapter written by Li Xueli and Yang Zhiqiang "The disturbing summer of the Anti-Extradition Bill movement: How will Hong Kong youth return to school?" (my translation) in Li Xueli (ed.) *Fiery Tides: The Hong Kong Anti-Extradition Movement and Its Impacts*, 73.

Chapter 8

1 CEAMSE is the acronym in Spanish for the Ecological Coordination Society of the State Metropolitan Area, the government agency that manages waste in the Buenos Aires Metropolitan Area. Here, it refers to the landfill where people rummage for food and goods to resell.
2 https://www.youtube.com/watch?v=u5PYXkNVQeM.
3 *Una tarde gris* (One Gray Afternoon) is a short produced by Code and a group of students in 2016. In it, a voice off-camera recounts how, on 3 February 2011, two of his friends were killed and one wounded in what is known as the Carcova Massacre, when the Buenos Aires province police fired tear gas, and rubber and live ammunition at a group of residents who had gone to a derailed train because of the poor state of the tracks to rummage in its cargo: https://vimeo.com/182132295.

Chapter 9

1 For example, 350.org is sponsored each year by the Rockefeller Foundation to the tune of $200,000 (US).
2 The law stated that a gathering of more than fifteen people using music equipment listening to rhythmic music outside in an unlicensed event was illegal.

Chapter 11

1 For Guattari's critique of what he saw as the excesses of Laing's approach at Kingsley Hall, see Guattari (1996b).

Chapter 13

1. Akira Asada's *Kozo to Chikara* (*The Structure and Force*, 2013) became a bestseller but no one knows how many readers could actually understand what was said in his writings. The content consisted of his 'bold and violent' summary of the theory of post-structuralism. There have been so far many criticisms against his work including his understanding of Deleuze and Guattari, especially from the new generation of Deleuzians in twenty-first-century Japan. But I do not know any other intellectual who can speak perfect French and English – even in front of Guattari, Žižek or Said – when debating or discussing complicated philosophical issues and everyday politics under info-semiocapitalism. This past 'enfant terrible' was Japan's Oedipus in both negative and affirmative ways.
2. One might recall another Tetsuo in a real action film with the same title: *Tetsuo*, directed by Shinya Tsukamoto (1989). Perhaps, there are intertextual connections but it is beyond the scope of this chapter to deal with this film.
3. In his seminar, I translated some chapters of the manuscript.
4. The translocal is not merely a synonym for the global or international. Kogawa started to utilize this term around the mid-1990s.
5. Augaitis, D and Lander, D. (1994). Radio Rethink – *Art, Sound and Transmission*.
6. His idea of narrowcasting was originally influenced by initiatives of public access channels in New York but elaborated later in the development of his performative workshops all over the world.
7. Based on this insight, and against the grain of interpretation on Deleuze, a Japanese Deleuzian, Masaya Chiba has a book entitled *Ugokisugitewa ikenai: Jiru doruzu to seisei henka no tetsugaku* [Don't Move Too Much: Gilles Deleuze and the Philosophy of Becoming] (Kawade Shobo 2017).
8. Recently, the emperor himself is appearing online to communicate with people.

Index

NOTE: Page references in italics refer to figures.

#stargazing   128
11 March Collective   185, 187

academic philosophers   91–2, 95, 98, 101
acceleration/accelerationism   228–31
accumulation, knowledge-based   57–61
addictive consumption   25
adolescence
   molecular revolution of   200–1
   reappropriation of a-signifying
      systems   203, 213
   self-expression of   206–13
affect   6, 42
aionic time   204, 210, 211–12
Akira (anime)   10, 218, 228
algorithmic governmentality   4, 20
Alice (fictional character: Carroll)   190–2
alter egos   127–30
Alternatik network   8, 103, 108, 109
amateur filmmaking and documentary
      production   201–2, 207–8
amateurism of artistic practice   50
Amazon   5, 17, 60, 170–1
Ambedkar, Bhimrao R.   6, 52
anarchism   154
androidization   228
anime and manga   10, 218, 229
Anna (film: Grifi and Sarchielli)   9, 183,
   189–90
Anthropocene   8–9, 149, 151, *153*, 157–8
   educational schema for   159–61
anthropology of disobedience   190
anti-psychiatric cinema   184–5, 194
   in Italy   185–9
anti-psychiatric documentaries   185
anti-psychiatry   9–10, 183
   in Italy   186–7
apocalyptic realism   9, 164
Apple   165, 170–1
arborescent thinking   99–100

Arc-en-ciel (AEC)   110–12, 114
Arendt, Hannah   171
artifactuality   57, 60, 62
artificial intelligence   62
   becoming AI   228
Asada, Akira   10, 218, 219, 225, 227–8
   Kozo to Chikara   239 n.1 (Ch 13)
a-signifying semiotics   10, 50, 70–1,
   201–4, 213
assemblages   6–7, 194, 221
   machinic   8, 44, 47–9, 119, 126–32,
      224, 226, 229
   rhizomatic   7, 69, 73, 77–8, 81–2
   of territory   45–7, 49
Asylum (documentary: Robinson)   185
atomic time   153
audiovisual practices   183–4
audiovisual production   8, 135
   the always-other other   138–40
   humour and irony in   140–1, 146–7
   other gaze and   136
aura   123–4, 238 n.3 (Ch 7)
automatic societies   21
autopoiesis   103, 104, 110–12, 114,
   237 n.2 (Ch 6)

Bachelard, Gaston   42–3
Backyard Brains (firm)   5, 17, 21
Badlands (film: Malick)   185
barbarian   135–6, 138, 144
Barthes, Roland   232
Basaglia, Franco   183, 185, 186–7, 188
Bataille, Georges   178
Bateson, Gregory   177
Baudrillard, Jean   136, 170, 173–4, 176
becoming   81–4, 168, 222
   becoming AI   228
   becoming-Japanese   213
   becoming minor in major
      language   210, 211–13

becoming other   136, 137–43
double-becoming   206
of a neighbourhood   142–3
Bellocchio, Marco   9, 183, 187–8
Benjamin, Walter   62–3, 123–4, 238 n.3 (Ch 7)
Bentham, Jeremy   56
Berardi, Franco   29, 35, 70, 73, 75, 86, 88, 90, 152, 165–7, 170, 172–3, 175, 176, 220
Bergson, Henri   204, 207
Be Water Movement (Hong Kong)   8, 119, 130–1, 133
Bezos, Jeff   164
Big Tech   60–1, 165–7
Bineham, Jeffery   90
Blanchot, Maurice   232
body
  in art   121–6
  body-flesh binary   211
  Freudian   168
  incorporeality   225–7
  innovative communication by   130
  potentiality of   223, 224–5
  separation of brain from   172–3
Body without Organs (BwO)   19, 222, 226, 228
Bookchin, Murray   150, 154, 160
Bourdieu, Pierre   132
bourgeois household/family   72–5
Braidotti, Rosi   147
Brand, Stewart   169
Branson, Richard   164
Brazil   236 n.1
Brecht, Bertolt   224
bricolage   189–90
broadcast media, Derrida's analysis of   62–3
Buchanan, Ian   235 n.1 (Ch 4)
Buenos Aires   136, 138–9, 238 nn.1, 3 (Ch 8)
Burroughs, William   16

caesura   204–5
capitalism   3–5. *See also* semiocapitalism; surveillance capitalism
  anarchist approach to   154
  in *Anti-Oedipus*   150–2
  financial capitalism   155–6
  industrial capitalism   57–8, 59
  information-age capitalism   70
capitalistic subjectivity   19, 69
  schizoanalysis of   9, 165–9
carbon trail   153
Carroll, Lewis, *Alice Adventures in Wonderland*   190–2
Cartesian philosophy   92–5, 99, 125, 236 n.3
Centre d'initiative pour de nouveaux espaces de liberté (CINEL) (Initiative Centre for New Spaces of Freedom)   106, 111
Cézanne, Paul, *Card Players*   121–2
chaos   45–7, 224–5, 229
chaosmos   63–4, 176–7
chaosmosis   19, 26
childhood sexuality   75–6, 79–80
chronosign   211
CINEL. *See* Centre d'initiative pour de nouveaux espaces de liberté
cinema, anti-psychiatry in. *See* anti-psychiatric cinema
cinematic culture in Italy   9, 183, 194
ciné-trance   205–6
Citizenship Amendment Act (CAA) (2019, India)   6, 40, 47
cockroach
  computer-aided subjectivity of   17–19
  deterritorialization   6, 34–5
  loss of freedom   22
  Umwelt of   19
coding   120–1
coexistence (in Japan)   10, 210–11
  Japanese-ness and   199–201
cogito   86, 92–5, 125
cognitariat   73
cognitive capitalism   2–3, 7–8
  ideological imperative of   58–9
  legitimacy of surveillance and   56–7
  notion of   57, 58
cognitive labour   70, 73
Cold Lazarus (TV drama: Potter)   15, 28–32
collective algorithmic unconscious   3, 20, 22, 30
collective assemblage of enunciation   48–9, 130–3, 192, 209–10, 224, 231–2
collective consciousness   16, 35

collective intelligence 16, 26–8
collective subjectivity 104, 105–6
collective tethering 30
communalism 40, 42, 51, 154
computation code 172–3
computer-aided subjectivity 17–19, 26–7
  dangers and possibilities of 16, 35
computer-generated art 8, 119–20
  body and identity in 121–6
  eyes in 125, 126–32
  human-machine collaboration 120–1
conceptual mapping 99–101
consent/consensus 4–5, 103–5, 107, 110–14, 192–3
consistency 33, 46–7, 76–8
  artificial consistency 72
conspiracy 176
control
  of object choice 172–3
  schizoanalytic cartography of 5–6, 17–26
coordination 108, 237 n.4
corporeality
  Kogawa's 225–7
  sign and 123–4, *125*
cosmos 45–6
counterpoint 45–6
COVID pandemic 51
  electronic surveillance and 122–3
  privacy and 55–7
  slum dweller and 141
Creative Autonomia movement 9, 183, 185–6, 187, 189–92, 220
creative involution 31–2
creativity 232
creolization 212
critical culture 64
critical postmedia 4–5
critical postmedia studies 1–2
Cronenberg, David 34
cultural senility 175
cybernetics, as unconscious 172
cyber utopia 169–70
cyborg 17, 22, 30

D'Alembert, Jean le Rond 28
Dallas 160
data 57–60

data doubles 171
data exhaust, commodification of 170–1
Dawkins, Richard 140–1
death 178
deceleration 228–30
de Certeau, Michel 132
deep ecology 154–5, 238 n.1 (Ch 9)
Deleuze, Gilles
  'Immanence: A Life' 227
  The Logic of Sense 190–1, 232
democratic centralism 8, 103, 104–5, 109, 112–14, 237 n.7
Derrida, Jacques 56–7, 62–4
Descartes, René 86, 92–5, 98, 99, 125, 236 n.3
desire
  alternative approach to 7–8, 83–4
  capitalism and 4–5
  'cinema of desire' 235 n.3 (Ch 4)
  commodification/coding of 171
  dissensual 80
  economy of the possible and 223
  Eros distinguished from 74–5, 77
  instrumental control of 172–3
  interconnections between power, social institutions and 188
  language and 193–4
  machinic assemblage of 47
  machinic theory of 31
  Oedipal restraints on 78–9
destining 61
deterritorialization 27, 34
  of becomings 81–2
  of digital ecology 49–50
  of knowledge 221
  of language 211–13
  of Little Hans phobia 78, 79
  of protest art 50
  of Shaheen Bagh (New Delhi) 40, 42–4
  of state power 130–2
Dickerson, Adam 95–6
Diderot, Denis 28
digital art. *See* computer-generated art
digital media, media flows 49–50
digital utopia 170–1
dissent/dissensus 1, 2, 8, 32, 113–14
  as experience of nonsense 105, 237 n.3

machinations of   47–51
postmediatic and postmodernist
    conceptions of   103–4, 109–10
space of   40, 42–4
use of technology to suppress   51
Dosse, François   219
double-becoming   206
doughnut economics   9, 158–9
dystopia   20, 147, 166–7, 170, 173, 174, 178

ecology   174–8
ecosophy   5
    aesthetic-politics of   232–3
    as virtual ecology   10, 219, 223–4
education
    of foreign nationals in Japan   197–9
    third synthesis of time and   9, 159–61
emperor system in Japan   230–2
encapsulation   73–4
enframing   61
entomological metaphors   15–16
environment, economy and   158–9
Eros   74–5, 77, 80, 81
erotic cinema   235 n.3 (Ch 4)
essentialism   211
ethics
    of brain research   15, 16, 30–1
    'ethics of the media'   213
    of responsibility   4, 32
    technological governmentality and   61
ethology   45
existential territory   6, 41–2, 72–3
    finite   17–19
    notion of   72
    of Shaheen Bagh (New Delhi)   40, 43–8, 51–2
exosomatization   30–1
experimental films, Italian   189–90
eye in art   125, 126–32

Facebook   50, 60, 128, 152, 165, 170–1
face masks, surveillance evasion and   127–30
faciality   76, 77, 78–9, 81, 93–4, 231–2
Fagioli, Marco   187–8
Faiz, Ahmed Faiz   49
family dwelling   72–3, 81

Family Life (film: Loach)   185
feeling   226
figuration   76–7, 80
finance subjectivity   156–7
financial capitalism   155–6
first-person narrative   142–3
Fists in the Pocket (film: Bellocchio)   9, 183, 187
Ford Motor Company   57–8
fossil-fuel industry   155–6
Foucault, Michel   52, 56, 62, 73, 87, 186
fourfold meta-model functors   17–19, 41–2
free radio   94, 108–9, 132–3, 222, 224, 229
    Kogawa's interest in   220
    media ecology of   190–4
Freud, Sigmund   7–8, 69–70, 73, 76, 78–82, 168–9, 176, 178, 235 n.1 (Ch 4)
functional subjectivity   89–90
futural unconscious   2, 4–5
future
    in art   124, *126*
    collective imagination of   24

Gandhi, Mahatma (Mohandas K.)   6, 52
General Motors   57–8
Génération Écologie (political party)   103, 112–13
Genosko, Gary   31–2, 71, 190
Gestell/enframing   30
Glissant, Edward   212
Goethe, Johann Wolfgang von   227
Goffman, Erving   186
Google   30, 57, 60, 165, 166, 170–1
Gorz, André   28
governmentality   87–8
grammatization   130
grassroots emperor system   230–2
Grifi, Alberto   9, 185–6, 189–90
group subjectivity   98–9
Guattari, Félix
    activism of   8, 103–4, 112–13, 219
    anti-psychiatric cinema and   184–5
    conceptualization of subjectivity   88
    co-opted attitude of   219
    Japan and   10, 227–8
    Les années d'hiver   236 n.1

notion of medium 90–1
postmedia project of 152–4
'Reflections on Institutional
   Psychotherapy for
   Philosophers' 86, 91
Guattari, Félix and Gilles Deleuze
   Anti-Oedipus 150–2, 188–9, 191
guilt and shame 75–6, 78, 81–2, 138–9, 141, 145–6

Han, Byung-Chul 20
handworks 227
(Little) Hans (Freud's case study) 7–8, 235 n.1 (Ch 4)
   escape from social subjection 71–2
   faciality traits of mother and 78–9
   family territory 72–4
   literality of 76–8
   mapping of 69–70
   phobic escape 81–3
   sexuality of 74–6, 79–80
Hardt, Michael 169–70
Heidegger, Martin 30, 42, 61, 63, 151, 225, 236 n.4
Hernot, Yann 109
heterogenesis 105–6, 112
heterotopia 51–2
Hindutva 6, 40, 46, 51–2
home 42–3
   creation amidst chaos 46, 49
   as place of privacy 56
Hong Kong protests (2019-2020) 8, 126–33
horse
   becoming-horse 81–2, 83
   as paternal signifier 80, 81
Houellebecq, Michel 174–5
human, Marxist vision of 167–8
human behaviour modification, technological mediation of 60–1, 62, 166, 171, 172
human-machine alliance 21–2, 24–5, 32, 120–1
humour and irony
   in art 124, *126*
   in audiovisual production 140–1, 146–7
Husserl, Edmund 225
hyalosign 211

ICTs. *See* information and communication technologies
identity
   in Big Data age 119, 121–2
   deconstruction of 8, 126–32
   immigrants in Japan and 10, 208–9, 211
   Japanese people and 199–200
   self-identity 122–3
   transformation of 123, *124*, 125–6
idiot media 9, 149, 150–1
Il Festival del proletariato giovanile al Parco Lambro (*The Festival of Proletarian Youth at Parco Lambro*) (film: Grifi) 189
image data augmentation 120
imaginary 77–8
imitation 207
immanence 227
immaterial labour 70
immediacy 95–6
immigrants in Japan
   barriers to attending school 198–9
   identity of 10, 208–9, 211
   as 'imagined Others' 200
   minoritarian self-expression of 206–13
   'school refusal' 197–8
   as threat to Japanese-ness 203–4
incel (Involuntary Celibate) 175–6
incorporeal universe(s) 18–19
industrial capitalism 57–8, 59
inevitablism 170
infantilized subjectivity 22–4, 32, 106–7
info-capitalism 219
information-age capitalism 70
information and communication technologies (ICTs) 103, 105–6, 107, 114
information society 57
info-semiocapitalism 5, 219
inner sides 210–11
Institute for Social Ecology 154
institutional vacuoles 232–3
Integrated World Capitalism (IWC) 31, 152, 165, 201
inter-corporeality 225–7
Internet 167

Investigation of a Citizen above Suspicion (film: Petri) 188
Italian neorealism 189

Jalib, Habib 49
Jameson, Fredric 219
Jamia Millia Islamia 40, 43, 45–6, 235 n.2
Japan
  Akihabara, Tokyo 229
  emperor system in 230–2
  in mid-1980s 218
Japan. Ministry of Education, Culture, Sports, Science and Technology (MECSST) 197–8
Japanese language
  minor treatment of 211–13
  proficiency of 197–9
Japanese-ness 10, 199–201
  foreign nationals as threat to 203–4
jianghu practices 120, 131–2
Jonas, Hans 32
Joyce, James 177
juridico-politics, surveillance and 6–7, 55–6, 60–2

Kafka, Franz 167, 219, 228
Kant, Immanuel 86, 95–7, 99
Kelly, Kevin 28
knowledge
  in Cartesian philosophy 93–5
  vs. data 57–60
  deterritorialization of 221
  and power relation 56
  through experience collecting 120
Knowles, Malcolm 59
Kogawa, Tetsuo 10, 218–20, 239 n.2 (Ch 13)
  on corporeality 225–7
  postmedia performance activism of 222–3, 227
kolam (art) 50

La Borde clinic (Cour-Cheverny, France) 185
labour, industrial-era and post-industrial 70–1
Lacan, Jacques 77–8, 172, 235 n.1 (Ch 4), 235 n.1 (Ch 5)

La classe operaia va in paradiso (film: Petri) 9, 183
Laing, Ronald David 185
La macchina cinema (TV series) 185
Land, Nick 151, 228, 238 n.2 (Ch 2)
landfill scavenging 138–41, 238 n.1
language 48, 144–5
  deterritorialization of 211–13
  as instrumental control of desire 172–3
  Radio Alice and 193–4
Lazzarato, Maurizio 70–1, 152, 204, 207, 237 n.4
lectosign 212–13
Lee, Bruce 130–1
Lefebvre, Henri 42
Les Verts (political party) 103, 104, 110, 112–13, 237 n.7
Lévy, Pierre 16, 26–7, 28
literality 76–7, 80, 84
lived space 42–3
Li Zi-Fong 8, 119–21
  The Cartesian Headgear 125, *127*
  The Copy 122–3
  Digital Foundation Makeup 123, *124*
  Disembody 123–4, *125*
  The Four Quadrants of an Elephant 125, *128*
  Salamander-Merfolk 124, *126*
  Sun Wukong in the Matrix 125–6, *129*
  Two Cézannes 121–6
  Your Left Eye Is My Right Eye 126–32
looking and being looked at 135–6
Lulu the Tool (*La Class Operaio va in Paradiso*) (film: Petri) 188–9
Lyotard, François 110

machinic assemblages 8, 44, 47–9, 119, 126–32, 224, 226, 229
machinic becoming 34, 35
machinic enslavement 7–8, 35, 70–2, 83
machinic phyla 18, 21–2, 24, 41–2, 49–50
machinic solitude 33, 35
machinic subjectivity 28
McLuhan, Marshall 169, 226
madness 187, 188
Marx, Karl 58, 59, 168, 221, 225

masculinity, and sexual politics   174–6
mass media
   on Buenos Aires slum-dwellers
     138–9
   fragmentation of   165–7, 169, 173–4
   Japanese-non-Japanese binary
     and   10, 197–8, 200–1, 203–4,
     213
   limitations of   171
   postmedia and   103–4
   reappropriation of   201–3, 213
   uses of   106–7, 114
Massumi, Brian   100, 226
Matti da slegare (*Fit to be Untied*)
   (documentary: Agnosti)   9, 185,
   187
mechanical surveillance
   juridico-politics of   6–7, 55–6, 61
   post-media and   62–4
mechanosphere   31–2, 35
media/mediation/medium
   climate change and   151, 157–8
   communicative/representational sense
     of   90, 99
   environmental sense of   90–1, 93,
     100, 152
   role in construction of subject   7, 86,
     92–5
   subjectivity and   236 n.4
   transformation of   156–7
media ecology   190–4, 201–2
megamachine   41
memes   140–1, 146–7
memory
   exploitation of   28–32
   manipulation and loss of   17–26, 35
mentality, change in   32–3
mental pollution   16, 23–4
Merleau-Ponty, Maurice   42–3, 125
Me-Too movement   174–5
Metz, Christian   184
micro-media   219
micro-radio   222
milieu   42, 45–7, 62
Mills, Charles Wright   169
mimesis   132
miniaturization of technologies   4, 21, 24
Minitel (*Médium Interactif par
   Numérisation d'Information
   Téléphonique*) 3615 ALTER   2, 8,
   103, 107, 108–9, 111, 114
minor cinema   9, 183, 185, 205–6
minority   62, 64
   becoming-minor   210, 211–13
   filmic practices of   205–6
   self-expression of   200–1, 203–4,
     211–13
minor utopia   9, 165, 167, 178
minor video, migrant adolescent self-
   expression as   206–13
Mises, Ludwig von   60
mnemotechnology   20–2, 28
Modern Times (film: Chaplin)   188
molar media   24, 75–6, 78–9, 81–3, 220,
   222, 224, 229
molecular revolution   8, 103, 105–6, 114,
   143–4, 170, 200–1
Monkey King (Sun Wukong)   125–6, *129*
moral gaze   138–9, 141, 145–6
motif   45–7
Moulier-Boutang, Yann   57
Mumford, Lewis   41
Musk, Elon   22, 28, 30
Muslim women   40
   subjectivation of   43

Naess, Arne   150, 154–5, 238 n.1 (Ch 9)
narrowcasting   222, 224, 239 n.5 (Ch 13)
nationalism   47
necromancy   30–1
Negri, Antoni   152, 169–70, 220
neighbouring assemblages, destabilization
   of   6, 42–4
NeuroLace/Neuralink   30
neuroscience, of RoboRoach device   5–6,
   15, 17, 21, 30
neuro-totalitarianism   5, 16, 165–6,
   171–2
new academism (*Nyu Aka*)   218
new aesthetic paradigm   167, 169, 221
news. *See also* mass media
   development of, for
     re-education   200–1, 203–4
   news production   192–3
nihilism   173
nihonjnron   199–200
noetic necromass   30–1
nomads   230

no media   8–9, 149, 150, 154, 160–2
nonsense   105, 190–2, 237 n.3
noosign   211
noosphere   22, 28, 31–2
normalization   167–8
novelty   136, 144
Noys, Benjamin   228

object choice   170–3, 175
occupy movements   42–4, 47
Oedipal family   69, 71, 72–6
Oedipalization   7–8, 70, 82–3, 167–8
   Eros and   74–5
   notion of   69
online identity   119
opsigns   204–5, 207, 210
optional matter   223–4, 225
Orgonauti, Evivva! (film: Grifi)   189–90
the Other
   the always-other other   138–40
   as barbarian   135–6, 138, 144
   'imagined Others'   200
   as the other   136–7
   as profane object   174
other gaze   8, 135
   an(other) gaze   146–7
   cartography of   136–7
Oury, Jean   232–3

panopticon   56, 63
paradox   190–2
paranoia   168–9, 173, 176–7
   provisional paranoia   169, 178
Parma Psychiatric Hospital (Colorno, Italy)   185
passivity, and mass media   106–7
passwords   48–9
penis   77, 79–80, 82, 83
performance activism, of Kogawa   222–3, 227
perversity   174–6
Petri, Elio   9, 183, 188–9
phallocene   153
phallus   79–80
philosophy   91–2, 101
   thinking subject and   93–9, 236 n.3
Philosophy 4 Children (P4C)   160
phobia   69–70, 73, 77
   escape from   81–3

Piccone, Paul   220
planetary computerization   221
planetary consciousness   21–2, 32–5
political activism
   of Guattari   8, 103–4, 112–13, 219
   of Kogawa   220
political communication   191–3
politico-ethico-aesthetic paradigm   177–8
politics, and schizoid personality   188–9
polymorphous   222–3, 224, 226
possible   223–5
postmedia   9, 119, 152–4, 169–73, 183, 221
   as anti-production   165
   critique of   69, 177
   mechanical surveillance and   62–4
   notion of   2, 104, 220–3, 236 n.1
postmedia activism   88
postmedia ecology   132–3
postmedia theory, and subjectivity   87–92
postmodernism   103, 106, 110
post-structuralism   239 n.1 (Ch 13)
potential/potentiality   221, 223, 224–5
power
   interconnections between desire, social institutions and   188
   and knowledge relation   56
precision advertising   170, 171
prehension   226
presuppositions   91–2
primordial deceleration   229–30
privacy
   juridical norms of   58
   need for   56–7
   notion of   55
   surveillance and   6–7, 55–6
proletarianization   20–1, 25, 26
protest art   6, 47, 50
protest movements. *See also* Shaheen Bagh (New Delhi, India) protests
   aesthetics and communication of   126–33
   use of Minitel by   108
protest poetry   49
protest space   42–4
proto-Fascism   188
proto-subjectivity   224
Proust, Marcel   78, 141

psychoanalysis   69–70, 77, 82–3, 167–8, 172
    capitalist subjectivity and   165
    cinema and   184
psychology, data economy model   60–1
puissance   210, 213

QAnon movements   176
quality of life   155

Radio Alice   9, 132–3, 183, 220
    choice of name 'Alice'   190–1
    media ecology of   191–4
Radio Tomate   108–9, 234 n.5
Radio Xilik   236 n.1
Rainbow network   8
Raworth, Kate   9, 158–9
real-imaginary-symbolic topology   77–8, 83–4
reality   92–3, 95–7, 99, 165
reconciliation   213
reflexivity   94–5, 236 n.2
remote control   17–26, 27, 35
reserve/reservoir   225
resingularization
    of democracy   8, 103, 104–5, 107, 109, 112–14
    of subject group   202–3
resistance   1, 4–5, 7, 40, 51–2, 63–4, 143–4. *See also* protest movements
reterritorialization   27, 28
    of Little Hans phobia   78
    of Shaheen Bagh (New Delhi)   42–4
revolutionary behaviour   156–7
rhizomatic collective assemblages   7, 69, 73, 77–8, 81–2
rhizomatic thinking   99–100
rhythm   6, 45–7, 50–1
right to privacy   56–7
ritournello   45–7
RoboRoach   5–6, 15, 17
Rouch, Jean   205–6

Sakamoto, Ryuichi   227–8
Sartre, Jean-Paul   104
schizoanalysis   1, 2, 4, 16, 35–6, 64, 137, 167
    notion of   35
    postmedia philosophy and   97–101

schizoanalytic cartography   136–7
    application of   5–6
    of audiovisual production   143–7
    of cockroach   16
    of existential territory of Shaheen Bagh (New Delhi)   40–7
schizoanalytic ecology   41–2
schizoid personality   188–9
schizophrenia   168–9, 173–4, 176, 177–8
school refusal   197–8
Schreber, Daniel Paul   176–7
science fiction   5, 15, 25
Searching (film: Chaganty)   122
self-awareness   97
self-expression
    of migrant adolescents   206–13
    of minority   200–1, 203–4
self-foundation/self-referentiality   237 n.2 (Ch 6)
self-identity, multiplicity of   122–3
self-learning   59
self-referencing   48
self-reflection   93–4, 236 n.2
semiocapitalism   9, 71, 73, 156–7, 161, 165, 169–70
semiotic collapse   78–9, 237 n.3
sexism   231
sexual body   74–5
sexuality   9, 183, 188
    childhood   75–6, 79–80
Shaheen Bagh (New Delhi, India)
    protests   6
    deterritorialization of   40, 42–4
    existential territory of   44–7, 51–2
    as intensive spatium   47–51
Shannon, Claude and Warren Weaver   169
sign/signifier   87, 168
    corporeality and   123–4, *125*
singularity   8, 48, 76, 137–8
    of the Anthropocene   151, *153*
    of Japanese society   231–2
singularization   111–12
social conflicts, and special segregation   42–4
social control   24–5, 166
social critique, in Italian cinema   187–9
social desires   74–5

social ecology   9, 149, 238 n.1 (Ch 9)
    Bookchin's approach to   154
    Naess's approach to   154–5
    a new ecology   150–5, 161–2
    notion of   149
social mediation   7
social practices   32–3
social subjection   70–2, 83, 202–3
sonsign   204–5, 207, 211–13
sound   9, 183, 188
    nondiegetic sound   212
spatial segregation   43
speed   228–30
spider narrator   141
standing reserve   225
stand-still dialectic   63
state power   130–1
Stiegler, Bernard   7, 20, 21, 28, 130
storytelling
    minor cinema   205
    otherness and   137
subject group   104–5, 172–3, 202–3
subjectivity
    in Cartesian philosophy   92–5, 99
    conceptualization of   86–7, 235 n.3 (Ch 5)
    deterritorialization of   49–50
    fourfold   17–19, 41–2
    group relations and   86
    in Kantian philosophy   95–7, 99
    mechanical surveillance and   63
    mediation and   236 n.4
    postmedia theory and   87–92
    production of   3, 6
    stages of   221
    under Japanese emperor system   230–2
subjugated group   104–5, 202–3, 232
substantial (nature of virtual)   223
Sugimura, Fredric   219
Super-8 film   201–2
super consciousness   30
superstring theory   237 n.1 (Ch 7)
surveillance
    ambiguous aspect of   55–6, 64
    Covid pandemic and   122–3
    evasion of   127–30
    legitimacy of   56–7

surveillance capitalism   7, 57–8, 170
    juridico-politics and   60–1
    privacy and   55–6
    and technological mediation of behaviour modification   60
surveillance technologies   51
symbolic   77–8

tangibility   226–7
Taussig, Michael   132
technical reproduction   63
techno-fix, for apocalypse   164–5
technological revealing   61, 63
technology
    Heidegger's critique of   61, 63
    impact on human psyche   2
    miniaturization of   4, 21, 24
    minor use of   62, 64
    social form of   31
    suppression of dissent and   51
    surveillance and   60–1
Teilhard de Chardin, Pierre   22, 28, 30
tekhne   227
Telegram   128–9
telematics   109
tele-technology   7, 57
    Derrida's conceptualization of   62–4
television   106–7
Telos (journal)   220
temporality   221–2
The Tenth Victim (film: Petri)   188
territorialization   42–5
    capitalist models of   168–9
territory   6, 40, 46–7, 51–2
    conceptualization of   42–4
    earth as   168
    family territory   72–4
Tetsuo (anime)   218
Tetsuo (film: Tsukamoto)   239 n.2
Theweleit, Klaus   176
thinking
    Cartesian   93–5, 99, 236 n.3
    Kantian   95–7, 99
    philosophy and   98
    rhizomatic and arborescent modes of   99–100
    in schizoanalysis   99, 100–1
third synthesis of time   9, 204–5

Tiffany & Co 126
time-image 204–5, 210–12
Tinguely, Jean 222
tool enhancement 153
Tosquelles, François 237 n.3
tracing 99–100
Trakl, Georg 151
transcendental empiricism 205
Transfert per camera verso Virulenta (film: Grifi) 189–90
transhumanism 5, 15, 16, 21–2
transversality 8, 103–5, 114, 177
trauma 5, 142–3
Trump, Donald 174–6
Turner, Fred 169
Twitter 50, 84, 152

umbrellas, and surveillance evasion 127–30
Una tarde gris (One Gray Afternoon) (short) 238 n.3
unconscious 168
  cinema's impact on 184
  four zones of 152–4
  futural role and nature of 2, 4–5
  Lacanian 172–3
  neuro-totalitarianism of 16
  Oedipalization of 7–8
universe of reference 21, 35, 41–2, 44
  emergence of 22–5
universes of value 18–19, 49
ur-materiality 228

utopia 2, 51–2, 172, 173
  cyber utopia 169–70
  digital utopia 170–1
  minor utopianism 9, 165, 167, 178

vacuole 232–3
Varian, Hal 170
Verifica Incerta (film: Grifi) 189
Vernadsky, Vladimir 22, 28, 30
video police 9–10, 186
violence, by capitalism 150
Virilio, Paul 22, 28, 29
virtual 210, 219, 223–4
vision, and identity politics 126–32
voluntary servitude 21, 24–5

wasp-orchid rhizome example 27
Watermelons and Humans (video) 208–13
Wells, H. G. 30
Whitehead, Alfred North 223, 226
Wiener, Norbert 19, 169
Weinstein, Harvey 174–5
women, participation in protest 40, 43, 46
World Brain 6, 16, 20–2, 28–32, 35

Zavattini, Cesare 189
Zhang Shiran 120
Zhuangzi 131
Žižek, Slavoj 20, 21, 22, 29, 164, 239 n.1 (Ch 13)
Zourabichvili, François 76–7
Zuboff, Shoshana 58, 60–1, 166, 170

www.ingramcontent.com/pod-product-compliance
Lightning Source LLC
Chambersburg PA
CBHW062130300426
44115CB00012BA/1876